POPULATION GEOGRAPHY

This book studies the origins and development of population geography as a discipline. It explores the key concepts, tools and statistical and demographic techniques that are widely employed in the analysis of population. The chapters in this book:

- Provide a comprehensive geographical account of population attributes in the world, with a particular focus on India;
- Study the three major components of population change – fertility, mortality and migration – that have remained somewhat neglected in the study of human geography so far;
- Examine the salient social, demographic and economic characteristics of population, along with topics such as size, distribution and growth of population;
- Discuss major population theories, policies and population–development–environment interrelations, thus marking a significant departure from the traditional pattern-oriented approach.

Well supplemented with figures, maps and tables, this key text will be an indispensable read for students, researchers and teachers of human geography, demography, anthropology, sociology, economics and population studies.

Mohammad Izhar Hassan is Senior Professor of Geography at Maharshi Dayanand University, Rohtak, Haryana, India. He also served as Professor at Ravenshaw University, Odisha, India (2014–17), and has been a recipient of the UGC Research Award on a project entitled *Demographic Situation in Odisha and its Development Implication*. His research mainly focuses on population studies in geography. Twelve Ph.D. scholars and seventeen M.Phil. students have obtained their degrees under his guidance. He has authored four books and three dozen research papers, published in journals of national and international repute. He is a life member of several professional bodies/societies including Indian Association for the Study of Population, Indian Regional Science Association, National Association of Geographers India, Institute of Indian Geographers, Geographical Society of India and Eastern Geographical Society.

POPULATION GEOGRAPHY

A Systematic Exposition

Mohammad Izhar Hassan

Routledge
Taylor & Francis Group
LONDON AND NEW YORK

First published 2020
by Routledge
2 Park Square, Milton Park, Abingdon, Oxon OX14 4RN

and by Routledge
52 Vanderbilt Avenue, New York, NY 10017

Routledge is an imprint of the Taylor & Francis Group, an informa business

British Library Cataloguing-in-Publication Data
A catalogue record for this book is available from the British Library

Library of Congress Cataloging-in-Publication Data
A catalog record for this book has been requested

ISBN: 978-0-367-44066-4 (hbk)
ISBN: 978-0-367-44154-8 (pbk)
ISBN: 978-1-003-00798-2 (ebk)

Typeset in Bembo
by Apex CoVantage, LLC

In the sacred memory of my parents
Mohammad Abul Hassan and
Nazra Khatoon

CONTENTS

List of figures *ix*
List of maps *x*
List of tables *xii*
Preface and acknowledgements *xvi*

1 Introduction 1

2 Sources of population data 15

3 Population distribution 28

4 Urban–rural distribution 49

5 Population growth 68

6 Age–sex composition 91

7 Literacy and education 120

8 Marital status 141

9 Economic composition 160

10 Fertility 176

11 Mortality and life table 210

12 Migration 242

13 Population theories 274

14 Population–development–environment interrelations 294

15 Population policy 307

Glossary *326*
References *335*
Index *345*

FIGURES

1.1 Trewartha's triad of geographical elements 4
3.1 Distribution of world surface area (A) and population (B) by major regions, 2017 35
3.2 Lorenz curve of inequality in population distribution in India, 2011 (based on district-level data of the 2011 Census) 44
4.1 Decadal change in urban and rural population in India, 1951–2011 59
4.2 Rural population by size class categories of villages in India, 2011 60
4.3 Urban population by size class categories, 2011 63
5.1 World population growth (beginning of Christian era to 2015) 71
5.2 Trends in population growth in India, 1901 to 2011 82
5.3 Trends in birth rate, death rate and rate of natural increase in India, 1901–11 to 2011–16 87
6.1 Age pyramid, India, 1961 and 2011 93
6.2 Trends in overall sex ratio in India, 1901–2011 111
8.1 Marital status of women (age 15–49 years) in India, 2016 (NFHS-4) 151
9.1 Percentage employment in agriculture, industries and services in the world, 2017 166
9.2 Per cent distribution of workforce in primary, secondary and tertiary activities in India, 2011 169
10.1 Trends in crude birth rate in India, 1901–11 to 2011–16 189
10.2 Duration involved in fertility transition from CBR < 30 to CBR < 20 191
10.3 Liebenstein's Model of Fertility Decline 206
10.4 Easterlin's Model of Modernisation and Family Size 209
13.1 Logistic Law of Population Growth 287
13.2 Demographic Transition Model 291

MAPS

3.1 World population density, 2017 36
3.2 Population distribution in India, 2011 43
3.3 Population density in India, 2011 46
4.1 Per cent urban population in the world, 2017 54
4.2 Per cent urban population in India, 2011 65
5.1 Rate of natural increase in population in the world, 2017 75
5.2 Stages of demographic transition reached by different countries in the world, 2017 81
5.3 Patterns of population growth in India, 2001–11 86
6.1 Dependency ratio in the world, 2017 96
6.2 Population ageing in the world, 2017 100
6.3 Dependency ratio in India, 2011 104
6.4 Sex ratio in the world, 2015 109
6.5 'All age' sex ratio in India, 2011 114
6.6 Child sex ratio (age 0–6 years) in India, 2011 116
6.7 Decadal change in child sex ratio in India, 2001–11 118
7.1 Adult literacy rate (age 15 years and above) in the world, 2015 126
7.2 Literacy rate (age 7 years and above) in India, 2011 139
8.1 Singulate mean age at marriage (SMAM) of females in the world, 2015 148
8.2 Singulate mean age at marriage (SMAM) of females in India, 2011 157
8.3 Proportion women (age 20–24 years) married before the legal age in India, 2015–16 158
9.1 Proportion population (age 15 years and above) in employment in the world, 2015 164
9.2 Percentage employment in agriculture in the world, 2017 167

9.3 Work participation rate (age 15–59 years) in India, 2011 – main and marginal workers combined 172

9.4 Proportion main workforce (age 15–59 years) engaged in primary activities in India, 2011 174

10.1 Total fertility rate in the world, 2017 183

10.2 Crude birth rate in India, 2004–10 196

11.1 Crude death rate in the world, 2017 224

11.2 Infant mortality rate in the world, 2017 226

11.3 Life expectancy of males at birth in the world, 2017 227

11.4 Life expectancy of females at birth in the world, 2017 228

11.5 Infant mortality rate in India, 2011 239

11.6 Under-five mortality rate in India, 2011 240

12.1 Triangular Slave Trade initiated by the British 257

12.2 Major human migrations in modern times, 1500–1900 259

12.3 International migrants as percentage of total population in the world, 2017 264

12.4 Population mobility in India, 2001 273

TABLES

2.1	Population-related topics covered in various NSS rounds	26
3.1	World distribution of population, 2017	34
3.2	Distribution of population and area by density levels in India, 2011	44
3.3	Population concentration index and density of population in India, 2011	45
4.1	Urban–rural distribution of population in the world – 1950, 2000 and 2015	52
4.2	Number of countries by per cent urban and world major regions, 2015	54
4.3	Urban–rural populations in India, 1951 to 2011	58
4.4	Distribution of rural population by size class categories of villages in India, 2011	60
4.5	Rural population by states/union territories in India, 2011	61
4.6	Urban population by size class categories in India, 2011	62
4.7	Urban population by states/union territories in India, 2011	64
4.8	Distribution of districts and their proportions in geographic area and population by urban–rural ratio in India, 2011	66
5.1	Past trends in world population growth	71
5.2	Adding the billions: actual and projected	73
5.3	Population growth in major regions of the world, 1950–2017	74
5.4	Scheme of classification of countries in different stages of transition on the basis of vital rates, 2017	81
5.5	Population growth in India, 1901–2011	84
5.6	Birth rate, death rate and rate of natural increase: states and union territories, 2016	89

6.1 Percentage distribution of population in broad age groups and dependency ratio in major areas of the world and some select countries 95
6.2 Index of ageing in major areas of the world and in some select countries, 2003 and 2017 100
6.3 Percentage distribution of population in broad age groups in India, 2011 101
6.4 Percentage distribution of population in broad age groups and dependency ratio by states and union territories, 2011 103
6.5 Sex ratio for world and major regions by broad age groups, 2016 (number of males per 100 females) 108
6.6 Trends in sex ratio in India, 1901–2011 110
6.7 Decadal change in sex ratio in states and union territories, 2001–11 113
7.1 Statistics on global literacy, 2016 124
7.2 Status of world educational attainment, 2005–15 124
7.3 Trends in literacy rates in India, 1901–2011 129
7.4 Literacy rate and levels of educational attainment in India, 2011 131
7.5 Literacy differentials in India, 2011 133
7.6 States and union territories arranged in descending order of overall literacy rates, 2011 135
7.7 Proportion population (age 25 years and above) with at least matric/secondary level education in India, 2011 136
8.1 Marital status of females (age groups 15–19, 20–24 and 25–29) in select countries 147
8.2 Mean age at marriage of women in years: select European countries (18th–19th centuries) and India (20th century) 149
8.3 Current marital status of women (age 15–49 years) in India, 2011 and 2015–16 150
8.4 Proportion single and singulate mean age at marriage of females in India, 1891–2011 152
8.5 Proportion single females in broad age groups and singulate mean age at marriage of females by states in India, 2011 154
8.6 Differentials in marital status of females (age 15–29 years) in India, 2011 155
9.1 Employment to population ratio and labour force participation rate in the world, 2015 164
9.2 Percentage of total employment in agriculture, industries and services in the world and major regions, 2017 165
9.3 Trends in work participation, share of marginal workers and proportion non-workers seeking/available for work in India, 1981–2011 (age 15–59 years) 168
9.4 Percentage distribution of main and marginal workers in primary, secondary and tertiary activities in India, 2011 169

9.5 Economic characteristics of population (age 15–59 years) in states and union territories in India, 2011 171
10.1 Crude birth rate and total fertility rate for the world and major regions, 2003 and 2017 182
10.2 Estimates of birth rates in India from various sources since 1901 188
10.3 Cumulative listing of major states with stages of fertility transition 190
10.4 Crude birth rate, general fertility rate (GFR) and total fertility rate in India and bigger states/UTs, 2016 194
10.5 Fertility levels by background characteristics of women in India, 2015–16 198
11.1 Period abridged life table for females, India, 2012–16 215
11.2 Estimates of mortality and life expectancy in the world and major areas, 2017 223
11.3 Estimated deaths by causes in the world, 2016 230
11.4 Persons living with HIV/AIDS, number of new cases and deaths due to AIDS in the world and major regions, 2018 231
11.5 Trends in average annual death rates and life expectancy in India, 1901–11 to 2015–17 233
11.6 SRS estimates on select mortality indicators in India, 2016 235
11.7 Social and economic differentials in infant and child mortality in India, 2015–16 236
11.8 Estimates on mortality rates in states and union territories, 2016 238
12.1 Temporal change in migration characteristics: Zelinsky's Model of Mobility Transition 253
12.2 Distribution of international migrants in the world, 2000 and 2017 262
12.3 Top 20 countries hosting the largest number of international migrants, 2000 and 2017 263
12.4 World distribution of population and international migrants by regions of their origin, 2017 265
12.5 Ten largest countries of origin of international migrants, 2017 265
12.6 Internal migrants as percentage to total population in India, 1961 to 2011 267
12.7 Distribution of internal migrants by streams and distance categories in India, 2011 (as per place of last residence criterion) 269
12.8 Reasons of migration by streams and distance categories in India, 2011 270
12.9 Rate of migration and inter-state migration in India and states/union territories, 2011 (based on 'place of last residence' concept) 272
14.1 Gross per capita food production (2004–06 = 100) in the world by regions 297
14.2 Prevalence of undernourishment (per cent) in the world and major regions 299

14.3 Percentage share in population, hazardous waste production and consumption of natural resources – developed vs. less developed world 301
14.4 Carbon dioxide emission and per capita energy use in the world and regions 303
14.5 WWF estimates on average per capita ecological footprints of the world and select countries, 2008 304

PREFACE AND ACKNOWLEDGEMENTS

An outcome of nearly three decades of teaching a course on population geography with special reference to India at the post-graduate level, this book is a thoroughly revised and enlarged version of a textbook entitled *Population Geography* published earlier in 2005 by Rawat Publications (India). The text has been completely redrafted in the light of recent developments and new data-set with two new chapters on *urban-rural distribution* and *economic composition of population*. In addition, several new sections on emerging issues have been incorporated in the existing chapters. Population geography as an independent sub-field of Human Geography has its origin in the early 1950s, and during this short period, it has grown into a major area of research and teaching in the overall scheme of systematic geography. In India, the teaching of the subject was started in the early 1960s, and at present, a paper on population geography is offered both at the undergraduate as well as post-graduate level in almost all the universities.

Interestingly, however, there are not many textbooks on the subject available in India. The ones that are available are heavily inclined towards the *pattern-oriented descriptive approach* covering a wide range of aspects on which data are easily available from conventional sources like census. These books lack *process-oriented* rigour with very scanty discussion on fertility and mortality. One apparent reason for this neglect is the absence of reliable data on vital rates at lower levels, a pre-requisite for any geographical analysis of population dynamics. This gap could always be bridged with the help of some indirect estimates based on the district-level census data on the age and sex structure of the population. This necessitates adequate emphasis on statistical and demographic techniques. For one or the other reason, geographers have always shied away from these techniques. In the teaching process, too, not much attention is paid on this component even at the post-graduate level. The apathy of geographers to demographic techniques has seriously impacted upon the utility and scope of geographical studies on population. Although the spatial mobility of population has engaged the attention of geographers for quite some time, contemporary international migration has by and large not received due attention.

Spread over 15 chapters, the present book is a humble attempt to overcome these shortcomings. Along with such topics as size, distribution and growth of population, the book provides a comprehensive treatment to components of population change and salient social, demographic and economic characteristics of population. In addition, separate chapters are devoted to 'population-development-environment' interrelations, population policies and population theories. Each chapter with an empirical component begins with a general introduction to basic concepts and exposes readers to various measures and techniques. This is followed by a discussion on the world scenario based on data for major regions and different countries, in general, and India's case based on state/union territory and district-level data, in particular. For world-level discussion, the latest available data up to 2017 have been used. Likewise, for India, while data from the 2011 census form the basis of discussion in some chapters, in still others, the latest data up to 2016 from sources like NFHS-4 and SRS have been used. The discussion is well documented with figures, maps and tables. As a unique feature, the book contains a *glossary* of terms used in demography and population studies for the benefit of students as well as instructors. Written in very simple language, the proposed book is likely to serve a very useful purpose for students and instructors in India and abroad. How far I have succeeded in this endeavour will be known only from the response of the readers.

Revising and updating a book on a subject like this is indeed an arduous task. Although the process of revision had begun much earlier, it gathered momentum only in 2017 when I was granted sabbatical leave for one year to accomplish the work. In the course of preparing this revised version, I have received assistance and encouragement from several individuals. First of all I must express my sincere gratitude to my teachers at JNU, New Delhi, particularly Prof. Aslam Mahmood and Prof. Saraswati Raju for their constant inspiration in all academic endeavours. My interaction with students both at Maharshi Dayanand University (Haryana) as well as Ravenshaw University (Odisha) – the latter, where I served as professor during 2014–17, has been a major stimulating force. I indeed owe a lot to them. My friends and colleagues, namely R. B. Bhagat, Binu Sangwan, K.V. Chamar, Sachinder, Parmod Bhardwaj, Pritirekha Daspattanayak, Sibabrata Das, Padarabinda Rath and Sushil Dalal, really deserve appreciation for their constant help and support at various stages. I am extremely appreciative of the team at Routledge for their enthusiasm in executing the project in the shortest possible time. I also thank the anonymous reviewers whose valuable comments were a great input.

Finally, I would like to put on record my sincere gratitude to my wife, Pritirekha Daspattanayak, a professor of Geography at Ravenshaw University, and our two children – Hena and Aman – for their unceasing support in this endeavour.

However, I alone shall be responsible for any shortcomings in the book. Constructive criticism and suggestions are welcome. They will be duly acknowledged and incorporated in future editions wherever necessary.

1

INTRODUCTION

Human elements in geography

Geography has traditionally been concerned with a man-environment relationship, and, therefore, man and his activities on the earth's surface have occupied an important place in the discipline for a very long time. Nevertheless, with a greater emphasis on physical aspects, human elements were by and large missing from the concern of geographers for quite some time. Towards the end of the 19th century, however, the foundation for what came to be known as 'human geography' was already laid. It was Friedrich Ratzel (1844–1904) who established the new subdiscipline i.e. human geography for which he coined the term 'anthropogeographie' (Kosinski, 1984:15).

In 1882, Ratzel, considered as the single greatest contributor to the development of the geography of man, published the first volume of his book, entitled *Anthropogeographie*, in which he traced the effects of different physical features on the course of history (James and Martin, 1981:169). The second volume of *Anthropogeographie* was published in 1891. His works were quite influential in attracting the attention of scholars to population and its various attributes. Ratzel had keen interest in the mode of life of different tribes, races and nations. During his visits to the United States and Mexico during 1874–75, he developed interest in the life of people of not only German origin but also other minority groups such as the Indians, the Africans and the Chinese. In fact, it was his visits to the New World that led him to formulate general concepts regarding geographical patterns resulting from the contacts between aggressively expanding communities and the retreating groups. It was such research experience that had aroused his interest in the study of human geography (Dikshit, 1997:68).

Ratzel had a large number of followers in Europe and North America, and his *Anthropogeographie* flourished in Germany and outside, especially in France and the

United States. But the views of Ratzel and his followers on man-environment relations were essentially deterministic in nature, wherein the population phenomena were explained in terms of the influence of physical factors mainly. However, some German geographers, notably Kirchhoff, using the opposite approach to the study of human geography focussed on man himself instead of describing the influence of the physical earth on human affairs (James and Martin, 1981:169). Ratzel's second volume of *Anthropogeographie* was written from this perspective (Dikshit, 1997:69; Hartshorne, 1961:91; James and Martin, 1981:169), but it is interesting to note that Ratzel came to be known as a deterministic more from his first volume than the second one.

Alfred Hettener, another German geographer and a contemporary of Ratzel, regarded the study of population as an integral part of the general field of human geography. In his analysis of the separate branches of human geography, he singled out population and gave it equal prominence with other popular topics of that time (Trewartha, 1953:75). Along with density and numbers, Hettener treated the dynamics of population, i.e. regional birth and death rates, in-migration and out-migration, with equal importance in studies on population in geography. He emphasised that geographers should not confine their studies to biological phenomena only but also look into the social qualities, as they are equally important depending upon prevailing economic, political and socio-psychological conditions. Hettener's observations on the significance of the study of population in geography are, thus, among the most direct and illuminating on the issue (Trewartha, 1953:75).

In France around the same time, a viewpoint, contrary to *determinism* and popularly known as *possibilism*, was emerging as a guiding point for studies in human geography. Paul Vidal de la Blache (1845–1918) is credited for the development of this 'new geography' in France. The concept of possibilism envisaged that nature sets limits and offers possibilities for human activities, but the way man reacts to these possibilities depends on *gene re de vie* or the way of living, or what we may call as *culture*. Vidal's monumental work *Principes de geographie humane* (or subsequently translated into English as *Principles of Human Geography*) was published posthumously in 1921. Vidal de la Blache devoted one whole part or, one third, of his book on the study of population (James and Martin, 1981:191–2; Trewartha, 1953:74).

The ideas of Vidal de la Blache on human geography were later elaborated and popularised by his disciple Jean Brunhes. While analysing the elements of human geography in his volume *Human Geography*, Brunhes gave a very high position to the unequal covering of population on the earth's surface. Brunhes was of the opinion that two world maps were of chief importance in the understanding of human geography – a map of water and a map of population. To him, any description of population can, however, only be made through the spatial distribution of the dwelling and the morphology of settlements.

The works of Vidal de la Blache and his followers were undoubtedly instrumental in generating interest among fellow geographers to study human beings and their activities. However, as Trewartha (1953) later pointed out, their emphasis was so much on the cultural landscape i.e. the product of human activities on the earth, that population itself was by and large neglected. Though Vidal de la Blache did incorporate population distribution in the scheme of *Human Geography*, he completely ignored other geographical aspects and made no attempt to arrange and classify its content (Trewartha, 1953:74). Jean Brunhes, too, completely ignored the qualities or characteristics of population in his treatment.

Though several studies dealing specifically with population did appear in Europe, the United States and Russia in the late 19th and early 20th century, on the whole population remained a neglected field in the overall scheme of human geography throughout much of the first half of the last century. In other words, population geography was largely subsumed within the descriptive Human Geography mainstream (Barcus and Halfacree, 2018:6). After the Second World War Kabo made an attempt to gain acceptance of the social geography of population as a separate discipline in 1947. In the year 1951, Pierre George, a French geographer, for the first time presented a very comprehensive treatment of the facts of population in geography. However, the emergence and recognition of population geography as a new sub-branch of human geography is largely attributed to the influential statement of Trewartha in the early 1950s.

Trewartha's case for 'population geography'

In his presidential address before the Association of American Geographers on the occasion of its 49th annual meeting held in Cleveland, Ohio, in 1953, Trewartha made a very forceful case for population geography. He was very critical of the neglect of the study of population in geographical studies. According to him, since geography is fundamentally anthropocentric in nature, the number, densities and qualities of population provide the essential background to all geography. In his view, thus, population is the pivotal element in geography, and around population all other elements are oriented. He said, 'population is the point of reference from which all other elements are observed, and from which they all, singly or collectively, derive significance and meaning. It is population which furnishes focus' (Trewartha, 1953:83). Trewartha proposed a three-fold sub-division of geographical science in place of the traditional two-fold classification – physical and cultural elements (Figure 1.1) – giving equal importance to man in relation to the physical earth and the cultural earth. He also said that 'the study of population is logically the single most important approach to geography and the one in which regional concept has the broadest application' (Trewartha, 1953:86). Therefore, any neglect to the study of population, according to him, will cause serious injury to the geographical science in general. Trewartha argued for a focus on man instead of concentrating on the cultural landscape alone. Trewartha presented a very comprehensive framework for geographical studies on population. The acceptance of the sub-field in human geography owes much to his influential appeal to his fellow geographers.

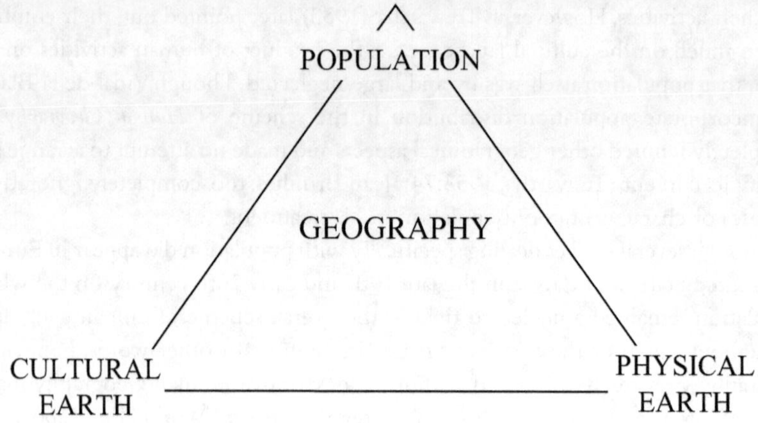

FIGURE 1.1 Trewartha's triad of geographical elements

Source: Based on Trewartha, 1953:81.

The roots of population geography

The early works of George (1951) and the influential statement of Trewartha before the annual meeting of the Association of American Geographers in 1953 are often considered as the turning point in the emergence of population geography as a separate field within geographical studies. The development, however, was not sudden. Nor was it unexpected. The roots of the sub-field can be located in developments that were taking place both within geography and outside during some earlier periods. While some can be traced, as early as in 19th century, others became potent forces in the first half of the 20th century. In addition to the growing recognition of the significance of human elements in geography, some other developments that were taking place in different parts of the world, and in different fields, helped a great deal in the emergence, and thereafter, growth and expansion of the sub-field.

As Kosinski (1984) and Clarke (1984) have suggested, growing availability of population statistics has played a crucial role in the emergence of population geography. Prior to the emergence of governmental and international agencies as sources of data, several private agencies, mainly in Europe, were involved in collection and compilation of population data. The UN agencies began publishing demographic statistics on a regular basis soon after the end of the Second World War. The UN also played a significant role in making the census data uniform and comparable across different countries by issuing guidelines and principles for census taking. The political and societal conditions both during and after the wars necessitated a geographical study of the ethnic composition of population of different regions. The need for a more detailed account of other demographic characteristics resulted in a switch over from macro- to micro-level studies, which in turn, facilitated population mapping. Population mapping has a long tradition in geography. In the earlier periods such maps were largely confined to distribution and density aspects. The growing availability of population data after the Second World War facilitated mapping of the other demographic attributes in different regions of the world.

Further, increasing use of quantification aided by access to computers helped geographers handle large data-sets. The onset of demographic transition in Europe sometime in the middle of the 18th century had resulted in population growth at a rate unknown previously in human history. By the turn of the 20th century, most of the developed countries had completed this transition. Around this time, death rates started declining in the less developed parts of the world. Remarkably, this decline, unaccompanied by a corresponding decline in birth rates, was much faster than what had earlier happened in the West. Thus, world population continued to grow at an increasing pace. Since most of the world humanity lives in the less developed parts of the world, a significantly larger proportion of the net addition in world population during the first half of the 20th century came from this part. There was a growing consciousness among the people regarding population expansion and its effects on economic development. The less developed countries had also begun experiencing redistribution of population within their boundaries from rural to urban areas. The emergence of large cities and their manifold problems became a compelling focus for research by geographers.

Admittedly, the consequences of these developments were not confined to geography alone. Other branches of study dealing with human population viz. demography and population studies were also undergoing parallel change. In fact, development in these related disciplines also played a crucial role in the emergence of population geography as a separate and independent sub-field in geography.

Population geography: definition, nature and subject matter

As noted earlier, population geography as an independent sub-field of human geography is a comparatively recent phenomenon. In the expression 'population geography', the term population signifies the subject matter and 'geography' refers to the perspective of investigation. Thus, 'population geography' can be interpreted as the study of population in spatial perspective. Etymologically, 'population geography' implies the investigation into human covering of the earth and its various facets with reference to physical and cultural environment. Population geography is concerned with 'the geographic organisation of population and how and why this matters to society. This often involves describing where populations are found, how the size and composition of these population is regulated by the demographic processes of fertility, mortality and migration, and what these patterns of population mean for economic development, ecological change and social issues' (Bailey, 2005:1).

In the academic world, any discipline is almost invariably defined by its subject matter (Johnston, 1983:1). The subject matter of population geography has been a matter of debate ever since Trewartha formally raised the issue in 1953. So is the case with the definition of the sub-discipline. According to Trewartha, population geography is concerned with the understanding of the regional differences in the earth's covering of people (Trewartha, 1969:87). 'Just as area differentiation is the theme of geography in general, so it is of population geography, in particular' (Trewartha, 1953:87). Population geography is the area analysis of population which implies 'a wider range of population attributes than most geographers have ordinarily included' in their analysis (Trewartha, 1953:88). Trewartha proposed a very comprehensive outline of the content of the sub-discipline, which many subsequent geographers seem to have adhered to. Broadly speaking, the concern of population geography, according to Trewartha, can be grouped into three categories:

1 a historical (pre-historic and post-historic) account of population,
2 dynamics of number, size, distribution and growth patterns, and
3 qualities of population and their regional distribution.

Regarding the historical account of population, Trewartha suggested that where direct statistical evidence is not available, geographers should adopt indirect methods, and collaborate with anthropologists, demographers and economic historians. In Trewartha's opinion, an analysis of world population patterns, population dynamics in terms of mortality and fertility, area aspect of over- and under-population, distribution of population by world regions and settlement types and migration of population (both international and inter-regional) form an important part of analysis in population geography. And finally, with regard to qualities of population he suggested two broad groups – physical qualities (e.g. race, sex, age and health etc.), and socio-economic qualities (e.g. religion, education, occupation, marital status, stages of economic development and customs, habits etc.). In his book entitled *A Geography of Population: World Patterns*, published in 1969, Trewartha arranged these topics in two parts. While the first included a geographical account of population in the past, the second incorporated all the characteristics of population including biological, social, cultural and economic characteristics.

John I. Clarke, who is credited with bringing out the first textbook on the sub-discipline in 1965 (at least after Trewartha had made the case of population geography in 1953), suggested that population geography is mainly concerned with demonstrating how spatial variation in population and its various attributes like composition, migration and growth are related to the spatial variation in the nature of places (Clarke, 1972:2). He opines that the main endeavour of population geography is to unravel the complex relationship between the population phenomena, on the one hand, and cultural environment, on the other. The explanation and analysis of these interrelationships is the real substance of population geography (Clarke, 1972:2). His book on *Population Geography* (1972) is spread over 11 chapters, and his treatment of the subject matter is in conformity with that of Trewartha, though not as comprehensive as that of the latter.

Zelinsky (1966) defines the sub-discipline as 'a science that deals with the ways in which geographic character of places is formed by and, in turn, reacts upon a set of population phenomena that vary within it through both space and time as they follow their own behavioural laws, interacting one with another, and with numerous non-demographic phenomena' (quoted in Hassan, 2005:8). On the delineation of the field of population geography, Zelinsky suggested that the list of human characteristics of practical interest in the population geography may be equated with 'those appearing in the census schedules and vital registration system of the more statistically advanced nations' (Clarke, 1972:3).

Daniel Noin in 1979, in his book *Geographie de la population*, while agreeing with the scheme of Trewartha, opined that distribution of population, components of its growth and characteristics are the main concern of population geography (Woods, 1986b:16). More recently, while discussing the methodological problems in population geography, Proyer suggested that population geography deals with analysis and explanation of the interrelationship between population phenomena and the geographical character of places as they both vary over space and time (Proyer, 1984:25). According to him, population phenomena include 'the dynamics of population distribution, urban/rural location, density and growth (or decline); mortality, fertility and migration; and structural characteristics including age-sex composition, ethnicity, marital status, economic composition, nationality and religion'.

Obviously, delineating the precise field of the sub-discipline has been a major problem before the scholars ever since its beginning. It has been argued that population geographers have spread themselves too thinly over too large a field that they have not been able to establish a niche for themselves in population studies (Woods, 1986b:17). Scholars have, therefore, suggested that population geography should narrow its focus and concentrate on the components of population change (Woods, 1979, 1982, 1986a; Jones, 1981; Woods and Rees, 1986). Woods (1986a) has made a distinction between broad definitions and narrow definition. The former is described as an elaboration of Trewartha's wide-ranging agenda in which certain primacy is given to spatial variation in population, while the latter refers to the approach which prefers analysis of population dynamics, namely fertility, mortality and migration only. Noin's survey in 1984 of the contents of population geography textbooks that appeared during the preceding two decades revealed that the broad definition has been most widely used (Woods, 1986b:16). Woods (1979) and Jones (1981) proposing the narrow definition have confined the main concern of population geography to the analysis of fertility, mortality and migration at various scales. They claim that the narrow definitions reflect a new process orientation, contrary to the traditional pattern orientation of broad definitions, and are more in line with current trends in geography as a whole (Clarke, 1984:2). Woods and Rees (1986) propose the term *spatial demography* in place of population geography, which differs from the latter 'mainly in terms of the equal emphasis on mortality, fertility and migration as components of population change and distribution . . . its use of the statistical demographic methods and its multi-disciplinary approach' (quoted in Heenan, 1988:282). For Barcus and Halfacree, 'studying Population Geography requires core demographic indicators such as births, deaths and migration not to be thought of in isolation but examined through their entanglements with the full panoply of diverse processes that construct everyday life' (Barcus and Halfacree, 2018:3). However, as pointed out by Heenan (1988), the distinction seems to be one of semantics rather than one based on critical or substantial epistemological or methodological differences.

From the preceding, it is, however, clear that the main difference of opinion is on the main thrust in the sub-discipline and not on approach and methodology *per se*. Woods himself says that 'the role of population geography is to provide the spatial perspective in population studies' (Woods, 1982:247), and that 'population geography should be what geographers active in teaching and research do' (quoted in Heenan, 1988:283). To quote Heenan, 'if that is so, then in view of apparently increasing erosion of disciplinary boundaries among subjects of common interest in population studies, a case might be made in favour of a definition encompassing any work in which the perspective is principally and explicitly a spatial one – in other words, such a definition would refer to a kind of approach and supporting methodology, rather than to a more or less exclusive disciplinary orientation' (Heenan, 1988:283). As Woods himself admitted, the two – broad and narrow definitions – are not mutually exclusive, rather they represent differences of emphasis (Woods, 1986b:17). They are complementary to each other, and taken together provide the full diversity of works undertaken by researchers in the field of population geography. It has been rightly remarked by Clarke that one cannot possibly do justice to all the aspects of population that appear in the census schedules or vital registration system (as suggested by Zelinsky), and that some will receive more treatment than others, partly because they are more central to the theme of population geography, and partly because they have attracted closer attention from geographers (Clarke, 1972:3). Newman and Matzke (1984) suggest that population geography is a relatively open field of inquiry with a recognisable core beyond which there may be many issues that relate to people and their wellbeing (quoted in Woods, 1986b:16). The core includes 'demographic variables, population change and distribution; while beyond may lie "social and economic indicators" (e.g. language, ethnicity, religion, occupation); residential characteristics (rural and urban); and "population in its broader human context" (e.g. resources, politics, policy)' (Woods, 1986b:16–17).

To conclude, the main concern of population geography revolves around the following three aspects of human population:

- size and distribution including the rural-urban distribution of population.
- population dynamics – past and present trends in growth and its spatial manifestation; components of population change viz. fertility, mortality and migration.
- population composition and structure. They include a set of demographic characteristics (such as age-sex structure, marital status and average age at marriage etc.); social characteristics (such as caste, racial/ethnic, religious and linguistic composition of population; literacy and levels of educational attainment etc.); and economic characteristics (such as workforce participation rate and workforce structure etc.).

In addition to the preceding, as government policies and measures in a country have significant bearings on population and its various attributes, a population geographer also concerns himself or herself with policies and programmes designed to regulate population size and its attributes. There exists a very intimate association between population size and economic development. Expanding population is generally viewed as a deterrent to economic progress in a country. Of late, deteriorating environmental quality the world over is also being attributed to rapid growth in population. However, the nature of the precise link between population growth, on the one hand, and economic development and environmental degradation, on the other, varies a great deal from one part of the earth to another depending upon various social and economic parameters. These and similar other issues, therefore, also form part of the overall concern of a population geographer.

Subsequent developments in population geography

If we take the early works of George (who brought out the first textbook on population geography in 1951) and Trewartha (who made a forceful case of population geography in 1953) as the beginning of population geography, the sub-discipline has witnessed enormous growth and diversification during the last six and a half decades. It has now become a multi-faceted field of study. The 1960s witnessed the emergence of a large number of textbooks on the theme (for instance by Clarke in 1965; Zelinsky in 1966; Beaujeu-Garnier in 1966; and Trewartha in 1969). Population geography as an independent sub-discipline was introduced at graduate and post-graduate levels in various universities of the world.

This was the time when Human Geography was witnessing significant reorientation in the wake of *quantitative revolution*. Population geography could not remain aloof from this development. Under the influence of *positivist* philosophy, scientific methods of analysis were increasingly replacing the 'empiricist-descriptive' approach in regional mode that had dominated the academic discourse for a long time. Population geography, thus, gradually moved away from the traditional focus on 'intrinsic nature and universal attributes of population' to a scientific analysis of demographic facts in spatial perspective (Barcus and Halfacree, 2018:7).

The development of population geography was, however, not as rapid as one might have expected in the 1970s, particularly in light of further addition to the existing textbooks on the sub-discipline. The research output was also not as focussed or as innovative as in some other aspects of geography, partly because the thrust was in areas somewhat peripheral to population geography (Clarke, 1977:137). Although there were studies on the relationship of population phenomena with social or economic development, much of the works continued to be descriptive in nature. Likewise, though fertility and mortality did attract attention, migration analysis engaged population geographers throughout much of the 1960s and the 1970s. Of many works on migration that appeared during the period, mention may be made of *People on the Move*, a collection of 23 papers by Kosinski and Prothero in 1975. A classic work on migration, it covered such wide-ranging topics as theoretical framework and typology of migration, problems of migration data, empirical and comparative studies of internal migration, issues related with different groups of migration etc. Undoubtedly, the aspect of population geography which developed the most in the early decades was migration analysis, an issue that never appealed to the demographers in the same way as did fertility, nuptiality and mortality.

The major thrust on migration analysis by geographers got further impetus in the wake of rapid world urbanisation during the 1960s and the 1970s particularly in the less developed parts of the world. Population redistribution and related government policies received increased attention of geographers. One remarkable development in the sub-discipline was a move away from mere population patterns to the study of processes especially migration. No sooner had the quantitative revolution engulfed academia in the late 1950s and early 1960s, strong criticism began to pour in. Thus, there was a switch over from the macro-analytic explanation of social physics towards the micro-analytic explanation of *behaviouralism*, though the former was not completely given up (Clarke, 1979:263). Behaviouralism, too, began to be criticised for not completely breaking away from positivism. There was a growing discontent among academia with the process as well as the contents or topics of research. By the close of the 1970s, thus, Human Geography scholarship started moving away from the 'abstracted and objectified value free conception' of positivism towards great diversity of *post-positivist* ways of thinking under the influence of *structuralism* and *humanism* (Barcus and Halfacree, 2018:8). However, the influence of these developments, particularly with regard to humanistic perspective, on Population Geography was not as immediate as in other sub-disciplines of Human Geography.

In the meantime, the preoccupation of population geographers with distribution and composition – the so-called traditional pattern orientation in population geography – attracted severe criticism by some geographers towards the close of the 1970s. The publication of two books – *Population Analysis in Geography* by Woods in 1979, and *A Population Geography* by Jones in 1981 – initiated a discussion on the need to reorder the emphasis in population geography. Woods and Jones emphasised that population geography should reflect process orientation, in line with the current trends in geography, with emphasis on population dynamics. Woods later suggested that the role of population geographers is 'not to describe the geography of population by emphasis on its distribution but to employ their spatial perspective in the analysis of demographic structures' (Woods, 1984:247). Criticising the broad definition, which makes population geography identical to human geography, Woods suggested that population geographers should redefine the core of the sub-discipline and master the modern techniques. He suggested that spatial variation in mortality, fertility and migration, together with those of population distribution, should form the core areas of the sub-discipline. The period that followed witnessed a reordering of emphasis and resultant significant contributions from population geographers in the areas of modelling and estimation, policy-oriented research designed to assess the impact of population programmes and causes of long-term demographic changes (Woods, 1984:248). Population geography thus became strongly demographic and moved in the direction of being redefined as *spatial demography* (Findlay, 1991:64).

Population geography's trajectory from the time empiricism and positivism had dominated academic discourse is marked with tremendous expansion and diversification under the influence of structuralism and humanism that swept all social sciences in the post-positivist period. Emphasis on diversity further got a boost in the 1980s from the philosophy of *post-modernism*. Post-modernism discarded all the grand theoretical perspectives and stressed upon individual experiences. For Human Geography it implied production of multiple spaces for diverse groups, thus, giving rise to *population geographies* rather than a single population geography (Barcus and Halfacree, 2018:10).

However, it is also true that the impact of these theoretical debates on population geography was not as pervasive as in the case of other sub-branches of human geography. Empirical and quantitative analysis of demographic phenomena continued to dominate the academic discourse in the sub-field which invited severe criticisms from some geographers (see for instance Findlay and Graham, 1991; White and Jackson, 1995; Graham and Boyle, 2001) who called the mainstream discourse in population geography as 'methodologically conservative, neglecting theories and dominated by migration studies' (cited in Barcus and Halfacree, 2018:12).

Other disciplines – demography and population studies

The study of population is by no means the domain of a single discipline. Along with population geography, other disciplines such as demography and population studies also deal with human population though in a different manner.

Demography is a term derived from two Greek words: *demos* meaning 'people', and *graphy* meaning 'to study'. Hence demography is the study of the science of population. Guillard first used the term in 1855 (Cox, 1976:1), and, if defined in its narrow perspective, demography refers to the statistical analysis of the components of population change, mainly marriages, births and deaths. For this a term *formal demography* is more commonly suggested. Thus, demography is different from 'population studies', which unlike the former, is concerned with not only the components of population change but also their interrelations with various social, economic, political and biological variables. In the words of Philip M. Hauser, demography is 'concerned with the statistical analysis of population size, distribution and composition, and with the components of variation and change', whereas population studies involve the interrelations of demographic variables with other systems of variables (Hauser, 1975:7). This distinction is, however, no more relevant as demographers have, of late, shown increasing concern with social, economic and political variables as they affect the demographic behaviour of population. According to Cox, demographers 'take interest in the influences of social, political and economic variables on the functions of the components of population change, in the interplay between them, and in their effect on the population as a whole'

(Cox, 1976:2). The boundary line between the two has gotten blurred so much that they are used almost interchangeably nowadays.

Irrespective of the distinction between the two, demography and population studies stand clearly different from population geography in terms of their approaches. In practice while demography, as also population studies, is concerned with number, size and demographic processes for political units as a whole, population geography is concerned with aerial variation in these attributes. Population geography is aimed at demonstrating how spatial variation in the distribution, composition, migration and growth of population are related to the spatial variation in the nature of places. A population geographer is also concerned with the dynamic aspects of spatial variations over time or how spatial relations or interaction between phenomena occur (Clarke, 1972:2). This emphasis on space is the distinguishing feature of population geography.

The spatial approach has, however, become equally popular among researchers in demography and population studies with increasing availability of micro-level data during the last few decades. The contributions of demographers to recent advances in population studies includes many examples where regional and national levels of mortality or fertility have been the subject of discussion; or where migration, fertility or mortality were combined to create interregional population growth models (Woods, 1979:1). It has, thus, become increasingly difficult to distinguish the works of geographers from that of other disciplines (Clarke, 1977:137).

Both population geography and demography or population studies are mainly empirical sciences wherein they are concerned with statistical data and the mechanism of analyses. In terms of the techniques of analysis, knowledge of demographic techniques becomes indispensable to a population geographer.

Population geography in India

The origin of population geography as a separate topical study in human geography in India can be traced back to the late 1950s. Geographers associated with Panjab University, Chandigarh, played a pioneering role in the development of the sub-discipline in the country. Over a short span of half a century, population geography has grown into a major area of research and teaching in the overall scheme of systematic geography all over the country. Though some studies on population distribution and density by geographers did appear earlier, Gosal's doctoral work entitled *A Geographical Analysis of India's Population* in 1956, under the supervision of G. T. Trewartha, was the first systematic and comprehensive analysis of India's population in a geographical perspective (Krishan, 1997:74; Chandna, 2009:58). On his return, Gosal initiated teaching and research in population geography at Panjab University, Chandigarh, in the early 1960s. Gosal's work provided an initial framework and was followed by a number of similar studies by his colleagues using data on lower level i.e. villages and towns (Gosal, 1984:206). Thus, Panjab University has the distinction of being the first university to incorporate a component on population geography in teaching at post-graduate level. Subsequently, the sub-discipline was introduced at graduate and post-graduate levels in several other universities. The first textbook on population geography *An Introduction to Population Geography*, was brought out by Chandna and Sidhu, both associated with Panjab University, in 1980. The subsequent additions to the list of textbooks on population geography in the country include Chandna (1986, 1987), Lal (1988), Ojha (1989) and Hassan (2005).

A general review of research reveals that population studies in geography in the country have essentially been empirical in nature with a major thrust on 'from facts-to-theory' approach (Gosal, 1984:204). The theoretical approach – from theory to facts – has by and large remained neglected. It is not to suggest that one is superior to the other, or there is any dualism between the two. The two are basically interrelated to and interdependent on each other (Gosal, 1984:204). A balanced application of the two approaches will, therefore, promote not only the development of population geography but also geography as a whole in the country.

The theoretical approach in research and teaching in geography requires an adequate training in quantitative techniques and exposure to facts and methods of other social sciences like psychology, economics, sociology and history (Gosal, 1984:204). The contents of research and teaching in population geography leave much to be desired on both these counts. A cursory look at the content of the textbooks on the sub-discipline would reveal that population geographers in the country have generally shied away from demographic techniques and model building. Most of the studies on population in geography generally do not go beyond the description of spatial patterns in population attributes on which data are available through secondary sources. The tradition of fieldwork in population geography has been conspicuous by its absence. Among various secondary sources, census publications have occupied the central position relating to population studies in geography in India. The Census of India, as the largest source of population data, has been instrumental in the growth and development of the sub-discipline in the country (Gosal, 1984:204). To some (e.g. Krishan, 1997; Chandna, 2009), easy availability of vast amounts of data from secondary sources, particularly the Census of India, has not only led to a greater dependence on secondary sources of data in research but also made geographers somewhat complacent about the use of primary data. Interestingly, the main concern of geographers has remained bounded by the nature and type of data available in census publications. Population distribution and growth, its composition in terms of various demographic, social and economic attributes and migration have been the most favourite topics of research and teaching in population geography. It is not to suggest that these do not hold any significance in population studies in geography. What is important to note here is the fact that due attention has not been paid to the analysis of vital events viz. birth and death rates. The actual accomplishments relating to population geography in India have, thus, remained incomplete in its content. This deficiency can be attributed to the unavailability of accurate data, on the one hand, and lack of expertise among geographers in demographic techniques. Any account of spatial pattern in vital rates requires data at least at the district level. The Civil Registration System, which provides district-wise data on birth and death rates, suffers from a great amount of inaccuracy. The Sample Registration System, which is based on the principle 'dual report' and which is more reliable, provides data only up to state/UT level. India is a vast country with a great amount of diversity from one region to another in terms of its geography, historical experience and resultant social, economic and cultural attributes. This diversity is often found to be of a greater magnitude within states than those between states. Any discussion based on state/UT level data is, therefore, not adequate. Demographers have evolved techniques to derive estimates on birth and death rates using census data on age and sex composition. Geographers in the country need to acquire adequate knowledge of these demographic and statistical techniques, and incorporate them in the contents of teaching of the sub-discipline.

To conclude, population geography in India has not only remained largely empirical-descriptive with some influence of positivism but has also responded very little to the development of social theories under structuralism, humanism, and post-modernism. According to Gosal, the actual accomplishments of the discipline are therefore incomplete in terms of both spatial spread and content (Krishan, 1997:75). It is essential, therefore, to cultivate a theoretical approach in research activities.

2

SOURCES OF POPULATION DATA

Main or prime sources of data

Concerned with the regional differences in the earth's covering of people and their characteristics, population geography is basically an empirical science. In order to achieve the objectives, it is necessary for a population geographer to have data or facts on human population. There are two main aspects of population on which geographers generally require data. These are the state of population at a given time for a territorial unit including its geographical distribution and its composition, and the dynamics of population in time and space as a result of the combined effects of births, deaths and migration. Data pertaining to these two aspects are collected in two different ways. While in the case of one, data are collected at a particular point of time, the other refers to the recording of events on a continuous basis. The former, generally known as *stock data*, is represented by census and various social surveys, and provides information on size, distribution and various social, demographic and economic attributes of the population. The latter, on the other hand, is known as *flow data* and relates to the registration of such events as births, deaths and migration.

The census

The census is the single largest source of data for population studies all over the world. Though the modern census is the phenomenon of a more recent time in the past – in the 17th and 18th centuries – evidences indicate that enumeration of people was carried out in different parts of the world even during the ancient period. The purpose of such enumeration was, however, very limited i.e. for tax collection, or military conscription, or both. The earliest example of a modern type of census is known to have been conducted in New France (present-day Quebec) in Canada, in 1665 and Iceland in 1703. The first periodical census began in the United States in 1790 and in Britain and France in 1802 (Cox, 1976:28; Woods, 1979:17). By the middle of the 19th century almost the whole of Europe had developed the system. At the present time, almost all the countries of the world, excluding a few exceptions (notably China), conduct census counting at regular intervals (Woods, 1979:19).

The modern population census has been defined by the United Nations as 'the total process of collecting, compiling and publishing demographic, economic and social data pertaining, at a specified time or times, to all persons of a defined territory'. In other words, enumeration of the entire population of a country or a region at a particular time is called a 'census'. Periodicity is an important characteristic of a census (Clarke, 1972:8) in that such counting is done at a regular interval. Most of the countries, including India, conduct a census every 10 years. Another characteristic feature of a census is simultaneity, which implies that the entire population is counted simultaneously at a specified point of time. Since census involves counting of all the individuals of a country or a region, the actual exercise is invariably spread over a period of time, say a week or a fortnight. The actual counts, however, refer to a particular date and time known as *reference date* or *census moment* or *census time*. This is achieved by adjusting the figures for the births, deaths and migration that take place between the actual counting and the reference date through additional inquiries soon after the reference date. Further, in the enumeration process, two approaches are adopted. These are *de facto* and *de jure*. In the *de facto* approach, used in Australia for instance, each individual is recorded at the place where he or she is found at the time of enumeration. As against this, in the *de jure* approach, as in the United States, people are recorded at their normal or usual place of residence. In some countries, however, a combination of both the approaches is used, for instance in Brazil and England.

One of the major problems for a population geographer concerning census data is the difference in the level of detail provided, the accuracy of returns and the period of coverage across different countries of the world. This renders any international comparison very difficult. However, with the initiatives of the United Nations, a good amount of comparability has been achieved in data, though limited to a small number of variables, of different countries. Furthermore, the census data of the more advanced countries are, in general, more accurate and reliable than those of the underdeveloped or developing countries. The censuses in such countries are nominative and require individuals or household to complete their own forms (Woods, 1979:19). After the Second World War, with the assistance of the United Nations, the developing countries have begun census operations in a more scientific manner, and the output is becoming more and more reliable.

Vital statistics

The data on vital events such as births, deaths, marriages, divorces, separations, annulment and adoption etc. are known as vital statistics. The continuous recording of such data is known as the vital registration system or civil registration system. Though a practice of collecting information on the list of baptisms, burials and weddings by churches is known to have existed from a much earlier time in Europe, the vital registration system is a matter of the 19th and 20th centuries only. The first civil registration system was introduced in England and Wales in 1836 and Scotland in 1854. Britain, however, cannot be regarded as the birthplace of official vital statistics (Cox, 1976:23). Even before Britain, in Sweden a law for the making of tabular records of population had come into existence as early as 1748. This law provided for the regular recording of births and deaths along with other ancillary information for each parish. In fact, in the Scandinavian countries, there has been a continuous system of registering births, deaths and marriages since the mid-18th century.

Along with vital events, vital statistics also provide several other ancillary information. In case of birth, for instance, additional details on sex of the baby, mother's age, the number of her previous children, the order of the birth, the residence of the parents etc. are also recorded. Likewise, in the case of death, information on date and place of death, sex, age and occupation of the deceased and the cause of death are recorded. The vital statistics are an important tool for studying the dynamics of the population of any country or region. However, as noted in the case of census data also, the vital statistics are marked with a great amount of inaccuracy in a larger part of the world, particularly among the developing countries including India. Many of the developing countries still do not have a system of continuous registration of vital events. This poses a serious problem for a population geographer while mapping the world patterns of vital events. The inaccuracy of data on vital events in developing countries due to poor coverage renders a researcher's attempt on the study of population dynamics a very difficult task.

Demographic sample surveys

Demographic sample surveys form another important source of population data. In sample surveys data are obtained from selected samples and the extent of statistical error in the data is minimised by regulating the size of the samples. The data thus obtained have several uses – in bringing up-to-date results of a complete count taken some time in the past, in checking the accuracy and in supplementing the data of the current complete count etc.

The collection of data through sample surveys has several advantages over periodic complete counts. It requires a smaller number of staff or interviewers, and thus, is less expensive. With the help of more skilled interviewers and properly designed questionnaires, information on some specific topics can be obtained in detail through sample surveys which are ordinarily not possible in periodic complete counts. The data obtained through a sample survey is more reliable. Further, sample surveys can be conducted more often and questions asked can be varied from time to time.

Despite these advantages, sample surveys cannot replace the complete counts. Sample surveys and periodic complete counts are basically complementary to each other. An efficient sampling requires stratification, and this can be achieved only if there is a suitable reference framework based on a recent complete count of some sort (Cox, 1976:42). Likewise, sampling becomes indispensable at every stage of census enumeration – at the planning stage, in the enumeration itself, in the course of processing and tabulation of data, and in the post-enumeration checks of the accuracy of the data.

Population registers

In the Scandinavian countries, and some other European countries like the Netherlands, Belgium and Finland, local registration bureaus maintain registers in which details about each individual are continuously recorded. These registers are known as *population registers* and they provide a comprehensive account of the changes that take place in population. In this system, a separate card for each individual is maintained from the time of his or her birth (or immigration) to his or her death (or emigration). On this card all the information pertaining to changes in the civil status, along with other details of socio-economic and demographic importance, are continuously entered. Some non-European countries like Taiwan and Korea are also known to maintain such registers. The primary objective behind this system is to establish the identity of the individuals and to keep a vigil on them (Bhende and Kanitkar, 2011:56). Population registers, however, are an important source of a wide range of population data ordinarily not available from both the census counting and the vital registration system. They also provide a very good account of the contribution of migration in population change of a country.

Sweden is said to be the first country to have started this system in the 17th century (Ramakumar, 1986:182). It is obvious that the population registers can be maintained more efficiently for small populations with a higher level of culture. However, even those countries which maintain such registers cannot afford to do away with periodic censuses. One of the disadvantages of the system is the fact that a register as detailed as this might constitute an infringement on individual liberty (Petersen, 1975:29). That is why only a few nations attempt to maintain population registers in spite of the wealth of population data that they provide.

International publications

The United Nations and its various organs, along with other international agencies such as the World Bank, publish population data for the world and for different countries at regular intervals. The most important of them is the *Demographic Year Book*, published by the UN. It provides data on such wide-ranging topics as population size, area, density, percentage urban population, population growth, age-sex composition, number of births and birth rate, number of deaths and death rate etc. Sometimes the volume is devoted to special topics, which include fertility, mortality, marriage, divorce, migration, and population census statistics. The special volume includes detailed statistics regarding the topic. Besides the year book, the UN also publishes the *Population and Vital Statistics Report* quarterly which includes the latest data on total population, total mid-year population and estimate of population for a recent reference year (Srinivasan, 1998b:56). Information on vital events includes total number of births, deaths, infant deaths, crude birth rates and crude death rates.

The United Nations Development Programme (UNDP) also publishes data on various social, economic and demographic aspects for the world and for different countries in its annual volume on *Human Development Report*.

Other international publications on world population data include *Production Year Book* of FAO, *Year Book of Labour Statistics* of ILO, *Statistical Year Book* of UNESCO, *World Population Datasheet* of Population Reference Bureau (PRB) and *World Health Statistics Annual* of the World Health Organisation (WHO). While the FAO publication provides information on agricultural population, the *Labour Statistics* of ILO gives detailed data on the economically active population. Similarly, the UNESCO publication provides data on education, literacy and school attendance for different countries of the world. The monthly periodical of WHO presents data on public health and mortality for different countries of the world. Apart from these sources, the World Bank also publishes data on various demographic, social and economic aspects in its annual volume entitled *World Development Report*.

Population data in India

As elsewhere in the world, data for population studies in India are obtained from census enumeration, vital registration and sample surveys. In the following sections a discussion on these sources and the nature of data is presented.

Population census

The first attempt to obtain the size of population in India was made during 1867–72. But this census counting was not synchronous, as it was not conducted at the same time in different areas. It did not cover the whole country also. However, as remarked later by Kingsley Davis, a famous demographer, this attempt was 'an auspicious beginning of census taking in India'. From 1881 onwards, census counting has taken place on a synchronous basis at an interval of every 10 years. The 2011 census is the 15th in the series and the seventh after independence. There are very few countries in the world with such a record of an unbroken series of decennial censuses (Bose, 2001). Up to 1931, the Indian census had adopted a *de facto* approach wherein enumeration was undertaken throughout the country on a single night. Obviously, apart from being very costly this method required deployment of an extremely huge army of enumerators. Hence, from 1941 onwards, the country switched over to an extended *de facto* canvasser method in which data are collected from every individual by visiting the household and canvassing the same questionnaire all over the country over a period of two to three weeks (RGI, 2011:4).

For a large and extremely diverse population like that in India, conducting a population census is a daunting task (Bose, 2001). Census enumeration is perhaps the largest administrative exercise in the world. The responsibility of conducting the decennial census rests with the Office of the Registrar General and Census Commissioner, India, under Ministry of Home Affairs, Government of India. Its main responsibility is to conceive, plan and implement census taking in the country. It is a union subject with the Ministry of Home Affairs in charge. A senior officer of the Administrative Services, with experience in census operation, is appointed as the Registrar General and Census Commissioner. Similarly, for each state/union territory an officer designated as Director of Census Operation is appointed. The responsibility of actual counting rests with thousands of enumerators who are drawn from primary and other schools, village *patwari* (in case of rural areas) and local offices. An enumerator is required to visit every household within the area allocated to him for collecting required information. The Indian Census Act of 1948 authorises the enumerators to ask the prescribed questions, and the respondents are legally required to furnish the details truthfully. The Act guarantees that the collected information will be confidential, and used only for statistical purpose, and not as evidence even in the court of law.

It may be of historical interest that although the population census of India is a major administrative function, the Census Organisation was set up on an ad-hoc basis for each census till the 1951 Census. The Census Act was enacted in 1948 to provide for the scheme of conducting population censuses with duties and responsibilities of census officers. The Government of India decided in May 1949 to initiate steps for developing systematic collection of statistics on the size of population, its growth etc., and established an organisation in the Ministry of Home Affairs under the Registrar General and ex-Officio Census Commissioner, India. This organisation was made responsible for generating data on population statistics including Vital Statistics and Census. Later, this office was also entrusted with the responsibility of implementation of the Registration of Births and Deaths Act, 1969 in the country.

The task of census taking begins with the notification of the government. A draft questionnaire is prepared and discussed in the 'Census Users' Conference' for finalisation. A pre-test in the form of a pilot survey is undertaken all over the country before finalisation of the questionnaire. Enumerators are appointed for the purpose and arrangements are made to provide training to enumerators along with all other functionaries. As a preliminary to the census counting, each house – residential or non-residential – is numbered and a list is prepared a few months prior to the actual enumeration. The house-list forms an important component of the enumeration as it provides a frame for the actual counting. It is used for collecting data on housing and household amenities. In order to facilitate house-listing, detailed 'national maps' and layout charts of all villages and towns are prepared. Finally, on the day of counting, the enumerators visit the households in areas allocated to them and collect data with the help of specially designed schedules. At the time of the 1991 census, 'household schedules' and 'individual slips' were used for the purpose. In the 2001 census, two schedules – one for 'house-listing' and another for 'population enumeration' were canvassed. The same was continued in 2011 also.

For the 2011 census, the house-listing phase began on April 1, 2010, and continued up to September 30, 2010. 'Population enumeration' was undertaken during the period February 8–28, 2011. A revisional round, as part of the post-enumeration check, was conducted during March 1–5, 2011, to adjust the figures for changes taking place between the exact time of the visit of enumerator to the household and 00.00 hours of March 1, 2011. It may be noted that the census data pertain to a well-defined point of time called a *census moment*. For the 2011 census, 00.00 hours of March 1, 2011, was the census moment.

A Post-Enumeration Check (PEC) is conducted immediately after the actual counting is over. This is designed to assess the level of accuracy of the count in terms of the 'coverage' and 'content' errors. Based on appropriate sampling procedures, PECs have formed an integral part of the census enumeration in the country since independence. PECs help in 'identifying areas that would need attention such as concepts and definitions employed, procedures of enumeration and related instructions to the field staff, etc. as well as in improving the conduct of future censuses. No attempts, however, are made to adjust the Census results based on the PEC results' (RGI, 2011:25).

Soon after the actual counting is over, the census organisation gets involved in the task of tabulation and publication of data. Initially, the preliminary results are announced and 'provisional' tables on aspects of immediate interest to researchers and planners are released. The same for 2011 was released by the office of the Registrar General and Census Commissioner on March 31, 2011, with perhaps the shortest time lag between actual counting and publication in the census history of India (Navaneetham and Dharmalingam, 2011). This is followed by publication of detailed final results. The census data are brought out in different volumes or tables, of which the most commonly used by population geographers are Primary Census Abstract (PCA), General Population Tables (A-Series), General Economic Tables (B-Series), Social & Cultural Tables (C-Series), Migration Tables (D-Series), Fertility Tables (F-Series) and Special Tables for Scheduled Castes & Scheduled Tribes (SC & ST Series). These tables are published at two levels: while the office of the Registrar General publishes 'all India' volumes, which provide state-wise data, the Directorate of Census Operation publishes data pertaining to lower-order administrative divisions i.e. districts, tehsils and blocks of the respective state.

The census provides data on a wide range of demographic, social and economic aspects. The demographic aspects on which data are available include size and distribution of population by sex and age for rural and urban areas separately. It also includes some information on fertility aspects such as number of births during the preceding year to currently married women, and children ever born and surviving related to ever married women. On the social aspects the information provided pertains to distribution of scheduled castes and scheduled tribes, population by religion, languages spoken, marital status, levels of literacy and educational attainment etc. They are given for males and females in both rural and urban areas separately. Likewise, on economic characteristics, the census provides data on workforce participation by sex and by broad age groups and distribution of workers in different industrial categories for males and females and for rural and urban areas, among others. These data are also available for scheduled castes and scheduled tribes separately. The 2001 census provided data on these economic characteristics along with levels of literacy and educational attainment for different religious groups also. This practice has continued in the 2011 census also. The 2011 census has, for the first time, provided data on population of transgender in the country. It may also be noted that the 2011 census has collected data on 'caste' after a lapse of 80 years on demand from various walks of life. Census of India collected data on 'caste' up to 1931 and thereafter it was discontinued. Migration or spatial mobility holds a very important place in the study on the dynamics of population change of any area. The census remains the single most comprehensive source of data on migration in the country. It provides data on volume of migration by sex and rural-urban status (both at the place of origin and the place of destination) on the basis of 'place of birth' and 'place of last residence' criteria. Migrants are further classified on the basis of 'duration of residence' at the place of enumeration. From the tables on migration data, a researcher can generate data on volume of migration in different streams and different distance categories. These are available for all the states/UTs and the districts of respective states. The census also provides information on reasons of migration, which was started in the 1981 census and has continued in subsequent censuses. The census also provides information on the characteristics of migrants in terms of their literacy status, levels of educational attainment, working status and distribution in different industrial categories at the place of destination for all the million-plus cities of India. In addition, the census provides information on houses, household amenities and assets separately for female-headed households and the slum population.

Vital or civil registration in India

The system of registration of vital events such as births and deaths in India was introduced by the British government way back in the middle of the 19th century. It was, however, concerned mainly with mortality data. This was the time when the death rates were very high in India due to poor sanitary and public health conditions. Any improvement in sanitary conditions, therefore, required complete and accurate data on mortality rates. It was with this objective that the British government had introduced the vital registration system. It was only in the then Central Provinces where a system of registration of births was also available as early as in 1866 (Bhende and Kanitkar, 2011:50). The Births, Deaths and Marriage Registration Act was promulgated in 1886 by the British government. The act, however, covered only areas ruled by the British. Moreover, as registration under this law was purely voluntary, the act served very little purpose. Coverage and quality of data were very poor. Furthermore, as the system was concerned mainly with collection of data on epidemic and diseases, it served very little purpose for the study of the dynamics of population change. The overall responsibility of recording and tabulation of data rested with the Sanitary Commissioner, and later with the Director of Health Services.

In the post-independence period, realising the importance of data on vital events in planning for social and economic development, the government took several remedial steps to improve the quality and coverage of the civil registration system. In 1960, the responsibility of collection, tabulation and publication was shifted to the Registrar General who also looked after census operation in the country. The Registration of Births and Deaths (RBD) Act was passed in 1969 to promote uniformity, and to ensure comparability in the registration of vital events and compilation of statistics thereof. The act replaced all the diverse laws that existed on the subject prior to its enforcement, unified the system of registration and made reporting and registration of births and deaths compulsory in the country (Singh, 2004:2435). Thus, the act provided for a compulsory registration of births, still births and deaths, and any failure to register such events was made punishable under the act.

The Registrar General is the central authority in charge of the registration system. The responsibility of overall coordination, providing technical guidance and setting standards for the uniform vital registration system in different parts of the country lies with the Office of the Registrar General. The Office of the Registrar General is entrusted with the task of consolidation, tabulation and publication of data on vital events. However, implementation of the provisions of the RBD Act is vested with the state governments, and registration of births and deaths is done by the functionaries appointed by the state governments. In each state there is a Chief Registrar who looks after the activities of civil registration. The actual registration of births and deaths is done by authorities as *panchayat secretaries* or station house officers (SHO) in the rural areas, and executive officers of the municipal councils/ *Nagar Panchayats* (municipal corporations have officers notified as registrars) designated as Local Registrars (LRs). The Directorate of Census Operations of a state/ UT is sub-ordinate to the Office of the Registrar General, and it is responsible of monitoring of the working of the act. Recently, the directors of census operations have been designated as the ex-officio Joint Registrar Generals under Section 3(2) of the RBD Act. The Office of the Registrar General publishes annual volumes on 'Vital Statistics in India' which provides data on the number of births and deaths, age of deceased persons, infant mortality rates, causes of deaths etc.

Despite the fact that any failure to register vital events has been made punishable, and that birth and death certificates are essential nowadays in legal disputes, for instance disputes involving property, the civil registration system in India is far from satisfactory. The data provided suffer from a great amount of inaccuracy owing mainly to underreporting of the events. Illiteracy and ignorance among people regarding the importance of such data are the main problems for the magnitude of underreporting. This is more so in the rural areas of the country.

Sample registration system

In order to make more reliable and accurate data available on vital events, the government of India introduced several measures during the Third Five Year Plan. One among them was the introduction of a system, known popularly as the 'Sample

Registration System' (SRS). The SRS data on births and deaths are more reliable, and are based on the technique of the 'dual report system'. In this, information about births and deaths is collected on a continuous basis from a sample of villages/urban blocks by a resident part-time enumerator who is usually an *anganwadi* worker/teacher. Then every six months a full-time supervisor, generally a regular staff of State Directorate of Census Operations, conducts an independent retrospective survey of the area. The data obtained through these two operations are matched. The unmatched and partially matched events are verified in a visit to the concerned household either by a third person or jointly by the enumerator and supervisor. Thereafter, an unduplicated count of births and deaths is obtained. The SRS provides estimates on births and deaths for various states and union territories for rural and urban areas separately. In addition, it also provides data for other measures of fertility and mortality viz. total fertility rate, infant and child mortality rates etc. at higher geographical levels.

The Sample Registration System was initiated by the Office of the Registrar General of India (RGI) on a pilot basis in some selected states in 1964–65. The system became fully operational during 1969–70 covering about 3,700 sample units. Just as in the case with the *civil registration system*, the Office of the Registrar General of India is the central monitoring authority. The Vital Statistics Division of RGI formulates and prescribes necessary standards, provides necessary instructions and guidance, and undertakes tabulation, analysis and dissemination of data. Results are published in the form of the *SRS Statistical Report* annually and *SRS Bulletin* twice a year i.e. in June and October. The sampling frame of SRS is revised every 10 years based on the results of the latest census. While doing so, issues like modification in the sampling design, wider representation of population, overcoming the limitations in the existing scheme, meeting the additional requirements etc. are taken into account (RGI, 2016:1). The first replacement of the sampling frame after the introduction of the system took place in 1977–78 while the latest one was undertaken in the year 2014.

The sample unit in the system in rural areas is a village or a segment of it if the population of the village is 2,000 or more. Smaller villages with a population size of less than 200 persons are excluded from the frame. Likewise, in the case of urban areas, the sample unit is a census enumeration block. At present, SRS covers a total of 8,853 sample units – 4,961 in rural areas and 3,892 in urban areas – in all the states and union territories of the country.

Sample surveys

Apart from the sources discussed previously, there are several socio-economic and demographic sample surveys conducted from time to time by various government and non-government agencies. They provide useful information on different aspects of population ordinarily not available in the census or vital registration system. Three of them deserve special mention here – the *National Sample Surveys* (NSS), the *National Family Health Surveys* (NFHS) and the *District Level Household Survey* (DLHS).

In 1950, the government of India set up a large-scale sample survey agency known as NSS (National Sample Survey) with an objective of collecting comprehensive data pertaining to various social, demographic and economic aspects on a regular basis through sample surveys on a nation-wide scale. Initially, much of the work related to surveys was entrusted to the Indian Institute of Statistics. However, in 1970, all aspects of survey-related work were brought under one organisation, namely the National Sample Survey Organisation, now called the National Sample Survey Office (NSSO) under the overall technical guidance of Governing Council. The NSSO comes under the jurisdiction of the Ministry of Statistics and Programme Implementation, and is headed by the Director General and Chief Executive Officer (DG & CEO) who is responsible for coordinating and supervising all activities of the organisation in assistance of a small secretariat called Co-ordination and Publication Division (CPD). Ever since its inception in 1950, NSSO has been a very important source of data on select aspects at the national and state levels separately for urban and rural areas. In NSS data are collected in its various rounds from samples drawn from different NSS regions. Each state is divided into one or more NSS regions, which are homogenous in terms of agro-climatic and socio-economic conditions. A proper representation is given to rural and urban areas. One round in the NSS covers a group of topics on which data are collected from the field and processed. The topics covered so far include, among others, births, deaths, morbidity, population growth, family planning, maternal and child care, details on physically handicapped persons, employment and unemployment, urban labour force, consumer expenditure patterns and poverty, housing conditions, literacy and participation in education etc. Table 2.1 presents a summary of population-related topics covered in the various rounds of the NSSO so far.

The first round of the NSS was conducted during the period October 1950 to March 1951, and so far 71 rounds have been conducted. Currently, NSSO is involved in its 72nd round, which is devoted to the survey of the service sector excluding trade and finance. Up to the 13th round, the duration of the survey varied from three to six months (nine months in the case of the 8th and 13th rounds). From the 14th round onwards, the duration of the survey work has been extended to one year with the exception of the 28th, 36th, 47th, 49th and 54th rounds. While the 28th round was spread over a period of nine months, the remaining covered six months only. From the 27th round onwards the quinquennial survey covering a larger number of households is conducted every five years. The last quinquennial survey was the 68th round conducted during July 2011–June 2012.

Availability of a reliable set of data on demographic and health outcomes at both national as well as state level is indispensable for formulation of effective policy measures. Introduction of the NFHS (National Family Health Survey), a Ministry of Health and Family Welfare project funded by the United States Agency for International Development (USAID), with its first round in 1992–93, was a landmark event in this direction. It provided invaluable data for researchers, planners and policy makers on population, health and nutrition with an emphasis on women and young children. So far, four rounds of the surveys have been conducted

TABLE 2.1 Population-related topics covered in various NSS rounds

Topics	*Round Numbers*
Vital statistics	7, 9 and 13, 22
Population, births and deaths	14, 15, 16, 17, 18, 19, 20, 21, 22, 23, 28 and 29, 30
Fertility, maternal and child care	17, 19, 28, 35, 39, 52
Socio-economic profile of aged population	42, 52, 60
Morbidity	17, 18, 28, 42, 52, 60
Migration	14, 15, 18, 27, 43 and 49, 55, 64
Family planning	16, 28 and 35
Literacy and participation in education	42, 47 and 50, 52, 55
Physically handicapped persons	16, 24 and 28, 36, 47, 58
Employment and unemployment	9, 10, 11, 12, 13, 14, 15, 17, 27, 32, 38, 43, 45, 46, 48, 50, 51, 52, 53 and 54, 55, 59, 61, 62, 64, 66, 68
Employment and unemployment of agricultural and other than agricultural labour household	11 and 12, 16, 19
Employment and unemployment of rural labour household	19, 20 and 29
Economic conditions of weaker section of rural population, slum population	25, 31, 58, 65
Urban labour force	16, 17, 18, 19, 20, 21 and 22

Source: Central Statistical Organisation, New Delhi.

in the country. Population Research Centres in different states and union territories in collaboration with selected Consulting Organisations or Field Organisations undertook the task of data collection. The International Institute for Population Sciences (IIPS), Mumbai, is designated as the nodal agency to coordinate the process of data collection in different states.

Based on uniform questionnaires and methods of sampling, NFHS provides an invaluable database on demographic and health-related parameters at national and state levels. The data collected in the NFHS are of a very high quality and are comparable with those of the Demographic and Health Surveys (DHS) conducted in many other countries. The DHS programme is an international project designed to collect comparable survey data across countries on fertility, family planning and maternal and child health (IIPS, 1993:11). In each successive stage, the quality and coverage of data have undergone marked improvements. Some of the issues covered in the first round of the survey (NFHS-1) were fertility and nuptiality, infant and child mortality, the practice of family planning, maternal and child health care and utilisation of services provided for mothers and children. Along with estimates on these aspects, NFHS-1 also provided data on demographic and socio-economic determinants of fertility, family planning, and maternal and child health. In addition, the second round of the survey (NFHS-2) that was conducted in 1998–99 provided information on nutritional status of women and the prevalence of anaemia among ever married women and their children below age three in the country. It also provided data on the quality of health and family welfare services, women's reproductive health problems, and domestic violence, along with information on the status of women, education and the standard of living. Along with the rural-urban estimates on select indicators, NFHS-2 provided regional estimates for five states (Bihar, Jammu and Kashmir, Madhya Pradesh, Rajasthan and Uttar Pradesh), separate estimates for three metro cities (Chennai, Kolkata and Mumbai) and estimates for slum areas in Mumbai. The third round (NFHS-3) conducted in 2005–06 still covered much larger issues than the previous surveys. For the first time, a separate module for men in the age group 15–45 was included and sensitive issues like sexual behaviour were covered in the survey (Rajan and James, 2008:33). NFHS-4, the latest in the series and conducted in the year 2015–16, was based on a much larger sample size than that in the previous three rounds covering all the six union territories in addition to the 29 states. NFHS-4 provides for the first time estimates of most of the indicators at district level for all 640 districts as per the 2011 census. This round of the survey has covered a range of health-related issues, including fertility, infant and child mortality, maternal and child health, perinatal mortality, adolescent reproductive health, high-risk sexual behaviour, safe injections, tuberculosis and malaria, non-communicable diseases, domestic violence, HIV knowledge and attitude towards people with HIV (IIPS, 2017).

The Government of India introduced the Reproductive and Child Health (RCH) programme in 1996 towards the overall goal of target-free, client-oriented and demand-driven approaches in family welfare programmes. An effective monitoring of RCH and formulation of appropriate strategies required micro-level data on utilisation of services provided by the government. The Ministry of Health and Family Welfare, therefore, introduced DLHS with its first round of survey, known as RCH-I, in 1998–99. Subsequently, three more rounds of the survey have been completed so far. The first two rounds were known as RCH-I & RCH-II (held in 2002–04), while third was called DLHS-3 and conducted in 2007–08. The latest round of the survey was conducted in 2011–12 and is known as District Level Household & Facility Survey-4. The International Institute for Population Sciences is the nodal agency for carrying out this national survey also. DLHS in its various rounds has included aspects like coverage of ante-natal care (ANC) & immunisation services, safe deliveries, JSY beneficiaries, contraceptive prevalence rate, unmet need for family planning, awareness about RTI/STI & HIV/AIDS and accessibility, utilisation and adequacy of health facilities.

In addition to the sample surveys discussed previously, there are several ad hoc sample surveys which provide demographic data for different regions in the country. They include surveys conducted by the Institute of Politics and Economics, Pune (1952–56), the Mysore Population Study (1953), the Patna Demographic Survey (1955) and the Family Planning Survey conducted by Operation Research Group (1970) among others (Bhende and Kanitkar, 2011).

3
POPULATION DISTRIBUTION

The world is the home of over 7.5 billion people distributed over the globe in a very uneven manner. On the one extreme, vast areas including the hot and the cold deserts, the polar areas, the mountain ranges etc. are either uninhabited or very thinly populated. As against this, the fertile plains with favourable climatic conditions are very densely populated. Less than one-fifth of the land surface accommodates nearly nine-tenths of the world population. Population geographers have traditionally been interested in this uneven spatial expression from region to region and from place to place. The present chapter discusses some of the salient features of population distribution in the world, in general, and in India, in particular. Factors affecting population distribution have also been examined. The terms – *distribution* and *density* – are frequently used in any discussion on the distribution of human population. It is, therefore, worthwhile to discuss the exact meaning of the terms and their various measures before we embark upon population distribution.

Density and distribution

Though density and distribution have precise and distinct connotations, they are sometimes used interchangeably. While distribution refers to the actual pattern of spacing of units of individuals over the earth's surface, density, on the other hand, is an expression of the ratio between number of people and land surface area.

Measures of density

Crude density, also known as *arithmetic density*, is the most commonly used measure of population density. It is expressed as the number of people divided by total surface area. India, for example, has an average density of 382 persons per square kilometre, as per the latest census of 2011. Crude or arithmetic density can be worked out separately for rural and urban areas. Being an average figure, crude density suffers from a serious limitation. Crude density is one-dimensional and tells little about the opportunities and obstacles contained in the relationship between people and land. Since it takes into account the total surface area, crude density presents a very misleading picture, and particularly when there is significant variation in density within a region. Egypt, for instance, with a population of 93.4 million in the middle of 2017 and a geographical area of 1,004.9 thousand square kilometres presents a crude density of over 90 persons per square kilometre. However, it has been estimated that nearly 98 per cent of Egypt's population occupies less than 5 per cent of the country's total area – in the Nile valley and delta where density is more than 1,000 persons per square kilometre – while the rest of the country is desert. Geographers have, therefore, devised other measures of density by modifying numerator or denominator or both to illustrate the actual variation in density of human occupation within a region.

When total population is viewed in relation to the amount of land under cultivation in a region we get *physiological* or *nutritional density*. This is a more meaningful index of population density in any area. In the case of Egypt, while the crude density is only 93, physiological density works out to be nearly 3,498 thousand persons per square kilometres of arable land according to PRB, 2017. This measure is very appropriate for a situation where agriculture is the mainstay of population. But it is also true that not all the people in a region or country are dependent on agriculture. Thus, physiological density also does not provide an accurate picture of population pressure on land. As a further refinement, *agricultural density* is worked out which refers to a ratio between the number of people earning their living or subsistence from working the land and the total amount of farmland. In the economically advanced countries, agricultural densities are very low as compared to the less advanced countries.

As cultivable and cultivated areas of a region or country are generally not of uniform value, agricultural density does not provide an exact account of man-land relations. Vincent, a French geographer, in 1946, therefore, suggested an index, which he termed as *comparative density* (Clarke, 1972:30). In the calculation of comparative density, total population of a region is related to the aggregate of weighted land under cultivation according to its productivity. Thus, it is type of physiological density taking into account the varying levels of productivity of cultivated lands in any area.

It is worthwhile to note here that the measures of density discussed earlier are of no practical value for areas which are more urbanised and industrialised. In the developed countries of the West vertical expansions of residential complexes invalidate the relationship between population and areas, and these measures, therefore, reveal nothing about the concentration of people within buildings. In such circumstances *room density*, or average number of persons per room, provides a useful index widely used by the planners and geographers.

Measures of distribution

A number of measures are used by geographers in the analysis of population distribution in any country or region. Of them, the ones relating to centrality, dispersion and concentration of population are very useful tools in the development plans of emergent nations. Like central tendency in a linear distribution, centrality of population distribution is measured in terms of its mean, median and modal centres. Calculation of these measures is, however, a complex and tedious exercise.

Mean centre, or as sometimes also called *mean point*, is the simplest measure of the centre of a population distribution. It is similar to the arithmetic mean of a linear distribution and is worked out very much in the same way. For the location of mean centre on a map showing distribution of points, it is necessary to device some way of quantifying the location of each of those points. This is done by calculating the co-ordinates of each point according to an arbitrary system. Geographers are familiar with the measurement of location in terms of latitude and longitude. The first step, therefore, involves superimposing a grid system on the map where the vertical and the horizontal axes are orthogonal, and lines are drawn at equal spacing. The point of origin is conventionally kept at the bottom left-hand corner. In the next step, the co-ordinates (*x*- and *y*-axes) of each point are calculated. The means of the two axes represent the mean centre of the points.

Mean centre can be considered as the centre of gravity of any spatial distribution. Geographers are generally interested in some average centre of the distribution of towns or villages in a region. These towns or villages differ in terms of population size from one another. The ones larger in size will, therefore, have a greater influence on the location of mean centre. It is, thus, necessary to incorporate this dimension in the formula for calculating the mean centre. This is done by assigning some weight (i.e. population size in the present case) to the *x*- and *y*-axes for each point, and then working out the weighted mean. The weighted means of the two axes, thus, represent the location of mean centre of the distribution. The final equations corresponding to the two axes of the mean centre are thus:

For the *x*-axis:

$$\sum_{i=1}^{n} x_i p_i \; / \; P \tag{3.1}$$

and, similarly, for the *y*-axis:

$$\sum_{i=1}^{n} y_i p_i \; / \; P \tag{3.2}$$

where 'x_i' and 'y_i' are the co-ordinates of the '$_i$th' town or village, 'p_i' is the population of that town or village and '*P*' is the total population of the region.

'Of the various measures of central tendency in a spatial distribution, mean centre is the most useful tool for studying the aerial shifts in population distribution over time. However, its main disadvantage lies in the fact that it is greatly affected by the settlements having extreme sizes of population' (Clarke, 1972:35).

Median centre is another measure of average location of population in a region. Just as the median in a linear distribution is a value which has half the values above it and half the values below it, the median centre in a spatial distribution is the intersection of two orthogonal lines each of which has equal population on either side. The main advantage of the median centre is the fact that it can easily be worked out without resorting to too much of mathematical calculations. However, it is important to note that the location of median centre of a population depends upon the orientation of the two lines. Once the orientation is changed, the location of the median centre gets changed. Since the location of median centre is not fixed, its use should be restricted to preliminary investigation only (Ebdon, 1985:133). Nevertheless, as Clarke (1972) has suggested, the median point is the best index of centrality for a population distribution, and is the most useful for comparing different distributions in the same area at the same time.

Similarly, a point can be located in the distribution from which the sum of distances to all the points is a minimum. Termed as the *centre of minimum travel*, the measure is helpful in the identification of the optimum location for some centralised services in a region. The location of the centre of minimum travel can be determined by the process of trial and error – i.e. by measuring the aggregate travel distances pertaining to several probable points and then selecting the one which gives the lowest value. As in most of the cases, mean and median centres are generally located close to the centre of minimum travel, so either of the two can be used as a starting point. Alternately, centre of minimum travel can also be determined by superimposing a transparent mask of concentric circles.

And finally, *modal centre* of a population is also an important measure of spatial analysis. According to Clarke (1972), modal centre refers to the maximum surface density in an area. As he suggests, in all large populations modal centre coincides with the principal peak of population potential (for the discussions on population potential please see Chapter 12). Evidences indicate that most of the countries of the world with one principal peak of population potential are uni-modal. London, Paris and Buenos Aires are striking examples of uni-modal centres in the United Kingdom, France and Argentina respectively. Some countries are bi-modal with two peaks of potential, for example, Sydney and Melbourne in Australia. India with the mega-cities of Kolkata, Mumbai, Delhi and Chennai presents the example of a multi-modal distribution.

Once mean, median and modal centres are worked out, various statistical techniques can be applied to examine the extent to which population in the region is dispersed around them. Calculation of these measures is a fairly complicated exercise. Of the several such measures of dispersion, *standard distance deviation* is the most commonly used one, and is very simple to understand. The standard distance deviation is similar to the standard deviation of linear distributions. It describes the areal spread of points around the centre. It is determined in the same way as in the case of a linear data, and is obtained by dividing aggregate of the square of distance between each point and the mean centre by the number of points, and then taking its square root. The equation is:

$$S_r = \sqrt{\sum\left(d^2\right) / n} \tag{3.3}$$

where S_r is the standard distance deviation, d is the distance of each point from the mean centre, and n is the number of points. The calculation of standard distance for points corresponding to settlements of varying size of population requires modification in the equation accordingly. In the modified equation the distance between each settlement and the mean centre is multiplied by its population and then aggregated. The sum is then divided by the total population in the region, and finally the square root is taken (for details see Ebdon, 1985).

Unevenness in distribution of population over the earth's surface both at a given time-point and as an evolutionary process form the main concern of geographers. Hypothetically, concentration of population in an area is maximum where the entire population is located at one point, and minimum where individuals are located at an equal distance from one another. The tendency of a population distribution in any region towards either of the two hypothetical extremes can be measured by means of a graphical device known as the Lorenz curve.

Developed by M. O. Lorenz in 1905, the *Lorenz curve* has originally been used to measure the inequality in distribution of wealth and income in a population. Population geographers make frequent use of this graphical measure to depict the state of population concentration, and changes therein, in any region. The Lorenz curve involves plotting cumulative percentages of one variable against cumulative percentages of the other variable on a graph. In the case of population concentration, the aerial units are first arranged in ascending or descending order in terms of its density, and percentages of area and populations of each of the units are, then, worked out. Thereafter, cumulative percentages are obtained separately for area and population. These cumulative percentages are plotted on a graph – for example, the area on Y-axis and population on X-axis. The points so obtained are then joined by a smooth free-hand curve. For comparison, a diagonal line, showing the line of equal distribution, is drawn joining the points of origin and end (Figure 3.2). The deviation of any curve from this diagonal line is in proportion to the level of inequality in the distribution of population in relation to area in the region.

The overall concentration found in any curve may also be measured in terms of a ratio of the area between the curve and the diagonal line, on the one hand, and the total area of the triangle formed by two axes and the diagonal line. This is known as Gini's coefficient and can be numerically expressed as:

$$G = [1/(100 \times 100)]\{\sum_{i=1}^{n} X_i Y_{i+1}\} - \{\sum_{i=1}^{n} X_{i+1} Y_i\} \tag{3.4}$$

where X_i and Y_i are the cumulative percentages of population and area in the $_i th$ unit. In the case of uniform distribution of population the curve would correspond to the diagonal line, and the ratio will be 0. As against this, if the entire population is concentrated at one point, the curve moves along the two axes making the area between the curve and the diagonal line equal to the area of the triangle. Thus, the ratio works out to be a perfect unity. Hence, the ratio varies between 0 and 1 (for details see Mahmood, 1998). The maximum vertical distance from the Lorenz curve to the diagonal line is the *index of concentration*.

Mapping population distribution and density

The most common type of population distribution map is the one based on the *dot method*. This distribution of population on a map is depicted by dots (see Map 3.2 showing population distribution in India as per the 2011 census). The main problems involved in the construction of a distribution map relate to the determination of the value, exact location and size of dots. The success of a map depends largely on the choice of the value of one dot. There is an inverse relationship between the value of one dot and the required number of dots to be placed in one spatial unit. This value should be so determined that it is not so low that it becomes difficult to place the dots, nor so high that there are units without dots. The exact location of dots on a map poses another problem. Location of dots should, as far as possible, correspond to the actual patterns of population distribution on land. Obviously this is the most difficult task. Similarly, the size of dots depends on the scale of the base map and the number of dots to be inserted. The size should neither be so big that a coarse generalised effect is produced, nor so small that a blur is produced in the areas of dense value. Howsoever carefully the previously mentioned problems are taken care of, the resultant distribution map is always a compromise to some extent. Sometimes, symbols like proportionate circles or spheres are combined with dots to depict larger settlements on such maps.

An alternative to distribution map is a population density map. Though density maps do reveal variation in population, they too suffer from a fundamental weakness. They represent averages for respective units within which there may be substantial variation. Obviously, the smaller the units of area used the greater is the extent of accuracy likely to be achieved. The other problem with density maps relates to the selection of class interval. Care must be taken in the selection of class interval to ensure that major density values are given full weight (for more details on this aspect see Monkhouse and Wilkinson, 1980).

Population distribution, as already noted, is also sometimes described in terms of *concentration index*, a ratio between the actual population of a spatial unit and the average population size. Average population is obtained by dividing the total population in the region by the number of spatial units used for the analysis. For instance, the average population size of a district or state and union territory in India can be obtained by dividing the total population of the country by the total number of districts or states and union territories. Apparently, an index so obtained fails to take into account the differences in the geographic area of the different spatial units. It is, therefore, not an appropriate measure of population concentration in a situation where significant differences occur in geographic areas of different spatial units. In India, for example, a marked difference can be seen in the geographic area of the states/union territories. Even at the lower level, districts vary a great deal from one another in terms of geographical area. For example, Kachchh in Gujarat, the largest district in the country in terms of area as per the 2011 census, is larger than the 66 smallest districts put together. For the present purpose, therefore, a modification is suggested in the measure to explain spatial pattern in population concentration.

The modified index is actually the ratio between two ratios – the ratio between the actual population and the average population, on the one hand, and the ratio between the actual area and the average area of the respective units, on the other. The index thus derived is identical to the measure of location quotient, and can be mathematically expressed as under:

$$CI = (P / \nabla P) / (A / \nabla A) \tag{3.5}$$

where CI is the concentration index, P and A are the actual population and area respectively of an aerial unit, and ∇P and∇A are the average population size and area respectively in the region.

World distribution of population

Table 3.1 presents the distribution of population and related statistics for the world. On a surface area of little more than 23 per cent, Asia alone accommodates nearly 60 per cent of the world population (see also Figure 3.1). On the whole, the Old World is more populous than the New World. On a surface area of little more than 23 per cent, Asia alone accommodates nearly 60 per cent of the world population. Asia and Europe put together account for nearly 70 per cent of humankind on this earth. North America and South America, on the other hand, with more than 30 per cent of the surface area, contain only 13 per cent of the world's population. Likewise, because of unfavourable geographical conditions, Africa is the home of only a little over 16 per cent of the population even though it represents more than one-fifth of the total surface area of the world.

TABLE 3.1 World distribution of population, 2017

Major Areas / World	*Mid-year (2017) Population Estimates (millions)*	*Percentage of the World Population*	*Surface Area (thousand square miles)*	*Density (per square mile)*
Africa	1,250	16.59	11,698	107
Asia	4,494	59.63	12,263,	366
Europe	745	9.89	8,876	84
Latin America and the Caribbean	643	8.53	7,947	81
North America	362	4.80	7,700	47
Oceania	42	0.56	3,307	13
More developed countries	1,263	16.76	19,815	64
Less developed countries	6,273	83.24	31,975	196
World total	7,536	100.00	51,790	146

Source: Population Reference Bureau, *World Population Data Sheet 2003* and *2017*.

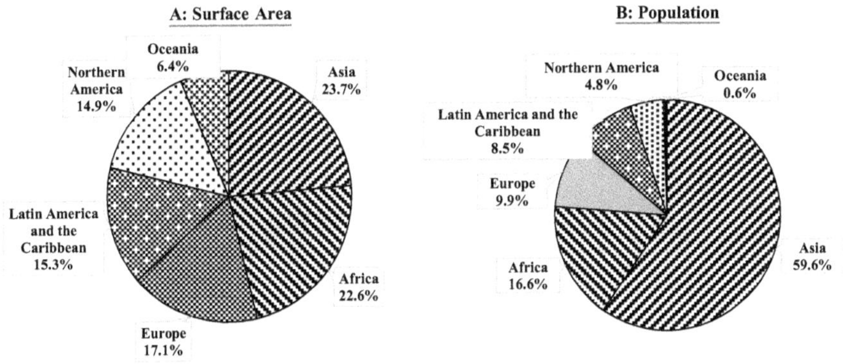

FIGURE 3.1 Distribution of world surface area (A) and population (B) by major regions, 2017

Source: Author.

The unevenness in the distribution of population is equally prominent within continents and countries. The southern and south-eastern parts in Asia are more populous than its counterparts in the north and west. Similarly, the north-western parts of Europe exhibit a greater concentration of population than the rest of the continent, and a majority of people in North America live along the Atlantic Coast in the east. Another striking feature of the world distribution of population is the disparity between the more developed and less developed countries of the world. Over 83 per cent of humankind resides in the less developed countries that account for only 61 per cent of the land surface area.

As already discussed population distribution over space is best represented by dots on a map. However, preparing a map depicting distribution of population in the world with the help of dots is not as easy as it might appear. Even when issues related to location and size of dots are resolved, unavailability of uniform data across the globe remains the single most important hindrance. Some authors tend to depict population distribution with the help of isopleth based on density figures while still others use density maps based on choropleth (see for instance Map 3.1). Nevertheless, some authors have described world population distribution with the help of dots. The work of Knowles and Wareing (1976) is one among them. Based on their description, three *primary concentrations* of humanity with outstandingly high population density on the globe can easily be identified. The first one can be seen in south and south-eastern parts of Asia where the world's two population giants – China and India – are located. This region alone accounts for more than half of the world's population on less than 10 per cent of its area. In the eastern part of Asia, the cluster adjoins the Pacific Ocean and penetrates towards the interior in the west along the river basins. Likewise, population concentration in south Asia reveals a coastal and riverine orientation. It is remarkable to note that the overwhelming majority of people in these areas are rural dwellers and depend

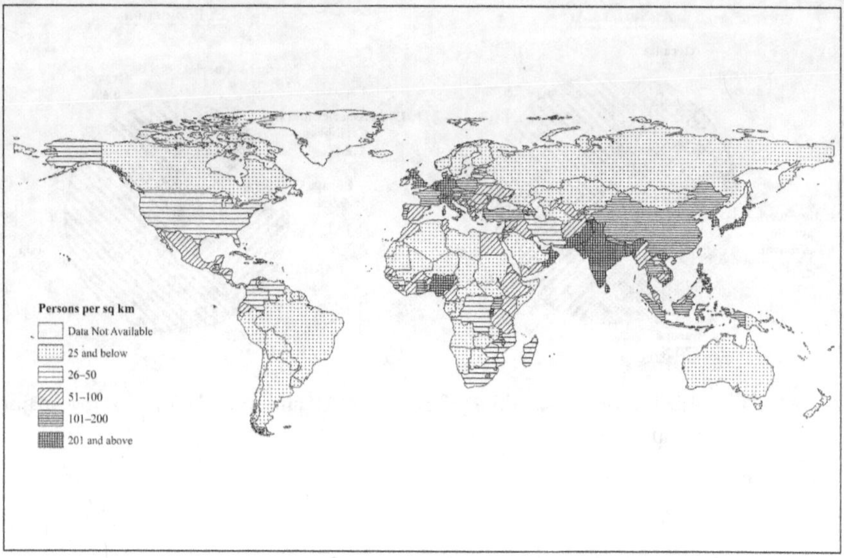

MAP 3.1 World population density, 2017

Source: Population Reference Bureau, *World Population Data Sheet, 2017*.

on farming, particularly in the coastal, lowland and the flood plains of major rivers (Norton and Mercier, 2016:159). The other two major concentration of dense population can be seen in north and north-western Europe and the east-central parts of North America. Unlike the population clusters of Asia, much of the population in these parts is concentrated in urban centres. Further, it is remarkable here to note that terrain and environmental factors in these parts have less to do with population concentration than in the case of Asian clusters. Unlike the Asian concentrations, which reflect correspondence with river valleys, the European population belt relates to the orientation of coalfields – the driving force behind the Industrial Revolution. These three regions of primary concentration taken together account for more than seven-tenths of the world's population. In addition to these areas of primary concentration, several patches of *secondary concentration* of population can be seen widely distributed over the globe. They include California, eastern Brazil, the river Plate lowlands, the Nile Valley, western and southern parts of Africa and the south-eastern parts of Australia. They account for anywhere between 5–10 per cent of the world population. Finally, there are numerous pockets of *tertiary concentration* of population scattered over the globe in the form of knots or strings. In contrast to these concentrations of high density, there are vast areas almost uninhabited by humankind. They are especially the high altitude areas located beyond 60° N latitude, mid-latitudes and tropical deserts, high mountains and plateau areas and areas of equatorial forests.

Ecumene and *non-ecumene* are the terms used by geographers to differentiate between the permanently inhabited parts and the uninhabited or very sparsely populated parts of the world. *Ecumene* was the term used by the ancient Greeks to signify the inhabited parts of the earth, thus distinguishing it from what they believed to be uninhabited in the equatorial regions and permanently frozen polar reaches of the earth (Knowles and Wareing, 1976:55). The term was revived by the German geographers in the early 19th century and has been subject to slightly differing interpretations. It has been estimated that approximately 60 per cent of the earth's land may be called *ecumene*, while the rest constitutes *non-ecumene*. The distinction between *ecumene* and *non-ecumene* is, however, not that sharp. Areas of high concentration of population gradually merge into sparsely populated areas. Even within the ecumene one may come across areas of very sparse population. Similarly the non-ecumene does contain dense settlement nodes in the form of oases, mining camps and other small communities. Perhaps the most anomalous case of settlement in the non-ecumene world is that of dense population in the Andes Mountains of South America and the plateau of Mexico. Further, the non-ecumene is not contiguous or vast as the ancient Greeks had once supposed. It is found in discontinuous patches spread over different parts of the globe and includes parts of tropical rainforest, mid-latitude deserts, high mountain areas, apart from the permanent ice caps in the polar region and large segments of the tundra and coniferous forests.

To conclude, the magnitude of unevenness in the distribution of world population can be outlined in the form of the following points:

- Almost 90 per cent of the world's population is found in the Northern Hemisphere, and two-thirds in the mid-latitudes between 20° N and 60° N.
- A large majority of the world's people occupy only a small portion of the land surface. More than 50 per cent of the population lives on merely 5 per cent of the land surface, two-thirds on 10 per cent and almost nine-tenths on less than 20 per cent.
- People tend to congregate in areas of low elevations. More than half of the world's population occupies areas below 200 meters above sea level, the zone containing less than 30 per cent of the land surface areas. Nearly 80 per cent reside below 500 meters.
- The margins of continents are more densely populated than interiors. Nearly two-thirds of the world's population is concentrated within 500 kilometres of the coast, much of it on the alluvial lowlands and river valleys.

Factors affecting population distribution

The irregular spatial distribution of population is the outcome of a continually changing pattern of adjustments by humankind to a variety of physical and cultural factors. Though of late, modern technologies have enabled people to live on any part of the earth surface, certain areas have tended to discourage human inhabitation due to adverse physical conditions and lack of sufficient opportunities of means of livelihood. It is, however, not to suggest that population distribution on the earth surface is determined by physical factors alone, for within the broad framework of physical attractions and constraints, cultural factors strongly influence the way humankind is distributed over the earth (Hornby and Jones, 1980:20). Apart from physical factors, numerous social, demographic, economic, political and historical factors affect population distribution. These factors operate not in isolation but in combination with each other. One cannot, therefore, isolate the influence of any one factor on population distribution. Further, the interplay between these determinants is generally very complex. The primary task of a population geographer, therefore, is to explain the irregularities in population distribution in terms of the influences of all these factors as an integral part of a dynamic process (Clarke, 1972:14).

Physical factors

Physical factors that affect population distribution include altitude and latitude, relief, climate, soils, vegetation, water and location of mineral and energy resources. It is important to note that most of the physical factors influence population distribution only indirectly through climatic conditions.

The influences of *latitude* and *altitude* on population distribution cannot be separated from one another. High altitude in general imposes an ultimate physiological limit upon human existence due to reduced atmospheric pressure and low oxygen content. Therefore, very few permanent settlements can be seen in the lofty mountains of the world at a height above 5,000 metres. Staszewski (1975) in his exhaustive analysis of the vertical distribution of population has shown that both numbers and densities in different parts of the world decline with increasing altitude. According to him a little more than 56 per cent of the world's population lives within 200 metres from the sea level, and over 80 per cent within 500 metres (for details see Clarke, 1972:18; Knowles and Wareing, 1976:58). However, in low latitude areas, which are otherwise hot and less favourable, high altitude provides suitable conditions for human habitation. Mountains in Africa and Latin America are much healthier than plains, and large cities have sprung up at high altitude. La Paz, the highest city in the world (3,640 m) and the capital of Bolivia, owes its existence to this factor. As against this, in the high latitude areas it becomes extremely difficult to live beyond a few hundred metres from sea level. It is in this context that we refer to 'mountains that repel and mountains that attract' (Knowles and Wareing, 1976:58).

Relief features also play an important role in influencing population distribution. The influence of altitude has already been noted. Among the other aspects of relief features which affect human habitation are general topography, slope and aspect. The main concentrations of human population are confined to the areas marked with flat topography. Rugged and undulating topography restricts the condensation of human population in any area. Abrupt changes in the density of population can be seen on the world map of population distribution where plains meet mountain ranges. Rising Himalayas, thus, mark the northern limit of dense population in the Ganga plain. Similarly, the Deccan plateaus with rugged and undulating topography appear distinct from the plains in respect of population concentration. In the mountainous areas valleys provide suitable locations for human settlements. Likewise sun-facing slopes provide favourable locations for the emergence and growth of settlements. This is particularly true in the temperate and other high latitude areas where insolation is very important. The river valleys may promote or restrict human settlements depending upon other geographic conditions. In Egypt nearly 98 per cent of the population is concentrated forming a ribbon along the Nile River. As against this, in tropical swamps and dissected plateaus, river valleys tend to repel population.

Of all the geographic influences on population distribution, *climatic conditions* are perhaps the most important. Climate affects population distribution directly as well as indirectly through its effects on soil, vegetation and agriculture that have direct bearings on the pattern of population distribution. Moreover, other physical factors like latitude and altitude also operate on population distribution through climatic conditions. Although climatic optima are difficult to define, extremes of temperature, rainfall and humidity certainly limit the concentration of population in any part of the earth. In the Northern Hemisphere, extreme cold conditions in the high latitude areas have prevented human habitation. Likewise, extremely high temperature and aridity in the hot deserts of the world restrict human habitability. Some of the geographers in past have, therefore, gone to the extent of claiming a deterministic relationship between climate and population distribution. It should, however, be noted that humans have the ability to adapt to different climatic conditions. This explains a high density in the tropics, which are otherwise marked with extremes of climatic conditions. Progress in science and technology has greatly augmented man's ability to adapt to different climatic conditions. Though limited in magnitude, the peopling of Alaska and Siberia during the last century owes to the scientific and technological advancements. The cases of Java and the Amazon Basin also serve to refute the deterministic stance of the relationship between climate and population distribution. Though both of them experience an equatorial type of climate, they differ markedly from one another in terms of population density. While Java is one of the most densely parts of the world, the Amazon Basin is marked with a very sparse population.

Similarly, quality of soils exerts an undeniable influence on the distribution of world population. The fertile alluvial and deltaic soils can support dense populations. Thus, most of the major concentrations of population in the world are located in the river valleys and deltas. Great civilisations of the world have almost invariably flourished on good fertile alluvial soils. Similarly, the *chernozems* of steppe grasslands and rich volcanic soils can support dense population. On the other hand, the leached soils of temperate lands, the *podsols*, which are very poor in terms of fertility, can support only a sparse population. In Canada, for instance, marked difference can be noticed in population concentration between areas of clayey soils and *podsol* soils. It is important to note that the influence of soils cannot be viewed in isolation, that is, soils influence population distribution in association with other physical factors, mainly climate. Moreover, progress in technology can alter the effectiveness of soil types on population concentration to a greater extent. Application of modern technologies during recent times has greatly enhanced the profitability of cultivation in many areas of the world which were hitherto not suitable for cultivation. Such areas have, thus, attracted population during the recent past. In association with climatic conditions, varying soil types give rise to a variety of vegetation cover on the earth surface. These in turn provide a contrasting environment for a variety of agricultural activities, and hence, lead to different population density. Tropical forests, savanna, tundra and taiga provide different media for human occupation and concentration.

Location of *mineral and energy resources* has led to dense population concentration in many parts of the world, which otherwise do not provide suitable conditions for human habitation. Large towns have grown up in inaccessible and extremely inhospitable areas such as deserts, polar regions or in the midst of forests where precious minerals and metals have been found. Kalgoorlie, a gold mining town in the Australian desert, is a very good example in this regard. Likewise, several other examples can be cited from elsewhere in the world including Canada, the United States and Russia. Location of coal, the most important fuel in the 19th and early 20th centuries, was the main factor behind industrial conurbation and dense population concentration in Western Europe. However, the influence of mineral and energy resources on population distribution depends upon a wide range of social and economic factors such as market demand, capital for development, availability of labour supply and transportation network. It is, therefore, important to note that the influences of all the physical factors outlined operate through a series of economic, social and political factors in the area concerned.

Economic, political and historical factors

Population distribution and density in an area depends to large extent on the type and scale of economic activities. The same geographic conditions provide different opportunities for people with different types and scale of economic activities. Technological and economic advancement can bring about significant changes in population distribution of an area. For instance, the prairies of North America offered different opportunities for the Native Americans with their hunting economy, the 19th-century ranchers, the later settled agriculturist and finally the modern industrialised and largely urbanised society. Each stage in economic development was marked with profound changes in population density and distribution in the region. Industrialisation and discovery of new sources of minerals and energy resources have, throughout human history, brought about redistribution of population through migration. In the pre-industrial agricultural societies, population distribution often fairly evenly distributed responds to the nature of crops grown and their relationship to physical conditions. The Industrial Revolution has resulted in considerable change in population distribution in many parts of the world. Dense population concentration has replaced long established patterns of dispersal and generally even distribution. Initially, sources of energy and mineral resources became the force of industrial growth and population concentration. Improved transport network, growing spatial mobility of labour and increasing trade in the wake of economic and technological advancements have led to a decline in the importance of place-bound industries. Growing commercial activities, for instance, in the developing world, accompanied by improvements in transport networks, have resulted in considerable redistribution of population and the emergence of mega-urban centres. It is aptly said that increasing complexity and diversification of economic activities the world over have led to a new pattern of population distribution.

During the more recent times, *government policies and political factors* have emerged as an important determinant of population patterns. With increasing state control over economic activities, government policies have led to a significant change in the patterns of population distribution in several parts of the world. In the erstwhile USSR, facilitated by advances in science and technology, population was directed to parts of the Siberian plain, which were hitherto not suitable for human habitation. Likewise, in China, planned colonisation of the interior, encouraged by the Communist government, has resulted in significant change in population patterns. In the late 1960s and 1970s, some 10 to 15 million people in the country were forcibly relocated to the rural communes in order to ease pressure on urban employment. Examples of government inducements encouraging migration to new areas can be cited from several developed countries of the West as well. In addition to government policies, *political events* have also caused redistribution of population throughout human history. Wars have forced a great number of people to migrate from one region to another all over the world. Post-partition redistribution between India and Pakistan, or displacement of several million Sudanese as a result of civil war, or expulsion of Asians from Uganda in the early 1970s are some of the instances of how political events can cause changes in population patterns.

Apart from the factors discussed, historical processes should also be taken into account while explaining the patterns of population distribution. Duration of human settlements is an important determinant of the magnitude of population concentration in any area. Most of the densely populated areas of the world have a very long history of human habitation, while sparse population in certain areas can in part be explained in terms of its recent habitation. It should, however, not be concluded that the highest densities are always to be found in areas with the longest history of habitation. There are several instances of formerly prosperous and densely populated areas which are now only sparsely populated. Parts of North Africa and Mesopotamia, the Yucatan Peninsula and eastern Sri Lanka are some such examples. Based on this, some scholars have talked about the *cycle of occupation*, whereby size and densities of population first increase and then decline only to be followed by another cycle of increase.

Distribution and density of population in India

India is the second-largest populous country in the world. Occupying a geographical area of 2.45 per cent of the world, the country accounts for over 17 per cent of its population in 2017 as per the estimates of the *Population Reference Bureau.* India's population stood at 1,210.85 million according to the final figures of the 2011 census. With a density of 382 persons per square kilometre as compared to the world average of a little over 50, India indeed is one of the most thickly populated countries of the world.

India is a vast country with a great amount of diversity from one region to another in terms of its geography, historical experience and the resultant social, cultural and economic attributes. This diversity is also manifest in the patterns of population distribution in the country. One of the unique features of India's population relates to its uneven distribution over space (Map 3.2). While the fertile alluvial plains in the north rank among one of the most thickly populated tracts of the world, the arid region of the *Thar* Desert in the north-western part of the country appear as almost uninhabited on the map. This unevenness in population distribution is best revealed in the fact that more than 55 per cent of India's population is concentrated in less than a quarter of its geographical area (Table 3.2). Likewise, more than one-third of the country accounts for only a little over 10 per cent of its population. Of the total 640 districts at the time of the 2011 census, the 100 most densely populated ones accommodated nearly 27 per cent of the population on an area that is less than 7 per cent of the country's total. The average density of these districts works out to be as high as 1,524 as against the nation's average of 382 persons per square kilometre. On the other extreme, the 100 least densely populated districts, covering nearly a quarter of the total geographic area, account for only 4 per cent of the country's population. The unevenness in the distribution of population in the country has been shown with the help of the Lorenz curve in Figure 3.2 on the basis of district-level data pertaining to the 2011 census.

Table 3.3 presents the *concentration index* and *density* of population of states and union territories corresponding to the year 2011. A great deal of regional variation can be seen in terms of both population concentration as well as density. As is evident, union territories are strikingly more densely populated than the states. Of the seven, as many as five union territories occupy the top slot in the country. The NCT of Delhi and Chandigarh top the list in terms of concentration and density of population. However, they account for barely 0.07 per cent of India's geographic area and 1.47 per cent of its population. Among the major states, Bihar ranks first followed by West Bengal, Kerala and Uttar Pradesh. It may be noted that the recent past has witnessed remarkable change in the ordering of top-ranking states in terms of density of population. Kerala, which had occupied the first rank till 1981, slipped to the second position in 1991, and finally to third position in 2001. After the creation of Jharkhand as a separate state, Bihar came to occupy the second position in the country in terms of density level in 2001 while West Bengal topped the list. At the time of the 2011 census, Bihar became the first ranking state while West Bengal slipped to second position.

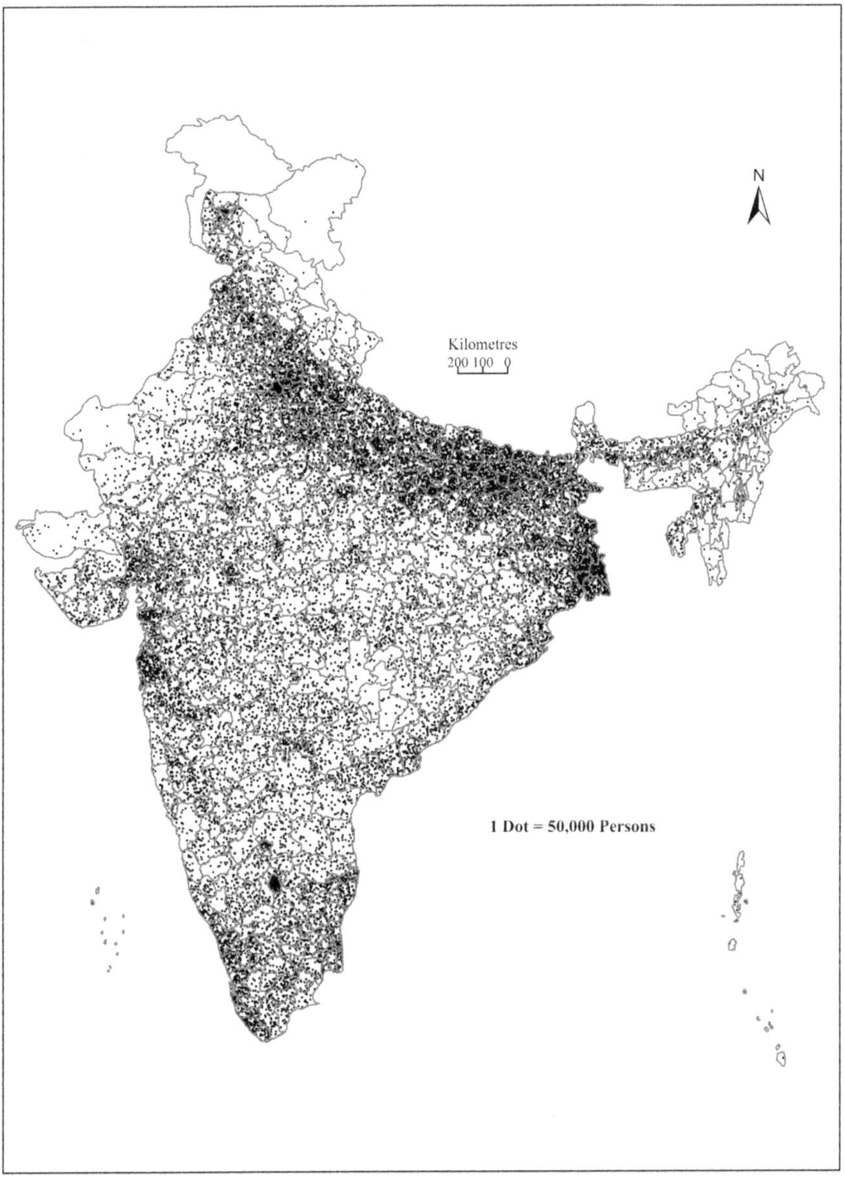

MAP 3.2 Population distribution in India, 2011

Source: Author.

Other states with higher density of population than the nation's average are Goa, Assam, Jharkhand, Punjab, Tamil Nadu and Haryana. From among union territories Dadar & Nagar Haveli also figure in the list. On the other extreme, from among the major states, Uttarakhand and Chhattisgarh report very low density. Jammu and Kashmir and Himachal Pradesh in the north, the north-eastern states barring Assam and

TABLE 3.2 Distribution of population and area by density levels in India, 2011

Density Levels (persons per km^2)	*Number of Districts*	*Percentage Share*		*Average Density*
		Population	*Area*	
Above 1,000	98	26.40	6.59	1,532
901–1,000	15	2.56	1.03	950
801–900	27	6.19	2.77	855
701–800	28	5.77	2.97	743
601–700	43	7.76	4.61	644
501–600	35	6.09	4.24	549
401–500	55	8.12	6.81	456
301–400	77	12.18	13.32	350
201–300	108	14.67	22.72	247
101–200	93	8.59	19.63	167
Below 100	61	1.68	15.32	42

Source: Computed by the author from *Table A-1, Census of India 2011.*

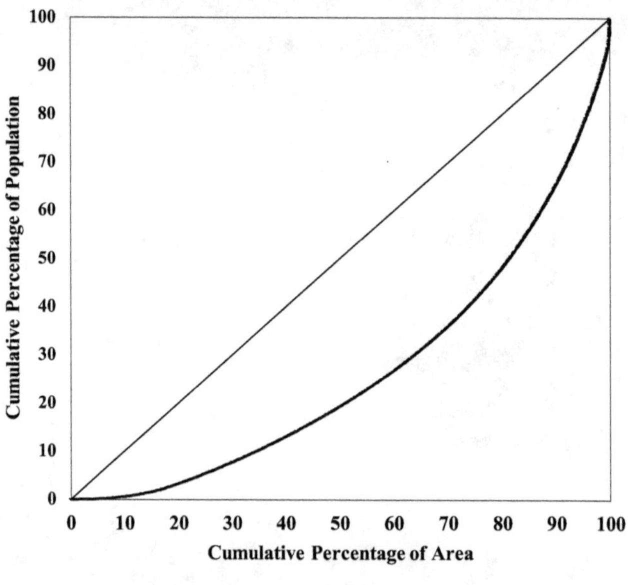

FIGURE 3.2 Lorenz curve of inequality in population distribution in India, 2011 (based on district-level data of the 2011 Census)

Source: Author.

Tripura, and the distantly located union territory of Andaman & Nicobar Islands in the Bay of Bengal also report an extremely low density of population and concentration index. So far as major states are concerned, besides Uttarakhand and Chhattisgarh, states like Rajasthan, Madhya Pradesh, Orissa, Andhra Pradesh, Gujarat, Karnataka, Tripura and Maharashtra also report lower density than India's average.

TABLE 3.3 Population concentration index and density of population in India, 2011

State/ Union Territory	*Concentration Index*	*Density (persons per km²)*
Andhra Pradesh	0.83	308
Arunachal Pradesh	0.04	17
Assam	1.08	398
Bihar	3.00	1,106
Chhattisgarh	0.51	189
Goa	1.07	394
Gujarat	0.84	308
Haryana	1.56	573
Himachal Pradesh	0.33	123
Jammu and Kashmir	0.15	56
Jharkhand	1.12	414
Karnataka	0.86	319
Kerala	2.33	860
Madhya Pradesh	0.64	236
Maharashtra	0.99	365
Manipur	0.35	128
Meghalaya	0.36	132
Mizoram	0.14	52
Nagaland	0.32	119
Odisha	0.73	270
Punjab	1.50	551
Rajasthan	0.54	200
Sikkim	0.23	86
Tamil Nadu	1.51	555
Tripura	0.95	350
Uttar Pradesh	2.25	829
Uttarakhand	0.51	189
West Bengal	2.79	1,028
Andaman & Nicobar Islands	0.13	46
Chandigarh	25.14	9,258
Dadra and Nagar Haveli	1.90	700
Daman & Diu	5.95	2,191
Lakshadweep	5.83	2,149
NCT of Delhi	30.73	11,320
Puducherry	6.91	2,547

Source: Computed by the author from *Table A-1, Census of India 2011.*

Notes: For Jammu and Kashmir, while the area under unlawful occupation of Pakistan and China has been included, population of the area was not included as the census could not be taken.

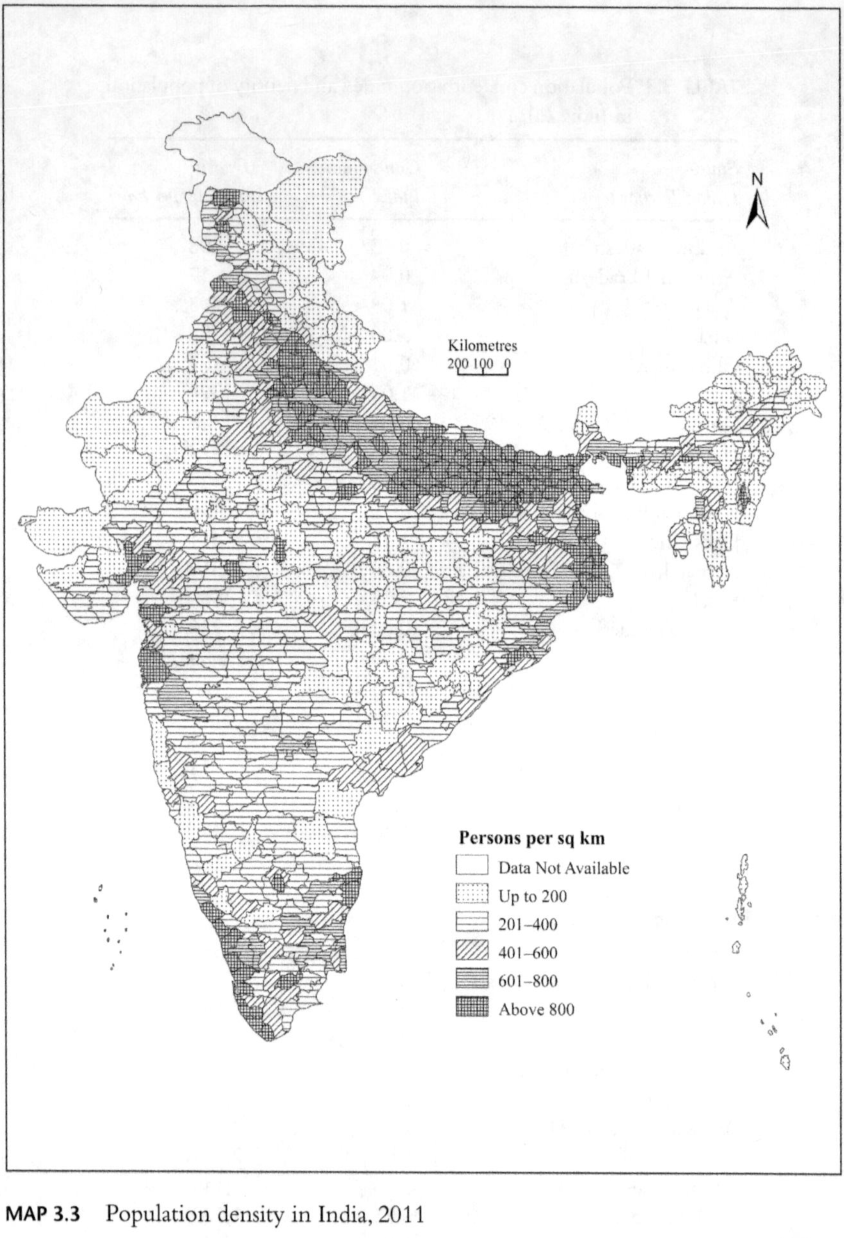

MAP 3.3 Population density in India, 2011

Source: Census of India, 2011.

Map 3.3 presents district-level patterns in crude density of population in 2011. Some of the most urbanised and industrialised districts like Chennai, Kolkata, Mumbai Suburban, Mumbai and Hyderabad appear with exceptionally higher density. Remarkably, excepting Mumbai Suburban, all the others are cent-per cent urbanised and, basically represent the mega-cities of the country. Likewise,

NCT Delhi, Chandigarh, Mahe in Puducherry, Bangalore in Karnataka and Ghaziabad, an adjacent district to NCT of Delhi, also report very dense population. Besides, other districts with a very high rate of urbanisation and industrialisation, and located in different parts of the country, also exhibit dense population. Prominent among them are Haora, Puducherry, Faridabad, Kanpur Nagar, Lucknow and Patna. Beyond these industrialised and urbanised districts, a significantly dense concentration of population can also be seen in the alluvial plains in the north, the coastal plains in the south and the Assam Valley in the north-east. Stretching from the river Yamuna in the west to the delta plains of West Bengal in the east, and bounded by the Himalayas in the north and the peninsular plateaus in the south, the northern plains are one of the most extensive and thickly populated regions of the world. The concentration of population becomes more conspicuous from west to east in the entire length of the plain. Average nutritional densities of over 3,500 persons per square kilometre exist in several areas of the plain where some 80 per cent of the population are engaged in agricultural activities (Tirtha, 1996:79). Within this region, there are several pockets where crude density exceeds a level of 800 – in some cases more than 1,000 – as against the national average of 382 persons per square kilometre only. Thus, if districts accommodating megacities like Chennai, Kolkata, Mumbai, Hyderabad, Delhi etc. and the ones with a large industrial base like Faridabad, Haora etc. are ignored, the dominance of the Ganga plain is evidently clear. Three distinct pockets with a density level of over 800 persons per square kilometre can be located on the map. The most extensive of them can be seen in the central part of the Middle Ganga plains spread over eastern Uttar Pradesh and Bihar plains. Remarkably, this is one of the least urbanised regions in the country where almost the entire population is concentrated in the rural areas. The economy is overwhelmingly dependent upon agriculture which is still subsistent in nature. With this amount of pressure on land, out-migration of people – particularly among landless labourers – to areas of prosperous agriculture in the Punjab and Haryana plains, and to other urban and industrial centres elsewhere in the country, has been a common phenomenon. Obviously, in the absence of this out-migration, the density levels in the region would have been still higher. The adjoining districts of West Bengal provide contiguity to this belt in the Lower Ganga plains. An extremely high density in this part can be attributed to in-migration of people from other areas in search of better job opportunities in the industrial centres in and around Kolkata and Haora. Finally, the third pocket with a density level of more than 800 persons per square kilometre can be seen in the extreme western part of the Upper Ganga plain and adjoining areas of Haryana. The districts of Moradabad, Meerut, Muzaffarnagar, Agra, Aligarh and Ghaziabad among others in Uttar Pradesh have density levels of even more than 1,000 persons per square kilometre. The adjoining National Capital Territory of Delhi along with Faridabad and Gurgaon in Haryana also report density levels above 1,000 persons. Further, towards the west, Ludhiana in the Punjab plain and the Union Territory of Chandigarh show distinctly higher density. In addition, the industrialised districts of Kanpur Nagar, Bhadohi, Lucknow (with the state capital) etc. are pockets of extremely high density scattered in the UP plains. Other pockets of heavy concentration of population, though less extensive than the Ganga plains, can be seen in the southern parts of the Indian peninsula along the coastal plains of Kerala and Tamil Nadu. In addition, the deltas of the Mahanadi, the Godavari and the Krishna along the eastern coast also exhibit a thick concentration of population.

Sharp-edged boundaries can easily be noticed between the areas of dense concentration of population in the alluvial tracts of the plains and deltas, on the one hand, and areas of relatively sparse population in the upland plateaus and the mountainous/hilly areas, on the other. The upland plateaus are characterised by rugged topography and poor soils. In addition, unfavourable climatic conditions and shortage of water for any large-scale agricultural activities have resulted in overall sparse population in the region. Some districts here and there with high values interrupt the monotony of a low density of population in the peninsular uplands. The southern parts of Chhattisgarh and its adjoining areas in Madhya Pradesh, Andhra Pradesh, Maharashtra and Orissa report very low density – less than 200 persons per square kilometre. Likewise, the arid and semi-arid districts of Rajasthan, Kachchh peninsula in Gujarat, the hilly areas of Jammu and Kashmir and Uttarakhand in the north, and the whole of Arunachal Pradesh, Mizoram, and parts of Manipur and Nagaland in the north-east report low density levels.

These patterns of population distribution in India have evolved over a long time as a response to a host of physical and cultural factors. Since nearly three-fourths of India's population still resides in the rural areas overwhelmingly dependent upon the agricultural sector, the pattern of population distribution in the country largely corresponds to the factors governing agricultural practices. Since medieval times, population distribution in the country was largely governed by factors such as consideration of defence, availability of water and caste affiliation in addition to geographical suitability of the area. Growing industrialisation and urbanisation, emergence of urban centres as foci of administrative and commercial activities, development of road and rail networks and expansion of irrigation facilities during some more recent times have led to significant amounts of redistribution of population in the country. Nevertheless, the broad patterns of population distribution as outlined previously have remained more or less unchanged over time.

4

URBAN–RURAL DISTRIBUTION

World population is distributed in an extremely uneven manner over space in the form of human settlements of varying sizes and nature across the globe. One of the most commonly used parameters of distinction in the attributes of settlements is its rural or urban character. Although there are some inherent difficulties in urban-rural classification (Clarke, 1972:46), settlements are invariably identified as towns (and also cities) or villages. Size, density and workforce structure of population form the bases of distinction between a town/city and a village. It is suggested that 'urban populations cluster in larger groups and live at higher densities than rural populations, pursue different occupations, and develop a different outlook on life' (Lowry, 1990:148). Principally agricultural settlements are usually called rural while those that are principally non-agricultural are called urban (Norton and Mercier, 2016:389). Income levels, and hence standards of living of the people, in urban areas are invariably higher than those in the countryside. This is particularly true in case of less developed parts of the world. Per cent population in urban areas is, therefore, commonly taken as an indicator of overall development. A discussion on relative proportions of urban and rural populations as it varies over space has, therefore, formed an essential component of the subject matter of population geography.

What constitutes an urban area differs markedly from country to country depending upon its history, culture, stages of economic development etc. Each country, therefore, has its own definition or concept of a town or city. Consequently, urban areas vary enormously in character and functions from one country to another. This renders any discussion on urban-rural distribution of population in the world very difficult. The Population Division of the United Nations, which provides estimates and projections of urban population for different countries in its regular publication *World Urbanization Prospects*, mostly accepts the data as supplied by individual countries, based on their definitions of urban (Alkema et al., 2013:292). As these definitions vary widely, the problem of comparability is unavoidable. In addition, the traditional urban-rural dichotomy is increasingly waning as improvements in transportation networks and communications collapse time and space, and the process of convergence in urban and rural lifestyles is making the distinction between urban and rural increasingly redundant (Cohen, 2004:24, 27).

However, the problem of variations in concepts and definitions of urban areas across the globe is outside the scope of this chapter. Using data from the UN publications, in the present chapter salient features of urban-rural distribution of population in the world are summarised. Care has been taken to avoid excessive encroachments into the realm of other sub-branches of human geography viz. urban geography or settlement geography. One simple way of analysing urban-rural distribution of population is in the form of percentages of population in urban and rural areas separately. One may also choose to confine to share of population in either of the two segments alone. For instance, percentage population residing in urban areas, often termed as *levels of urbanisation*, is a very handy measure in this regard. It is worked out as under:

$$\text{Percent urban} = \left(P_U / P_T\right) \star 100 \tag{4.1}$$

Where P_U is population living in urban areas of a region and P_T is the total population of the region.

Urban-rural distribution of population can also be analysed in terms of a ratio between urban and rural populations as mentioned here:

$$\text{Urban - rural ratio} = P_U / P_R \tag{4.2}$$

Where P_R refers to the population residing in rural areas while the other notation is same as that in equation (1).

As is obvious, urban-rural ratio is 'zero' in both the situations when the entire population of a region is concentrated in either urban or rural areas only. This creates a problem at the interpretation level. This problem can be taken care of by treating such cases as a separate category. The ratio is near unity when the size of urban as well as rural population is almost identical. A perfect 'unity' results only when exactly half of the population lives in urban areas and another half in rural areas. In the present chapter urban-rural distribution of world population is discussed based on both the measures i.e. per cent urban population and urban-rural ratio. In addition, in India's case distribution of population across size class categories of towns and villages is discussed.

The world scenario

Human settlements came into existence with the introduction of permanent agriculture some 12,000 years ago. Some of these settlements later experienced change in their economic functions in the wake of agricultural development with the passage of time. Initially the main function was to produce food for subsistence which later gave way to distribution of surpluses. This change eventually led some settlements to develop into centres of trade and commerce in due course of time. The first large permanent settlement based on non-agricultural activities began to develop about 3,500 years ago due to improvement in farming practices and expansion of trade networks which freed some people from agriculture to engage in non-agricultural pursuits (Norton and Mercier, 2016:389). However, for several thousand years the change from rural to urban remained very slow. In fact, until very recently in world history, almost the entire population of the world lived in rural areas (Weeks, 2018:36). The few urban centres that were in existence in different parts of the world appeared like tiny islands in the ocean of rurality. It was only after the onset of the Industrial Revolution in Europe during the 18th century that the pace of transition from rural to urban got momentum. However, it was not until the 19th century that the rate of growth in urban population became distinctly higher than that in rural population induced mainly by migration from countryside to towns and cities. Decline in mortality levels, in general, and in rural areas in particular, triggered population growth which induced the shift of population from countryside to urban areas. Immigration also played a key role in growing concentration of population in urban centres in the present-day developed parts of the world.

Urban transition that gathered momentum only after the middle of the last century in less developed parts differs from the experiences of the more developed world in many respects – first, the scale and pace are unprecedented; second, there is a mismatch between average income levels and pace of urban transition in individual countries; and finally, nature and direction of urban transition is more linked with the global economy now than before (Cohen, 2004:24). Rapid growth of cities is a recent phenomenon that has followed different trajectories in more developed and less developed parts of the world (Norton and Mercier, 2016:388). Till 1800 only about 3 per cent of the world population lived in urban areas. Over a period of another 50 years, i.e. by 1850 the share increased to only 6.5 per cent. By the year 1900, nearly 16 per cent of the world population was urban, and there were 16 cities in the world with a population of more than 1 million each. The period of a hundred years from 1850 to 1950, particularly its later half, witnessed a decided shift in urban-rural balance in human history, and by 1950, as much as 29 per cent of the world's population lived in urban places (Lowry, 1990:150). By 2007, world population was for the first time in history evenly distributed between urban and rural areas. Currently, a majority of world population (i.e. 55 per cent) resides in urban places, and there are almost 500 cities with population of over 1 million each. The average size of the world's 100 largest cities that was only 0.2 million in 1800 is now more than 5 million. According to the projection of the UN, two-thirds of world population will be urban by the middle of the present century.

Table 4.1 summarises transition in distribution of urban-rural populations in major geographic regions of the world during recent times. As early as the mid-20th century, the more developed regions that were spread over Europe, Northern America and Oceania were already 'urban majority', while the world average

TABLE 4.1 Urban–rural distribution of population in the world – 1950, 2000 and 2015

World/ Major Regions	*Mid-Year Population (thousands)*		*Per cent Urban*	*Urban-Rural Ratio*	*Mid-Year Population (thousands)*		*Per cent Urban*	*Urban-Rural Ratio*	*Mid-Year Population (thousands)*		*Per cent Urban*	*Urban-Rural Ratio*
	Urban	*Rural*			*Urban*	*Rural*			*Urban*	*Rural*		
	1950				*2000*				*2015*			
World	750,903	1,785,372	29.61	0.421	2,868,308	3,276,699	46.68	0.875	3,981,498	3,401,511	53.93	1.171
More developed regions	446,284	368,581	54.77	1.211	883,880	306,625	74.24	2.883	979,089	274,118	78.13	3.572
Less developed regions	304,619	416, 791	42.23	0.731	1,984,428	2,970,075	40.05	0.668	3,002,409	3,127,393	48.98	0.960
Less developed regions, excluding China	235,263	921,933	20.33	0.255	1,501,700	2,140,671	41.23	0.702	2,201,145	2,500,296	46.82	0.880
High income countries	393,682	279,214	58.51	1.410	821,849	248,281	76.80	3.310	955,213	224,848	80.95	4.248
Middle income countries	345,035	1,389,446	19.89	0.248	1,935,345	2,712,144	41.64	0.714	2,825,252	2,733,012	50.83	1.034
Low income countries	11,933	116,164	9.32	0.103	109,161	315,968	25.68	0.345	198,536	443,323	30.93	0.448
Africa	32,659	196,011	14.28	0.167	285,998	531,568	34.98	0.538	491,531	702,839	41.15	0.699
Asia	246,193	1,157,869	17.53	0.213	1,399,722	2,330,648	37.52	0.601	2,119,873	2,300,024	47.96	0.922
Europe	284,085	265,290	51.71	1.071	516,725	210,476	71.06	2.455	547,147	193,667	73.86	2.825
Latin America and the Caribbean	69,759	99,159	41.30	0.704	397,062	128,733	75.52	3.084	505,392	126,989	79.92	3.980
Northern America	110,300	62,302	63.90	1.770	247,471	65,374	79.10	3.785	290,616	65,387	81.63	4.445
Oceania	7,906	4,742	62.51	1.667	21,329	9,900	68.30	2.154	26,938	12,605	68.12	2.137

Source: Based on *World Urbanization Prospects: The 2018 Revision*, United Nations Population Division.

Notes:

(i) More developed regions comprise Europe, Northern America, Australia/New Zealand and Japan.

(ii) Less developed regions comprise all regions of Africa, Asia (except Japan), Latin America and the Caribbean plus Melanesia, Micronesia and Polynesia.

(iii) The country classification by income level is based on 2016 GNI per capita from the World Bank.

indicated only one-third of the population as urban. More developed regions accounted for nearly 54 per cent of the world's urban population while the rural population accounted for barely 19 per cent. The highest urban-rural ratio was seen in Northern America followed by Oceania and Europe. By the year 2000, the size of the urban population in Northern America i.e. the United States and Canada was almost four times as large as its rural counterpart. The pace of urban transition was particularly rapid in Latin America and the Caribbean between 1950 and 2000. During this period, Latin America and the Caribbean became not only 'urban majority' but the ratio between urban and rural populations also increased from 0.704 to as high as 3.084. In other words, urban population that was barely 70 per cent of its rural counterpart till 1950 became three times larger than the latter by the end of the 20th century. As a result, it occupied the second position in 2015 after Northern America in terms of proportion population in urban areas. On the other extreme, in Asia and Africa a majority of population is still rural-based with only 48 per cent and 41 per cent of the population in urban areas respectively. With the current rates of urbanisation, it is expected that by 2030 close to 54 per cent population in Asia and Africa will be living in urban areas. Interestingly, the size of urban population in Asia is more than twice those of Africa, Latin America and the Caribbean put together. Not only this, Asia alone accommodates more than 53 per cent of urban dwellers of the world. Thus, much of the future urban-rural mix of population in the world at aggregate level will depend upon the nature and pace of urban transition in Asia. Nevertheless, a marked correspondence between levels of development, on the one hand, and per cent urban population and urban-rural ratio, on the other, has existed throughout the period. The rate of growth in urban population has been particularly very high in the less developed parts of the world since 1950. As a result, the relative contributions of major regions in the world's urban and rural population have also undergone a corresponding change over time. The more developed areas that accounted for about 60 per cent of the world's urban population in 1950 now contribute less than a quarter.

One comes across a still wider range of variation in urban-rural mix of population based on country-level data (see also Map 4.1). Out of the total 232 countries for which the UN provides estimates, as many as 31 are more than 90 per cent urban which also includes 12 countries where the entire population resides in urban areas (Table 4.2). Many of them are small island countries located in different parts of the world accounting for a negligible proportion of world urban population. However, mention must be made of Hong Kong, Singapore and Kuwait with substantial size of populations. Basically city-states located in East Asia, Hong Kong and Singapore are among the world's top trading cities. Concentration of the entire population in urban areas in the case of Kuwait should be viewed in context of its oil resources. A careful perusal of Table 4.2 evidently reveals a significantly higher concentration of population in urban areas in more developed countries of Northern America and Europe. As can be seen, in Northern America more than 80 per cent of population is concentrated in towns and cities while the countryside accommodates barely one-tenth of the population. Although substantially different, in Europe also

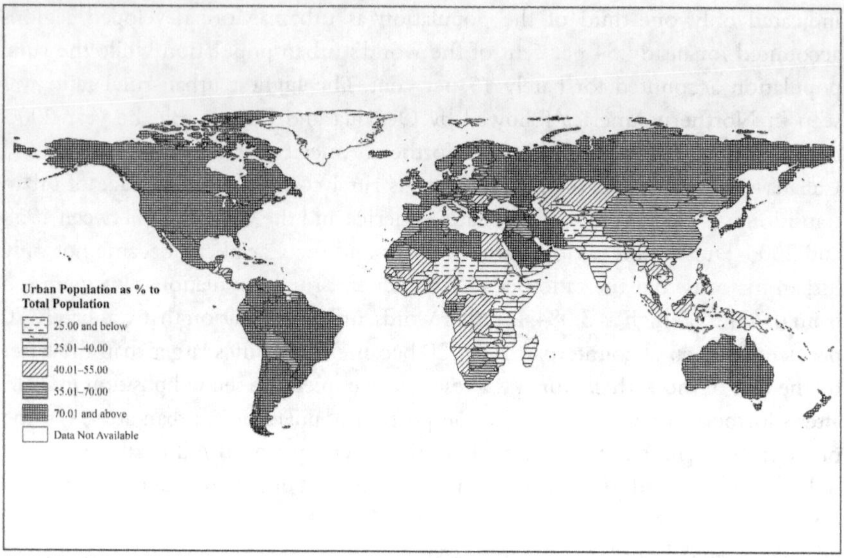

MAP 4.1 Per cent urban population in the world, 2017

Source: Population Reference Bureau, *World Population Data Sheet, 2017.*

TABLE 4.2 Number of countries by per cent urban and world major regions, 2015

Major Regions	*Number of Countries by per cent Urban*									*Total*
	Above 90.01	*80.01– 90.00*	*70.01– 80.00*	*60.01– 70.00*	*50.01– 60.00*	*40.01– 50.00*	*30.01– 40.00*	*20.01– 30.00*	*Below 20.00*	
Africa	1	2	5	7	6	16	8	7	6	58
Asia	8	6	6	5	8	2	9	5	2	51
Europe	9	6	10	9	9	3	1	-	1	48
Latin America and the Caribbean	9	7	7	8	6	4	3	2	1	47
Northern America	1	4	-	-	-	-	-	-	-	5
Oceania	3	3	3	3	3	-	-	4	4	23
Total	31	28	31	32	32	25	21	18	14	232

Source: Based on *World Urbanization Prospects: The 2018 Revision*, United Nations Population Division.

nearly one-third of the countries are more than 80 per cent urban. The present status of urban-rural distribution of population in developed countries has its roots in massive urban-ward migration both internal as well as international in the wake of forces unleashed by the Industrial Revolution in the mid-18th century. Industries located in urban areas acted as magnets attracting surplus population from the countryside. This happened first in north-west Europe, mainly England, and then spread to the rest of Europe. Across the Atlantic Ocean, North America, particularly the United States, was witnessing a similar change. Urban population in these highly developed countries will continue to grow through migration as well as natural increase in the future also. But once every one in these countries lives in cities, not much can occur other than de-urbanisation – a decrease in the proportion of population living in cities (Norton and Mercier, 2016:394).

From among the less developed regions of the world, Latin America and the Caribbean rank very high in terms of urban-rural ratios. Figures on 'per cent urban' in this region are quite comparable with those in North America and many European countries. Some of the Latin American countries, e.g. Argentina, Chile and Uruguay, were already highly urbanised by the mid-20th century while Brazil witnessed a remarkable pace of urban transition only in the latter half of the century. Along with natural increase, rural-urban migration played a significant role in the accelerated rate of urban transition in many countries in the region. This was facilitated by government policies that induced industrial growth and restricted dependence on imports through trade barriers. Most of the industries were concentrated in large urban centres, many of which were the national capital cities. The number of million-plus cities in the region, thus, drastically increased from just 6 in 1950 to more than 50 in 2000. Some of the largest cities in the region witnessed unprecedented growth in population during the period resulting in disproportionately higher concentrations of urban population in major cities of the region as compared to other less developed parts of the world. Migration from rural to urban areas is likely to continue, and the coming decades will witness an onset of shrink in rural population. There are, however, clear indications of slowing down in the rate of growth of some of the largest cities in the region. As per the UN revised estimates, size of urban population of the region is expected to be a little over 600 million in 2018 (UN, 2018). Among major countries in the region, mention may be made of Uruguay, Puerto Rico and Argentina where more than nine-tenths of the population is urban. They are followed by Venezuela, Chile and Brazil in that order. Urban populations in these countries are more than six times that of rural populations in size. One must note that several Caribbean island countries still report a majority of their population in rural areas. The lowest ladder in terms of per cent urban population is occupied by Saint Lucia, Antigua and Barbuda, Guyana, Barbados and Grenada. However, many of them are small island countries with little implication for urban-rural mix of population in the region at the aggregate level.

Asia comes next to Latin America and the Caribbean in terms of 'per cent urban' at the aggregate level. With a vast geographic expanse, Asia alone is the home of 2.12 billion urban dwellers which comes to about 54 per cent of the world total of 3.98 billion in 2015. However, in terms of per cent urban the continent ranks only marginally ahead of Africa. A stark contrast can be seen in urban-rural mix from one part of the continent to another. Countries in West Asia, along with its eastern counterparts, appear quite distinct from the rest of the continent in terms of urban transition. With more than 70 per cent population as urban dwellers at present, West Asia has been the home of some of the oldest cities of the world like

Damascus, Istanbul and Baghdad. However, much of urban transition in the region has occurred only after 1950. Rapid industrialisation and high levels of immigration to oil-rich Gulf States are the underlying reasons of higher concentration of population in towns/cities in countries like Kuwait, Qatar, Bahrain, United Arab Emirates and Saudi Arabia, which are all more than 80 per cent urban. The only country with majority rural in the region is Yemen. On the eastern side of the continent, as already noted earlier, Hong Kong and Singapore – the two city-states – are among the world's largest trading cities. Japan with more than nine-tenths of its population as urban occupies the next position. Although at the aggregate level, China ranks lower than these countries, the last three decades have witnessed incredibly rapid urban transition in its coastal regions since the adoption of the government's open policy and establishment of Special Economic Zones (SEZs). However, spatial redistribution of population in the country, on the whole, continues to be under strict regulation by the state. South-eastern Asia presents a different picture. Countries like Thailand, the Philippines, Vietnam, Laos, Myanmar and Cambodia continue to be 'rural majority'. The process of urban transition has been conspicuously slow in South Asia, although some of the largest cities are located in this part of the continent. In 1950, barely 16 per cent of the population in South Asia was urban, which increased to a little over 34 per cent despite a nearly eight-fold increase in the number of urban dwellers during the same period. The rural base continues to be very large, although the rate of growth in rural population has slowed down considerably during the recent past. Urban transition in the region is largely dominated by India, which alone accounts for over 68 per cent of urban population in South Asia. Remarkably, per cent urban population in India is lower than those in its neighbouring countries such as Bhutan, Pakistan and Bangladesh.

Africa, with barely 40 per cent of its population in urban areas, presents perhaps the smallest range of variation in urban-rural mix of population from one part to another. Countries in its northern parts are, however, more urbanised than Sub-Saharan Africa. Western Sahara, Libya and Algeria from the western parts and Reunion (an island country in the Indian Ocean) and Djibouti from eastern Africa are the only 'urban majority' countries with more than 70 per cent of their population in urban areas. Almost all of Eastern Africa, much of the western and central parts along with Egypt and Sudan from Northern Africa, are 'rural majority'. Even in its southern parts, barring only Botswana and South Africa, the size of the urban population does not exceed that of its rural counterpart in any country. Much of the continent forms part of the least developed areas of the world with persisting dependence upon primary sectors of the economy which are still subsistent in nature. Nevertheless, absolute size of urban population has undergone more than a 15-fold increase since 1950. According to the revised estimates of the UN, the continent will become predominantly urban only after 2030. It may be recalled that much of Africa remained a colony of European powers till as late as 1960s. Just as in the case of India, colonial rule in Africa also led to the formation of a new urban system focussed on exploitation of minerals and other agricultural produce. All these had serious implications for urban processes after these countries achieved independence from the colonial rule later. Urban population in these countries began growing through both natural increase as well as migration from the countryside unaccompanied by any significant industrialisation. Apart from economic reasons, in many African countries, rural to urban migration was also fuelled by long-persisting civil wars.

Urban-rural distribution of population in Oceania is dominated by Australia and New Zealand, both having substantial population of European origin. These two countries account for around 71 per cent of the total population in the region while their share in total urban population is over 90 per cent. Individually, they are more than 85 per cent urban. Nearly half of the urban population in Australia lives in its four large cities viz. Sydney, Melbourne, Brisbane and Perth alone. Likewise, Auckland, the largest urban area in New Zealand, is the home of 1.63 million urban dwellers of the total of 3.98 million in the country. On the other extreme, there are as many as eight countries in Oceania where more than three-fourths of the population lives in the countryside. The largest of them is Papua New Guinea, which accommodates over one-fifth of the total population in the region and where as much as 87 per cent of the population is rural-based.

India's case

Being the land of one of the world's oldest civilisations, India possesses a long tradition of an urban way of life. In terms of per cent population living in urban areas, India was far ahead of the Western world even at the turn of the 15th century. Much before the urban revolution began in the West, the presence of several large and flourishing port and commercial cities in India including Cambay, Calicut, Vijayanagar, Bidar etc. can be found in the foreign travellers' accounts as early as 1419 (Crane, 1955:469). Vasco da Gama had described Calicut as the greatest commercial city of South India when he reached India in 1498. The mention of several other cities such as Surat, Burhanpur, Agra, Fatehpore among others as great cities of trade and administration can be seen in the writings of some of the early Englishmen visiting India during the Moghul period. While most of these cities were seats of administration or centres of handicraft, trade and commerce, some were centres of religious importance. Advent of the Europeans on the sub-continent, however, brought about a steady decline of these cities. Soon the regional structure of the economy began changing, and there emerged a new urban landscape dominated by port cities that facilitated exploitative trade and commerce of the British. The interactive system that had previously evolved through ages between large numbers of centres of handicraft or service or trade and commerce, on the one hand, and their hinterland of primary production, on the other, as well as the one between large cities and smaller towns over space, were the main casualties (Kundu, 2011:3). A hierarchy of newly established urban centres came into existence which mainly served as satellites of the port cities. Regional inequalities became much sharper during the British period. Declining rural economy and lack of employment opportunities led to a shift of population from countryside to major port cities. With independence in 1947, India adopted a policy of planned economic development, and balanced regional development was accorded the top priority in terms of public sector investment in backward areas. However, regional imbalances in the levels of development persisted, leading to a continued shift of population from rural areas to large cities. Spatial structure and rural-urban distribution of population in contemporary India have its roots in the colonial period.

Despite a long tradition of urban life on the sub-continent, India currently ranks very low with regard to per cent population in towns and cities. India adopts a fairly average definition of urban areas (Kundu, 2011:5) based on administrative and demographic criteria. While 'urban' is often specifically defined, 'rural' is treated simply as a residual category (Bhagat, 2005:61). All those places which have urban local bodies like Municipal Corporation, Municipality, Notified Area Committee and so on are taken as towns. In addition, places with a population size of 5,000 or more, density of not less than 400 persons per square kilometre and at least 75 per cent of the male main workforce in non-agricultural activities are also treated as towns. Thus, there are two types of urban centres or towns in India – *statutory towns* that fulfil administrative or statutory criteria i.e. the presence of urban local bodies, and *census towns* that fulfil census criteria concerning size and density of population and workforce structure. All other places which do not fall under these categories are considered as villages.

Although the absolute size of India's urban population is much larger than that of the United States, the majority of the population in India still resides in rural areas. With nearly seven-tenths of the population living in rural areas, it is rightly said that India lives in villages (Table 4.3). Being the second largest populous country after China, the size of India's rural population is two and a half times that of the total population of the United States, about six times that of the Russian Federation

TABLE 4.3 Urban–rural populations in India, 1951 to 2011

Census Years	*Urban Population*		*Rural Population*		*Urban-Rural Ratio*	*Urban-Rural Growth Differentials (URGD)*
	Absolute Size (thousands)	*As % to total population*	*Absolute Size (thousands)*	*As % to total population*		
1951	62,444	17.29	298,644	82.71	0.209	-
1961	78,937	17.97	360,298	82.03	0.219	5.77
1971	109,114	19.91	439,046	80.09	0.249	16.37
1981	159,463	23.34	523,866	76.66	0.304	26.82
1991	217,566	25.70	628,855	74.30	0.346	16.40
2001	286,120	27.81	742,617	72.19	0.385	13.42
2011	377,106	31.14	833,749	68.86	0.452	19.53

Source: Census of India for various years.

Notes: As census enumeration could not be held in Assam in 1981 and Jammu and Kashmir in 1991, interpolated figures for these states were taken in respective years.

and 'six and a half' times that of the total population of Japan (Sekhar and Padmaja, 2013:157). Figure 4.1 shows the size of urban and rural populations in the country for the period 1951 to 2011. According to the first census after independence, nearly 83 per cent of the population lived in rural areas, and the remaining 17 per cent only in towns and cities. In other words, in terms of absolute size urban population constituted barely one-fifth of the rural population. The rural and urban distribution of population in any region is the function of differentials in rate of growth in the two segments. Since the urban population grew at a faster pace as compared to rural population, per cent population living in urban areas witnessed a steady increase, and by 1971, for the first time in the history of the Indian Census, nearly one-fifth of the population in the country became urban. The rate of urban growth continuously increased since 1951 and reached its peak in the 1970s. This is revealed in the URGD (Table 4.3). However, thereafter, the pace of urban growth has steadily declined except on the occasion of 2011 when there was a marginal increase. Pace of growth in the rural population, on the other hand, has decelerated and the decade 2001–11 witnessed one of the lowest growth rates in rural population. A reversal in the trend of URGD during 2001–11 has more to do with this deceleration in the pace of growth in rural population than any acceleration in growth of the urban population. For the first time in the history of census taking in the country, net gain in urban population was larger than that in its rural counterpart. According to the latest census of 2011, rural areas account for a little less than 69 per cent of population. In the forthcoming sections, the salient features of the urban and rural distribution of populations in India are presented separately. Since rural areas accommodate a much larger share of population, it is in the fitness of things to take up rural population first and then urban population.

Rural population: In 2011, nearly 833.75 million people lived in as many as 597,608 villages of varying sizes across the length and breadth of the country. The

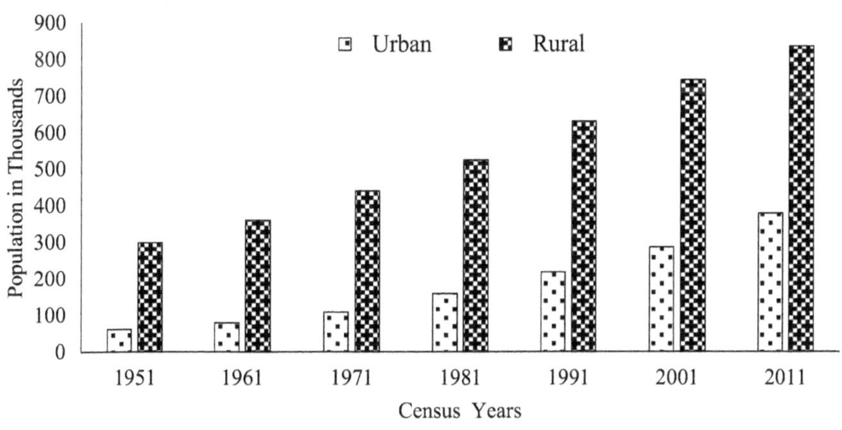

FIGURE 4.1 Decadal change in urban and rural population in India, 1951–2011

Source: Author.

average size of villages, thus, works out to be 1,395 persons. Census of India classifies villages into seven categories on the basis of size of population. Table 4.4 presents distribution of rural population across size class category of villages for the year 2011 (refer to Figure 4.2 also). Nearly six-tenths of the rural population lives in villages with population between 1,000 and 5,000 persons. Another one-fourth of the total rural population lives in villages with a size of 5,000 or more persons i.e. the cut-off size for defining urban areas. It is obvious that because of stagnant economies and persisting dependence on agriculture and allied activities, these villages did not quality as census towns. Such villages tend to be out-migrating in character causing redistribution of population over space. At the same time some of these villages are likely to qualify as urban centres in subsequent censuses once sufficient transformation in workforce structure takes place.

TABLE 4.4 Distribution of rural population by size class categories of villages in India, 2011

Size of the Villages	*Number of Inhabited Villages*	*Percentage Share in Total Villages*	*Population (thousands)*	*Percentage Share of Total Rural Population*	*Average Size of the Village*
Less than 200	82,151	13.75	8,180	0.98	100
200–499	114,732	19.20	39,685	4.76	346
500–999	141,800	23.73	103,321	12.39	729
1,000–1,999	139,164	23.29	197,536	23.69	1,419
2,000–4,999	96,428	16.14	288,774	34.64	2,995
5,000–9,999	18,652	3.12	123,877	14.86	6,642
10,000 and above	4,681	0.78	72,375	8.68	15,461
Total	597,608	100.00	833,749	100.00	1,395

Source: Census of India, 2011, Table A-3.

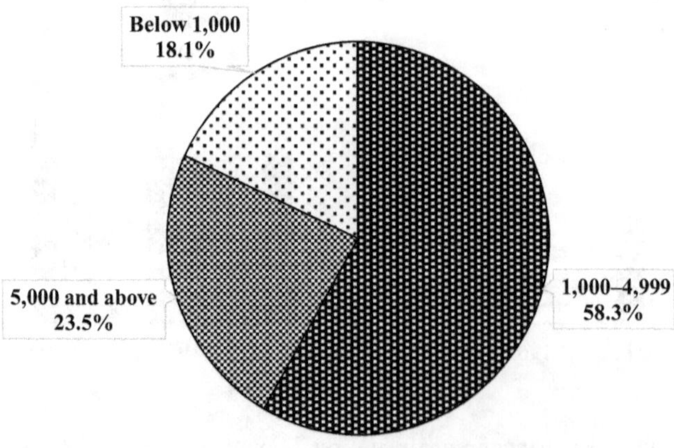

FIGURE 4.2 Rural population by size class categories of villages in India, 2011

Source: Author.

There appears to be a close correspondence between geographical conditions and distribution of rural population across size class categories (Table 4.5). Difficult terrain, higher elevation and other associated physical factors result in concentration of population in small-sized settlements. The hilly states of Himachal Pradesh

TABLE 4.5 Rural population by states/union territories in India, 2011

States/ Union Territories	*Rural Population as % to Total Population*	*Rural Density (per km²)*	*Per cent Population in Villages by Size Class*			*Average Size of Villages*
			Less than 1,000	*1,000 to 4,999*	*5,000 and Above*	
Andhra Pradesh	66.64	211	8.05	55.97	35.98	2,144
Arunachal Pradesh	77.06	NA	79.78	19.63	0.58	203
Assam	85.90	347	25.32	66.13	8.54	1,057
Bihar	88.71	1,005	8.07	49.87	42.07	2,363
Chhattisgarh	76.76	149	31.61	65.55	2.84	1,002
Goa	37.83	188	11.38	70.18	18.45	1,724
Gujarat	57.40	184	10.52	64.68	24.80	1,944
Haryana	65.12	391	5.83	60.34	33.83	2,486
Himachal Pradesh	89.97	111	70.82	27.78	1.40	345
Jammu and Kashmir	72.62	91	17.78	63.43	18.79	1,437
Jharkhand	75.95	324	36.13	56.12	7.75	850
Karnataka	61.33	202	19.45	59.73	20.82	1,368
Kerala	52.30	559	0.01	1.27	98.72	17,179
Madhya Pradesh	72.37	175	31.66	60.52	7.82	1,012
Maharashtra	54.78	206	17.52	61.92	20.56	1,503
Manipur	70.79	91	31.57	51.57	16.85	804
Meghalaya	79.93	107	74.19	23.92	1.89	367
Mizoram	47.89	26	49.37	48.36	2.27	746
Nagaland	71.14	86	28.96	56.46	14.57	1,005
NCT of Delhi	2.50	1,284	1.26	51.49	47.25	4,068
Orissa	83.31	230	40.54	55.66	3.80	734
Punjab	62.52	362	18.26	66.36	15.38	1,425
Rajasthan	75.13	153	24.53	61.79	13.67	1,190
Sikkim	74.85	65	30.59	63.72	5.69	1,075
Tamil Nadu	51.60	320	6.02	59.73	34.25	2,474
Tripura	73.83	269	2.97	55.73	41.30	3,143
Uttar Pradesh	77.73	666	14.70	66.15	19.15	1,588
Uttarakhand	69.77	134	49.19	36.23	14.57	447
West Bengal	68.13	744	14.52	57.22	28.26	1,660
A and N Islands	62.30	29	34.17	60.43	5.40	599
Chandigarh	2.75	6,486	0.00	28.82	71.18	5,798
D and N Haveli	53.28	411	3.64	67.28	29.08	2,817
Daman & Diu	24.83	967	5.37	35.45	59.19	3,179
Lakshadweep	21.93	1,542	2.31	44.50	53.19	2,357
Puducherry	31.67	1,178	0.44	43.70	55.86	4,391

Source: Census of India, 2011, Tables A-1, A-3.

and Uttarakhand in the north, and north-eastern states like Arunachal Pradesh, Meghalaya, Mizoram, Manipur and Nagaland report relatively smaller average size of villages. On the other hand, states in the fertile tract of northern plains and coastal areas are marked with larger average size of villages with a resultant larger share of rural population in large-sized villages. For instance, Kerala, which tops the list with respect to average size of villages, reports almost 99 per cent of its rural population in villages of the size of 5,000 persons and above. Obviously many of these large villages are on the borderline on the rural-urban continuum, and with diversification of their economy they might up-grade their status to the urban category in the future. Among the other major states with large average size of villages, mention may be made of Haryana, Tamil Nadu, Bihar, Andhra Pradesh, Gujarat, West Bengal etc. in that order.

Urban Population: More than 377 million persons that constitute a little over 31 per cent of the population live in 7,933 towns and cities across the country (Table 4.6). The Census of India classifies urban centres into six size classes. These six classes are generally regrouped into three broad categories viz. large, medium and small urban centres (Figure 4.3). Remarkably, more than seven-tenths of the urban dwellers live in Class I cities/urban agglomerations (those with population above 100,000). On the other hand, barely 13 per cent of the urban dwellers live in small towns with a population size of less than 20,000 persons. Small towns constitute as much as 62 per cent of all towns and cities. Further, as seen in the case of rural population, urban population in the country is also unevenly distributed over space. Nearly half of the urban dwellers in the country come from only Maharashtra, Uttar Pradesh, Tamil Nadu, West Bengal and Andhra Pradesh (Table 4.7). It is because of sheer geographic expanse that brings Uttar Pradesh in the list, otherwise in terms of per cent urban the state ranks very low. However, the presence of Maharashtra and Tamil Nadu is justified by their much higher levels of urbanisation as compared to the national average. These five states taken together account for less than one-third of the geographic area of the country.

TABLE 4.6 Urban population by size class categories in India, 2011

Size Class Categories	*Number of Urban Centres**	*Percentage Share in Total Urban Centres*	*Population (thousands)*	*Percentage Share of Total Urban Population*	*Average Size*
Class I – 100,000 and above	505	6.37	227,893	60.43	451,274
Class II – 50,000–99,999	605	7.63	41,328	10.96	68,311
Class III – 20,000–49,999	1,905	24.01	58,175	15.43	30,538
Class IV – 10,000–19,999	2,233	28.15	31,871	8.45	14,273
Class V – 5,000–9,999	2,187	27.57	15,883	4.21	7,262
Class VI – Below 5,000	498	6.28	1,956	0.52	3,928
Total	7,933	100.00	377,107	100.00	47,536

* Including Urban Agglomerations

Source: Census of India, 2011, Table A-4.

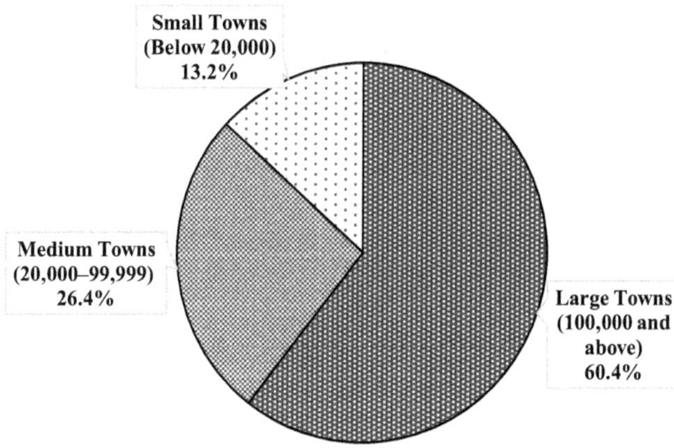

FIGURE 4.3 Urban population by size class categories, 2011

Source: Author.

In terms of per cent urban population also a wide range of variation across states and union territories can be seen. The union territories, in general are more urbanised than the states. Southern states are having higher levels of urbanisation than the northern states. Nine out of every 10 persons in the National Capital Territory of Delhi and Chandigarh live in urban areas. These two are followed by Lakshadweep, Daman & Diu and Puducherry. Along with these union territories, the states of Goa and Mizoram are also 'urban majority'. However, barring only NCT of Delhi, all these states/union territories account for a very small share of urban dwellers in the country.

Among the major states, Tamil Nadu, Kerala and Maharashtra with already more than 45 per cent of population as urban are expected to join the group of 'urban majority' very soon. In addition to these, Gujarat, Karnataka, Punjab, Haryana, Andhra Pradesh and West Bengal rank higher than the nation's average in terms per cent urban. On the other extreme, Bihar and Uttar Pradesh with a considerable size of population continue to be largely rural-based. The other major states which occupy a very low position are Odisha, Chhattisgarh, Jharkhand, Rajasthan etc. where less than one-fourth of the population is urban. Taken together, while these six states are home to nearly four-tenths of the population, they account for barely one-fourth of the urban dwellers. Interestingly, however, more than half the urban dwellers in these states live in large cities reflecting the degree of primacy at a very low level of urbanisation. Contrarily, in states like Goa, Tamil Nadu and Kerala with a much larger concentration of urban population in urban centres, the share of large cities is not that high. But urban structure in other more urbanised states like Maharashtra and Gujarat is characterised by a similar dominance of large cities.

Urban-Rural Mix: A marked regional variation in 'rural-urban' mix of population based on state-level data is evident from the foregoing discussion. The NCT

TABLE 4.7 Urban population by states/union territories in India, 2011

States/ Union Territories	*Urban Population as % to Total Population*	*Urban Density (per km²)*	*Per cent Population by Size Class*			*Average Size of Town*
			Large Towns[1]	*Medium Towns*[2]	*Small Towns*[3]	
Andhra Pradesh	33.36	3,593	67.97	26.41	5.62	79,941
Arunachal Pradesh	22.94	NA	0.00	44.42	55.58	11,754
Assam	14.10	3,491	37.54	28.53	33.93	20,554
Bihar	11.29	5,058	57.45	37.16	5.39	59,086
Chhattisgarh	23.24	1,826	55.85	22.37	21.78	32,622
Goa	62.17	1,186	0.00	39.74	60.26	12,954
Gujarat	42.60	3,477	72.52	19.55	7.93	73,980
Haryana	34.88	4,475	68.02	22.86	9.11	57,416
Himachal Pradesh	10.03	2,542	24.63	29.74	45.63	11,670
Jammu and Kashmir	27.38	2,755	56.31	19.37	24.32	28,141
Jharkhand	24.05	3,273	54.56	27.29	18.16	34,794
Karnataka	38.67	3,928	67.74	24.32	7.94	68,086
Kerala	47.70	2,097	20.42	61.76	17.81	30,644
Madhya Pradesh	27.63	2,591	55.62	27.32	17.06	42,163
Maharashtra	45.22	5,588	76.68	17.82	5.50	95,165
Manipur	29.21	4,647	33.23	21.21	45.56	16,356
Meghalaya	20.07	2,105	24.05	51.40	24.55	27,066
Mizoram	52.11	974	51.32	31.68	17.01	24,860
Nagaland	28.86	2,345	21.51	49.32	29.17	21,960
NCT of Delhi	97.50	14,153	82.54	13.60	3.86	144,858
Orissa	16.69	2,090	45.13	34.91	19.96	31,407
Punjab	37.48	4,136	57.17	30.27	12.56	47,922
Rajasthan	24.87	2,570	61.48	29.45	9.07	57,401
Sikkim	25.15	4,015	65.30	0.00	34.70	17,064
Tamil Nadu	48.40	2,561	39.64	36.83	23.53	31,830
Tripura	26.17	2,453	41.60	14.34	44.06	22,892
Uttar Pradesh	22.27	5,884	61.04	25.41	13.56	48,628
Uttarakhand	30.23	3,381	45.98	28.77	25.25	26,516
West Bengal	31.87	5,676	61.95	16.89	21.16	32,006
A and N Islands	37.70	3,784	75.31	0.00	24.69	28,698
Chandigarh	97.25	9,371	94.56	0.00	5.44	171,077
D and N Haveli	46.72	3,514	0.00	61.19	38.81	26,766
Daman & Diu	75.17	3,769	0.00	66.09	33.91	22,856
Lakshadweep	78.07	2,416	0.00	0.00	100.00	8,389
Puducherry	68.33	5,517	63.85	32.99	3.16	85,275

Source: Census of India, 2011, Table A-4.

Notes: [1]. Large Towns: Class I cities; [2]. Medium Towns: Class II and Class III; [3]. Small Towns: Class IV to VI.

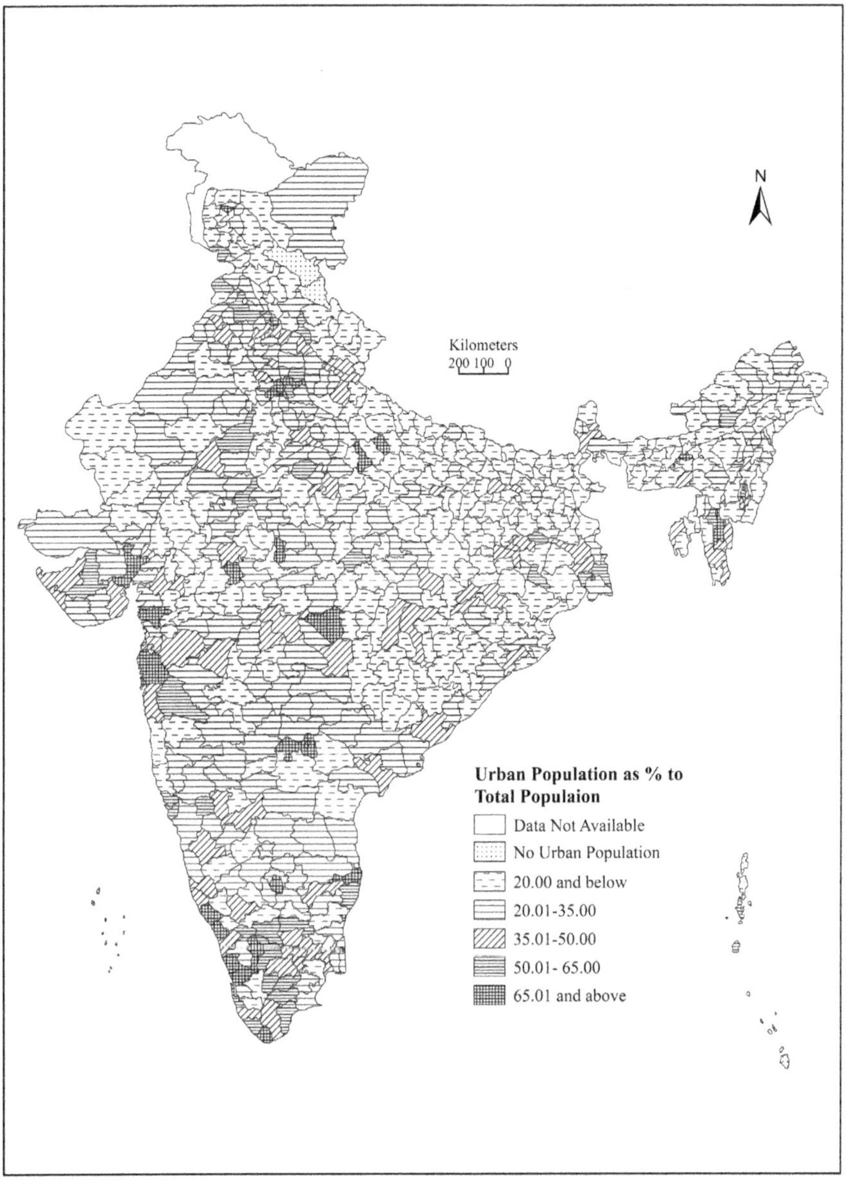

MAP 4.2 Per cent urban population in India, 2011

Source: Census of India, 2011.

of Delhi along with the union territories, in general report a comparatively larger share of their population concentrated in urban areas. In NCT of Delhi and the union territory of Chandigarh urban population is more than 35 times larger than its rural counterpart in terms of size. The developed states both in the north as well as the south report a larger share of their population as urban. On the other extreme are major states like Madhya Pradesh, Rajasthan, Jharkhand, Chhattisgarh, Uttar Pradesh, Odisha and Bihar which continue to be predominantly rural. In fact, these major states along with Jammu and Kashmir and north-eastern states barring only Mizoram account for nearly half of the total population in the country but urban population, on the whole, is hardly 40 per cent of its rural counterpart. The regional disparity in rural-urban distribution of population in the country becomes even sharper when analysed at district level.

Table 4.8 presents distribution of districts and their proportions in geographic area and population of the country by urban-rural ratios. Seven districts viz. Kolkata in West Bengal; Mumbai Sub-urban and Mumbai in Maharashtra; Hyderabad in Andhra Pradesh (presently in Telangana after bifurcation of Andhra Pradesh); Chennai in Tamil Nadu and Yanam and Mahe in Puducherry are cent-per cent urban. Including three of the metro cities of the country, they account for above 2 per cent of India's population, although their share in geographic area is negligible. On the other extreme, there are three districts which do not have any urban centre within their boundaries. Two of them are located in the hilly terrain of Himachal Pradesh while the third forms part of Andaman & Nicobar Islands. Consequently, their proportion in India's total population is negligible.

Between the two extremes all the other districts are located. Although at the aggregate level less than one-third of the population resides in urban areas, in as many as 66 districts urban population is either equal or larger than its counterparts in rural areas. Taken together these districts account for more than one-fifth of the

TABLE 4.8 Distribution of districts and their proportions in geographic area and population by urban–rural ratio in India, 2011

Urban/Rural Ratio	*Number of Districts*	*Geographic Area*			*Total Population*		
		Absolute (km²)	*As % to India's Total*	*Cum. %*	*Absolute (thousands)*	*As % to India's Total*	*Cum. %*
Entirely Urban	7	1219.00	0.04	0.04	25,627	2.12	2.12
Above 1.000	66	230680.99	7.28	7.32	205,070	16.94	19.05
0.900–0.999	10	44360.00	1.40	8.72	21,510	1.78	20.83
0.800–0.899	6	23930.00	0.76	9.48	11,031	0.91	21.74
0.700–0.799	17	72891.89	2.30	11.78	41,145	3.40	25.14
0.600–0.699	20	95981.81	3.03	14.81	45,712	3.78	28.91
0.500–0.599	29	288233.00	9.10	23.91	59,108	4.88	33.79
0.400–0.499	41	237956.00	7.51	31.43	81,903	6.76	40.56
0.300–0.399	56	381031.01	12.03	43.46	130,646	10.79	51.35
0.200–0.299	129	710458.31	22.44	65.90	206,186	17.03	68.38
Below 0.200	247	1057795.01	33.44	99.30	382,764	31.61	99.99
Entirely Rural	3	22083.00	0.70	100.00	153	0.01	100.00
Total	631*	3166620.02	100.00	-	1,210,855	100.00	-

* NCT of Delhi and Union Territory of Daman & Diu have been treated as 1 unit each.
Source: Census of India, 2011.

population of the country if fully urban districts are also included. Many of these districts accommodate large cities that are either state capitals or centres of industrial and commercial activities. On the whole, nearly one-fourth of the country with over 33 per cent of population is characterised by urban population that is at least half the size of rural population. However, the fact remains that a significantly larger portion of the country is predominantly rural in character. Covering a little less than 56 per cent of the geographic area of the country, the urban population constitutes less than 30 per cent of its rural counterpart. Spread over as many as 376 districts and accommodating marginally short of half of the total population of the country, this feature can be seen in agriculturally dependent regions of states like Uttar Pradesh, Bihar, Madhya Pradesh, Odisha, Jharkhand, Rajasthan etc. apart from the hilly states in the north and north-east (see also Map 4.2). Interestingly, the relatively backward districts in otherwise more urbanised and developed states also display this feature.

5

POPULATION GROWTH

Population geographers have traditionally been concerned with the analysis of trends and patterns of growth in world population. However, lack of reliable data on size of the population during early times renders their task very difficult. It may be recalled that the first census operation began in a few countries in Europe only in the beginning of the 19th century, and as late as the middle of the 20th century, several countries of the world had never conducted any census. Even at present times, reliable estimates are not available for many areas or regions in the less developed parts of the world. Despite this limitation, several attempts have been made to chart the trends and patterns of world population growth using some indirect evidences. These indirect sources include archaeological remains, inferences from the population structure of some modern societies with economies similar to those of earlier groups, and for more recent periods, written records and estimates based on surveys of different kinds (Hornby and Jones, 1980:4). These estimates help us construct trends in world population growth in the past and identify its spatial patterns. The present chapter presents an account of the trends in growth of world population and its spatial manifestations. But, before we embark upon that it is necessary to discuss the various measures used in the analysis of population change.

Measures of analysis of population change

Any change in population size of an area over a certain period of time is expressed in the form of rate of growth per annum. Here population at time $t + 1$ is considered as a function of population at time t. Rate of growth in a population is generally worked out in three different ways. In the case of all these measures all that is required is the figures on population size at any two time points. The simplest and the most commonly used measure is *arithmetic rate of increase* in population. As is implied, this measure is based on the assumption that population grows arithmetically by a constant number. According to this, population at time t would equal to:

$$P_t = P_0(1 + rt) \tag{5.1}$$

where P_0 is population at the base year, r is rate of growth and t is the interval between base year and terminal year. In other words, the arithmetic rate of growth in population between any two time points would be:

$$r = (P_t - P_0)/P_0 \tag{5.2}$$

where the notations are the same as those in Equation 5.1. Since population of an area actually grows geometrically i.e. in a compound fashion (just as money accrues in an investment account if the interest is not paid out), it is suggestible to apply *annual compound rate of growth,* while analysing change in population size. Annual compound rate of growth in a population can be expressed in the following manner:

$$P_t = P_0(1 + r)^t \tag{5.3}$$

Equation 5.3 is also known as *geometric law* of population growth. Malthus in his classic treatise on population in 1798 had postulated that population grows geometrically, and, therefore, population following such a pattern of growth is sometimes called as *Malthusian Population* (Pathak and Ram, 1998:2). Under the assumption of geometric growth, a population growing at a rate of 1 per cent per annum will double its size in 70 years (and not in 100 years as in the case of arithmetic rate of growth), and at 2 per cent rate of growth in 35 years. The duration involved is called *doubling time*, and can be worked out by dividing 70 i.e. the time required for a population to double its size at a rate of 1 per cent per annum, by the prevailing rate of growth. If figures on population size at two time points are available, the annual compound rate of growth can be worked out and population size pertaining to any time between the two extremes can be estimated using Equation 5.3. Similarly, if some accurate assumption about future compound rate of growth can be made, population size can easily be projected at any time into the future.

Still another measure of the analysis of change in population size is *exponential rate of growth*. This measure is based on the assumption that population growth follows an exponential distribution, which is a generalisation of the geometric function when time t is considered to be a continuous variable (Srinivasan, 1998b:134). Exponential rate of growth can be worked out using the following equation:

$$P_t = P_0 \cdot e^{rt} \tag{5.4}$$

Past trends in world population growth

For most of human history, the size of world population, in general, remained very small and virtually stagnant due to extremely high death rates. The present rate of growth in population is, thus, a recent phenomenon. Rates of growth in population over a long time in human history remained very small, and occasional decline in numbers, due to such events as wars, epidemic and famines, was a common phenomenon. The history of growth in world population is marked by three distinct periods of sudden acceleration in the growth rate – while the first was witnessed around 8000 BC, the second and the third occurred sometime in the middle of the 18th and 20th centuries respectively. The period around 8000 BC is said to be a turning point in human history when man learnt the art of domesticating plants and animals. With this development, he was no more a food gatherer or a hunter. Rather, he became a food grower himself. Likewise, the year 1750 is marked with revolutionary changes in economic systems, generated by, first the Agricultural Revolution and then the Industrial Revolution in Europe, which, in turn, unleashed profound changes in demographic trends. Finally, the middle of the 20th century coincides with the onset of demographic expansion in the less developed parts of the world, as a result of the spread of medical technology. Thus, each of these periods of sudden spurts in the growth rate is linked with technological advances, which increased the capacity of the earth to support human population.

Archaeological and other evidences suggest that in the year 8000 BC the size of the world population was between 5 to 10 million only. Up to this time, the economy of the societies, widely scattered in different parts of the world, was largely based on food gathering and hunting. For several hundred thousand years from the emergence of humankind, the population of the world had increased by only 0.0015 per cent per year. The period of technological advancement, often known as the *Neolithic Revolution* when man became a farmer in place of a food gatherer or hunter, drastically altered the human-environment relationship. The transition from the stage of food gathering and hunting to the stage of domesticating animals and growing crops was, by no means, a sudden phenomenon. The change had its beginning as early as some 12,000 years ago. With its first manifestation in the Tigris Euphrates valleys of present-day Iraq (Norton and Mercier, 2016:150), the transition spread farther over space, and by 7000 BC, a vast region of high population density, the first of its kind in human history, had appeared on the earth. It stretched from Greece to Iran including Egypt. By 4000 BC permanent sedentary life had appeared on the Mediterranean coast and in different locations in Europe. Other locations where a similar type of 'human-nature' relations appeared were in Mexico, Peru, China and India. Prior to this transformation, human population remained almost stable, marked with mild increases for some time and then interrupted by a decrease, depending upon cultural advances and physical constraints. However, as food availability improved and became stable with this transformation of 'human-nature' relations, human population started growing faster.

From the time of the Neolithic Revolution to the beginning of the Christian era, world population grew at an average annual rate of 0.6 per cent only. In the year 1 AD the world population is estimated to have been nearly between 250 to 280 million (see Figure 5.1 and Table 5.1). The subsequent periods witnessed further rise in the pace of growth, and the world population reached the 500-million

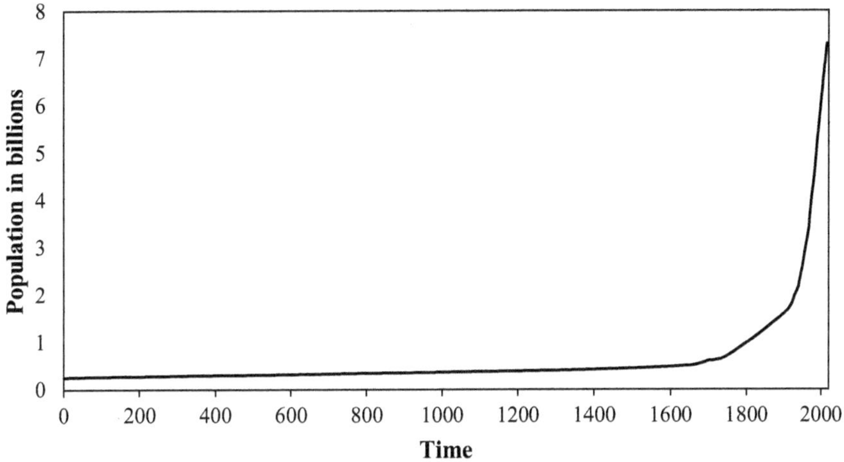

FIGURE 5.1 World population growth (beginning of Christian era to 2015)

Source: Author.

TABLE 5.1 Past trends in world population growth

Year	*Population*	*Per cent Annual Increase**	*Year*	*Population*	*Per cent Annual Increase**
10000 BC	10,000–10 million	**	1950	2.5 billion	1.10
5000 BC	5–20 million	**	1960	3.0 billion	2.00
1 AD	256 million	**	1965	3.3 billion	1.96
1300 AD	400 million	**	1970	3.7 billion	2.06
1650	0.5 billion	0.1	1975	4.1 billion	2.03
1700	0.6 billion	0.1	1980	4.4 billion	1.77
1750	0.7 billion	0.3	1985	4.8 billion	1.67
1800	1.2 billion	0.5	1990	5.3 billion	1.74
1900	1.6 billion	0.6	1998	5.9 billion	1.40
1920	1.8 billion	0.65	2005	6.5 billion	1.45
1930	2.0 billion	1.07	2010	6.9 billion	1.23
1940	2.2 billion	1.11	2015	7.3 billion	1.16

Sources: (i) Figures up to 1998 are borrowed from Bhende and Kanitkar, 2011 (Table 3.3, p. 68). (ii) United Nations, *World Population Prospects: Highlights, The 2004 Revision* (iii) United Nations, *World Population Prospects: Key Findings and Advance Tables, The 2015 Revision.*

Notes: * Annual rate of increase since the previous year. **Insignificant rate of increase.

mark in the year 1650. The rate of growth, however, fluctuated through time and between different groups. The year 1750 marks the beginning of the second spurt in the growth rate. The Industrial Revolution that began in the middle of the 18th century in north-western Europe and spread to the rest of Europe and North America by the early 19th century led to the emergence of a new economic system and an irreversible change in demographic behaviour. With revolutionary changes in agriculture, medicine and industry, death rates started declining, while the birth rates responded only with a time lag, leading to a sudden surge in the rate of growth in population. The annual rate of increase, thus, rose to 0.8 per cent in the early 20th century (Findlay, 1995:155). By the time most of the developed countries began experiencing a slackening in the growth rate towards the close of the demographic transition, the spread of medical technology to the less developed parts of the world since the early 20th century led to a similar decline in the death rates. The world population, therefore, continued to grow at an accelerating pace. The annual rates of increase reached around the 2 per cent level towards the middle of the century. The year 1950, thus, appears as yet another stage of surge in population growth. After the end of the Second World War, following economic recovery, Europe and North America witnessed a rise in the birth rates. This phenomenon of the rise in birth rates after the end of the Second World War is often called as the 'baby boom'. Around this time almost all the less developed countries had gained independence from colonial rule. They began concerted efforts to improve the social and economic conditions of their people. Death rates declined sharply with technological advances, prevention and control of diseases and growth and expansion of public health services. Interestingly, however, death rates in these countries declined without achieving a certain level of social and economic development unlike the experiences of the developed countries. This was due to the fact that the measures for control of mortality rates were largely borrowed from the developed countries and grafted in these countries with the assistance of various UN agencies. As a result, the decline in death rates was not accompanied by a corresponding reduction in birth rates. Thus, though the baby boom in the developed countries disappeared by the close of the 1950s, world population began to grow at an unprecedented rate after 1950. The less developed countries, thus, experienced a far more rapid increase in population than did the European countries in the 19th century. The average annual rate of growth in population, which was only 0.8 per cent during 1900–50, rose to over 2 per cent during 1955–65. Some countries in Latin America and Africa recorded a growth rate of even more than 3 per cent. Remarkably, after 1975 there has been a definite declining trend in the rate of growth in world population. The rate of growth came down from 1.8 per cent during the 1970s to 1.7 per cent in the early 1980s. Between 1995 and 2000 the world population is said to have grown at the rate of 1.3 per cent per year. Much of the decline in the growth rate occurred due to the enforced population policy in China since the 1980s. India too has exhibited a declining trend in the rate of growth in its population during the recent past. Remarkably, the annual population increment has also declined from its peak of 86 million in 1985–90 to the current 78 million (Bhende and Kanitkar, 2011:72).

TABLE 5.2 Adding the billions: actual and projected

Billions	*Year Reached*	*Years Taken*
1	1800	
2	1930	130
3	1960	30
4	1974	14
5	1987	13
6	1999	12
7	2011	12
8	2023	12
9	2042	19

Source: Norton and Mercier, 2016:153.

However, populations in some of the countries in Latin America and Africa continue to grow at an alarming rate.

A rapid growth in the world population during the recent past can also be appreciated by looking at the duration involved in an increase in population of a certain magnitude. It is interesting to note that while it took some hundreds of thousands of years for the world population to reach the 1 billion mark sometime in the early 19th century, the next billion was added in just about a little more than a hundred years (Table 5.2). With further acceleration in growth rates, the duration involved became increasingly shorter – the third billion was added in only 30 years, the fourth in 14 years and the fifth in 13 years. The world population is said to have crossed the 6 billion mark sometime in 1999 and the 7 billion mark towards the end of 2011, the interval between the two being 12 years. Although the next billion is expected to be added after 12 years (i.e. 2023), the duration involved in further addition is expected to increase.

Growth differentials

One of the salient features of growth in the world population during the recent past has been its uneven pace between different regions and countries. Though the rates of growth have varied over space throughout human history, the differential growth since the middle of the last century has been more conspicuous. The most important dimension of this uneven growth in world population is the contrasts between the developed and less developed regions of the world. Between 1950 and 2000, nearly 90 per cent of the net addition of 3.4 billion people in the world population came from the less developed regions. The contribution of the less developed regions happened to be still higher towards the close of the 20th century. For instance, during 1995–2000 less developed regions contributed as much as 97 per cent of the net increase in the world population. On the other hand, Europe, Northern America and Oceania put together contributed nearly 14 per cent of the net addition in world population during 1950–75. This share has come down to a little over 6 per cent between 1975 and 2010. The UN projections indicate that the less developed regions will account for the whole of the net increase between now and 2050 because the developed regions will experience overall decrease in their populations.

This unevenness in the growth rate is reflected in the shift in the distribution of population among different regions, countries and continents during the recent past (Table 5.3). While Europe and North America have witnessed a steady decline in their share in the world population, Africa, Latin America and Asia have recorded an increase in their share. In 1950, Europe and North America had accounted for 28.5 per cent of the world population, which came down to 17.6 per cent in 1998 and 14.69 in 2017. If other developed countries like Japan, Australia and New Zealand are also included, the share of the more developed regions is reported to have declined from over 32 per cent in 1950 to barely 20 per cent in 1998 and 15.25 per cent in 2017. According to the medium variant projection of the UN, their share will further decline to 13 per cent by 2050. Meanwhile, the share of Africa in the world population has gone up from 8.8 per cent to 16.59 per cent during the same period, and is projected to reach 19.8 per cent in 2050. The population of Africa that was less than half the size of Europe in 1950 surpassed the latter in the mid-1990s. Latin American countries present another case of disproportionate concentration of growth in population. In Latin America, the share is found to have gone

TABLE 5.3 Population growth in major regions of the world, 1950–2017

Major Areas	*Population (millions)*				
	1950	*1975*	*2005*	*2010*	*2017*
Africa	224	416 (3.43)	906 (3.93)	1,030 (2.74)	1,250 (3.05)
Asia	1,396	2,395 (2.86)	3,905 (2.10)	4,157 (1.29)	4,494 (1.16)
Europe	547	676 (0.94)	728 (0.26)	739 (0.30)	745 (0.12)
Latin America and the Caribbean	167	322 (3.71)	561 (2.47)	585 (0.86)	643 (1.42)
Northern America	172	243 (1.65)	331 (1.21)	344 (0.79)	362 (0.75)
Oceania	13	21 (2.46)	33 (1.90)	37 (2.42)	42 (1.93)
World	2,519	4,074 (2.47)	6,465 (1.96)	6,892 (1.32)	7,536 (1.33)

Sources: (i) United Nations, *World Population Prospects: The 2004 Revision*, and (ii) Population Reference Bureau, *World Population Datasheet*, 2010 and 2017.

Note: Figures in parentheses are annual rate of increase over the previous time-point.

up from 6.62 per cent in 1950 to 8.53 in 2017. Africa and Latin America, taken together, will account for a little less than 30 per cent of the world's population in 2050. The share of Asian countries, too, has increased from 55.6 per cent in 1950 to around 60 per cent in 2017. However, it may be noted that the last decade or so has witnessed a decline in the share of Asia in the world population *albeit* marginal. The pace in decline in the share is expected to increase further in coming decades. Though continuing as the main contributor in absolute terms, Asia's net addition population is likely to be 1.68 billion during 1998–2050 as compared to 2.18 billion during 1950–98.

Patterns in natural rate of increase at individual country levels are shown in Map 5.1. It is interesting to note that almost the whole of Eastern Europe including Russia is experiencing a decline in population size. According to the UN data there are 17 countries estimated to have fewer people now than in 2010, and 14 of them are located in Eastern Europe (Weeks, 2018:46). These populations are marked with more deaths than births annually, a phenomenon that is not occurring elsewhere in the world barring few exceptions. Ukraine and Russia, for instance, are losing about 340,000 and 950,000 people every year due to higher death rates. A surplus of deaths over births in such populations can largely be attributed to its age structure. Outside this region, Germany, Japan and Cuba are other countries witnessing a similar demographic phenomenon (Weeks, 2018:46). It may be noted that 18 per cent of Europe's population is in the age group '65 years and above' as against a world average of only 9 per cent.

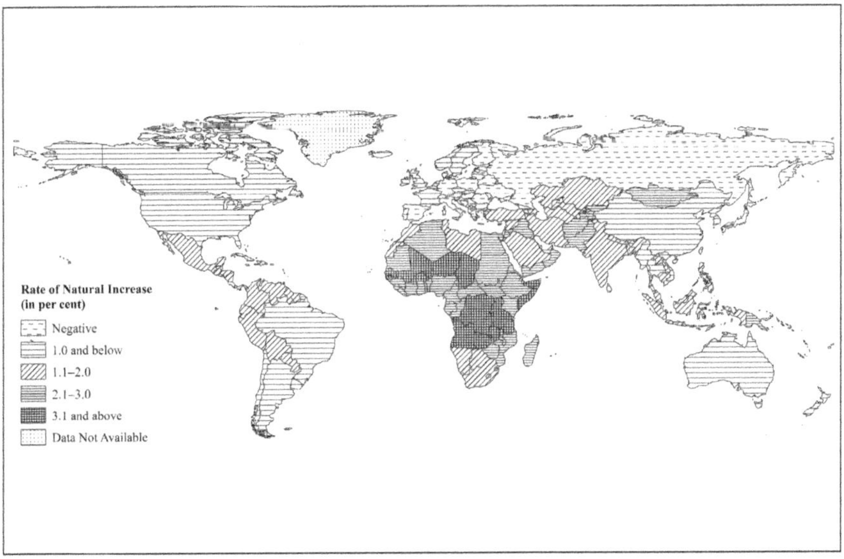

MAP 5.1 Rate of natural increase in population in the world, 2017

Source: Based on Population Reference Bureau, *World Population Data Sheet, 2017*.

On the other extreme are African countries marked with persistently very rapid growth in their populations. Barring a few countries almost the whole of Africa still reports a natural growth rate of over 2 per cent annually. Some countries are even growing at a rate of more than 3 per cent per annum. Nigeria is the most populous country of the continent followed by Egypt, Ethiopia and Congo Democratic Republic. While Egypt is located in Northern Africa, the other three form part of Sub-Saharan Africa. The average total fertility rate in Nigeria and Congo Democratic Republic is still as high as 6 children per woman while in Ethiopia the corresponding figure is 4.5 children. Taken together these three countries account for 30 per cent of the population of Africa. With the current rate of growth, Nigeria is expected to emerge as the third largest populous country of the world by 2050, and Ethiopia is expected to move into the top 10 closely followed by Congo (Weeks, 2018:50). The neighbouring countries like Tanzania, Uganda and Kenya with similar fertility levels are also expected to rank among top 20 largest populous countries by the middle of the present century. The Islamic countries in West Asia also report growth rates of the same magnitude. In fact, the entire belt stretching westward from Pakistan to Africa's Atlantic coast, and dominated by Islamic countries, is marked with high growth of population due to drastic decline in mortality rates since the middle of the last century. Evidences indicate that since 1950, the population of 40 countries where Muslims account for more than half of its population has more than trebled. Increase in youthful population in the region has been substantial due to delay in the onset of fertility decline. Turkey is, however, an exception where fertility levels have drastically declined to below replacement level, and life expectancy is identical to that in Europe.

South and Southeast Asia is the home of one-third of world humanity. The Indian subcontinent dominates the demographic conditions of the region with India, Pakistan and Bangladesh. While the rate of natural growth in population is well below 2 per cent per annum in most of the countries in the region, it is still above 2 per cent in Afghanistan and Pakistan. Singapore, Thailand and Vietnam are growing at a rate below 1 per cent. East Asia with over one-fifth of the world population presents unique demographic conditions. China alone is the home of over 85 per cent of people in the region. Although fertility decline in China began way back in the 1960s, it got an unprecedented push with the state-enforced 'one-child policy' implemented in 1979. Although total fertility rate declined to below replacement level sometime in the 1990s, population continues to grow at a rate of 0.6 per cent. However, China and also Japan, South Korea and Taiwan are likely to have fewer people in 2050 than now (Weeks, 2018:52).

Just as in parts of Africa and South Asia, some countries in Oceania also exhibit an annual growth of over 2 per cent per year. It is worth mentioning here that in all these countries death rates have undergone a sharp decline during the recent past while birth rates continue to be very high. A major part of the growth, thus, results from high levels of natural increase in the wake of the high birth rate and youthful age structure. However, all these countries are very small in size. It may be noted that people of European origin form a substantial portion in population of many countries in the region, and the rate of natural increase in such countries is much smaller as compared to others. Australia is the largest country in terms of size of population followed by Papua New Guinea and New Zealand. The population of Australia has been growing through immigration mainly from Asian countries.

Remarkably, countries in Latin America and South America report the natural rate of increase below 2 per cent. With a population of 129.2 million and 207.9 million respectively, Mexico and Brazil dominate the demography of the region. Mexico, which alone accommodates over 72 per cent of the population of Latin America, witnessed a decline in birth rates since the 1970s encouraged by a change in government policy promoting small family size. Likewise, Brazil, which accommodates nearly half of the population in South America, witnessed a spectacular reduction in total fertility rate from more than 6 children per woman to below replacement level since the 1960s. As a result population is growing at a natural rate of increase of just 0.7 per cent per annum. Besides, countries with a substantial population of European origin e.g. Argentina, Chile and Uruguay also have almost similar fertility levels as well as a rate of growth in population to that of Brazil. With relatively higher fertility levels, the rest of the countries in South America report a higher rate of increase in population.

Demographic transition

On the basis of evidences on the trends of fertility and mortality, and resultant change in population size in Europe during modern times, demographers have suggested a scheme of transition from a stage of high birth and high death rates to eventually a stage marked with low birth and low death rates. This transition occurred in different stages and is best summarised in the *demographic transition model* (see Chapter 13). Though further evidences have shown that particular countries in many cases do not conform in detail to all aspects of the sequence of transition, the model provides a useful indication of change and a yardstick to examine the experience of individual countries (Hornby and Jones, 1980:6). In other words, while the demographic transition model is essentially a descriptive rather than an analytical tool, it provides a simple way of summarising the state of demographic development reached across the globe (Champion, 2003:196).

It is important to note that the transition did not begin simultaneously in the whole of Europe. Evidences indicate that the transition first began in north-western Europe sometime in the middle of the 18th century. Thereafter, it gradually spread to the rest of Europe and, a little later, to countries outside Europe such as the United States, Canada and Australia whose populations have strong links with Europe in terms of their origin. Some Asian countries like Japan and Singapore also experienced a 'European' type of demographic transition. In the rest of the world, the transition is said to have set in only towards the middle of the 20th century.

Demographers are of the opinion that European countries have passed through four main stages of transition. Until about the middle of the 18th century both birth and death rates in most of the European countries were very high and fluctuated between 30 and 40 per thousand. Periodic wars, famines and epidemics resulted in occasional rise in death rates. Birth rates, on the other hand, remained stable at a high level. Thus, whenever death rates exceeded birth rates, there was occasional decline in number. However, the long-term effect of high birth and high death rates was a very slow change in population size. This represented the *first stage* of demographic transition.

From 1750 onwards the demographic situations in Europe began to experience a significant change. Improved food supply and increased political stability led to the onset of decline in death rates. This declining trend in mortality levels further got strengthened with improvements in sanitation, personal hygiene and increased medical knowledge. Remarkably, there was no corresponding decline in birth rates. Rather, there was an occasional rise in birth rates, as for instance in the UK. The growing difference between birth and death rates resulted in sudden and rapid growth in population. This situation represented the *second stage* and prevailed for over roughly a century up to the middle of the 19th century. In most of the European countries this was the period of population growth on a scale not previously known, though there were variations in terms of timing and magnitude of growth.

As standards of health and sanitation further improved, and more and more diseases were brought under control, death rates continued to decline. Towards the middle of the 19th century, birth rates which so far had remained at a high level began declining. With the onset of this decline European population is said to have entered the *third stage* of transition. Though death rates continued to decline, there was a perceptible deceleration in the pace. Population size, therefore, continued to grow but with decreasing rate. Decline in birth rates, however, is less easily understood than the earlier decline in death rates. In most European countries this decline appears to be the outcome of the emergence of a predominantly urban-industrial society in which the desire for, and possibly the economic value of, additional children decreased. In addition, growing availability of improved methods of birth control made it possible for the parents to limit the size of their family if they so desired.

By the middle of the 20th century the European countries are found to have reached the *fourth* or *final stage* of the transition where both birth and death rates became stable at a very low level. A small difference between birth and death rates again meant a very slow rate of natural increase in population – generally below 1 per cent per annum. However, unlike stage 1 where death rates were marked with a fluctuating trend, stage 4 was characterised by fluctuation in birth rates. Of late many of the developed countries have experienced a rise in the death rates because of a growing concentration of persons in old age groups. Death rates in many of them have become higher than birth rates, as result of which population size has begun shrinking once again.

Demographic transition spread to southern, eastern and south-eastern Europe by the end of the 18th century. A similar change occurred in North America also. Outside Europe, Australia and New Zealand in Oceania, and Japan and Singapore in Asia also experienced similar changes in demographic behaviour. Much interest is now focussed on the demographic transition in the less developed parts of the world. Though recent evidences do show a decline in the pace of population growth, some countries still continue to experience very rapid growth in their populations. Demographic transition in the less developed world began only in the 20th century. Just as it had happened in Europe, the timing of the onset of this transition varied from country to country. While some countries, for example India, began experiencing a decline in death rates as early as the 1930s, in most of the LDCs this change could begin only towards the middle of the century. The decline in death rates in the LDCs was much more rapid than those experienced in the developed countries. As a result of this, the LDCs achieved a decline in mortality rates of a magnitude in just 50 years, which had earlier taken more than 150 years in Europe. Further, this transition was not accompanied by the kinds of social and cultural changes that had occurred in industrialised countries earlier and led to fertility decline. Birth rates continued at a very high level.

The reduction in mortality, unaccompanied by a decline in fertility levels, resulted in an accelerating population growth since the 1950s. The growth rate reached an 'all-time' high during the 1960s. Many developing countries recorded rates of increase as high as 3 per cent a year exceeding by two- or three-fold the highest ever experienced by European populations. At this rate of growth population would double every 23 years. Terms like *population bomb* and *population explosion* were aptly suggested for this phenomenal growth. Some of the highest growth rates were recorded in Latin America and in Asia. Since then, these regions have recorded substantial declines in birth rates along with continuing mortality decline. The most dramatic decline has been seen in China where the growth rate has come down from over 2 per cent in the 1960s to about half of that in the 1980s. India, another population giant, too, has witnessed significant decline in birth rates during the recent past. As we shall see later, annual growth in population in the country has come down to below 2 per cent for the first time since independence. Meanwhile, most of the African countries continue to experience a rapid growth in population due to belated declines in death rates unaccompanied by any reduction in birth rates.

In an early work, Chung (1970) made an attempt to map the diffusion of the demographic transition across the globe since the early years of the 20th century. He classified the countries of the world into three categories representing three stages of transition. Chung's scheme was based on a very simple framework in which the criteria for classification were a death rate of 15 and a birth rate of 30 per thousand persons. While a death rate of 15 per thousand persons was taken as the dividing line between stages 1 and 2, a birth rate of less than 30 per thousand persons demarcated the boundary between stages 2 and 3. In other words, in Chung's scheme of demographic transition, countries in stage 1 were marked with death rates of more than 15 per thousand persons. Similarly, stage 2 represented a situation where the death rate was less than 15 but the birth rate was over 30. And finally, birth and death rates below 30 and 15 per thousand persons characterised countries in stage 3 of the transition respectively.

In Chung's scheme of classification, a majority of the present-day less developed countries appeared in stage 1. The industrialised countries of the West, on the other hand, had already reached the final stage of demographic transition. Since then, the demographic situation across the globe underwent significant change. While, on the one hand, many less developed countries graduated to higher stages, the birth rates in the developed West, at the same time, further declined. Many of the less developed countries appeared in the third and final stage of transition along with developed countries according to this scheme. This produced a great amount of diversity among the countries in the final stage.

Though the death rates among the countries in the final stage were closely aligned to 6–10 per thousand (excepting European countries where death rates had recently gone up due to its typical age structure of population), the birth rates showed a wide range of variation. Some countries in Africa, Latin America and Asia were still marked with birth rates only a short way below the 30 per thousand threshold. As against this, in a large number of European countries the birth rates did not exceed 10 per thousand. Thus, in order to reflect the post–1960s changes, and to differentiate the situations in developed countries from the rest of the countries in the final stage, Champion (2003) later divided stage 3 into two phases – the dividing line being a birth rate of 15 per thousand. Following this modified scheme, an attempt was made by this author earlier (Hassan, 2005) to summarise the demographic situations reached across the globe towards the beginning of the present 20th century using the PRB (2003) estimates on vital rates.

The demographic situation over the last one and a half decade has further changed both in the developed as well as less developed countries. The rise in death rates with further ageing of population accompanied by either stagnant, or in some case increasing birth rates, characterised the process of transition in the developed world. As per the PRB (2017) estimates, of the total 32 countries with birth rates below 10 per thousand persons, 12 countries reported higher death rates than their birth rates (and hence negative natural rate of increase), and another 6 had equal birth and death rates resulting in zero rate of natural increase. Further, as many as 18 countries have experienced a rise in death rates between 2003 and 2017 i.e. over a period of roughly one and a half decade. Barring only 8, all such countries are located in Europe with the largest concentration coming from its southern parts. Outside Europe, Asia was represented by 6 countries namely Hong Kong, Japan, South Korea, Singapore, Taiwan (in its eastern parts) and UAE (in the western part of the continent). The other two were Mauritius and Puerto Rico from Africa and the Caribbean islands respectively. During the same time, less developed countries continued to witness decline in both birth and death rates. As a result, the gap in death rates between the developed and the less developed worlds has almost disappeared. At the same time some of the developed countries are now reporting death rates that are higher than those prevailing in the less developed world.

Any exercise to classify countries in different groups (roughly representing different stages of transition) on the basis of vital rates, therefore, becomes very complicated. In order to capture the given wide diversity among countries in terms of prevailing vital rates, a three-fold classification of stages of transition, with further two sub-groups in each stage, based on PRB estimates (PRB, 2017) is proposed here. The same is presented in Table 5.4.

It is obvious that 'birth rate' is the main criterion of classification at the first level while death rate forms the basis of identification of sub-groups at the second level. As could be seen in the Table 5.4, the cut-off points for first-level classification are crude birth rates of 15 and 30 per thousand persons. In other words, according to this scheme of classification, stage 1 consists of countries with a birth rate of 30 and above while stage 2 represents counties with a birth rate between 15–29, and stage 3 with a birth rate below 15 per thousand persons. Thereafter, each stage is split into two parts – the cut-off point being a death rate of 10 per thousand persons, excepting for stage 3 where the criterion for separation is different. It may be

TABLE 5.4 Scheme of classification of countries in different stages of transition on the basis of vital rates, 2017

Groups / Stages	*Sub-groups*	*Birth Rate (per 1,000 persons)*	*Death Rate (per 1,000 persons)*	*Number of Countries*
I	A	30 and above	10 and above	18
	B	30 and above	Less than 10	30
II	A	15–29	10 and above	3
	B	15–29	Less than 10	77
III	A	Less than 15	Up to 10	66
	B	Less than 15	Equal or higher than birth rate	16

Source: Author.

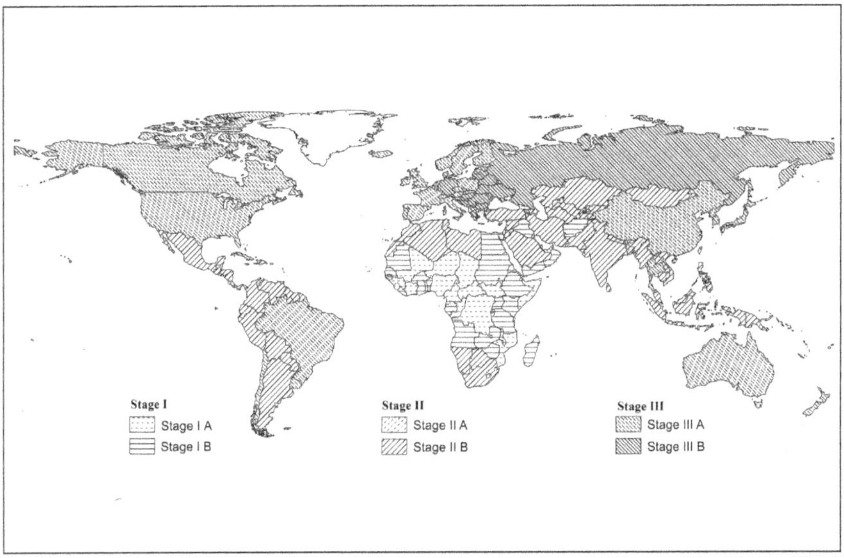

MAP 5.2 Stages of demographic transition reached by different countries in the world, 2017

Source: Population Reference Bureau, *World Population Data Sheet, 2017.*

recalled that among the European countries the process of demographic transition had already come to an end in the 20th century. With the passage of time the population of these countries grew older in the wake of long-term declining trends in birth and death rates. Consequently, death rates once again began increasing in such countries, and in some of them it crossed birth rates resulting in negative growth in population towards the end of the century. In order to differentiate these countries from others in the final stage of transition, a death rate that is either 'equal to' or 'greater than' birth rate prevailing in individual countries was taken as the basis for division between two sub-groups in the final stage. Map 5.2 shows the stages of demographic transition reached by individual countries as per latest data of PRB (2017) data on vital rates.

Population growth in India

According to the final figures of 2011, India's population has grown at an exponential annual growth rate of 1.64 per cent during 2001–11, down from 1.97 per cent during 1991–2001 (Figure 5.2). In fact, the pace of growth in population has undergone a continuous deceleration over the last four decades. When the 1991 census had revealed a decline in the growth rate, some scholars (e.g. Premi, 1991; Tyagi, 1991; Goyal, 1991) treated it as an outcome of the onset of a faster decline in birth rates. They had argued that the declining trend will continue in the future also. However, Ashish Bose, a famous demographer, was of the opinion that the decline is not real, and the growth rate would continue to increase (Das and Bhavsar, 1991:227). In this context, a continuous decline in the pace of population growth for the fourth consecutive decade is indeed an important achievement. This has validated the proposition that birth rates in India have begun to decline at a faster pace, and India's population is fast approaching the end of the third stage of transition. As could be seen in Table 5.5 net decadal addition in the population that increased uninterruptedly since 1931 has undergone decline for the first time in 2011. This implies that although India's population continues to grow in size as a result of population momentum and somewhat impeded fertility, the pace of net addition is on the decrease.

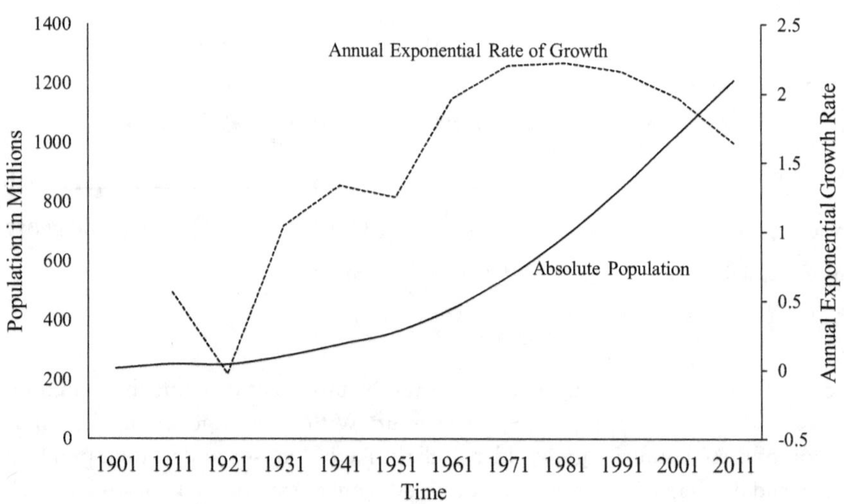

FIGURE 5.2 Trends in population growth in India, 1901 to 2011

Source: Author.

In fact, since ancient times India has been the home of a considerably large size of population. Though census taking in the country is a matter of only the recent past, based on archaeological and historical evidences scholars have tried to construct the trends in population growth since ancient times. A land of one of the world's earliest civilisations, India possessed a fairly high level of technological knowledge to support a large and dense population even some 3,000 to 7,000 years ago. Kingsley Davis in his pioneering book *Population of India and Pakistan* has remarked that 'before Christian era, India had a substantial population, first because of its advanced technology and second because of the fertile environment for the application of this technology' (Davis, 1968:29). One estimate puts India's population in the range of 100 to 140 million in 300 BC (Bhende and Kanitkar, 2011:89). The population size, however, appears to have remained more or less static for almost another 2,000 years. The underlying reasons for this static population size were the same as that which checked population growth elsewhere in the world during the pre-industrial stage – i.e. an abnormally high death rate. According to Davis, the population of the country remained in the neighbourhood of 125 million until the middle of the 19th century, and thereafter a gradual acceleration in the growth rate began taking place. The first census in the country was conducted during 1867–72. However, it was neither synchronous nor did it cover the whole country. This was followed by another census count in 1881, which was synchronous and covered a much wider area. Since then, every 10 years census enumeration has been conducted in the country. In the early stage, however, with each census additional territories were covered and improvements effected in the methodology of data collection. It will, therefore, be more meaningful to confine the present discussion on the trends in population growth during the more recent times to the post–1901 period.

Population growth in India since 1901

The history of growth in India's population can be divided into four distinct phases – the points of division being 1921, 1951 and 1981. Prior to 1921, India's population was characterised by a chequered growth. Decades of substantial growth regularly alternated with decades of small increase or even negative growth. The Census Commissioner for the 1951 census, therefore, rightly called 1921 as the year of *Great Divide*, which differentiated the earlier period of fluctuating growth rates from a period of moderately increasing growth rates. The second point of division was 1951, which differentiated the period of earlier moderate growth from a period of rapid growth in the post-independence period. This phase of rapid growth in population continued up to 1981. Thereafter, though population continues to grow, the rate of growth has undergone a continuous deceleration.

Table 5.5 presents the trends in population growth in India during the last 110 years. The figures for the pre-independence period have been adjusted to take care of partition of the country in 1947. The rate of inter-censal growth in India's population remained very low till 1921, and in fact, the rate of growth was negative during 1911–21. The first 20 years of the 20th century, thus, witnessed a growth rate of only 5.42 per cent in India's population. Severe famines, plague, cholera and influenza epidemics contributed to this phenomenon, and the rate of growth was slow (Amonker, 1974:196). The decade 1901–11 was struck by several local famines. For instance, one such famine occurred in 1907 in areas of what later came to be known as Uttar Pradesh. In addition, plague claimed a heavy toll of life during the decade in Bengal and Bombay Presidencies. Further, in Uttar Pradesh and Punjab plague and malaria caused a considerable number of deaths. The northern zone – comprising Haryana, Himachal Pradesh, Jammu and Kashmir, Punjab, Rajasthan, Chandigarh and Delhi – had, in fact, recorded a negative growth in its population during the decade. The situation was even worse during 1911–21 when India's population at the aggregate level recorded a shrink in its size in the wake of the influenza epidemic, which had struck in 1919. It has been estimated that the epidemic claimed the life of nearly 7 per cent of the population in the country. A continuous belt extending from the Ganga plain down to the Mahanadi delta; part of Rajasthan desert plains; Punjab plains; and Upper Godavari, Krishna and Tungabhadra basins in Maharashtra and Karnataka plateaus witnessed strikingly heavy loss of population during 1901–21 (Premi and Tyagi, 1985:25). From 1921 onwards, a progressive control of the epidemics of cholera and plague resulted in acceleration in the rate of population growth. The decadal rate of growth in population increased from 11 per cent during 1921–31 to over 14 per cent during

TABLE 5.5 Population growth in India, 1901–2011

Census Years	*Population (millions)*	*Decadal Change*		*Annual Exponential Growth Rate (%)*
		Absolute	*Percent*	
1901	238.40	-	-	-
1911	252.09	13.70	5.75	0.56
1921	251.32	–0.77	–0.31	–0.03
1931	278.98	27.66	11.00	1.04
1941	318.66	39.68	14.22	1.33
1951	361.09	42.42	13.31	1.25
1961	439.23	77.68	21.51	1.96
1971	548.16	108.92	24.80	2.20
1981	683.33	135.17	24.66	2.22
1991	846.42	163.09	23.87	2.16
2001	1,028.74	182.32	21.54	1.97
2011	1,210.85	182.12	17.70	1.64

Source: Census of India for various years.

1931–41. Over a period of 30 years i.e. 1921–51 population grew at an exponential rate of growth of 1.21 per cent.

The year 1951 marked the beginning of a rapid growth in the population in the country, as a result of a sharper decline in death rates after independence. The acceleration in the growth rates continued up to 1981. During 1951–81, India's population grew at annual exponential rate of 2.15 per cent. After 1981, although population continued to grow, the pace of growth underwent a definite deceleration. It is expected that this deceleration will continue in the future also as decline in the birth rates becomes sharper in more and more states. Thus, the year 1981 can be called as yet another year of great *divide* in the demographic history of the country. The annual exponential growth rate declined to 1.92 per cent during 1981–2011. The rates separately for the three decades were 2.16 per cent, 1.97 and 1.64 per cent respectively.

During the recent past, states like Bihar, Jharkhand, Uttar Pradesh, Uttarakhand, Madhya Pradesh, Chhattisgarh and Rajasthan have reported faster growth in population than the nation's average. Popularly known as *BIMARU* states (an acronym meaning 'sick' as coined by Ashish Bose), these states account for over 42 per cent of India's population in 2011. Ranking very low in terms of socio-economic development, these states along with Odisha and Assam were designated as Empowered Action Group (EAG) states for initiating appropriate interventions in demographic situations. Despite a general slowing down in the pace of population growth in the country after 1981, states like Bihar, Uttar Pradesh and Rajasthan experienced further increase during the 1990s while in other EAG states, the rate of growth remained almost stagnant. As against this, all the non-EAG states experienced deceleration in the pace of growth in the 1990s. However, of late the EAG states have also witnessed the onset of change in the demographic situations. During 2001–11, for the first time the growth momentum of EAG states has given the signal of slowing down with a decline by about 4 percentage points in decadal growth rate (RGI, 2011:49). This, along with a similar decline in growth rate elsewhere in the country, brought down the decadal growth rate from 21.54 per cent during 1991–2001 to 17.70 per cent during 2001–11.

The spatial pattern in decadal rate of growth of population in the country has of late been characterised by a marked 'north-south' divide. Northern plains have generally recorded faster growth as compared to their counterparts in the south during the recent past. Although the decade 2001–11 has witnessed a general deceleration, the 'north-south' divide in the patterns of growth continues to exist (Map 5.3). Roughly 20° N latitude separates regions of higher growth in the north from regions of lower growth in the south. As can be seen on the map, parts in Bihar and Uttar Pradesh plains, western and central Rajasthan, and areas in and around the national capital territory of Delhi are conspicuous with a significantly faster growth in population. To the contrary, almost the whole of Kerala and Tamil Nadu, major parts of Karnataka, Maharashtra and Andhra Pradesh have witnessed a lower growth than the nation's average. It is in these southern regions that the pace of growth in population has undergone further deceleration. The deceleration has been more

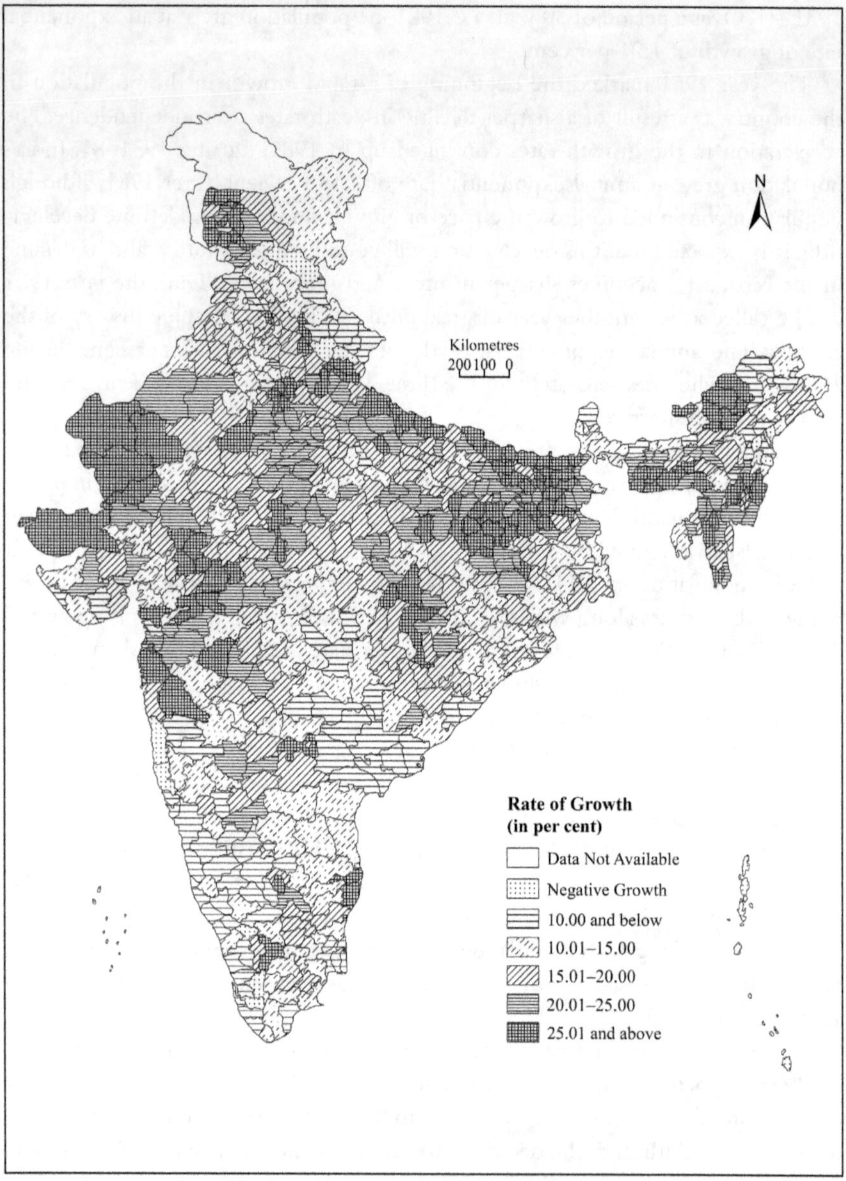

MAP 5.3 Patterns of population growth in India, 2001–11

Source: Census of India, 2011.

conspicuous in the states of Kerala and Tamil Nadu. A remarkably lower annual growth rate in the states of Kerala and Tamil Nadu is indicative of the fact that they have reached an advanced stage of demographic transition. With substantial declines in the birth rates during the post-independent period, these states have long back reached *replacement-level fertility* in the country.

Demographic transition in India

It is important to examine the process of demographic transition in India in order to anticipate future trends in growth in population. Although past and contemporary trends indicate a great amount of variation in pattern, sequence and timing of the transition from one population to another, the model is a very important tool to assess the dynamics of population in any country. One striking similarity between the Indian experience and the experiences of other countries with respect to the transition is the fact that the decline in mortality rate has preceded the fall in fertility (Visaria, 1995:3). If one examines the trends in vital rates in the country it appears that India is fast approaching the completion of the third stage of transition with a death rate already at a low level and a rapidly declining birth rate (Figure 5.3). Since the rate of natural increase, which speeded up in the initial phases, has now shown a tendency to narrow down during the last three decades, a stage is set to enter the next phase to bring about a new balance between mortality and fertility at lower levels. However, the speed with which India achieves this stage depends on the transition of vital rates in some of the major states, which appear to be still in the initial phases of transition.

The process of demographic transition in India is said to have set in some time in the late 1920s and early 1930s when death rates started declining. Prior to that, India's population was in the first stage with very high birth and high death rates. The death rate fluctuated from year to year, and as a consequence, the size of population remained almost stationary. With the onset of decline in the death rates, India's population entered the second stage of transition. Birth rates responded

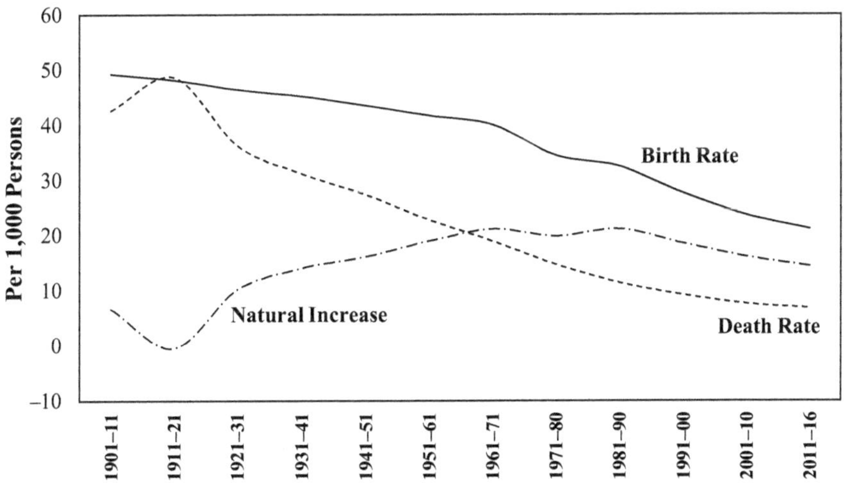

FIGURE 5.3 Trends in birth rate, death rate and rate of natural increase in India, 1901–11 to 2011–16

Source: Author.

only in the second half of the 20th century. Evidences indicate that the decline in birth rate remained only marginal for over 50 years since the turn of the last century. A definite dent in the birth rate was noticed only from 1961–70 onwards, which marked the end of the second stage or the *early expanding stage*. Thus, India's population entered the third stage of transition i.e. the *late expanding stage* sometime towards the close of the 1960s. As decline in the death rates was rapid, the rate of natural increase in the population went up from 1.2 to 1.3 per cent during 1921–51 to 2 to 2.2 per cent during 1951–81.

As elsewhere in the less developed parts of the world, the decline in death rates was more rapid in India than what had happened in the more developed countries earlier. By the close of the 1980s, the death rates had already declined to the neighbourhood of 10 per thousand, a rate very similar to those prevailing in the developed countries. Interestingly, around the same time the decline in birth rates also gathered momentum. The decline in birth rates was experienced almost throughout the country, though there were significant regional variation in its pace. In fact, at the aggregate level, fertility declined at a faster pace than was actually expected (Visaria, 1995:5). The continuing deceleration in the pace of population growth in the country over the last three decades is indicative of the fact that India's population is closing towards the end of the *late expanding stage* of demographic transition. The average rate of natural increase has undergone a significant decline largely because of the decline in the crude birth rate since the late 1980s.

The demographic scenario at the aggregate national level, however, conceals many of the regional peculiarities. India is a vast country with a great amount of regional diversity in terms of its geography, historical experience and socio-cultural attributes including demographic situation. An analysis of the state-level trends in fertility and mortality reveals that the transition has not occurred at a uniform pace, nor the period and pattern have been identical in different parts of the country. As a result, different states are, in fact, at different stages of demographic transition. On an average, the peninsular India appears to be ahead of its counterpart in the north with respect to the transition. Earlier, this author (Hassan, 2005) had grouped the major states in the country in three broad categories on the basis of the levels of birth and death rates and resultant rate of natural increase using SRS data for the year 2001. Currently, crude death rates among most of the states are aligned to 6–7 per thousand persons while birth rates vary a great deal. Therefore, grouping states/union territories in stages of transition is a more complicated exercise now than before. As mortality levels are marked with a smaller range of variation across different regions, for the present purpose, states and union territories have ben categorised in three groups roughly representing three stages of transition based on fertility levels in the year 2016 (Table 5.6).

States like Kerala, Punjab, Tamil Nadu and Goa are at the verge of completing the transition. From among the major states Kerala has the distinction of being the leading one in the country in demographic transition. Decline in mortality rate in the state began in the late 1940s, and currently the crude death rate is one of the lowest not only in the country but also in the entire world. With an impressive decline, total fertility rate in the state reached replacement level as early as 1988.

TABLE 5.6 Birth rate, death rate and rate of natural increase: states and union territories, 2016

States	*Birth Rate*	*Death Rate*	*Rate of Natural Increase*
Group I: Birth Rate up to 15.0			
A and N Islands	11.7	5.2	6.5
Goa	12.9	6.7	6.2
Manipur	12.9	4.5	8.4
Tripura	13.7	5.5	8.2
Chandigarh	13.9	4.5	9.4
Puducherry	13.9	7.2	6.7
Nagaland	14.0	4.5	9.5
Kerala	14.3	7.6	6.7
Punjab	14.9	6.0	8.9
Tamil Nadu	15.0	6.4	8.6
Group II: Birth Rate 15.1–20.0			
West Bengal	15.4	5.8	9.6
NCT of Delhi	15.5	4.0	11.5
Mizoram	15.5	4.2	11.3
Jammu and Kashmir	15.7	5.0	10.7
Maharashtra	15.9	5.9	10.0
Himachal Pradesh	16.0	6.8	9.2
Andhra Pradesh	16.4	6.8	9.6
Uttarakhand	16.6	6.7	9.9
Sikkim	16.6	4.7	11.9
Telangana	17.5	6.1	11.4
Karnataka	17.6	6.7	10.9
Odisha	18.6	7.8	10.8
Arunachal Pradesh	18.9	6.2	12.7
Lakshadweep	18.9	6.0	12.9
Group III: Birth Rate 20.1 and Above			
Gujarat	20.1	6.1	14.0
Haryana	20.7	5.9	14.8
Assam	21.7	6.7	15.0
Chhattisgarh	22.8	7.4	15.4
Jharkhand	22.9	5.5	17.4
Meghalaya	23.7	6.6	17.1
Daman & Diu	24.0	4.6	19.4
Rajasthan	24.3	6.1	18.2
Dadar & Nagar Haveli	24.5	4.0	20.5
Madhya Pradesh	25.1	7.1	18.0
Uttar Pradesh	26.2	6.9	19.3
Bihar	26.8	6.0	20.8

Source: *Sample Registration System Bulletin*, Vol. 51, No. 1, September 2017.

The state which remained marked with one of the most rapid growth up to 1971 has, since then, witnessed a substantial decline in the pace of growth in population. This rapid decline in the pace of growth became the subject of much discussion and debate at both national and international levels. A rapid fertility transition in Kerala is generally attributed to a high level of female literacy for many decades, and a remarkably higher status of women in the society. Kerala is, therefore, often considered as a unique case. Tamil Nadu, too, has witnessed a rapid transition during the recent past. During the 1980s and 1990s, the annual exponential growth rate in the state has been only marginally higher than that in Kerala. Unlike Kerala, Tamil Nadu is very close to the average Indian situation. It is, therefore, sometimes suggested that Indian policy makers should look at the experience of Tamil Nadu as a model for achieving demographic targets in other states. Some of the smaller states like Manipur, Nagaland and Tripura are also near completion of the transition with birth rates of less than 15 and death rates below 10 per thousand persons. Remarkably, these states have a substantial proportion of Christians in their population. A rapid transition in fertility and mortality rates in these states can be attributed to the works of 'Christian Missionaries' which have been operational for a long time now. The union territories of Chandigarh, Andaman & Nicobar Islands and Puducherry are also characterised by a similar demographic situation.

On the other extreme, the *BIMARU* or 'sick' states – Bihar, Madhya Pradesh, Rajasthan and Uttar Pradesh – in the Hindi belt of the north are still in the *expanding stage* of transition. Though death rates in these states are already below 10 per thousand persons, birth rates are still around 25 per thousand persons. As a result of this, the natural rate of growth in these states continues to be very high ranging from 1.8 to more than 2.1 per cent per annum. Since they account for over 35 per cent of the country's population, India's performance at the aggregate level will continue to depend on demographic behaviour in these states for quite some time. Other states and union territories in the country fall between these two extremes. Interestingly, Odisha, which still ranks very low in the levels of development in the country, figures higher in the ladder of transition than some of the more developed states. It may be noted that Odisha has throughout been characterised by mortality conditions that are almost similar to those in *BIMARU* states like Bihar, Madhya Pradesh, Rajasthan and Uttar Pradesh. In view of their demographic situations, these states were later identified as Empowered Action Group (EAG) of states for appropriate interventions in health planning. However, in terms of birth rate Odisha presents a completely contrasting picture. Crude birth rate in the state is even lower than that of developed states like Gujarat and Haryana. The state achieved replacement-level fertility way back in 2012.

6

AGE–SEX COMPOSITION

Population geographers have traditionally been interested in the composition of population or population structure as it varies over space. Population composition refers to the characteristics of population in which distribution by age and sex holds a very important place. An analysis of age and sex composition, in fact, forms an integral part in any study on population. Age and sex are the biological characteristics of population, which are different from other achieved characteristics acquired by the individuals during the lifetime. Information relating to age and sex composition is generally gathered at the time of periodic censuses. It is also collected through regular registration of births, deaths and migration. Age and sex composition of a population affects not only the other demographic attributes but also the social, economic and political structures. Sex and age composition has significant bearings on such demographic processes as fertility, mortality and migration. It goes without saying that a young population i.e. a population in which young persons are relatively more numerous, is more fecund, less susceptible to many causes of death and is usually more migratory than an old population. In almost all the societies of the world, procreation is allowed only in a marital bond. The number of marriages possible in monogamous societies, and also the number of legitimate births, depends in part on whether there are as many men as women of marriageable ages. A marked and growing disparity in the balance between males and females in the population has often been viewed as a threat to family and social stability.

Age structure

Age is a very important biological characteristic of an individual. The United Nations defines age of an individual as 'the estimated or calculated interval of time between the date of birth and the date of census, expressed in completed solar years' (quoted in Bhende and Kanitkar, 2011:154). Since age determines the physical capacity and mental maturity of an individual, every society uses age as an integral part of social organisation. Social roles and responsibilities are assigned in accordance with an individual's age. Kingsley Davis, a renowned demographer, had earlier commented that 'all societies recognize age a basis of status, but some of them emphasize them more than others' (quoted in Weeks, 2018:300). The age structure of a population determines the number of persons available for different social categories. For instance, the size of the labour force available in a population depends on its age structure. Planning for various social and physical amenities in a region also requires data on age distribution. In addition, age is biologically related to fertility and mortality.

The interrelations between age structure and a wide range of social, demographic, economic and political phenomena make the classification of a population by age groups especially important. The age distribution of a population provides the basis of all detailed demographic analysis. For instance, the fertility and mortality levels of two populations can meaningfully be compared only when the age structures of the populations are taken into account. Data by age distribution is indispensable for the construction of life tables and for making projections.

Keeping in mind the significance of age structure, the question on age is included in all censuses and surveys the world over. Data on age are, however, less reliable. In the underdeveloped societies, the illiterate or semi-literate persons do not know the exact age, and, therefore, at the time of counting, the enumerators generally resort to guess. Even in developed societies, there is a deliberate tendency to concentrate on certain ages, e.g. number ending 0 or 5 or some other even numbers. Age preference in varying degree can be seen in almost all the societies. This results in the concentration of an abnormally large number of individuals on certain ages. This problem is known as *age heaping* of data. Errors in data on age can also occur because of carelessness in reckoning age, misunderstanding of the question or deliberate attempt to conceal the real age. Before such data are put to any analysis, the user must make necessary corrections.

Measures of age structure

The age structure of a population can be analysed in number of ways. The most commonly used method is the one in which percentage distribution of population in various age groups is worked out. Once the percentage distribution in different age groups is available, one can compare the age structures of two populations, or examine the temporal changes in age structure of a single population. The percentage figures are sometimes plotted on a special type of bar graph, which is known as an *age pyramid*. In an age pyramid, various horizontal bars represent successive ages from the lowest at the bottom to the highest at the top, and the scale is shown along the horizontal axis at the bottom. In an age pyramid one can show the age structure separately for the two sexes, and for rural and urban areas. Age pyramids are generally wider on the bottom and gradually taper towards the top, an outcome of above-replacement fertility and increasing mortality with increasing age

(Newbold, 2010:63). However, with the passage of time, the shape of the age pyramid of a population undergoes change in the wake of transition in vital rates. The base of a pyramid becomes narrower due to decline in fertility levels, while the top gets broader with reduction in mortality rates and increased longevity. At the same time a bulge in between two extreme ages gradually develops (Figure 6.1 summarises changes in India's age structure between 1961 and 2011). The age pyramids of developed countries are more rectangular in shape.

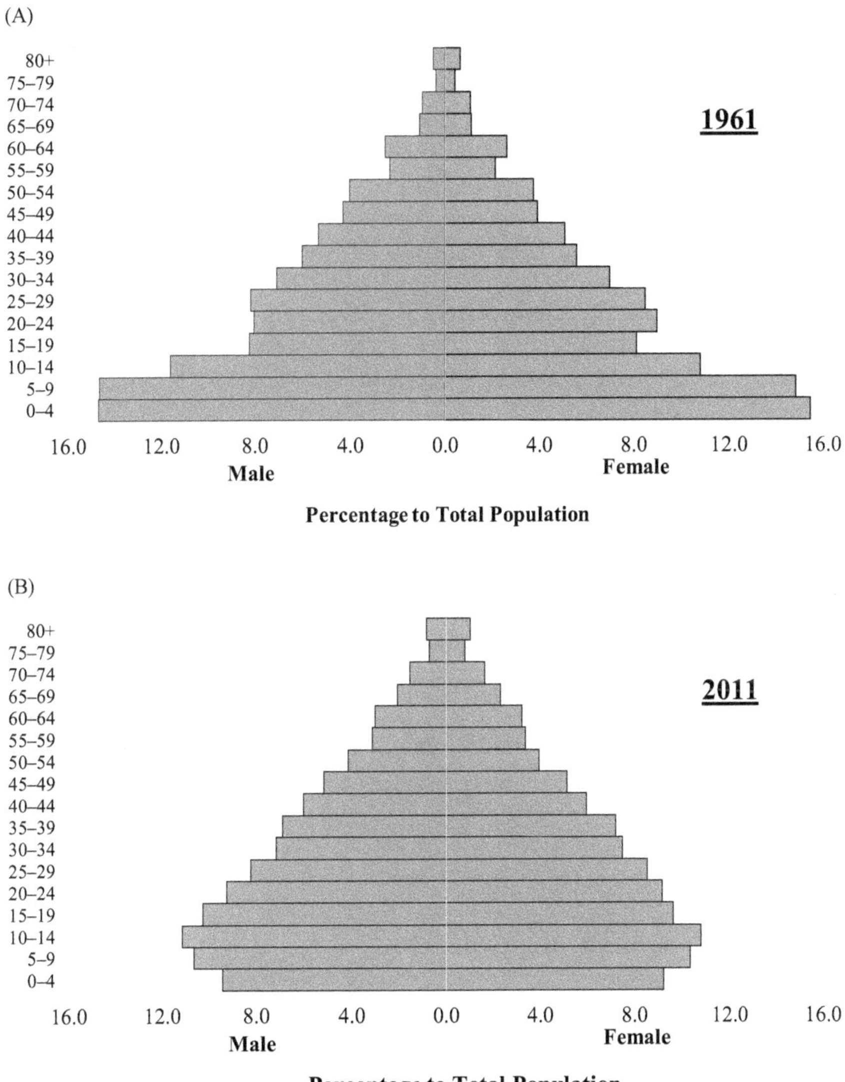

FIGURE 6.1 Age pyramid, India, 1961 and 2011

Source: Author.

In addition, various measures of central tendency viz. mean, median and mode can also be used for the analysis of age structure. However, the most commonly used measure of central tendency is the median age of population. Median age of a population is the age that divides all the individuals of the population in two equal halves. Since data on age composition are normally available for various five-year age groups, the median age can be calculated using the conventional statistical formula for the grouped data (see for instance Mahmood, 1998).

Another measure to study the age structure of a population is what is commonly known as the *dependency ratio*. The dependency ratio of a population provides the number of dependents in the population for every 100 working persons. Here, children below age 15 years and persons age 60 years and above (or sometimes 65 years depending upon the prevailing social and economic conditions and quality of life) are considered as dependent on people in the working age group i.e. between 15 and 59 years (or 64 years). The ratio is computed in the following manner:

$$\text{Dependency Ratio} = \{(P_{0-14} + P_{60+}) / P_{15-59}\} \star 100 \quad (6.1)$$

where $P_{0-14,}$ P_{60+} and P_{15-59} refer to populations in the age groups 0–14, 60 years and above and 15–59 years respectively. In cases where the lower limit of dependent age is 65 years, necessary modifications are done accordingly in the numerator and denominator in the formula.

With decline in the birth and death rates the phenomenon of *population ageing* has attracted widespread attention, particularly in the developed parts of the world, during the recent past. Population ageing is defined as the process whereby the proportion of children in the population decreases and that of old people increases. The ageing of population can be shown with the help of the median age of population. Sometimes, simple percentage share of 'dependent aged' in the population is also used. However, such percentages do not provide an accurate estimate of ageing as they are determined by the relative size of population in all other age brackets. Migration of population, which is highly age selective, may affect the proportion of 'aged dependents' in the population. Petersen (1975) has, therefore, suggested a measure, which he called as 'index of ageing'. This can be worked out in the following manner:

$$\text{Index of Ageing} = (P_{65+} / P_{0-14}) \star 100 \quad (6.2)$$

Please note that the notations are same as those in Equation 6.1.

Age structure of population in the world

The prevailing age structure of any population is the result of past trends in birth, death and migration. Populations characterised by very high fertility levels are marked with a larger share of children in the population. A high rate of mortality results in lower expectation of life. The dependent aged persons, thus, form a very small share in the population. If for some specific reason, there is an abnormally high death rate in a particular age bracket, the overall age structure gets affected. Migration is a highly age-selective phenomenon. People in certain age groups have a higher propensity to migrate than others. The age structure of population is, therefore, determined to a great extent by the process of migration. It is, then, rightly remarked that age structure of a population reveals the entire demographic history.

The age structure of different populations is usually compared with reference to three broad age groups corresponding to 'dependent young' (less than 15), 'working' (15 to 59 or 15 to 64 years) and 'dependent aged' (60 or 65 and above). There is a great amount of variation in the age structure from one country to another. On the one extreme, there are less developed countries where high birth and high death rates have resulted in a very large proportion of children and a small proportion of aged persons in the population. On the other extreme, there are developed countries where birth and death rates are very low and children constitute a very small portion of the population. The proportion of 'dependent aged', however, is much larger in such populations. This typical age structure in economically developed countries has resulted from a major fertility decline, which has had the effect of sharply reducing the proportion of children and increasing the proportion of persons in the working age group and in old age groups.

Table 6.1 presents the percentage distribution of population in three broad age groups for the world major areas. As evident, on an average, children constitute 26 per cent of the world population, down from 30 per cent in 2003. Elderly dependents account for another 9 per cent. The less developed countries of the world report much larger share of children in their populations as compared to more developed regions. Consequently, the share of elderly persons in such countries is

TABLE 6.1 Percentage distribution of population in broad age groups and dependency ratio in major areas of the world and some select countries

Major Areas and Countries	*Percentage Population in Broad Age Group (years)*			*Dependency Ratio*
	< 15	*15–64*	*65+*	
World	26	65	9	53.8
More developed	16	66	18	51.5
Less developed	28	65	7	53.8
Africa	41	56	3	78.6
Asia	24	68	8	47.1
Europe	16	66	18	51.5
Latin America and the Caribbean	26	66	8	51.5
North America	16	66	18	51.5
Oceania	23	65	12	53.8

Source: Based on Population Reference Bureau: *World Population Data Sheet*, 2017.

less than half of that in the more developed regions. In some of the countries in Africa like Niger and Uganda, nearly half of the population is represented by children. Remarkably, barely 3 per cent of the population of these countries survive up to the age of 65 years. On the other extreme, the more developed countries of the world report just 16 per cent of its population in the age group 'below 15 years'. Countries like Japan, Germany and South Korea report barely 12–13 per cent of their populations below the age of 15 years. But at the same time the share of elderly persons in the population of these countries is very large. Though on average, the share of elderly persons in the population in the more developed countries is 18 per cent, in some European countries like Italy, Germany, Bulgaria, Finland, Portugal, Greece more than one-fifth of the population constitute elderly persons. However, the highest proportion of elderly is seen in Japan (28 per cent) in East Asia and Monaco (26 per cent), a small country in Western Europe. The difference in the age structure of population is the result of the long-term effect of declining fertility and mortality levels in the developed countries. Dependency ratio, a ratio between dependent population (i.e. children and elderly dependents) and economically active population (i.e. adult population), is a very good summary measure of age structure of a population. With a greater proportion of population in the young age groups, the populations in the less developed parts of the world are marked with a higher dependency ratio than those in the developed countries (Map 6.1).

Interestingly, before the onset of demographic transition in Europe in the 18th century, the age structure of various populations of the world did not reveal much of a difference (Bhende and Kanitkar, 2011:161). They had a typical age pyramid

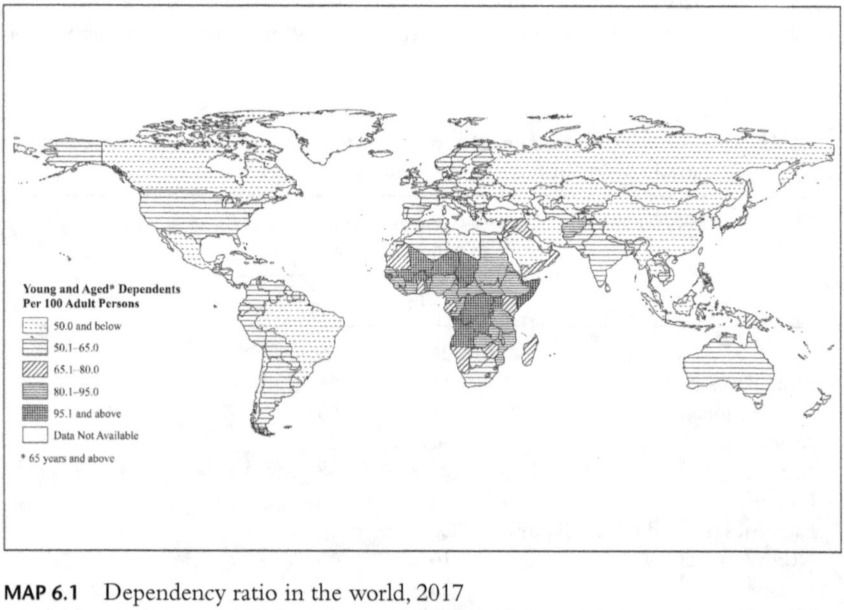

MAP 6.1 Dependency ratio in the world, 2017

Source: Population Reference Bureau, *World Population Data Sheet, 2017.*

with a broad base and tapering top indicating high fertility and high mortality levels. With the onset of demographic transition, the age structure of population in north-western Europe first began to undergo change. Gradually, this change spread to the rest of Europe and to countries outside Europe with the onset of demographic transition. These populations became increasingly older with a marked gain in the share of elderly people in the population. The example of Sweden, which experienced an early transition in vital rates, is worth noting in this context. At the time of the onset of transition, children and elderly people constituted 33.5 per cent and 5.2 per cent of the population respectively. The adults constituted a little over 60 per cent of the population. The age structure, thus, was hardly different from those in many of the less developed countries today. But by the turn of the 20th century population in Sweden had already become aged. Currently, children and elderly persons constitute 18 per cent and 20 per cent of the population respectively. Similar transformation in age structure has taken place in other developed countries also. It should be noted here that though age structure in less developed parts of the world has also undergone change during more recent times, the transformation has been only marginal. For illustration, let us take the case of India. India was one of the first countries from the less developed parts of the world to have experienced transition in vital rates. The proportion of children in India's population is found to have declined from 39 per cent in 1921 to nearly 31 per cent of the population in 2011. The proportion of elderly persons (aged 65 years and above) during the same time has increased from 2.43 per cent to a little over 5 per cent. Thus, over a period of nine decades, the age structure of India's population has undergone only a marginal change.

Age transition

Current demographic trends are having profound effects on population composition all over the world. Perhaps the most fundamental of all transformations is the one that is taking place in the age structure of population. Two of the most crucial manifestations of this age transition are what we know as *demographic dividend* or *youth bulge* and *population ageing*. While the former refers to a demographic situation likely to prevail in a society for a given period, the latter is a continuous process of change occurring in any population.

Demographic dividend is generally defined as an increased potential for economic growth due to shifts in age structure of population towards working age groups in the wake of long term declining trends in birth rates. In other words, demographic dividend refers to a situation where size of the economically active population is larger than that in the dependent age groups. An outcome of a sudden decline in fertility rates, this situation manifests itself in the form of a bulge in young age groups in the age pyramid. It is also sometimes called demographic *gift* or *bonus* (James, 2008:63). This situation of demographic advantage lasts only for some period depending upon the speed of demographic transition, and, therefore, it is called 'window of demographic opportunity' (Navaneetham, 2010:72). This 'window of opportunity' can be exploited in three different ways – firstly, by making the available labour force productively employed, which will enhance GDP; second, through increased savings (an outcome of declining dependency ratio) and investments in the productive sector; and finally in the form of more investments in human capital formation, which results in better resource utilisation (Navaneetham, 2010:72). In the wake of improved longevity, the proportion of 'aged dependents' eventually becomes large and together with 'young dependents' results in a high dependency ratio once again. If the fertility decline is slow and steady as it happened in developed countries of the West, this phase may even pass unnoticed (James, 2008:64). But among developing countries, for example in China, and also in India, it is due to a sudden and rapid decline in fertility levels during the recent decades that has made the transformation in age structure more vivid. Till the 1960s, China's demography was marked with very high fertility rates, although decline in it had set in. The age pyramid was characterised by a typical broad base and tapering top indicating high proportion of children prior to the introduction of state-enforced One-Child policy in 1979. The 1980s witnessed a drastic decline in fertility rates in the country resulting in a big bulge in the young adult ages by the end of the century. Not burdened by many young and aged dependents, this age structure provided an unprecedented economic advantage to the economy. The age structure helped accelerate the process of economic reforms in the country. China was successful in reaping the benefits of demographic dividend because of its efforts in human resource development in the form of spreading education among its younger population. The demographic window in China will remain open for another decade or so before the bulge shifts to middle adult ages. As the bulge moves to upper age brackets, the consumption patterns of the population will undergo change, and productivity gains of the bulge would begin declining. China wants to extract the maximum benefits before the window closes, and this explains the 'aggressiveness with which China is pursuing its current global economic expansion' (Weeks, 2018:320). Similar were the experiences of Taiwan and South Korea also. Japan had already enjoyed earlier a demographic dividend of this kind.

In most of the countries of the world, particularly in the developed parts of the globe, *population ageing* has become a dominant trend. As life expectancy has significantly gone up, more and more people are surviving till higher age brackets. With reduction in the birth rates, the proportion of children in the population has continuously declined. The overall impact of this process can be seen in the concentration of people in the elderly age groups. The trend continued uninterrupted in the developed world despite the temporary rise in the birth rates, for example, after the end of the Second World War. Already many of the developed countries of the world have moved a long way from the traditional 'pyramid' age structure and indeed are beginning to look distinctly 'top heavy' (Champion, 2003:211).

According to estimates based on UN figures (see Champion, 2003), the median age (in years) of the world population increased only marginally from 23.5 in 1950 to 26.6 in 1998. However, thereafter the pace of transformation in age structure gathered momentum, and by the year 2015, the median age reached 29.6. Median age of population is expected to rise further to 37.8 by the year 2050. It should be noted that the median ages vary a great deal across the world depending upon key socio-economic and demographic situations. The process of population ageing is primarily the result of long-term trends in declining mortality and fertility rates accompanied by increasing longevity. Though, the current average levels do not sound very alarming, the situation in the developed regions has already attracted serious attention since it has created a number of social and economic problems. In agricultural economies, societies have a familistic social organisation where elderly persons are not only maintained within the family household but they also enjoy a very high social status. By contrast, in industrial societies the aged persons are in a much less enviable position. Challenges resulting from ageing include, on the one hand, problems at micro level related to individual 'aged dependents' like poor health, loneliness, social isolation as well as challenges at aggregate level for the society, on the other, such as depletion of labour force, increased dependency ratio, rising expenditure on health care for aged, intergenerational conflict etc. among others (Pakulski, 2016:112). The median age of population in developed countries is much higher (e.g. 46.9 years in Japan, 46.8 years in Germany and above 50 in European Principality of Monaco) at present, and the number of elderly persons (65 and above) has already exceeded that of the children (aged below 15) in a number of countries in Europe like Monaco, Bulgaria, Greece, Germany, Italy, Portugal, Finland, Latvia and Spain to name a few. A number of other countries are fast approaching this distinction. Japan, which was the only country from Asia with this distinction till some recent times, is joined by Hong Kong and North Korea (all from East Asia) by 2017 with more elderly dependents than children in their populations. Europe, in fact, will remain the most affected region in the coming future with regard to the transformation of age structure.

So far, population ageing in the less developed countries has been very slow with median age at aggregate level increasing from 21.3 to 24.4 only over the last 50 years. We have already seen a very marginal change in the age structure of population in such countries in the earlier discussion. But the projected estimates indicate that the next half a century would see a far greater change in the age structure of population in the less developed regions than that in the developed regions. By the year 2050, the median age of population will increase to 36.7, up by 12.3 years as compared to only 8.1 in the developed parts (Champion, 2003:212).

Table 6.2 gives the indices of population ageing for the world and its major areas (please also refer to Map 6.2). It is evident that the index of ageing varies a great deal from country to country. As against the world average of only about 35.00, the developed parts of the world report an index as high as 112.50. Among the continents, Europe tops the list followed by North America in terms of index of ageing. In India, index of ageing is still very low, in fact, much lower than the world average, and also the average for all the less developed countries taken together. Of late,

TABLE 6.2 Index of ageing* in major areas of the world and in some select countries, 2003 and 2017

Major Areas and Select Countries	*Index of Ageing*	
	2003	*2017*
World	23.33	34.62
Africa	7.14	7.32
Asia	20.00	33.33
Europe	88.24	112.50
Latin America and the Caribbean	18.75	30.77
North America	61.90	78.95
Oceania	40.00	52.17
More developed	83.33	112.50
Less developed	15.15	25.00

* Based on formula suggested by Petersen (1975).
Source: Calculated by the author from PRB, *World Population Data Sheet*, 2003 and 2017.

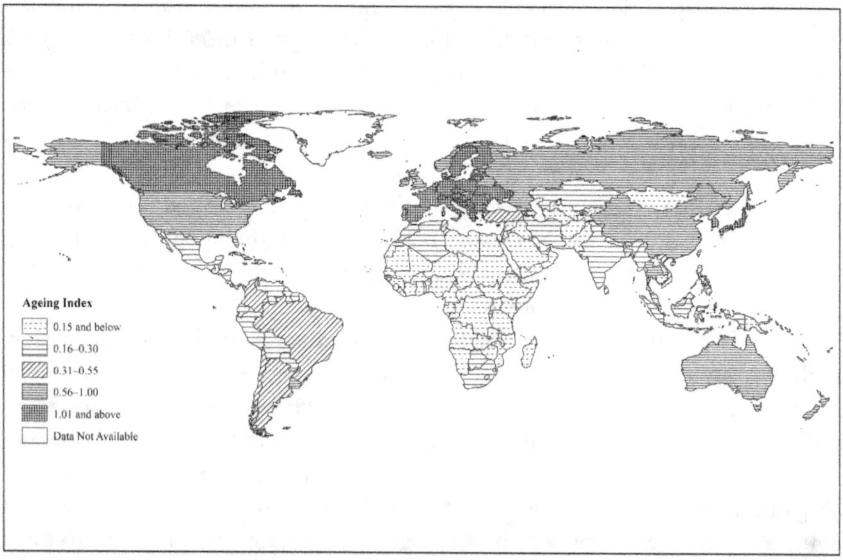

MAP 6.2 Population ageing in the world, 2017

Source: Population Reference Bureau, *World Population Data Sheet, 2017.*

the ageing of population has assumed a serious proportion in Japan. With an index of more than 233, the country ranks even higher than many European countries, which have long been facing the problems of ageing. In fact, Japan has witnessed the sharpest increase in the ageing index during the last 15 years or so. Japan is followed by Monaco, a small country in Western Europe.

Age structure of India's population

India's population is characterised by a typical age structure prevailing in the developing countries. Table 6.3 presents the distribution of India's population in broad age groups as per the 2011 census. As is revealed in the table, children in the age group 'below 15 years' account for as high as 31 per cent of the total population in 2011. Population in the age group '0–9 years' alone accounts for almost one-fifth of the population. It is interesting to note that the proportion of children in the population has recorded a decline by nearly 5 percentage points between 2001 and 2011 as compared to only 2 percentage points between 1991 and 2001. This can be attributed to a faster decline in the levels of birth rate in the country during the decade. The rural areas report a higher share of children in its population because of a generally higher birth rate than that in the urban areas. In addition to a higher birth rate in rural areas, out-migration of population, which generally takes place in the working age groups, is also responsible for a higher share of children in the population in the rural areas. The percentage share of population in different age groups declines sharply as one moves up in the age hierarchy. Elderly people i.e. persons age '60 years and above' account for nearly 9 per cent of the population in 2011 up from 7 per cent in 2001. As noted earlier, a relatively higher death rate and a resultant lower expectancy of life in the developing countries result in a very small share of population in the higher age groups. Strikingly, the rural areas in the country report a marginally higher share of population in the age group '60 and above' than their counterparts in the urban areas. It will, however, be erroneous to attribute this difference to a differential in life expectancy between rural and urban areas. The reason for a higher share of population in the old age groups in the rural areas again lies in migration. In developing countries, migration from rural to urban areas constitutes a significant proportion. Since this migration is highly age selective, rural areas suffer net loss of people in the working age group. This inflates the share of 'dependent aged' in the population. This is also seen in a distinctly higher share of persons in the working age groups in the urban areas.

TABLE 6.3 Percentage distribution of population in broad age groups in India, 2011

Age Groups (in years)	*Percentage of Population*		
	Total	*Rural*	*Urban*
0–9	19.80	21.20	16.69
0–14	30.76	32.82	26.21
15–59	60.29	58.04	65.27
60+	8.58	8.79	8.10
Age not stated	0.37	0.35	0.42
All ages	100.00	100.00	100.00
Dependency ratio	65.24	71.68	52.57

Source: C-14, *Social and Cultural Tables*, Census of India 2011.

This age distribution of population in the country produces a very high dependency ratio. For every 100 persons in the working age groups, there are over 65 dependent persons in the country as a whole. It may be noted that dependency ratio in the country has undergone a very sharp decline by as much as 10 percentage points between 2001 and 2011. As is expected, rural areas report a higher dependency ratio of population than their counterparts in urban areas. This differential in the dependency ratio reveals the differences in economic dependency in the population in rural and urban areas.

India is a vast country with a great amount of diversity in various attributes of population. The same is true for the age structure of population also. A marked variation in the age structure can be noticed from one state to another depending upon time of onset and pace of demographic transition. Table 6.4 presents the distribution of population in broad age groups for states and union territories of India. As could be noted, union territories in general report lower dependency ratio than the states. Similarly, the southern states reflect a lower dependency ratio than their counterparts in the north. The states of Kerala and Tamil Nadu report the lowest dependency ratio. It may be recalled here that these states report one of the lowest fertility levels in the country. They are, in fact, the two leading states in the country as far as transition in fertility behaviour is concerned. Children constitute less than one-fourth of population in these states. As against this, Bihar, Jharkhand Uttar Pradesh and Rajasthan have very youthful age structures. In Bihar, for example, children still constitute more than 40 per cent of its population. Birth rates in all these states continue to be very high. The other major states with a higher share of children than the nation's average are Madhya Pradesh, Chhattisgarh and Assam. The dependency ratios, therefore, are distinctly higher among these states.

It is interesting to note that the percentages of 'aged dependents' in the population reveal a much smaller range of variation across the major states. To the contrary, the proportion of children shows a much wider variation from one state to another. Much of the regional variation in dependency ratio in the country, therefore, can be attributed to variation in the proportion of children in the population. The spatial patterns in the dependency ratio will provide a good insight into the population dynamics in the country. Map 6.3 presents the same based on 2011 data. As could be seen, on an average, the northern plains and the interior uplands report a higher dependency ratio. The coastal districts in the peninsula reveal a generally lower dependency ratio. In the north, the whole of Middle Ganga plain, the north-western parts of the Chhotanagpur plateau and its adjoining districts in eastern Madhya Pradesh report a very high dependency ratio. A narrow belt running in a south-western direction connects this region with a very high dependency ratio in the central and western parts of Madhya Pradesh. It should be noted here that these areas are marked with very high fertility levels. In addition, they have also been characteristically out-migrating areas in the country. Since this out-migration mostly occurs in working age groups, it results in an increase in the dependency ratio. Another extensive pocket with a very high dependency ratio can be seen in Rajasthan, particularly in its western and eastern parts. This region of a very high dependency ratio extends into the bordering districts of Haryana and Madhya

TABLE 6.4 Percentage distribution of population in broad age groups and dependency ratio by states and union territories, 2011

States / Union Territories	*Percentage Population*				*Dependency Ratio*
	< 15	*15–59*	*25–59*	*> 59*	
Andhra Pradesh	26.00	64.12	44.76	9.88	55.95
Arunachal Pradesh	35.69	59.71	38.89	4.60	67.50
Assam	32.86	60.48	41.30	6.66	65.37
Bihar	40.23	52.33	35.42	7.44	91.08
Chhattisgarh	32.07	60.08	40.53	7.85	66.44
Goa	21.84	66.93	50.13	11.23	49.41
Gujarat	28.98	63.07	43.72	7.95	58.55
Haryana	29.74	61.60	40.88	8.66	62.35
Himachal Pradesh	25.90	63.84	45.11	10.26	56.64
Jammu and Kashmir	33.85	58.78	39.63	7.37	70.13
Jharkhand	36.17	56.66	38.30	7.17	76.50
Karnataka	26.25	64.27	44.81	9.48	55.61
Kerala	23.47	63.97	48.16	12.56	56.33
Madhya Pradesh	33.50	58.62	39.09	7.88	70.58
Maharashtra	26.72	63.36	43.96	9.92	57.83
Manipur	30.26	62.72	42.75	7.02	59.44
Meghalaya	39.78	55.53	34.89	4.69	80.09
Mizoram	32.46	61.28	41.03	6.26	63.19
Nagaland	34.35	60.45	38.51	5.20	65.40
Odisha	28.85	61.63	43.21	9.52	62.27
Punjab	25.58	64.08	43.88	10.34	56.06
Rajasthan	34.75	57.77	37.64	7.48	73.12
Sikkim	27.23	66.08	44.06	6.69	51.32
Tamil Nadu	23.60	65.99	48.41	10.41	51.55
Tripura	27.72	64.39	44.49	7.89	55.29
Uttar Pradesh	35.98	56.23	35.73	7.79	77.84
Uttarakhand	31.07	59.98	39.18	8.95	66.72
West Bengal	27.14	64.37	44.83	8.49	55.35
A and N Islands	24.37	68.94	50.49	6.69	45.06
Chandigarh	25.26	68.38	47.00	6.36	46.23
Dadra and Nagar Haveli	31.40	64.55	42.01	4.05	54.91
Daman & Diu	22.64	72.68	45.97	4.68	37.58
Lakshadweep	25.57	66.24	48.44	8.19	50.97
NCT of Delhi	27.22	65.94	45.48	6.84	51.66
Puducherry	23.93	66.41	49.48	9.66	50.58

Source: C-14, *Social and Cultural Tables*, Census of India 2011.

Pradesh. A very high dependency ratio in this region can be attributed to persisting high fertility rates, for instance in Rajasthan, and out-migration of people in working age groups, for instance in southern parts of Haryana. Interestingly, the districts located in the western Uttar Pradesh are also marked with a very high dependency ratio. This region of a very high dependency ratio extends into northern and

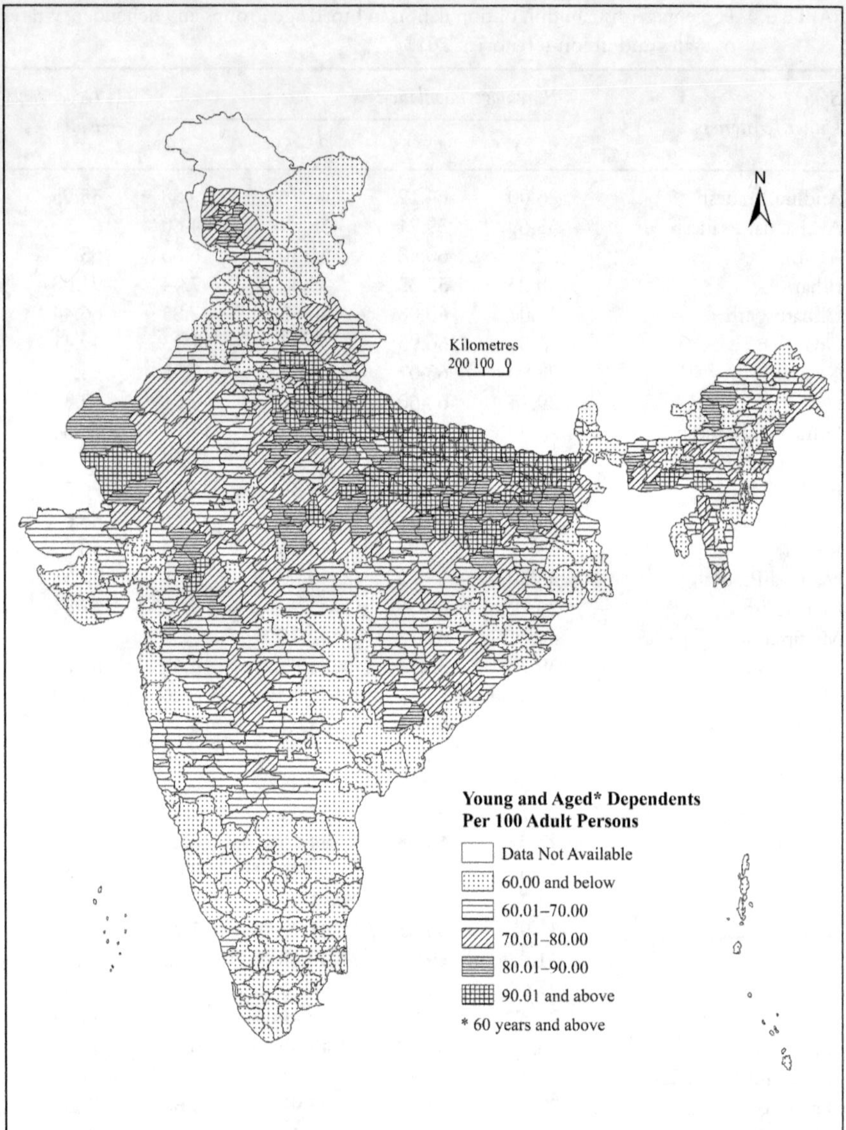

MAP 6.3 Dependency ratio in India, 2011

Source: Census of India, 2011.

central parts of Haryana. In the north-eastern region also pockets of very high dependency ratio can be noticed. In the peninsular uplands, the only pocket with a very high dependency ratio can be seen over Maharashtra and Karnataka plateaus. On the other extreme, southern Kerala and central Tamil Nadu in the south and Goa along the western coast report a very low dependency ratio. In addition, the district of Sabar Kantha in the eastern Gujarat appears conspicuous with a very low dependency ratio.

Demographic Dividend: Age structure of a population is governed largely by the process of long-term trends in fertility and mortality levels at the aggregate level. Demographic transition in India is said to have set in sometime in the 1920s when death rates began declining. However, a perceptible decline in birth rates was visible only towards the close of the 1980s. Thus, the period with declining mortality but persisting high fertility was marked with a high dependency ratio because of a relatively large proportion of 'young dependents' i.e. children under age 15 in the population. With the decline in fertility levels towards the end of the last century, transformation in the age structure set in. With an increasingly smaller number of children being added to population, the dependency ratio started declining. Consequently, the age structure of population witnessed a gradual bulge in the working ages. This has apparently several economic advantages as economically active population outnumbers dependent population. Decadal growth rate in population that was on an increasing trend began declining after 1981. Initially this did not attract the attention of academia because of the persisting high rate of growth in population. But an accelerated pace of decline in fertility levels with resultant reduction in decadal growth rate in population in subsequent decades led to a widespread discourse on the favourable demographic situation often called as *demographic dividend*. The window is said to be already open for India, and is expected to last for roughly one to two decades. The share of population in the 15–59 age group that has already crossed the 60 per cent (refer to Table 6.3) mark is expected to further rise to a level between 65–70 per cent in another two decades and will remain at that level for some time. The share of peak working ages i.e. 25–59 years that has already crossed the 40 per cent level as per the 2011 census is expected to be around 50 per cent by that time.

Evidences indicate that the rate of growth in total population in the country was higher than that in working age population in India till 1971 meaning thereby that the 'demographic bonus' was negative prior to 1971. After 1971, however, the working age population has increased at a faster pace than the total population resulting in a positive 'demographic bonus'. It has also been earlier suggested that the demographic bonus in India would be at its peak during 2001–11, and after 2031 the demographic bonus would become negative once again. Inter-state variation in share of population in working age groups i.e. 15–59 or 25–59 years is in tune with the timing of onset and pace of demographic transition. States like Tamil Nadu, Karnataka, Andhra Pradesh, Punjab and Kerala, which were the leading states in terms of demographic transition, report significantly higher share of population in peak working age groups (Table 6.4). For many of these states, the 'demographic window' is already shut or near closure. Contrary to this, Bihar, Jharkhand, Uttar Pradesh, Madhya Pradesh etc. are yet to pick up. For these states the window opened only recently and will last up to 1931. In other words, India will not be able to derive economic advantage on a large scale as one would expect with the given size of population at the aggregate level. Rather, as the demographic window is open for different regions at different points of time, India will derive only moderate benefits for a longer period of time. Whether or not India is able to reap the benefit of the demographic gift in the coming future depends on the success of human resource development and expansion of productive employment to growing youths of the country. If appropriate interventions are not made during the period, it would have negative implications for the economy and society (Navaneetham, 2010:73). As noted already, China was successful in deriving maximum benefits of the demographic situation because of its efforts in educating youth on a massive scale. In fact, the present demographic situation is both a challenge as well as an opportunity. 'The challenge is to ensure human development and optimum utilization of human resources. The opportunity is to utilize available human resources to achieve rapid economic development and improvement in quality of life' (Naagarajan, 2010:92).

Sex composition

Sex is an easily identifiable characteristic of an individual, and, hence, data by male and female are available in almost all the countries of the world. Sex composition of a population refers to the balance between male and female in any population. It can be expressed either in the form of proportion of a particular sex in the population or as a ratio between the population of two sexes. Of the two, sex ratio is the most commonly used measure in the analysis of sex composition the world over. If we denote the number of males in the population by P_m and the number of females by P_f, sex ratio can be calculated in either of two ways:

$$\left(P_m / P_f\right) \star 100 \tag{6.3}$$

$$\text{or, } \left(P_f / P_m\right) \star 100 \tag{6.4}$$

As is obvious, the first one gives the number of males per hundred females in the population and is the most widely used measure of sex ratio the world over. On the contrary, the second provides the number of females per 100 males in the population. In some of the countries in Europe, the sex ratio is expressed in the latter form. In some of the countries, like India, sex ratio is defined as the number of females per 1,000 males. This requires an addition of one zero in the constant in Equation (6.4).

In any population, distribution by sexes is generally unequal. The balance between males and females in any population at a given point of time, in fact, depends on three factors. They are sex ratio at birth, sex differentials at death and sex ratio among migrants. In addition, in a country, like India, differential counting of males and females at the time of enumeration also produces an artificial imbalance in sex composition of the population.

Sex ratio at birth is a biological phenomenon, and there is always a predominance of male babies over female babies at birth. There are indications that there is a general preponderance of male foetuses over female at the time of conception. It is also suggested that male foetuses are more susceptible to loss or death. Nevertheless, on the basis of data collected from different parts of the world it has been estimated that, on an average, there are 105 male babies born for every 100 female babies. In fact, this ratio varies from 103 to 107 in different populations. The greater vulnerability of male foetuses means that the better the conditions of gestation and birth, the more likely it will be that the baby is boy. Although genetic factors do determine sex ratio at birth, the inter-group variation in sex ratio at birth, and also a temporal change within a group, should also be examined in terms of the influences of the social, economic and cultural environment on the incidence of foetal death.

The other determinant of sex ratio in a population is the differentials in the death rates of males and females. In normal circumstances, there is a higher rate of mortality among males than females, not only because they are generally more susceptible to disease but also because their vocations are typically more dangerous. As a result, females would outnumber males in the population if the social system were based on gender equality. This is, however, not the case in most parts of the world. In societies, particularly in the less developed parts of the world, gender biases result unequal treatment of the two sexes. Females are accorded an inferior status to males. A female child is considered as a burden while a male child is regarded as a source of wealth. Discriminatory customs and traditions, and the resultant unequal allocation of resources between males and females, offset the advantage of biological or physiological superiority. A general neglect of females results in a higher death rate not only in childhood but also during childbearing age groups. It is only in the older age groups that such populations reflect a favourable sex ratio for females. Sex ratio in a population is, therefore, sometimes considered as a very good indicator of the status of women in such societies (Hassan, 2000:61).

Migration or spatial mobility of population is another very important factor affecting sex composition of a population. Migration, whether internal or international, is highly sex selective. In long-distance migrations males tend to outnumber females. However, in short-distance migrations there is a general preponderance of females. Much of the regional variation in the sex ratio in India, for example, is attributed to spatial redistribution of population.

Sex composition of the world population

Evidences indicate that the overall sex ratios (i.e. the number of males per 100 females) of most of the countries fall within the range of 95 to 105 males per 100 females. Any deviation from this is generally considered to be extreme and is attributed to some such unusual circumstances as heavy war casualties and/or excessive immigration or emigration. Table 6.5 presents sex ratios – both overall and by broad age groups – for the world and for major regions as per the latest data available. On an average, the world population reflects a sex ratio of 102 males per 100 females. Thus, the disparity in the distribution of males and females in the world population is not that

TABLE 6.5 Sex ratio for world and major regions by broad age groups, 2016 (number of males per 100 females)

Major Areas and Regions	*All Ages*	*< 15*	*15–64*	*65+*
World Total	102	107	103	82
Africa	100	103	99	82
Latin America and the Caribbean	98	104	98	78
Northern America	98	105	101	80
Asia	105	110	105	88
Europe	93	105	98	69
Oceania	100	106	101	87

Source: Calculated from *UN Demographic Yearbook, 2016*:49–50.

wide. However, there exists a marked preponderance of males in the younger age groups. This preponderance declines sharply with increase in age. Sex ratio in the developed societies, in general, are found to be in favour of females, while in the less developed societies, populations are marked with a preponderance of males. With regard to sex ratio, Asia stands quite distinct from the rest of the world with a striking preponderance of males in the population. Western Asia reports the largest preponderance of males in the population. Some of the world's most adverse sex ratio can be seen in the Middle East. Qatar reports the largest preponderance of male in its population. Qatar is followed by United Arab Emirates and Bahrain. South-central parts of the continent are only slightly better than their western counterparts (see Map 6.4). This may be attributed to a generally higher mortality rate among females than males. Countries in this part of Asia are long known for gender biases. More recently, they have witnessed an increased masculinity at birth, which has further widened the gap between the numerical strengths of males and females. Guilmoto (2009) has reported indications of a rise in sex ratio at birth (SRB) during the recent past in some West Asian countries like Azerbaijan, Georgia, Armenia etc., and hence sex composition of population at the aggregate level is expected to further worsen. Demographic manifestations of persisting son-preference can also be seen in several countries in Eastern Asia. For instance, with existing gender bias and preference for sons in China, the enforced 'one child norm' since the 1980s has led to millions of girl children going missing through sex-selective abortions. Sex ratio at birth had, thus, reached a level of 111 male babies for every 100 female babies as early as 1986–87 (Heer and Grigsby, 1994:72). Thereafter, it crossed the 115 mark during the 1990s and 120 in 2000 (Guilmoto, 2009:522). Almost around the same time, a rise in SRB was witnessed in South Korea also. However, since the early 1990s there has been a gradual decline in SRB in South Korea as a result of which overall sex ratio is very close to normal. For the same reason, in India also, the recent past has witnessed a growing imbalance in sex ratio at birth. As a result, despite improvement in sex differentials in mortality rates, overall sex ratio continued to decline in the country till some recent times. Other countries with

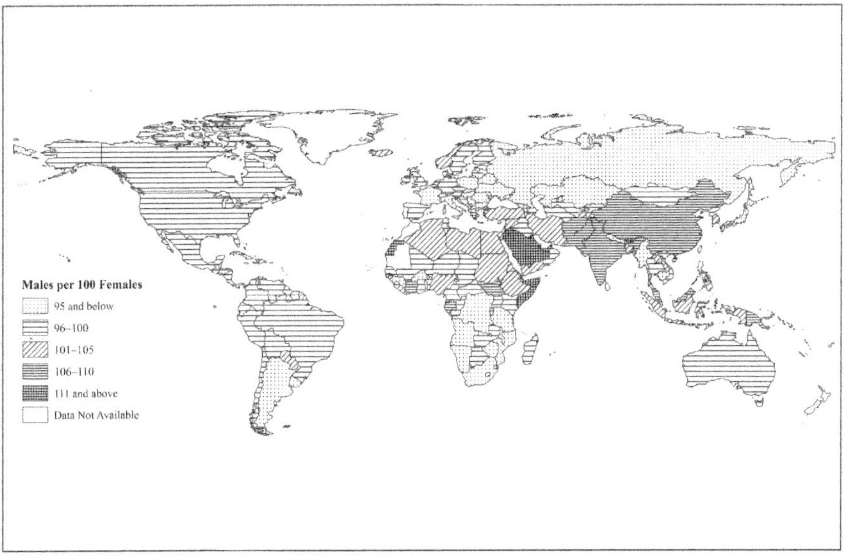

MAP 6.4 Sex ratio in the world, 2015

Source: United Nations, *Demographic Yearbook, 2016.*

extremely adverse sex ratio in the south and south-eastern part of Asia are Maldives, Bhutan, Pakistan, Afghanistan, Malaysia etc.

In Africa, Latin America and Caribbean, though females outnumber males, the disparity is not that wide. In Africa, it is only in the northern and western parts that the population reports a sex ratio adverse to females. In the developed parts of the world the sex ratio is generally lower. In other words, with more equitable gender relations and a better status of women, the developed societies report a general preponderance of females in the population. In fact, Europe reports the lowest sex ratio in the world. In Europe, the eastern parts report even a greater preponderance of females in the population. Elsewhere, in North America, Australia and New Zealand also sex ratios are in favour of females although with a very small margin. A deficit of males in the populations of many European countries can, in part, also be attributed to war-related deaths and an excessively male-dominated emigration to different parts of the world in the past.

Sex composition of India's population

India's population has been marked with a large and growing deficit of females ever since the turn of the last century. This has been a matter of much investigation and speculation among researchers and policy makers (Visaria, 1968; Mitra, 1979; Fisher and Ifeka, 1984; Kundu and Sahu, 1991; Rajan et al., 1991; Agnihotri, 2000; Premi, 2001; Bhat, 2002a, 2002b). Sex ratio, measured in terms of the number of females per thousand males in the population, has recorded a continuous decline in the country throughout the last century (Table 6.6) except on two occasions – the

TABLE 6.6 Trends in sex ratio* in India, 1901–2011

Census Years	*All Age*		*0–6 Years*#	
	Sex Ratio	*Decadal Change*	*Sex Ratio*	*Decadal Change*
1901	972	910	-	-
1911	964	872	-	-
1921	955	846	-	-
1931	950	838	-	-
1941	945	831	-	-
1951	946	860	-	-
1961	941	845	976	-
1971	930	858	964	−12
1981	934	879	962	−2
1991	927	894	945	−17
2001	933	900	927	−18
2011	943	929	918	−9

*Number of females per 1,000 males. # Based on single-year age returns from 1961 to 1981.
Sources: (i) Census of India, 1991, Series 1, Paper 2 of 1992; (ii) Premi, 2001 and (iii) Census of India, 2011, Primary Census Data Highlights, India.

first, when the 1951 census revealed an improvement in the sex ratio by one point over 1941, and the second, when the 1981 census saw an increase by four points over 1971 census data (please also refer to Figure 6.2). As far as the improvement in sex ratio in 1981 over 1971 is concerned, experts have called it a statistical phenomenon and, therefore, not real (Raju and Premi, 1992:911). It has been suggested that at the time of the 1971 census there was a relatively greater extent of female undercount. Sex ratio, therefore, came down by an unusually larger margin between 1961 and 1971. Female undercount of the 1971 census, thus, artificially led to an improvement in sex ratio in 1981. Thus, if a marginal increase by one point at the time of the 1951 census is ignored, sex ratio in the country appears to have monotonically declined at least up to 1991. When the 2001 census revealed an improvement in the sex ratio by six points from 927 in 1991 to 933, it brought some relief to the scholars. The improvement continued in the present century also when the sex ratio increased by as much as 10 points. However, what is still worrisome for many is the fact that the sex ratio among children in the age group 0–6 years has undergone a drastic decline from 945 in 1991 to 919 in 2011. Thus, it can be suggested that improvement in overall sex ratio from 933 in 2001 to 943 in 2011 was largely due to narrowing down of sex differentials in mortality rates, mainly to age group '7 years and above'. Deterioration in the child sex ratio, on the other hand, can be attributed to prenatal elimination of a girl child along with persisting survival disadvantages for daughters, both having their roots in prevailing gender bias and strong son-preference. Growing norms for small family size have only aggravated the problem. Trends in overall sex ratio in the country are, therefore, expected to undergo a reversal once again in the future when population in the bottom of the age pyramid gradually moves to higher age brackets.

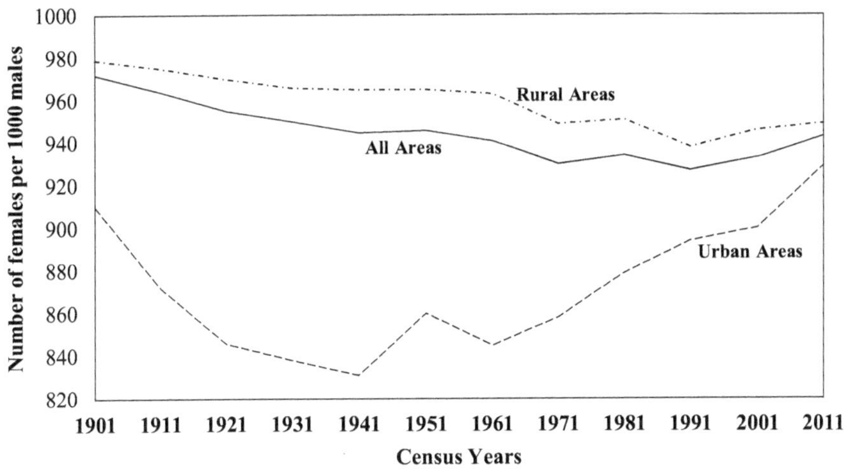

FIGURE 6.2 Trends in overall sex ratio in India, 1901–2011

Source: Author.

Sex composition of population in a country at the aggregate level depends on the trends in sex ratio at birth, differential mortality of males and females, sex composition of international migrants and differential coverage of sexes at the time of census counts. Long-term trends in the sex ratio in India cannot be explained in terms of one single determinant. The sex ratio at birth (SRB) in India has become excessively masculine only during some recent times. International migration is not likely to affect the sex composition of the population at the aggregate level in any significant manner. Sex differentials in mortality rates did affect sex composition of population in the past but of late a significant improvement in the mortality conditions of females has occurred. As the process of demographic transition in the country gathered momentum in the late 1980s, decline in birth rates became more conspicuous. This had several 'beneficial effects on the survival of women in reproductive age groups, through fewer births and a reduction in the associated mortality risk' (Krishnaji, 2000:1161). Sex differentials in life expectancy at birth do confirm this trend. Life expectancy at birth for females in the country surpassed that of males sometime in the late 1980s, and since then the difference between female-male life expectancy has been gradually widening (Premi, 2001:1874). For quite some time in the past, 'under-enumeration of females' remained as the most plausible explanation for the adverse sex ratio. Estimates of percentage of undercount by sex derived from post-enumeration checks (PECs) of the past censuses, however, indicate that sex differentials of undercount have indeed decreased over time (Premi, 2001:1876). Moreover, a careful examination of the imbalance in the sex ratio reveals that under-enumeration of females cannot explain more than a small part of the deficit of females in the population. Therefore, the lowest-ever female-male ratio as revealed in the 1991 census came as a big shock when a reversal was expected. It was soon realised that 'larger female deficits were occurring at birth itself' (Krishnaji,

2000:1161). Thus, the growing deficit of females during some recent times drew the attention of demographers towards increased masculinity at birth.

Decline in fertility levels has undoubtedly led to reduction in excess mortality of adult females, but at the same time it resulted in a new form of discrimination against female children. Desire of a small family size and patriarchy-induced strong *son-preference* ultimately led to a widespread practice of female foeticide reflected in increased preponderance of male babies at birth. Prenatal elimination of a girl child came to be identified as the main reason underlying the growing deficit of females in more recent times. Although initially this proposition was contested by some demographers (see for instance Rajan et al., 1991, 1992; Srinivasan, 1994), with more and more evidences pouring in, there was soon a general unanimity among scholars regarding the adverse effects of the modern facilities for sex determination techniques on sex composition of population in several parts of the country. A continuous deterioration in child sex ratio, as will be seen in the subsequent sections, over several decades has only confirmed the prevalence of the practice of sex-selective abortion and its impact on sex composition of population in the country during some recent times.

In view of the preceding, sex ratio is rightly considered as a manifestation of gender relations in a society. Ours is a male-dominated society where human relations are governed by patriarchal structures. Male-dominated social ethos discriminate against females in several ways. This was earlier manifest in the sex differentials in mortality rates, both during childhood and childbearing age groups. With the passage of time as mortality conditions improved, however, the nature of gender bias in our society has taken a new shape. Post-natal elimination of a girl child through survival disadvantage for daughters slowly gave way (but not disappeared completely) to pre-natal elimination in the form of sex-selective abortions. In the Indian context, sociological evidences indicate varying gender relations in different social groups. It is argued that male-dominated ethos are more conspicuous among the upper-caste Hindus than the other social segments. The scheduled tribes enjoy somewhat more equitable gender relations than that in the general population. The scheduled castes come somewhere in between. One would, therefore, expect a corresponding difference in sex ratio among the three social groups, and some evidences did earlier confirm this pattern (see e.g. Agnihotri, 1995), although the gap in female ratios among these social groups has of late narrowed down.

Spatial patterns of sex ratios, and also other demographic features in India, have been characterised by a 'north-south' divide. As compared to its southern counterpart, the 'north' has been traditionally marked with higher fertility and mortality rates along with a larger sex differential in death rate. Strikingly, female work participation in this part also has been on a lower side. All these indicate a somewhat lower status of women. Unlike this, in the south where paddy is the main crop, work participation of females is higher. This along with other cultural factors, including marriage pattern, have led to a more respectable position for females in the south, and hence families are less patriarchal in the south than in the north (Krishnaji, 2000). It is, however, important to note that the recent past has witnessed the remarkable spread of the practice of elimination of a girl child in the south also. As a result, the contrast between north and south in terms of demographic features has been gradually thinning. Scholars have used the term *regional* convergence for the phenomenon.

In general, the northern Hindi belt, particularly the north-western states, have been marked with a larger deficit of females than its southern and eastern counterparts (Table 6.7). Despite remarkable improvements between 2001 and 2011, states

TABLE 6.7 Decadal change in sex ratio* in states and union territories, 2001–11

States / Union Territories	*All Age*			*0–6 Years*		
	2001	*2011*	*Change*	*2001*	*2011*	*Change*
Andhra Pradesh	978	993	15	961	939	–22
Arunachal Pradesh	893	938	45	964	972	8
Assam	935	958	23	965	962	–3
Bihar	919	918	–1	942	935	–7
Chhattisgarh	989	991	2	975	969	–6
Goa	961	973	12	868	871	3
Gujarat	920	919	–1	938	942	5
Haryana	861	879	18	883	890	7
Himachal Pradesh	968	972	3	819	834	15
Jammu and Kashmir	892	889	–4	896	909	14
Jharkhand	941	948	8	941	862	–79
Karnataka	965	973	8	965	948	–18
Kerala	1058	1084	26	946	948	3
Madhya Pradesh	919	931	12	960	964	4
Maharashtra	922	929	7	932	918	–14
Manipur	974	985	11	913	894	–19
Meghalaya	972	989	17	957	930	–27
Mizoram	935	976	40	973	970	–3
Nagaland	900	931	30	964	970	5
Odisha	972	979	6	964	943	–20
Punjab	876	895	19	953	941	–11
Rajasthan	921	928	7	798	846	48
Sikkim	875	890	15	909	888	–20
Tamil Nadu	987	996	9	963	957	–6
Tripura	948	960	12	942	943	1
Uttar Pradesh	898	912	14	966	957	–9
Uttarakhand	962	963	1	916	902	–13
West Bengal	934	950	16	908	890	–17
A and N Islands	846	876	30	957	968	11
Chandigarh	777	818	41	845	880	35
Dadra and Nagar Haveli	812	774	–38	979	926	–54
Daman & Diu	710	618	–92	926	904	–22
Lakshadweep	948	946	–2	959	911	–48
NCT of Delhi	821	868	47	967	967	1
Puducherry	1001	1037	37	957	968	11

* Number of females per 1,000 males.

Sources: Census of India, 2011, Primary Census Data Highlights, India.

like Punjab and Haryana continue to report some of the worst sex ratios in the world. As compared to this, the southern states, except Maharashtra, as well as the eastern parts of the country, are characterised by much better sex ratios. If a line connecting the southern-most tip of Gujarat in the west and the southern extent of Dinajpur district of West Bengal in the east is drawn, the areas lying to the north of this line appear with a more conspicuous deficit of females in the population (Map 6.5).

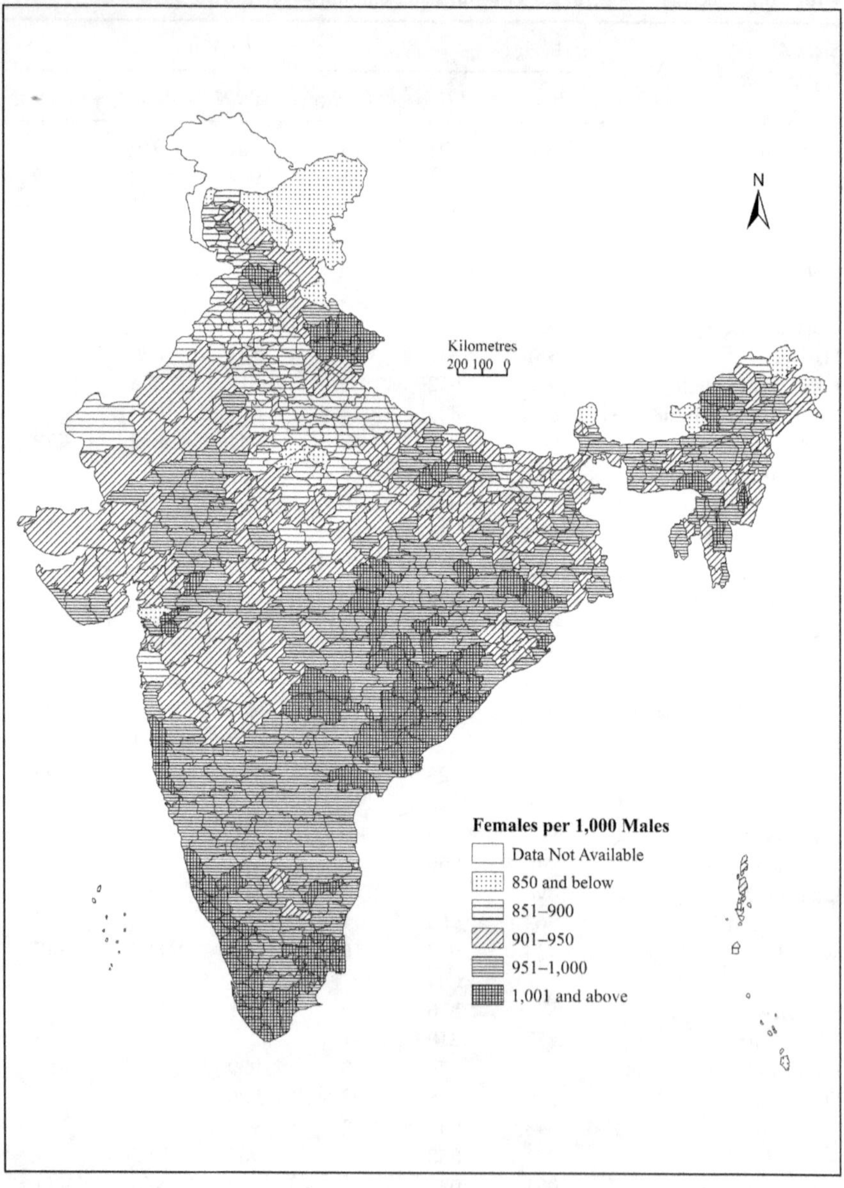

MAP 6.5 'All age' sex ratio in India, 2011

Source: Census of India, 2011.

However, within this vast stretch of low sex ratio, there are some pockets with distinctly favourable sex ratio to females. Likewise, among the southern and eastern states also one comes across several pockets with serious deficit of females. In fact, as already noted, the boundaries between regions of low sex ratios in the north and north-west vis-à-vis high sex ratios in the south have become blurred during the recent past.

It may be noted that variation in all-age sex ratio at the regional level is determined to a large extent by spatial mobility of population. Much of the regional variations, as noted previously, in sex composition of population in the country can be attributed to male selective spatial redistribution of the population. The characteristically out-migrating areas in the Bihar and Uttar Pradesh plains, and areas elsewhere in the north-eastern parts of the peninsula, are marked with better sex ratios. A favourable sex ratio to females in the hilly parts of Uttaranchal can also be attributed to male selective out-migration from the region to the plains in search of better employment opportunities. Some of the lowest sex ratios in the country, for instance in the metropolitan areas of Mumbai and Delhi, and also in Chandigarh, are related to the inflow of male migrants seeking work in industrial, commercial and other related sectors of the economy.

Child Sex Ratio in India: Unlike the overall sex ratio, the sex ratio among children is not influenced by spatial mobility of population. Migration in this age group normally occurs with family. Sex ratio among children is, therefore, considered as a better indicator of the nature of gender relations in a population. The main determinants of sex composition in this age group are sex ratio at birth (SRB) and sex differentials of mortality rates among children. Though sex ratio at birth is primarily a biological phenomenon, the recent experiences are testimony to the adverse effects of gender preference on the balance between the number of male and female babies at birth. Evidences indicate that improvements in the social, economic and cultural environments in some parts of the country after independence had led to a reduction in male foetal losses, resulting in increased preponderance of male babies at birth. With development making its inroads into new areas, a similar demographic process is expected to have occurred in different regions at different points of time. Besides, unequal treatment of male and female children in a society characterised by a male-dominated social ethos inevitably results in higher death rates among female children leading to an adverse sex ratio in this age group.

An adverse and rapidly declining sex ratio among children in the age group 0–6 years has indeed been a disturbing feature of sex composition of India's population. It may be noted here that for the first time the 1991 census tabulated data by sex separately for the age group 0–6 years. This was done mainly for the purpose of obtaining estimates of literacy rates according to revised procedure. Since the data are available down to village level, it led to a widespread use by experts in analysis of sex composition of population separately for the children. From the single age returns, however, it has always been possible to derive comparable estimates for the earlier censuses but only up to state level. Based on the same, trends in child sex ratio (hitherto called CSR) in the country since 1961 are shown along with 'all age' sex ratio in Table 6.6. A monotonous decline in CSR is evidently clear over the last five decades. The decline has, however, been more rapid during the 1980s and 1990s. More than 60 per cent of the decline in CSR since 1961 is reported to have occurred only during these two decades.

From the regional patterns of sex ratio among children in the country one comes across a sharper contrast of the 'north-south' divide (Map 6.6) discussed

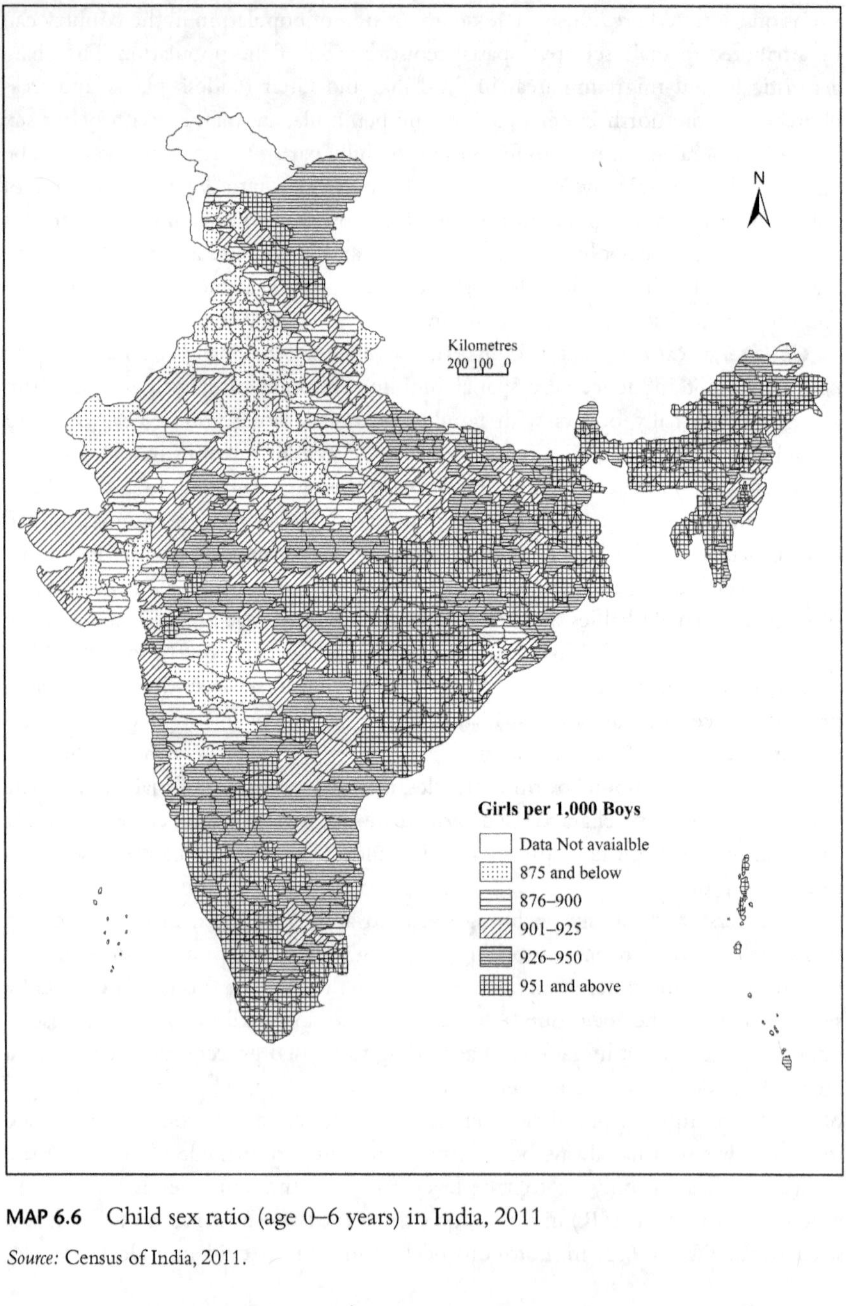

MAP 6.6 Child sex ratio (age 0–6 years) in India, 2011

Source: Census of India, 2011.

earlier. The north-western parts of the country once again appear as the single largest pocket with significant deficit of female children in the population. In fact, this region holds the distinction of having one of the lowest child sex ratios not only in the country but also perhaps the entire world. The largest deficit of female children is found in the states of Punjab and Haryana. Parts of Himachal Pradesh, Gujarat and Madhya Pradesh along with NCT of Delhi also report one of the lowest sex ratios among children in the country. As one moves towards the south and south-eastern parts the sex ratio among children gradually improves, although patches of adverse CSR can be seen over parts of Maharashtra and Tamil Nadu. Barring some small patches here and there, the whole of Kerala, Andhra Pradesh, Chhattisgarh and Jharkhand, and southern Karnataka along with upland Orissa and hilly states of the north and north-east, report better child sex ratios than the nation's average.

During 2001 and 2011, CSR at the aggregate level has declined by 9 points. Map 6.7 presents the regional dimension of the deterioration in child sex ratio in the country. It is alarming to note that the child sex ratio has declined with varying magnitude over wide and diverse areas across the country. Districts located in the plains of north, the peninsular uplands, the hilly areas in the north or the coastal plains on the two sides of the peninsula have all witnessed declines in CSR during the decade. As is obvious, some of these areas are characterised by the dominance of agriculture with a low level of urbanisation and development while others are highly urbanised and industrialised. The 'north-south' divide with regard to economy, culture and demographic attributes as discussed earlier in the section seems to be neutral to the patterns in changing child sex ratio. The sharpest decline can be seen in the hilly areas of Jammu and Kashmir, Uttarakhand and north-eastern states as well as in the central parts of Maharashtra in the Deccan plateau and in the coastal Tamil Nadu. Southern states have traditionally been known as female friendly, and in this context deterioration in child sex over vast areas in the peninsula, particularly in Andhra Pradesh and some areas in Tamil Nadu, is a matter of great concern. Likewise, in the eastern part of the peninsula CSR has undergone decline over a greater part of Odisha, which otherwise has reported throughout favourable sex ratios. The decline in CSR in the state can be seen over tribal-dominated inaccessible areas on the uplands as well as in relatively more developed coastal areas. Another striking feature is improvement in CSR in parts of north-western states otherwise characterised by very unfriendly socio-cultural practices to women since long ago. As a great surprise to demographers, the whole of Punjab and a greater part of Haryana have witnessed a rise in CSR between 2001 and 2011. Nevertheless, in the rest of the Hindi belt of the north, barring only a few districts, deterioration in CSR continues in the whole of Madhya Pradesh, Uttar Pradesh and Rajasthan during 2001–11 also. The same is true in Maharashtra which has always behaved differently from the southern states in terms of demographic attributes.

Much of this decline in CSR can be attributed to further masculinisation of births during the recent past. The role of female infanticide in declining child sex ratio can also not be ruled out, as it was prevalent earlier in parts of the Hindi belt of the north. There are indications of its persistence in contemporary times, though in

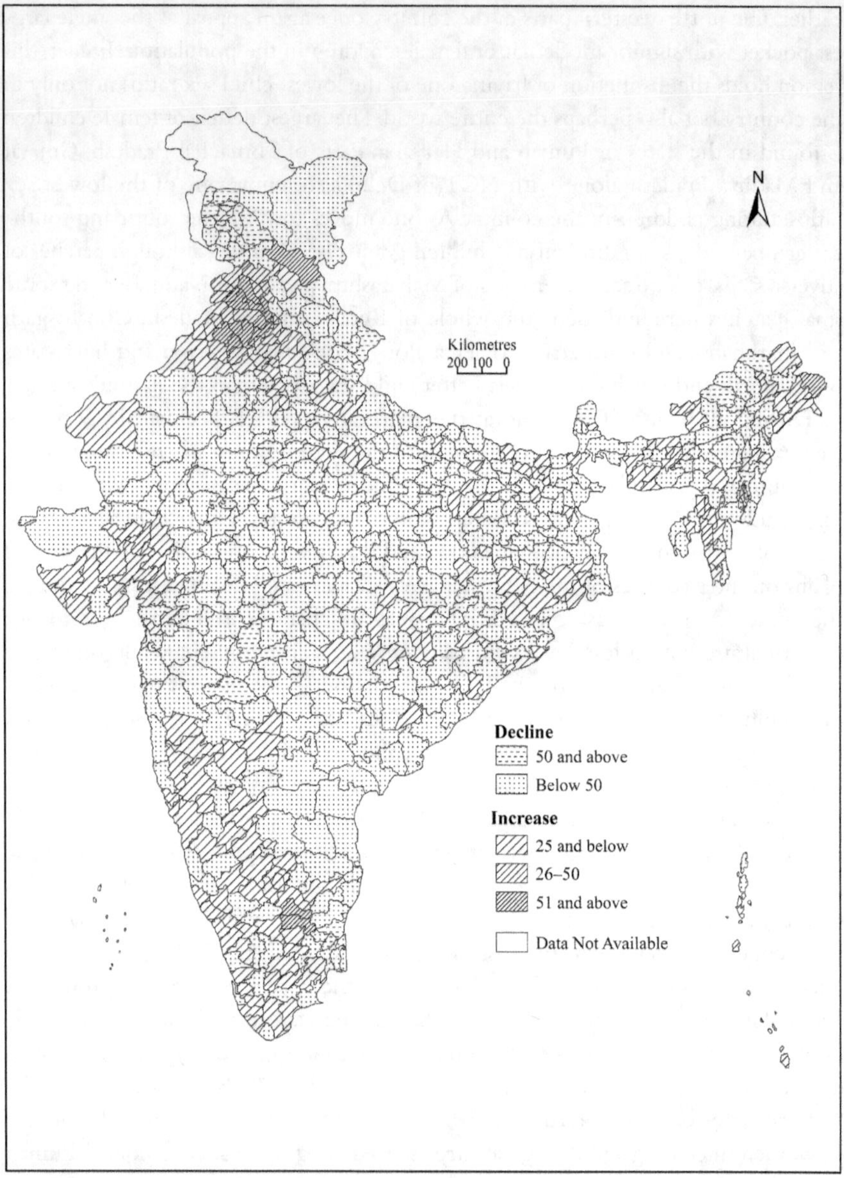

MAP 6.7 Decadal change in child sex ratio in India, 2001–11

Source: Census of India, 2011.

its indirect form (George and Dahiya, 1998:2194). It may be noted that sex determination techniques are known to have existed in the region for quite some time now. A large part of the increased preponderance of male children at birth can, thus, be related to widespread incidences of sex-selective foeticide. The recent past has, therefore, witnessed a growing concern regarding the misuse of medical technology for sex determination (George and Dahiya, 1998; Hassan, 2000). Some of the early indications of the adverse effects of sex-selective foeticide on sex ratio came from Kundu and Sahu (1992) and Raju and Premi (1992) in the early 1990s. Riley (1997:15) mentioned that 'nearly all aborted fetuses in Indian hospitals are female'. Similarly, UNICEF also remarked that female foeticide is the cause of adverse sex ratios in some of the districts in India (George and Dahiya, 1998:2191). An easy availability of doctors for ultrasound tests and a better transport network along with the ability to pay for the services are the factors responsible for the rampant practice of female foeticide even in the rural areas of the region. Gender preference is pervasive throughout the country although in varying degree. The social evil has gradually crept into some of the southern and eastern states like Tamil Nadu, Kerala and Odisha also. Widespread decline in CSR between 2001 and 2011 in Andhra Pradesh also points in the same direction. Saravanan (2002) has cited several studies confirming the practice of female infanticide in several parts of Tamil Nadu. In the backward regions, however, growing preponderance of male births should also be examined in terms of improvements in the social, cultural and economic conditions affecting reproductive health and hence reduced loss of male foetuses.

7

LITERACY AND EDUCATION

In common parlance, literacy is defined as the ability to read and write at least a simple message in any language; illiteracy, conversely, refers to the lack or absence of this ability. In other words, if a person possesses the dual skill of reading and writing, he or she is called literate. Similarly, a literate society is one in which all or most of its adult members can read and write with some amount of understanding, in any language. The proportion of literate persons in a population is termed as *literacy level*. The invention of written language involved a gradual development from the use of pictures, known as pictography, to the use of an alphabet. This development is said to have occurred in ancient Sumer around 3600 BC (Murphy, 1970:775). People who lived prior to this development, however, cannot be called illiterate. The distinction between the terms like *preliterate*, *nonliterate* and *illiterate* is important in this regard. According to Murphy (1970), societies that existed prior to the invention of written language are called *non-literate* rather than illiterate. Even after the invention of written language, at present times, there are societies that have never encountered any written language. The people of such societies are referred to as *preliterate*. Finally, people in societies that otherwise have written language, but due to one or the other reason, who do not possess the ability to read and write are best described as *unliterate*. Thus, the terms *preliterate* and *unliterate* basically form two sub-groups of the general category of *illiterate*.

It goes without saying that mere ability of a person to read and write at a low level of proficiency does not equip him or her effectively to meet the challenges of daily life in modern complex societies. Therefore, a further distinction is generally made between a person who is simply literate and a person who is functionally literate. To function effectively in the modern societies, a person must be able to read newspapers, magazines and books of non-specialised nature with a fair amount of understanding. He or she should also be in a position to write legible letters or comparable statements. This level of competence is referred to as *functional literacy*.

According to William S Gary, an authority on the subject, 'a person is functionally literate when he has acquired the knowledge and skill in reading and writing which enable him to engage effectively in all those activities which literacy is normally assumed in his culture or group' (Cortright, 1982:17). Measurement of functional literacy in any society, however, is a very complex exercise. Obviously, the level of proficiency required for a person to qualify as functionally literate is culture-specific. Different cultures impose different levels and it is very difficult to quantify the same. Some analysts are, therefore, of the opinion that functional literacy is achieved upon the completion of a specified minimum of formal education. For instance, United Nations Educational, Scientific and Cultural Organisation (UNESCO) assumes functional literacy as normal consequence of four or more years of formal education (Murphy, 1970:775). The problems of comparability of levels of functional literacy among different societies, however, remain unresolved. What may constitute functional literacy in one society with a low level of technological development may be far from functional in advanced societies based on high levels of industrial and urban development.

Literacy plays a very crucial role in the social and economic development in a country. It goes without saying that literacy promotes social awareness and critical enquiry, the two key factors in the process of social change. Literacy stimulates initiatives and enables humankind to appropriate nature in the best suitable manner with technical knowhow and mastery over human relations. Rightly remarked by Bataille (1976), 'literacy is not end in itself. It is fundamental right' (quoted in UNESCO, 2006:154). A low level of literacy in a population retards the progress along the path of social and economic development and political empowerment. Illiteracy, particularly among adults in a society, results in stagnation of technology, social and cultural lags, weakened national security, and over all stagnation of economic progress. Illiteracy in a society is primarily an obstacle to peaceful and friendly international relations and to democratic processes within a country (Murphy, 1970:412). Evidences indicate a very close association between literacy skills among people in a society, on the one hand, and the nature of society's occupational skills, on the other. In fact, the invention of written language, itself, is said to be the outcome of increased occupational diversification and the emergence of the earliest forms of urban settlements. The presence or absence of writing has, therefore, been rightly regarded as an important criterion of differentiating civilisation from tribal societies. In view of this, population geographers have traditionally been concerned with factors determining literacy level in a society, and the conditions under which the diffusion of literacy takes place.

Information on the extent of literacy forms an integral part of census enumeration in countries where census counts are taken on a regular basis. However, in countries where census counting is not a regular feature, one has to depend on various other estimates. Some of these estimates are sometimes superior to the average census in terms of accuracy. Quality of data in the underdeveloped parts of the world remains far from satisfactory. Differences in definition of literacy and in enumeration procedures render data on literacy across different countries incomparable.

Though most of the countries use the simple definition proposed by the United Nations Population Division, some countries sometime apply a somewhat stricter definition of literacy. The Population Commission of the United Nations defines literacy as 'the ability of people to read and write a simple message in any language with some understanding' (quoted in Hassan, 2005:153). With more and more countries now switching over to the definition proposed by the UN Population Commission, international comparison has become increasingly easier. The Indian census has been using the UN definition. Another problem of comparability of data on literacy relates to differences in the techniques of tabulation of literacy statistics. Some countries compute the rate of literacy taking into account the total population. In India, this technique was in vogue up to 1981 census. It is, however, argued that since children, particularly in the early age groups, do not possess potential to acquire literacy in the true sense of the term so as to qualify as functionally literate, they should be excluded from the population while computing literacy levels. In some countries, therefore, population below five years of age is ignored while computing the proportion of literate in the population. In still others, population below 10 or sometimes 15 years is not taken into account. In India, from 1991 onwards, population in the age group 0–6 years is excluded while calculating the literacy rate. The UNESCO Institute of Statistics publishes data on adult literacy rate (aged 15 years and older) and youth literacy rate (aged 15–24 years) for different countries of the world in its annual factsheets. Based on the estimates of UNESCO, the United Nations Development Programme (UNDP) provides data on literacy, enrolment ratios and educational attainment in its annual publication *Human Development Report*. Besides, the Population Reference Bureau and World Development Review also provide data on select aspects of literacy and education.

The process of dissemination or spread of literacy among the people in a society is known as *literacy transition*. This process does not occur uniformly across different groups. Some people by dint of their location, age, gender and affiliation to certain social and economic groups (e.g. caste, creed, religion etc.) are privileged to acquire literacy skills earlier than others do. The young adult urban dwellers aiming for skilled occupations generally acquire literacy much earlier than people residing in the rural areas. Literacy transition in a population, thus, is accompanied by growing differentials among different social and economic groups in the initial stage. In general, throughout the transition some literacy differentials within the population are predictable. However, the extent of differentials in the literacy rate among different groups in a population has a tendency to decline with the progress of transition. For example, the developed countries of the West, which have completed the transition, exhibit the lowest differentials among various groups. As against this, in the least developed countries where the transition has just begun, the differentials are found to be one of the largest. In between these two extremes fall those countries that are in the middle of the literacy transition. Thus, by looking at magnitude of literacy differentials among males and females, among urban and rural dwellers and among different social and ethnic groups, one can have a fairly good idea about the stage of literacy transition reached in a country.

World scenario

The world's transformation from largely illiterate to moderately literate began in the industrial countries of the Western Europe (Murphy, 1970:414). This literacy transition then gradually spread to other developed countries of the West. By now, all these countries have already achieved universal literacy. The less developed parts of the world have also witnessed improvements in literacy and education. After the Second World War, UNESCO has played a leading role in spreading literacy with a major focus on less developed countries. The initial emphasis on 'mass literacy campaign' was later shifted to 'human capital models of education'. Literacy came to be viewed as a necessary condition for economic growth and national development leading to the concept of functional literacy (UNESCO, 2006:154). According to UNESCO, 'a person is functionally literate who can engage in all those activities in which literacy is required for effective functioning of his group and community, and also for enabling him to continue to use reading, writing and calculation for his own and the community's development'. Spread of literacy and quality education got a further boost since 2000, when Millennium Development Goals (MDGs), later replaced by Sustainable Development Goals (SDGs) in 2015, were adopted by the world community.

The UNESCO data indicate that since 1950, adult literacy rate at the world level has undergone remarkable improvement. Adult literacy in the world has increased by almost five percentage points every decade since 1950. In the year 1950, adult literacy rate was around 56 per cent, which has gone up to nearly 86 per cent in 2015. However, improvements in literacy levels in the past have not been uniform across regions. In the less developed parts of the world, which account for more than three-fourths of its population, the problem of illiteracy still remains a serious problem. In fact, mass literacy is not only a recent phenomenon, but is still confined to a select few countries of the world. It may be noted that world population has increased during all these years and the rates of growth were exceptionally very high during the 1950s and 1960s. As a result, absolute size of 'illiterate' continued to grow at least till 1990, and thereafter; although it has declined, the number is still larger than what it was in the year 1950 despite decades of universal education policies and literacy interventions. Renewed efforts are, therefore, needed to realise 'literacy-education' related targets of *Sustainable Development Goals* (SDG), which envisions 100 per cent literacy among youth and a substantial portion of adults as literate by 2030. According to estimates of UNESCO 750 million adults in the world – nearly two thirds of whom are women – still remain illiterate (Table 7.1). The main tasks before the world community is to expand education fast enough to take care of rapid growth in population. As long as large portions of the children in the world have no prospect of being exposed to fundamentals of education, progress in literacy and education at the aggregate level will continue to be slow.

There exists a wide regional variation in the levels of literacy among adult and youth across major regions and across broad groups of countries on the basis of levels of development (Table 7.2). While the developed countries of the world

TABLE 7.1 Statistics on global literacy, 2016

Indicators/ Parameters	*Adults (age 15 years and older)*	*Youth (age 15–24 years)*
World literacy rate (%)		
Total	86	91
Men	90	93
Women	83	90
Gender parity index	0.92	0.96
Illiterate population (millions)		
Total	750	102
Men	277	44
Women	473	58
Share of women (%)	63	57

Source: UNESCO Institute for Statistics, June 2017.

TABLE 7.2 Status of world educational attainment, 2005–15

Major Divisions/ Regions	*Adult Literacy Rate Age 15 and Above*	*Youth Literacy Rate Age 15–24 years*		*Population with at least Some Secondary Education Age 25 Years and Above*
		Male	*Female*	
World average	84.3	92.1	89.1	64.9
Developing countries	83.3	91.8	88.7	57.7
Least developed countries	63.3	78.9	74.3	25.7
Regions				
Arab States	80.7	94.6	91.6	47.0
East Asia and the Pacific	95.7	98.9	99.0	69.9
Europe and Central Asia	98.1	99.7	99.4	81.7
Latin America and the Caribbean	93.2	98.0	98.4	58.1
South Asia	70.3	89.5	84.8	47.9
Sub-Saharan Africa	64.3	78.3	71.1	29.6

Source: UNDP *Human Development Report*, 2016:233.

Note: Based on the data of individual countries for the most recent year available during the period specified.

have already achieved universal literacy, nearly one-third of the adult population in least developed countries is yet to be brought under the net of literacy and education. The lowest literacy rates are found in Sub-Saharan Africa and South Asia. Although better than Sub-Saharan Africa in terms of literacy rate, South Asia is the home of nearly half of the world illiterate population (49 per cent). Sub-Saharan

Africa accounts for another 27 per cent of the world illiterate population. East and South Asia (10 per cent), Northern Africa along with West Asia (9 per cent) and Latin America and the Caribbean (4 per cent) follow in that order. Remarkably, Latin America and the Caribbean countries fare far better than other less developed parts of the world. The gaps in literacy rates exist despite remarkable progress made during the recent past in the less developed parts of the world. Annual regional-level estimates of UNESCO Institute of Statistics indicate that Eastern and South-eastern Asia, Southern Asia, Northern Africa and Western Asia have made the greatest progress in adult literacy since 1990. On the basis of the preceding, although continent-level literacy data are not available it may safely be concluded that North America and Europe are on top in terms of literacy levels among adults and youth while Africa occupies the lowest position. Further, Latin America and the Caribbean are far ahead of Asia with regard to literacy levels.

With regard to patterns in world literacy it may be noted that the unavailability of comparable data for all the countries of the world renders our task very difficult. Till recently, for much of the less developed parts of the world, data on literacy and education were not available. Further, because of the differences in definition and in enumeration procedure, no actual figure can be accepted with complete certainty. A relatively more accurate estimate on literacy rates are available for the developed countries of the world. However, as most of these countries have attained universal literacy, they seem to have discontinued publishing data on literacy. Therefore, in the statistics provided by UNESCO Institute of Statistics, which is the main source of data on literacy and education, 'data not available' is shown against the industrialised countries. The problem becomes tricky in view of non-availability of data for some other countries as well which do not belong to the 'more developed' group of nations. However, their number is small and hence patterns in world literacy can still be attempted. Based on the estimates of UNESCO Institute of Statistics published in Human Development Report 2016, the forthcoming section presents the patterns in world literacy.

The lowest literacy rates in the world can be seen in the northern parts of Sub-Saharan Africa in the form of a contiguous belt running from the western coast to the eastern margin of the continent (Map 7.1). This belt of extremely low literacy rate is located to the north of the equator. Spread over a dozen countries, the belt starts from the coastal countries of Guinea, Sierra Leone and Liberia in the west and extends towards the east covering vast stretches of land over Côte d'Ivoire, Burkina Faso, Benin, Mali, Niger, Chad, Central African Republic, South Sudan and Ethiopia in the east. Adult literacy rate in the belt is less than 50 per cent. Niger occupies the lowest position with a literacy rate of only 19 per cent, up from 16.5 per cent in 2003. In other words, more than four-fifths of the adults in the country are still illiterate. Interestingly, the situation in the neighbouring countries in the belt seems to have improved during the last 15 years but Niger's position is almost stagnant. The only country with an adult literacy rate of less than 50 per cent outside this belt is Afghanistan in South Asia. Earlier, Human Development Report (2003) had indicated the lowest *Education Index* for Niger. The index is worked out on the

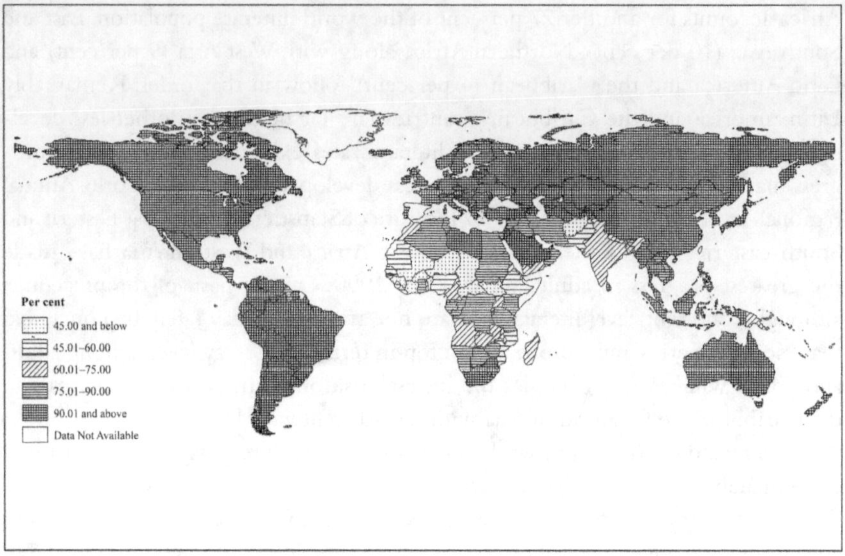

MAP 7.1 Adult literacy rate (age 15 years and above) in the world, 2015

Source: UNDP, *Human development Report, 2016.*

basis of the adult literacy rate and the combined primary, secondary and tertiary gross enrolment ratios of an individual country (for details see UNDP, 2003:341). The index varied from over 0.90 in the developed countries to as low as 0.17, for instance, in Niger. In the adjoining countries of Mauritania, Senegal, Gambia, Guinea-Bissau and Nigeria in Western Africa, the literacy rate is somewhat better but less than 60 per cent. Barring only Mozambique in Eastern Africa, the rest of the continent reports literacy rates above 60 per cent. The highest literacy rates are found in South Africa followed by Libya in the north. Remarkably, these are the only countries with more than 90 per cent adults literate in the continent.

In Asia, the situation is somewhat better. The literacy rate is below 60 per cent in only two countries viz. Afghanistan and Pakistan in South Asia. In general, South Asia reports the lowest literacy levels. It is only Maldives and Sri Lanka in South Asia that report literacy rates of more than 90 per cent. Remarkably, a greater part of Western and Central Asia has already achieved universal literacy. Countries like Japan, South Korea, Hong Kong, Singapore, etc. are also likely to have reached the stage of cent per cent literacy rates. China with more than 96 per cent adults as literate is also likely to achieve universal literacy within a decade. India, the second-largest populous country after China, is far behind the other developing countries. India's literacy rate is markedly lower than that of Sri Lanka, its neighbour. Other countries in South and Southeast Asia like Myanmar, Malaysia, Indonesia, Thailand, Vietnam etc. also have much higher literacy rates than in India.

In terms of literacy rates, the Latin and South American countries along with Caribbean countries fare far better than the rest of the developing world. In some of the countries from this part of the world, the adult literacy rate is only marginally short of the rates in the industrialised countries of Europe and North America. In Argentina and Uruguay, for instance, more than 98 per cent of its adult population is already literate. Some other South American countries with more than 90 per cent literacy rates are Bolivia, Colombia, Chile, Venezuela, Paraguay, Suriname, Peru, Brazil and Ecuador. Likewise, among the Caribbean and Central American countries also literacy rates are very high. Cuba and Antigua report almost universal literacy rate. In addition, many other Caribbean countries like Barbados, Saint Kitts and Nevis, and Trinidad and Tobago seem to have achieved universal literacy during the recent past.

The preceding discussion reveals a marked contrast in the levels of literacy between the developed and less developed parts of the world. As against universal literacy in almost the whole of Europe, North America (excluding Mexico), Central and Eastern Asia, and Australia and New Zealand in Oceania, in a major part of Africa literacy transition is still in its early phases. The situation in South Asia by and large is only marginally better. The industrialised countries account for a disproportionately higher share in the world literate population. In fact, literacy transition in the world had first begun in the early industrialised countries of north-west Europe sometime in the latter half of the 16th century itself. From here the transition gradually spread to the rest of Europe and other industrialised countries of the world. The United Kingdom was perhaps the first country in the world to have experienced the process of transition in literacy. At the beginning of the 19th century, over half of the adults in England and Wales were illiterate. By the year 1850, the share of illiterate adults came down to 45 per cent. The transition was more rapid in the second half of the 19th century, and by the year 1910, the incidence of illiteracy was almost eliminated from the country. Less than five per cent of its adults that were still classified as 'illiterate' were mostly concentrated in the old age groups. In southern Europe, literacy transition had a late start. For example, in Italy the proportion of illiterate in the age group '10 and above' was as high as 75 per cent according to the 1861 census. However, over a period of nearly a century, the country was able to achieve universal literacy. Similarly, in Greece, the illiteracy rate that remained above 60 per cent – in the age group 8 and above – till 1907 declined to the neighbourhood of 25 per cent in 1951. Towards the east, in the erstwhile USSR also the transition began only towards the close of the 19th century. In the year 1897 nearly 67 per cent of the country's population age '9 and above' was illiterate but by the middle of the 20th century illiteracy had completely disappeared.

Universal literacy became a reality in early industrialised countries of the world towards the end of the 19th and beginning of the 20th century. However, at the aggregate level growth in literacy levels that was rather slow gathered momentum only after the middle of the 20th century. With the completion of transition, literacy differentials in the industrialised countries have completely disappeared. Although separate data for rural and urban areas are not available, it can safely be argued that even rural areas in such countries have attained universal literacy. Another aspect of literacy differentials relates to male-female gaps. In the industrial countries, the gap between male and female literacy rates has long been eliminated, while the same in the least developed countries is alarmingly wide. In England, for instance, gender gaps in literacy rates disappeared by the end of the 19th century. Other countries, for example, the United States took a little longer to eliminate gender gaps. Till some recent past, in almost the whole of Africa and in a large part of Asia, male literacy rates are still higher by more than 20 percentage points than female literacy rates (Nagle, 2000:437). Female literacy rate constituted only 70 per cent of male literacy rate in the least developed countries, on the whole. Remarkably, in South Asia this share was as low as 67 per cent. Even in the western parts of Asia, among the Arab states, the gap between male and female literacy rates was of the same magnitude. With overall progress in spread of literacy, the last one and a half decade has witnessed narrowing down of the gap between male and female literacy rates. Nevertheless, countries like Congo, Mauritania, Benin, Côte d'Ivoire, Mali, Liberia, Sierra Leone etc. which report the lowest literacy rates are marked with male-female differentials of 15 percentage points or more in youth (15–24 years) literacy rate. In western part of Asia, Yemen and Afghanistan also report differentials of the same magnitude. It is expected that similar differentials exist between the urban and rural areas of these countries. Future literacy gains for the world as a whole, therefore, would depend heavily on the extent to which highly illiterate segments of these countries get involved in literacy transition.

Literacy and education in India

Census is the main source of literacy data in India. Data on literacy have been collected ever since the counting began in the country in 1872. However, the concept of literacy and education has undergone significant change over time. Up to the 1891 census, population was classified into three groups – literate, illiterate and 'under instruction'. The last of the three included persons attending schools or colleges or private institutions. This three-fold classification of population had some inherent problems of interpretation. Therefore, the Census of India switched over to a two-fold classification of population into literate and illiterate, thus dropping the category of 'under instruction'. The other change effected in 1901 was to define literacy in more concrete terms. Earlier, mere ability to read and write determined whether a person was literate or illiterate. But in 1901 literacy was clearly defined as 'the ability to read and write a letter to a friend'. This definition was continued in subsequent three censuses. The 1941 census marks yet another stage in the evolution of the concept by introducing a question on specific educational attainment or the highest examination passed. Literacy came to be defined as 'the ability of person to read and write at least a simple message with some amount of understanding in any language'. This was in line with the guidelines of the United Nations, and the same has continued in the subsequent censuses also. However, the procedure for working out literacy rate in the country changed later at the time of 1991 census. Prior to that the entire population was taken in denominator while calculating the share of literate in the population. It was realised that since population in the early age groups does not possess potential to acquire literacy, they should be excluded while calculating literacy rates. Hence, from the 1991 census onwards, children up to the age of 6 years are ignored while working out literacy rates in the country.

Despite the fact that India has been a land of ancient tradition of literacy and education, the country's population was marked with an abysmally low level of literacy at the time census operation began in the country. A low level of literacy in the country in the past has generally been attributed to factors like the caste-based social system, primarily agricultural-based economy, low rate of population mobility, predominantly rural society, unfavourable social values towards education and literacy, prejudice against female education and mobility, extreme poverty and above all rapid growth in population.

At the beginning of the 20th century, India's literacy rate was only 5.35 per cent (Table 7.3). In other words, as many as 95 out of every 100 persons in the country could not read and write. For nearly 30 years, the level of literacy remained below 10 per cent. Thereafter, particularly after India got independence in 1947, with overall development in various social and economic fields, literacy rate in the country began increasing. Literacy rate that was only 16.67 per cent in 1951 increased to 36.17 per cent in 1981. Up to the 1981 census literacy rates were derived on the basis of total population. This is called *crude literacy* rate. Thus, when the 1991 census revealed a rate of over 52 per cent, based on the revised procedure for the

TABLE 7.3 Trends in literacy rates in India, 1901–2011

Census Years	*Literacy Rates (literate as % of total population)*			*Male-Female Gaps*
	All Persons	*Male*	*Female*	
1901	5.35	9.83	0.60	9.23
1911	5.92	10.56	1.05	9.51
1921	7.16	12.21	1.81	10.40
1931	9.50	15.59	2.93	12.66
1941	16.10	24.90	7.30	17.60
1951	16.67	24.95	7.93	17.02
1961	24.02	34.44	12.95	21.49
1971	29.45	39.45	18.69	20.76
1981	36.17	46.89	24.82	22.07
1991	52.21	64.13	39.29	24.84
2001	64.84	75.26	53.67	21.59
2011	72.98	80.88	64.63	16.25

Sources: (i) Census of India, 1981, *Provisional Population Totals*, Paper 1 of 1981.

(ii) Census of India, 2001, Directorate of Census Operation, Orissa.

(iii) Census of India, 2011, *Primary Census Abstract*.

Notes: (i) Figures corresponding to the 1991 census onwards relate to population age '7 years and above', unlike previous decades when total population was taken into account.

(ii) Excludes Assam in 1981 and Jammu and Kashmir in 1991 where the respective censuses were not conducted.

first time, many took it as the result of massive strides made in nation-wide literacy drives. However, much of the jump in the literacy rate from 36 per cent in 1981 to 52 per cent in 1991 was because of the fact that children below 7 years of age were excluded from the denominator while working out the rates. The revised procedure leads to what is known as the *effective literacy* rate. In the remainder of the chapter a common term *literacy rate* has been used to denote crude literacy rate and effective literacy rate interchangeably. When total population is taken into account overall literacy in the country in 1991 works out to be 42.84 per cent. Nevertheless, it cannot be denied that the 1990s really witnessed significant progress in literacy transition. The 2001 census had indicated a literacy rate of 64.84 per cent up by over 12 percentage points over the previous census. The final figures of the 2011 census reveal a literacy rate of nearly 73 per cent. The most significant aspect of the progress in literacy rate in the country at the time of the 2001 census was the fact that for the first time since independence, the absolute number of illiterate in the country had shown a decline to the tune of nearly 32 million (press release of the office of the Registrar General of India, quoted by Krishnan, 2002:52). The momentum has continued in the subsequent decade also with a further decline in the absolute number of illiterates by over 31 million between 2001 and 2011.

Another aspect of the progress in literacy transition in the country relates to the fact that for the first time the female literacy rate had crossed the 50 per cent mark at the time of the 2001 census. Further, according to the 2011 census, of the net addition of literate population during 2001–11, females for the first time outnumber males. Although gender differential in the literacy rate continues to exist, female literacy has recorded a much larger increase as compared to that in male literacy. As a result of which, the gap between male and female literacy rates has narrowed down by a much larger margin during 2001–11 as compared to the previous decade. Nevertheless, as Table 7.3 reveals, the goal of universal literacy in the country is still far from being met. Even after more than 70 years of independence, nearly one-fifth of males and over 35 per cent of females in the country are not able to read and write even a simple message in any language. The situation appears even worse when literacy rate among adults and other parameters of levels of educational attainment are taken into consideration (Table 7.4). A little less than three-fourths of the population in the age group 25 and older does not possess even matric/secondary levels of education in the country. 'Graduates and above' constitute barely one-tenth of the population age '25 years and above'. The policy makers will have to further strengthen literacy drives in areas where improvement has not been satisfactory, and among those segments of the population which are yet to benefit from the fruits of development. This brings us to the issues of regional disparity in literacy levels and gaps between different segments of population. There exists a wide regional disparity in literacy levels in the country. Similarly, one can see a marked difference in literacy levels between males and females, between rural and urban areas and between different social and economic segments of the population. We shall return to regional disparity a little later, first we examine differentials in literacy rate in the country.

TABLE 7.4 Literacy rate and levels of educational attainment in India, 2011

Levels of Literacy/Educational Attainment	*Age Group (years)*	*Percentages*			*Male-Female Gap*
		All Persons	*Male*	*Female*	
Overall literacy rate	7+	72.98	80.88	64.63	16.25
Adult literacy rate	15+	69.65	79.28	59.57	19.71
Youth literacy rate	15–24	86.14	90.04	81.85	8.19
Population with at least matric/ secondary level education	25+	26.89	34.15	19.43	14.72
Population as graduate and above	25+	9.11	11.45	6.71	4.74

Source: Census of India, 2011, Social and Cultural Tables, C-2 and C-13.

Literacy differentials in India: One of the most important aspects of literacy differentials in the country relates to male-female gaps in literacy rates. Gender differential in literacy rates is so pervasive that it exists in total population as well as in the rural and urban areas, and in different social segments, though in varying magnitude. Referring back to Table 7.3, it can be seen that there has been a wide and increasing gap between male and female literacy rates throughout much of the last century. If a marginal decline in the differential on the occasions of the 1951 and 1971 censuses is ignored, the gap between the two is found to have monotonically widened at least up to 1991. As already noted earlier, with the onset of literacy transition in a society, literacy differentials have a tendency to gradually widen, and as the transition proceeds, it tends to narrow down, disappearing ultimately with the completion of transition. With a decline in the gender gap in literacy rates to the tune of over 3 percentage points in 2001 as compared to 1991, and over 5 percentage points in 2011 as compared to 2001, one may suggest that literacy transition in the country is fast approaching the advanced stage. But, there still exists a significant gap in literacy rates between rural and urban areas, and between different social segments. The 2011 census reveals an overall literacy rate of 84.11 per cent in the urban areas and 67.77 per cent in rural areas. The rural-urban differential in literacy rates results from the social and economic differentials in the two areas. The economy of the rural areas is predominantly dependent upon primary sectors, and does not prescribe any formal level of literacy skills for entry into workforce. Unlike this, the urban economy largely based on secondary or tertiary activities necessitates a minimum level of literacy and education skills for entry into the workforce. The social values and attitude towards literacy and education in the countryside are not congenial for the spread of literacy. One can also see a marked disparity in the levels of educational facilities between rural and urban areas of the country. In addition, it is also argued that a continuous migration of literate persons from the rural to urban areas in search of better employment opportunities also results in a low level of literacy in the villages. The rural-urban gap in literacy rates that was of the order of over 20 percentage points till 2001 has come down to a little over 16 percentage points in 2011.

In addition to gender and rural-urban differentials, there exists a wide gap in the literacy levels among different social groups. Indian society has traditionally been governed by the institution of the caste system. The position of an individual in the society and his or her sphere of social interaction and code of conduct have been strictly determined by his or her caste affiliation (Ahmad, 2002:180). The caste system, originally an instrument for division of labour in the society, emphasised that educational skills were to be acquired only if they had any functional relevance. The caste system prescribed for a four-fold hierarchical order with the *Brahmans* on the top and the *Shudras* at the bottom. The system accorded the *Brahmans* the monopoly of acquiring knowledge and imparting it to the younger generation on a selective basis. In other words, only the children of upper castes were entitled for getting education. The *Shudras* who were assigned to carry out unclean jobs and to serve the people of higher castes were prevented from acquiring any knowledge and skill. After independence, the government initiated several measures for improving the social and economic conditions of the socially deprived groups. Although Indian society has undergone significant transformation, and although the caste system has increasingly weakened during the post-independence period, considerable differences can still be seen in the levels of literacy among different caste groups. Though the census of India discontinued caste data after the 1931 enumeration, it can safely be argued that the higher castes in India exhibit a very high literacy rate, while the lower castes are largely illiterate. Table 7.5 presents a comparative picture of the literacy levels among scheduled castes, scheduled tribes and among non-scheduled caste/tribe population in the country. The table provides estimates on literacy rates among these groups for the 2011 census. As can be seen, the scheduled tribes in the country report the lowest rate. Despite significant progress made during the 1990s, more than four-tenths of the population among the scheduled tribes is illiterate at the time of the 2011 census. In fact, growth in literacy among the scheduled tribes till recent times has been very slow compared to that in the general population, as a result of which the gap between the two has constantly widened (Mohanty, 2003:95–6). The scheduled castes are only marginally ahead of the scheduled tribes in terms of literacy rate. However, nearly 35 per cent of the SC population in the country is still illiterate. The corresponding figure for 2001 was 45 per cent, thus indicating a remarkable progress in literacy among SCs between 2001 and 2011. Female literacy rates among these two groups are still lower. Females among scheduled castes and scheduled tribes report just 83 and 72 per cent respectively of literacy rate among non-SC/ST females in the country. As compared to a rate of over 68 per cent in non-SC/ST women, only 49 per cent of ST women and 56 per cent of SC women can read and write. It may, however, be noted that the gap in female literacy rates of the three groups has significantly narrowed down since 1991. Although enrolment of SC and ST children as percentage of total children

TABLE 7.5 Literacy differentials in India, 2011

Population/Sub-groups	*Literacy Rate*		
	All Persons	*Male*	*Female*
Total population			
All areas	72.98	80.88	64.63
Rural	67.77	77.15	57.93
Urban	84.11	88.76	79.11
Scheduled castes			
All areas	66.07	75.17	56.46
Rural	62.85	72.58	52.56
Urban	76.17	83.32	68.64
Scheduled tribes			
All areas	58.95	68.51	49.36
Rural	56.89	66.80	46.94
Urban	76.78	83.16	70.32
Non-SC/ST population			
All areas	76.06	83.47	68.19
Rural	70.74	79.92	61.08
Urban	85.51	89.73	80.96
Religious groups			
Hindus	73.27	81.70	64.34
Muslims	68.54	74.73	62.04
Christians	84.53	87.70	81.47
Sikhs	75.39	80.03	70.31
Buddhists	81.29	88.31	74.04
Jains	94.88	96.78	92.91
Others	59.90	70.89	49.07

Source: Census of India, 201, Social and Cultural Tables, C-8 and C-9.

is said to have perceptibly increased during the last few decades particularly at primary level, the dropout rates among these children continues to be very high. The main reason for this high rate of dropout among SC and ST children is the poor economic conditions of the communities, which compel the children to join the chunk of the labour force to supplement the meagre family income. The Census of India provided literacy data by religion for the first time in 2001, which has continued in the 2011 census also. Despite remarkable progress made during the recent past, significant literacy differentials can still be noticed among different religious groups in the country. The Jains occupy the top position in the country with a literacy rate of nearly 95 per cent. Christians who report 84.53 per cent of their population as literate are only next to the Jains. The other religious groups in that order are Buddhists (81.29 per cent), Sikhs (75.39 per cent), Hindus (73.27 per cent) and Muslims (68.54 per cent). It is important to note that during a period of 10 years from 2001 to 2011, the gap between the most literate community and the least literate community has come down from over 35 percentage points to

26 percentage points. In terms of literacy rates among females also, the different religions in the country occupy more or less the same position. Apparently, Muslims occupy the lowest position in the country in terms of literacy rate. However, spread of literacy among Muslim women has been quite impressive during 2001–11, and much of the decline in literacy differentials among religious groups can be attributed to this progress. The future prospects of literacy transition in the country, thus, heavily depends on the pace with which the unprivileged weaker sections of the society are brought to the fold of literacy in the coming decades.

Patterns in literacy and education: Literacy in India is marked with a great amount of regional variation from one part to another. The regional variation in literacy levels in the country has resulted from the regional diversity in various social, cultural and economic attributes along with a marked difference in the historical experience of different regions. Both the timing and the pace of literacy transition have varied over space, as a result of which while some areas particularly in the south have reached a situation of near universal literacy, in others the transition still appears to be in infancy. Table 7.6 presents the estimates on literacy rates with male-female break-ups in the states and union territories of the country for the 2011 census. Separate estimates on adult and youth literacy rates are also given in the table. Likewise in Table 7.7 the proportion of population age '25 years and above' with at least matric/secondary level education among the states and union territories is shown.

With regard to literacy level, Kerala occupies the first position in the country. Although the state does not rank very high in terms of economic development, Kerala has occupied a leading position in literacy transition in the country. As much as 94 per cent of the population age '7 years and above' are literate in the state. With 96 per cent of the males and 92 per cent of the females as literate, the state reports a very small gender gap in literacy rates. A very high literacy rate in the state can be attributed to a very long tradition of education facilitated by its native rulers, Christian missionaries and British administrators. In the post-independence period also various state governments have accorded a very high priority to education, particularly at primary level. Among the other factors that have contributed to very high literacy rate in the state are early commercialisation of the economy and expansion of trade, social movements of lower castes demanding educational facilities and, above all, a very high status of women in the society.

Kerala is closely followed by Lakshadweep and Mizoram. Lakshadweep is a union territory, and it is remarkable to note that union territories, in general, report higher literacy rates than the states. Out of the seven union territories (including NCT of Delhi), as many as six figure among the first 10 most literate states/union territories. In all of them the overall literacy rates are above 85 per cent. They are Lakshadweep, Andaman & Nicobar Islands, NCT of Delhi, Chandigarh, Puducherry, and Daman & Diu. The only union territory that ranks relatively lower in terms of literacy level is Dadar & Nagar Haveli. The unique position of Mizoram should be viewed in terms of the fact that over 80 per cent of the population in the state consists of Christians. It should be noted here that Christians are far more

TABLE 7.6 States and union territories arranged in descending order of overall literacy rates, 2011

States / Union Territories	*Literacy Rates (7 +)*				*Adult Literacy Rate (age 15+)*	*Youth Literacy Rate (age 15–24)*
	All Persons	*Male*	*Female*	*Male-Female Gaps*		
Kerala	94.00	96.11	92.07	4.04	93.48	99.04
Lakshadweep	91.85	95.56	87.95	7.61	91.65	98.30
Mizoram	91.33	93.35	89.27	4.08	91.32	93.40
Goa	88.70	92.65	84.66	7.99	87.74	96.15
Tripura	87.22	91.53	82.73	8.80	85.77	94.30
Daman & Diu	87.10	91.54	79.55	11.99	86.07	92.50
Andaman & Nicobar Islands	86.63	90.27	82.43	7.84	85.04	96.66
NCT of Delhi	86.21	90.94	80.76	10.18	84.82	93.17
Chandigarh	86.05	89.99	81.19	8.80	84.85	92.31
Puducherry	85.85	91.26	80.67	10.59	84.41	97.49
Himachal Pradesh	82.80	89.53	75.93	13.61	80.39	96.41
Maharashtra	82.34	88.38	75.87	12.51	80.25	93.66
Sikkim	81.42	86.55	75.61	10.94	79.00	94.20
Tamil Nadu	80.09	86.77	73.44	13.33	77.46	96.09
Nagaland	79.55	82.75	76.11	6.64	78.88	88.21
Uttarakhand	78.82	87.40	70.01	17.40	75.47	92.03
Gujarat	78.03	85.75	69.68	16.07	74.99	89.17
Manipur	76.94	83.58	70.26	13.33	75.75	87.90
West Bengal	76.26	81.69	70.54	11.15	73.27	87.25
Dadar & Nagar Haveli	76.24	85.17	64.32	20.86	72.06	86.78
Punjab	75.84	80.44	70.73	9.71	73.03	89.75
Haryana	75.55	84.06	65.94	18.11	71.99	89.96
Karnataka	75.36	82.47	68.08	14.39	71.88	90.79
Meghalaya	74.43	75.95	72.89	3.07	72.86	84.76
Odisha	72.87	81.59	64.01	17.58	69.40	86.03
Assam	72.19	77.85	66.27	11.58	68.96	82.41
Chhattisgarh	70.28	80.27	60.24	20.03	65.34	87.45
Madhya Pradesh	69.32	78.73	59.24	19.49	63.95	83.71
Uttar Pradesh	67.68	77.28	57.18	20.10	62.46	81.57
Jammu and Kashmir	67.16	76.75	56.43	20.32	62.71	83.15
Andhra Pradesh	67.02	74.88	59.15	15.73	62.18	87.02
Jharkhand	66.41	76.84	55.42	21.42	60.35	79.62
Rajasthan	66.11	79.19	52.12	27.07	60.28	81.73
Arunachal Pradesh	65.38	72.55	57.70	14.85	62.04	80.69
Bihar	61.80	71.20	51.50	19.70	55.41	72.29

Source: Census of India, 2011, *Primary Census Abstract*.

TABLE 7.7 Proportion population (age 25 years and above) with at least matric/secondary level education in India, 2011

States/ Union Territories	*Percentage*		
	All Persons	*Male*	*Female*
Andhra Pradesh	25.10	33.55	16.89
Arunachal Pradesh	23.58	30.71	15.54
Assam	22.21	27.01	17.14
Bihar	19.92	28.24	11.12
Chhattisgarh	19.10	26.69	11.55
Goa	45.35	50.72	40.04
Gujarat	27.76	34.38	20.84
Haryana	35.19	45.11	24.55
Himachal Pradesh	38.96	48.33	29.74
Jammu and Kashmir	29.97	38.41	20.38
Jharkhand	21.35	29.16	13.22
Karnataka	30.93	38.49	23.39
Kerala	41.70	43.41	40.22
Madhya Pradesh	19.82	26.41	12.93
Maharashtra	34.99	43.18	26.50
Manipur	37.54	44.61	30.51
Meghalaya	19.58	22.12	17.03
Mizoram	25.29	28.58	21.91
Nagaland	26.14	30.71	21.16
Odisha	20.27	26.53	13.89
Punjab	37.28	42.85	31.44
Rajasthan	18.61	27.09	9.93
Sikkim	26.59	30.54	21.85
Tamil Nadu	32.06	39.13	25.15
Tripura	21.30	26.43	15.87
Uttar Pradesh	23.60	32.17	14.57
Uttarakhand	34.56	44.44	24.85
West Bengal	21.87	27.05	16.39
Andaman & Nicobar Islands	33.56	36.72	29.77
Chandigarh	57.89	62.64	52.21
Dadar & Nagar Haveli	32.63	40.45	22.41
Daman & Diu	40.19	46.92	29.76
Lakshadweep	27.74	35.60	19.27
NCT of Delhi	53.78	60.58	46.13
Puducherry	44.05	53.25	35.44

Source: Census of India, 2011, Social and Cultural Tables, C-8.

literate than any other religious groups (excepting Jains) in the country. Among the states, with an overall literacy rate of 89 per cent, Goa ranks third after Kerala and Mizoram. The case of Goa can be explained in terms of a very high level of economic development in addition to the fact that Christians constitute a little less than one-third of its population. An almost negligible gap between general literacy rate and adult literacy rates only indicates a longer tradition of literacy and education in these states. Interestingly, barring only Mizoram, all these states/union territories rank very high in the country in terms of share of population age '25 years and above' possessing at least matric/secondary level education (Table 7.7). Himachal Pradesh, Maharashtra, Sikkim and Tamil Nadu come next with literacy rates of over 80 per cent. Although Himachal Pradesh does not figure among developed states, in terms of levels of educational attainment, it is only marginally behind the state like Kerala.

Interestingly, Punjab and Haryana, which rank very high in India in terms of per capita income, next only to Goa, do not figure in the list of the first 10 most literate states. Some of the less developed states like Himachal Pradesh, Tripura and Uttarakhand report even higher literacy rates than that of Punjab and Haryana. Even in terms of adult and youth literacy rates, the two states rank much lower. It is generally argued that out-migration of educated persons from the state, and a simultaneous in-migration of large numbers of labourers from other states who are largely illiterate, have led to an average literacy rate in these two states. It should also be noted that Punjab, along with Kerala, is often cited as a model of a mismatch between the processes of social and economic development. While Punjab occupies one of the top positions in terms of per capita income, it appears at 21st position in literacy rate. Similarly, Kerala, which has always shown a lower per capita income than the nation's average, ranks first in literacy rate. Haryana, a neighbouring state of Punjab, which has also experienced rapid economic transformation particularly since the mid-1960s, does not rank very high in literacy rate in the country.

As is evident, in 11 states the overall literacy rates are lower than the nation's average. Prominent among the states with miserably low literacy rates is Bihar with a literacy rate of only 61 per cent in 2011. Overall literacy rate in Bihar has been miserably low throughout the past. The rate of growth in literacy in the state has also been very slow as compared to other states occupying the lowest positions. For instance, at the time of the 1971 census there were as many as five states having lower literacy rates than that in Bihar. This number came down to two in 1981, and finally, since 1991, Bihar has enjoyed the distinction of being the least literate state in the country. Barely 55 per cent of its adults and 72 per cent of its youth can read and write at present despite significant improvements elsewhere in the country. Remarkably, till 2001, Bihar was the only state in the country with an illiteracy rate of over 50 per cent. Marked with a feudal social structure, low level of urbanisation and extreme poverty, the state also reports a very high level of literacy differentials. The other major states with literacy rates lower than the nation's average are Rajasthan, Jharkhand, Andhra Pradesh, Uttar Pradesh, Madhya Pradesh, Chhattisgarh and Odisha. Odisha, however, lags behind the nation's average by only a slender margin. Interestingly, all these states, with the only exception of Andhra Pradesh, rank very low in the country in terms of the levels of economic development also. It is strange to find that Andhra Pradesh, which otherwise fares better with regard to other social and demographic indicators, ranks so low in literacy rate. The percentage share of literate population in the state has been lower than even that in Orissa and Madhya Pradesh since the 1991 census. Despite more than six decades of planned development and massive strides made on social and economic fronts, barely one-fifth of the adult population in these states possesses at least matric/secondary level education. Rajasthan occupies the lowest rank while Bihar, Chhattisgarh and Madhya Pradesh are only marginally ahead. Proportion of adults with at least matric/secondary level education in these states is even less than half of those in states like Goa and Kerala.

Literacy patterns in India based on district-level data are more revealing (Map 7.2). The level of overall literacy in the country varies from as high as 98 per cent in Serchhip and Aizawl in Mizoram, to a low of only 36 per cent in Alirajpur in Madhya Pradesh. It is important to note that there are 22 districts in the country where the overall literacy rates are very high i.e. over 90 per cent. In as many as 11 of them, literacy transition is near completion. As is expected, the districts with very high rates of literacy are located mainly in Kerala and Mizoram. On an average, peninsular India, mainly its western parts, reports better literacy rates. The entire western coast from Kerala in the south to the northern extreme of Maharashtra appears as a contiguous belt of high to very high literacy rates. With a literacy level of 80 per cent, this belt of high literacy rates turns abruptly eastwards along the northern margins of Maharashtra. As against this, the eastern coast of the peninsula is marked with relatively lower literacy levels. It is only in Tamil Nadu and in the coastal districts of Orissa that one comes across a literacy level of 'above 80 per cent'. In Tamil Nadu along with the coastal districts, some districts in the interior as well as in the extreme south also report high literacy levels. In Orissa, districts surrounding the state capital are conspicuous with high levels of literacy. In the northern parts of the country, high levels of literacy can be seen in and around NCT of Delhi, in southern parts of Himachal Pradesh and in the adjoining districts of Punjab and Haryana, and in some hilly districts of Uttaranchal. In addition, individual pockets of high literacy levels can also be seen scattered elsewhere in the country. While most of them are centred on the capital cities of individual states, others find some highly industrialised and urbanised districts as its nuclei.

On the other extreme, there are as many as 15 districts in the country where the overall literacy rates are still below 50 per cent. Although widely scattered, one prominent concentration of such districts with very low levels of literacy can be seen in the bordering areas of Odisha, Chhattisgarh and Andhra Pradesh. Inhabited largely by a tribal population, it is one of the least developed regions of the country. Outside this, very low levels of literacy can also be seen in western Madhya Pradesh along the adjoining border with Gujarat and along the *tarai* districts in Uttar Pradesh. Remotely located, they represent one of the least developed regions in the country. Areas of literacy rates in the range of 50–60 per cent can be seen in the

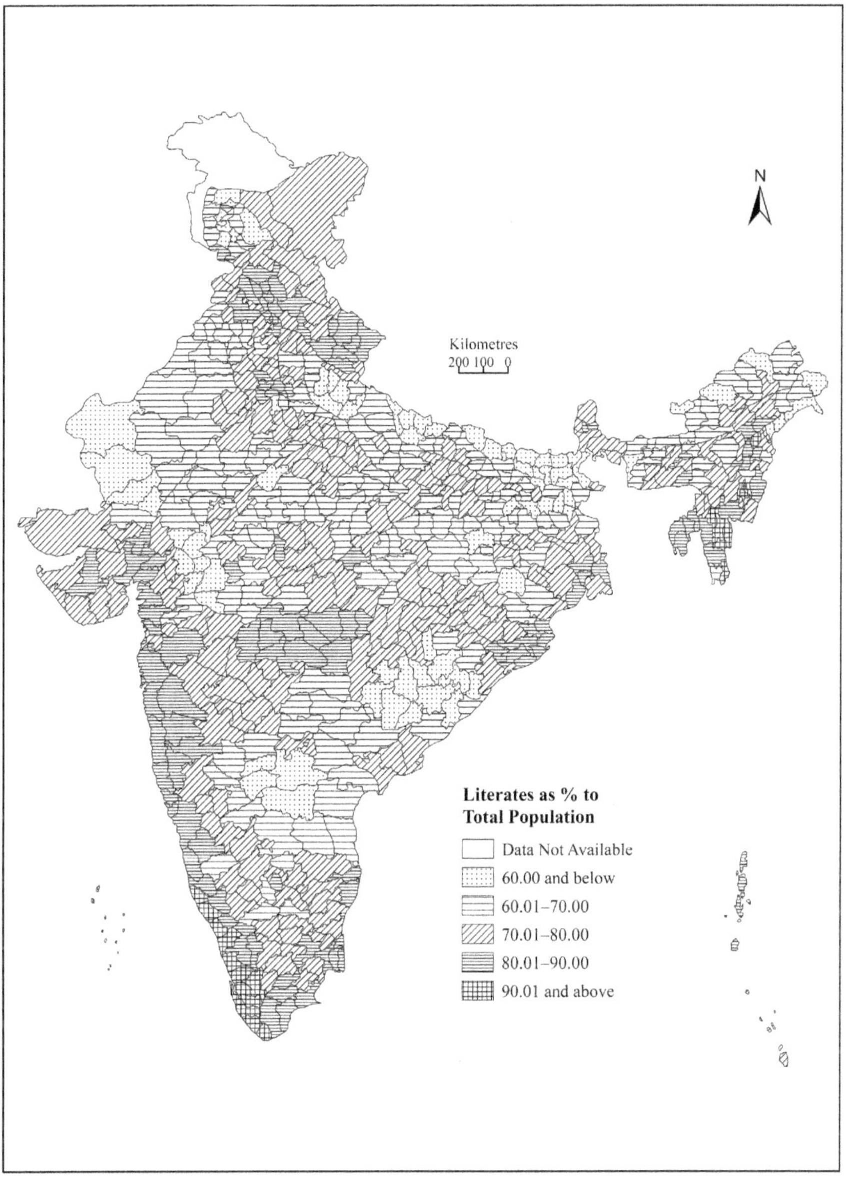

MAP 7.2 Literacy rate (age 7 years and above) in India, 2011

Source: Census of India, 2011.

western parts of Rajasthan, bordering areas of Madhya Pradesh and Gujarat, parts of western Uttar Pradesh, northern Bihar plains, isolated pockets in the Chotanagpur plateau, southern Odisha and bordering districts of Andhra Pradesh and Karnataka. These areas of 'extremely low' to 'low' literacy are surrounded by regions of relatively higher literacy rates i.e. 60–70 per cent. In addition, much of interior

Karnataka and Andhra Pradesh, northern parts of Orissa uplands and its adjoining districts in Jharkhand report literacy levels between 60–70 per cent. In the north, in a greater part of Rajasthan, and in Uttar Pradesh and Bihar plains also we have the same levels of literacy. In the north-eastern states, in some districts of Arunachal Pradesh, literacy rates vary in this range.

8

MARITAL STATUS

Although population geographers have traditionally been interested in the spatial analysis of population characteristics, marital status has not attracted adequate attention from them. An analysis of the marital status of people in a society holds a very important place in any study on the population composition and structure. The distribution of population according to marital status in any area has significant bearings on the components of population change viz. fertility, mortality and migration.

In almost all the societies of the world, childbearing is allowed only in a marital bond. Thus, the proportion of married persons in a population has profound effects on fertility behaviour. Fecundity i.e. the biological capacity of a woman to reproduce children is not uniform across the entire length of her reproductive span. The reproductive span in the life of a woman commences from menarche i.e. the first menstruation in the early or mid-teens and terminates at menopause i.e. the permanent cessation of menstruation that occurs, on an average, in her late 40s. Evidence indicates that the fecundity level of a woman that is at its lowest level in the early years of her reproductive span undergoes a six- to seven-fold increase in her 20s, and again tends to decline only to stabilise at a very low level in her late 40s. An early marriage of a woman, thus, means not only a longer duration of childbearing but also more frequent childbirth. Age at first marriage of a woman, therefore, becomes a crucial determinant of fertility levels in a population. In societies where marriage is a universal phenomenon, and where contraceptive prevalence rate is very low, raising age at marriage holds a prime position in population control programmes.

Similarly, marital status exerts a significant influence on the health and morbidity conditions of an individual. Based on data from some European countries, Cox (1975) has shown that bachelors' mortality exceeded that of married men by a considerable margin in all ages. The end of marriage by the death of one of the partners brings about sudden change in the mode of living of the survivor whose vitality is temporarily influenced and may even be impaired (Cox, 1975:121). Thus, both bereaved men and women suffer poorer health than those still married, and mortality rate among them is invariably higher. Also, marriage of a woman, particularly when it occurs in the initial years of her childbearing span, exposes her to extra risk to health from childbearing, sometimes leading to death. The less developed societies characterised by the practice of early marriages report a significantly higher incidence of maternal mortality. Further, infants born to very young mothers have a much higher probability of dying during the first few weeks or months. The National Family Health Survey (NFHS), in its second round, reports that neonatal mortality (within the first four weeks of the birth) of infants born to mothers below 20 years of age in India is higher by nearly 42 per cent than among those born to mothers age 20–29 years (IIPS, 2000:192). Even the child mortality rate (up to 5 years of age) is higher in cases where mothers' age at childbirth is less than 20 years. Thus, age at marriage in a society plays a very crucial role in the mortality conditions of children and infants. Finally, change in marital status of an individual may induce migration. Although not much is known about the precise link between marital status and migration, the common understanding allows us to argue that marital status does have its influence on the spatial mobility of population. In the patrilocal societies, brides move to grooms' places after marriage. Such societies, therefore, exhibit a greater mobility among females than males. In India, too, as shall be seen later in the chapter on migration, females are more mobile than males. Migration is at the same time highly age-selective. People in the working age groups have a higher propensity to migrate than among others. A bachelor is more likely to out-migrate in search of job opportunities or better education facilities than a person who is tied in a marital bond. Instances, however, are also not uncommon where a man chooses to out-migrate after marriage for better earnings to meet the additional responsibilities of maintaining a family. In some cases, for instance in India, end of marriage by death of the spouse, particularly when it occurs soon after marriage, often results in the return of the widow to her parents' place.

Data and measures

Information on marital status of population in a country is obtained in its periodic censuses. The data are usually obtained under five broad categories recommended by the United Nations (UN). These categories are as under:

1 single persons i.e. *never married*,
2 currently married persons,
3 persons divorced and not remarried,
4 persons widowed and not remarried, and
5 persons legally separated.

The last four of these categories put together represent *ever married* persons in a population. In addition to these five categories, sometimes yet another category is added for the persons who do not report their marital status. For example, in India, a sixth category on *not specified* can be seen in the tables on marital status. In India, data on marital status are provided in the 'Social and Cultural Tables'. In some countries where extra-legal consensual unions are common, additional categories are incorporated in the census counts. The Caribbean data on marital status often include 'visiting and common-law unions' in addition to the conventional categories (Wilson, 1985:135). Apart from the periodic censuses, various demographic surveys – especially fertility surveys – also provide data on marital status in specific populations. *The Demographic Yearbook*, the annual publication of the UN, provides data on marital status for different countries collected by periodic censuses and other sources.

The data on marital status of population are usually given for males and females separately by broad age groups starting from some minimum age. In India, up to the 1951 census, data on marital status were compiled for all age groups including children. However, from the 1961 census onwards, persons below 10 years of age are returned as single irrespective of their actual marital status. The most commonly used measure in the analysis of marital status is the percentage distribution of population in different categories. However, from the point of view of the marriage pattern, it is more useful to look into the proportion single in some early age groups. A change in the proportion single over time indicates the trend in the average *age at marriage*. The average age at marriage can be separately worked out for a population, where the measure is known as *mean age at marriage*. Mean age at marriage i.e. the average age at which an individual in a population gets married, refers to a cohort of persons. The calculation of mean age at marriage, thus, requires data on exact age at marriage of individuals in a cohort. From the periodic censuses information on exact age at marriage is not available. A widely used variant, therefore, is what is known as *singulate mean age at marriage* (SMAM). The measure uses census data on proportion of persons never married in each age group to create a synthetic estimate of mean. The measure, thus, provides the average number of years lived single by a group of individuals in a population. First proposed by Hajnal in 1953, the measure is based on certain assumptions. These assumptions are:

1 that the population is closed to migration.
2 that there are no mortality differentials in the population by marital status, and
3 that the age pattern has not undergone any abrupt change over time.

Agarwala (1962) later suggested that migration and mortality differentials do not cause any serious error in the estimates. The measure is, therefore, very useful for making comparison across different groups or regions (Goyal, 1982:109).

Hajnal's method of calculating singulate mean age at marriage is very simple and can be expressed as follows:

$$\mathrm{SMAM} = [\sum_{i=10}^{50} \mathrm{nSx} - \mathrm{Sk}\ (\mathrm{K})] / 1 - \mathrm{Sk} \qquad (8.1)$$

where nSx is the proportion single in the age group x to x + n, K is the upper limit of the age under which marriage occurs (in most of the studies this limit is taken as 50 years), Sk is the proportion single at age k, and n is the interval of the age groups.

The previously mentioned two commonly used measures viz. proportion single in a specified age group and SMAM can be worked out for both male and female separately. However, in most of the studies, measures on marital status are generally confined to females only as it is more appropriate for the analysis of demographic characteristics.

Determinants of marital status

The distribution of population in different categories pertaining to marital status and the mean age at marriage in a population depend on the interplay between a large number of social, economic and cultural factors. The practice of universal marriage in India for example has its roots in religious prescriptions. For Hindus, who constitute over 82 per cent of the population in the country, the principles of 'Purusarthas' prescribe four stages in the life of an individual – *brahmacharya, grhastha, vanaprastha and samnyasa* – each having its own duties and functions (Kapadia, 1966:27). For Hindus, marriage is essential for a man to accomplish the duties of *grahasthashram* – the second stage of life. For a woman, marriage is essential because it is the only sacrament that she is allowed in her lifetime, unlike a man who goes through several sacraments (Bhende and Kanitkar, 2011:169). Cultural practices have traditionally favoured an early marriage in India as a result of which the proportion single particularly among females in the age group '15 and above' is one of the lowest in the world. Similarly, some religions prescribe strict sanctions against divorce. In countries inhabited predominantly by Roman Catholics, for whom divorce is not permitted, one can see a very insignificant proportion of *divorced and separated* in the population. As shall be seen later, the countries in Western Europe have been marked with unique marriage patterns, which find their roots in social and economic conditions and historical experiences. The example of Ireland will suffice to illustrate this. The Irish society has a long history of a neolocal family system. Possession of land and establishment of an independent house are preconditions for an individual in the agrarian population for marriage. Land could be acquired through inheritance or through reclamation of wastelands. Laws governing sub-division of land in Ireland and also in many other European countries were very strict. Inheritance was permitted to only one son – usually the eldest one and the rest of the sons were required to seek employment outside. This practice was known as *institution of primogeniture* (Bhagat, 2002:19). The ones who were not allowed share in the father's land were compelled to delay marriage till they got jobs. Even the eldest son had to wait till such time when his father was willing to resign both authority and property. As a result, age at marriage for both males and females in the country became one of the highest towards the middle of the 19th century after the institution was reinforced. Unlike this, in European Russia where land was in abundance, marriage of young persons was a precondition for getting land. Landowners were interested to maximise labour supply by encouraging their serfs to marry their children early.

Scholars are of the opinion that the system of joint and extended family has been responsible for early marriage in many of the developing societies of the world. It is also argued that late marriage has been associated with the nuclear and conjugal family system. In societies characterised by a joint family system, an individual is not required to make an independent arrangement of housing and livelihood, and the responsibilities of maintaining a family are shared by the extended family system. As against this, in the nuclear family system, an individual is required to be in a position to provide support independently, which ultimately delays entry into wedlock. The joint family system has never been a feature of the European countries. Unlike this, in most of the developing societies of the world, the joint or extended family system has been a predominant feature. The weakening of the system during some recent time has, therefore, been accompanied by a rise in the age at marriage in such societies.

Among other social and economic determinants of marriage patterns, mention may be made of literacy and employment levels among females, prevalence of the dowry system, economic status of the people etc. In a developing country like India, literacy and levels of educational attainment among females appears to be a very important determinant of age at marriage (see for instance Malaker, 1978; Pathak, 1980; Pandey, 1984). Similarly, involvement of women in gainful employment may influence their average age at marriage. In addition, in India, although there are differences of opinion, some scholars have suggested inter-caste differentials in age at marriage. Though the European experiences have been different, evidences indicate that improvement in material prosperity in the less developed parts of the world has led to a rise in age at marriage.

Among the demographic factors that influence marriage pattern, levels of urbanisation, mortality rates and numerical balance between male and female in the population are important. The process of urbanisation erodes old practices and traditions, and brings about a new set of social values that are amenable to industrial societies. Again, though the European experiences were different, in the less developed societies the process of urbanisation has definitely led to rise in age at marriage. In Europe, even during the 19th century age at marriage was higher in rural than in urban areas. In the non-European realm, social values, customs and practices in rural areas invariably favour an early marriage. Several studies have established a marked rural-urban differential in age at marriage. In India, too, the instances of early marriages are more common in the rural areas. It has also been suggested that one of the reasons of early marriage in many societies in the past has been the high mortality rate. Early marriages were preferred in order to maintain population size. Decline in mortality rates, thus, motivated delay in marriage. Finally, marriage depends on whether there are as many men as women in the marriageable age group in the population. Hajnal (1965) has pointed out that mortality and migration have played an important role in the European marriage pattern. In India, growing imbalance in sex ratio over the past few decades in its north-western parts has compelled people to seek brides from other regions during the recent years. The average age at marriage is also likely to have undergone an increase in the areas marked with deficit of females in the marriageable ages.

World patterns

World patterns in marriage have historically been characterised by a marked contrast between the European realms and the rest of the world. In one of the earliest studies, Hajnal (1965) categorised world patterns in marriage into two types – European and non-European. The European type has been characterised by a generally higher age at marriage and an equally greater proportion of single persons in the population. The non-European type, on the contrary, has been marked with a universal marriage practice and a low age at marriage (see also Srinivasan, 2017). Hajnal was, however, of the opinion that the European type of marriage did not prevail all over Europe. The countries in the eastern part deviated from this European model. Female age at marriage in many countries in Western Europe during the 18th and 19th centuries was around 30. The proportion of single people in the population was normally above 10 per cent, and in some countries it was as high as 25 to 30 per cent. Based on the marriage index, Coale (1973) has also highlighted the sharp contrast between the European and non-European countries. Coale was also of the opinion that even within Europe there was a marked difference in marriage pattern. For instance, France and Spain deviated markedly from the European pattern of marriage. Sklar (1974) has, however, cited examples of a reasonably higher age at marriage even in some eastern European countries, which were earlier classified as the non-European type.

The marriage pattern in Europe has undergone a marked change during some more recent times. Female age at marriage in many of the European countries declined considerably after the end of the Second World War. The marriage rate is also found to have increased during the post-war period, a phenomenon termed as *marriage boom* by many scholars (Bhagat, 2002:15). The magnitude of regional variation in age at marriage significantly narrowed down as compared to what prevailed towards the close of the 19th century.

The marital status of women in five-year age groups from 15 to 34 years for select countries of the world including India is presented in Table 8.1. The effects of an early, and almost universal, marriage in India are quite evident from the table. In Indian culture, a daughter's marriage constitutes one of the prime responsibilities of parents. Among *Hindus* giving a daughter in marriage as a virgin i.e. *kanyadaan* is one of the greatest merits of the parents. Universal and early marriage, therefore, has been an integral part of Indian society and culture, although the recent past has witnessed significant changes in it. It needs no mention that the institution of marriage has increasingly become weak in Western societies, and the same process is slowly making inroads into parts of the rest of the world. Dissolution of marriage or separation is more common in Europe and populations of European origin (Srinivasan, 2017:121–2). The incidence of

TABLE 8.1 Marital status of females (age groups 15–19, 20–24 and 25–29) in select countries

Country/ Year	*Age Groups*	*Percentage Females*				
		Single	*Consensual Union*	*Married*	*Divorced/ Separated*	*Widowed*
France	15–19	99.7	-	0.2	0.0	0.0
2012	20–24	93.9	-	5.7	0.3	0.1
	25–29	73.9	-	24.4	1.6	0.1
	30–34	52.5	-	43.0	4.3	0.3
India	15–19	80.1	-	19.5	0.2	0.2
2011	20–24	30.4	-	68.5	0.5	0.6
	25–29	8.8	-	89.1	0.8	1.3
	30–34	3.3	-	93.2	1.1	2.5
Ireland	15–19	98.9	0.7	0.4	0.0	0.0
	20–24	84.8	10.7	4.4	0.1	0.1
	25–29	53.6	23.4	22.5	0.3	0.3
	30–34	33.1	16.8	49.1	0.8	0.6
Russia	15–19	92.1	3.5	4.0	0.3	0.0
	20–24	57.2	10.2	28.9	3.5	0.2
	25–29	26.3	11.1	52.8	9.1	0.7
	30–34	14.7	11.3	58.6	13.9	1.6
United Kingdom	15–19	97.0	2.5	0.4	0.1	0.1
2011	20–24	73.8	19.0	6.9	0.2	0.1
	25–29	42.5	27.6	28.7	1.1	0.1
	30–34	26.3	21.0	49.5	3.1	0.2
United States of	15–19	98.5	-	1.3	0.2	0.0
America	20–24	85.6	-	12.5	1.9	0.1
2014	25–29	57.9	-	35.7	6.2	0.2
	30–34	34.7	-	53.5	11.4	0.4

Sources: (i) Census of India 2011, Social and Cultural Tables (C-2), Marital Status by Age and Sex. (ii) United Nations, Department of Economics and Social Affairs, *World Marriage Data, 2015.*

Notes: (i) The column on 'Divorced/Separated' in the case of France and the United Kingdom refers to only 'Separated' as separate data on 'Divorced' are not available. (ii) Columns on 'Single' and 'Married' for India correspond to 'Never Married' and 'Currently Married' categories of the Census of India. (iii) For the United States it refers to the sum of 'married spouse absent' and 'married spouse present'.

divorce or separation in India is, therefore, much lower than that in the developed countries of the West. It may be noted that the proportion of single people in the age group 30–34 years among both European countries, as well as countries with a population of European origin, is not only relatively higher but has also recorded an increase over the last two to three decades. Some of the largest increases since the early 1980s can be seen in countries like France, Denmark, Australia, New Zealand and Sweden.

So far as mean age at marriage for females is concerned, while countries in Africa, on an average, rank very low in the world, European countries top the

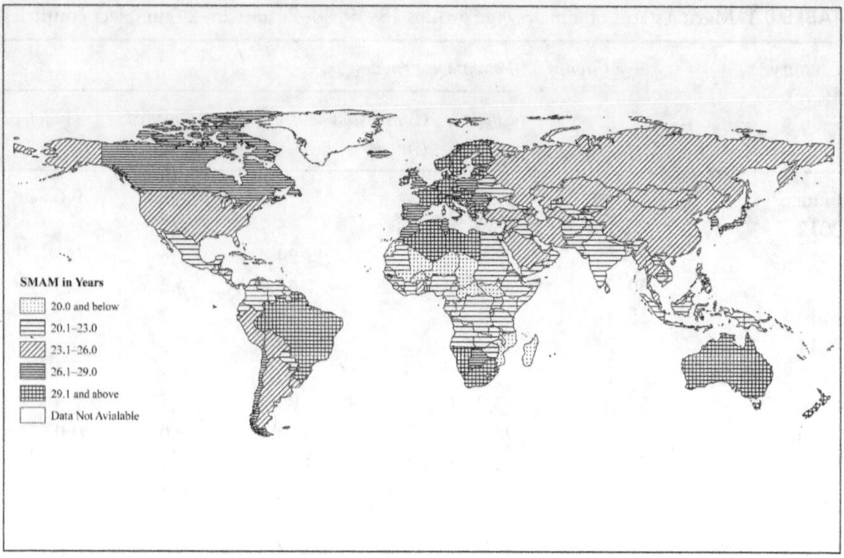

MAP 8.1 Singulate mean age at marriage (SMAM) of females in the world, 2015

Source: United Nations, Population Division, *World Marriage Data, 2015.*

list with the highest mean age at marriage (Map. 8.1). As per the *UN World Marriage Data 2015*, female mean age at marriage in Africa is around 22 years. Asia occupies the next position in terms of female mean age at marriage with a large range of variation from one part to another – the lowest being just 19 years in Bangladesh while the highest is around 30 years in a developed country like Japan. It is important to note that countries in the southern parts of the continent report the lowest mean age at marriage. India located in South Asia reports one of the lowest female age at marriage in the world. India's figure (20.7 years) is next only to Bangladesh. Even in Sri Lanka, the mean age at marriage of females is 24 years. Countries in the eastern parts of Asia report a fairly higher female age at marriage (the average centred around 28 years) than that in the rest of the continent. In Southeast Asia, female mean age at marriage varies from nearly 20 years in Laos to 28 years in Singapore. Mean age at marriage for Singapore was around 24 during some one and a half decades ago (Bhagat, 2002:16). The Latin American countries including the Caribbean Islands report a higher mean age at marriage of females as compared to Africa and Asia. European countries occupy the distinctly highest positions in terms of age at marriage. Mean age at marriage among the northern and north-western countries in Europe, on average, is centred around 30 years. As compared to this, East European countries report lower age at marriage.

So far as the linkage between economic development and age at marriage is concerned, European experiences are perceptibly different from those in the non-European countries. Evidences indicate that among the European countries, age at marriage was higher even prior to the Industrial Revolution, and a

TABLE 8.2 Mean age at marriage of women in years: select European countries (18th–19th centuries) and India (20th century)

Country	*Time Period*		
	Pre-1750	*1740–90*	*1780–1820*
Belgium	25.0	24.8	27.9
England	25.0	25.3	24.2
France	24.6	26.0	26.7
Germany	26.4	26.9	27.5
Scandinavia	26.7	25.5	29.8
India	1901–11	1941–51	1971–81
	12.0	15.4	18.4

Source: Srinivasan (2017), Table 6.1, p. 114.

portion of females remained single throughout their lives (Srinivasan, 2017:114). Even as early as 1700, the mean age at marriage of females in many European countries was higher than what India reports now after more than three centuries (Table 8.2) Further, unlike in the less developed parts of the world, the agricultural population in Europe was not marked with any higher marriage rate than its counterpart in the urban areas. However, a rise in the age at marriage in most of the non-European countries during the recent past has been associated with the process of industrialisation and urbanisation. In many of the European countries, on the other hand, age at marriage recorded increases during the time of economic depression in the 1930s, and during the war periods. When the situation improved, age at marriage again declined. The same trend was experienced in other non-European countries like the United States, New Zealand and Australia, which had close ties with Europe in terms of the origin of its population.

India's case

Census is the main source of data on marital status in the country. In addition, National Sample Survey (NSS) and various Demographic Sample Surveys, e.g. National Family Health Survey, provide estimates on marital status in the country. Information on marital status for the period prior to census taking in the country is purely descriptive and is based on religious texts mainly (Bhagat, 2002:59). Agarwala (1962) made one of the earliest attempts on the study of marriage patterns in the country. He derived the estimates on proportions single and female mean age at marriage based on census data for the period 1891 to 1951. This was followed by similar attempts by many other demographers. One of the latest studies on the marriage patterns in India is by Bhagat (2002). The study has the distinction of being the first attempt by a geographer. Bhagat has presented a very comprehensive account of early marriages and its social and economic correlates in India in a spatial perspective.

Marriage in India is nearly universal, and barely 1 per cent of females remain 'never married' by age 45–49 (Table 8.3). Age at marriage has steadily increased in the past as a result of the process of modernisation. However, early marriage is still an undistinguishable feature of India's culture. A little less than one-fifth of females age 15–19 years were reported 'currently married' at the time of the 2011 census. Obviously, many such marriages must have been solemnised before the brides attained the age of 18 years, and hence could be categorised as child marriages. Nevertheless, it is also true that marriages below 18 years of age have steadily declined over the past. NFHS estimates indicate a drastic decline in proportion of females age 15–19 years reported as 'currently married' between its third and fourth rounds – from over 43 per cent in 1998–99 to around 16 per cent in 2015–16. In the past, high mortality rates and the prohibition of widow remarriage among higher castes resulted in a decline in proportion 'currently married' women beyond the age of 30 years (Srinivasan, 2017:115). This feature still persists as seen in the table. The share 'widowed' females undergoes a sharp increase beyond age 30. As noted already earlier, the incidence of divorce is more limited in India as compared to the developed countries of the West. The share of women age 15–49 years reported as 'divorced/separated or deserted' is barely 1 per cent.

Figure 8.1 shows marital status of women aged 15–49 years in India as per NFHS-4. India's population has since long been marked with one of the lowest age at marriage in the world. It is important to note that till sometime in the recent past, child marriage was a widespread practice in the country. Even in modern times, instances of child marriage are reported in the media despite the fact that marriage below the minimum age (21 years for boys and 18 years for girls) is a cognisable

TABLE 8.3 Current marital status of women (age 15–49 years) in India, 2011 and 2015–16

Age Groups	*Percentage Distribution of Females*							
	Never Married		*Currently Married*		*Widowed*		*Divorced/Separated/ Deserted*	
	Census (2011)	*NFHS-4* (2015–16)*	*Census (2011)*	*NFHS-4 (2015–16)*	*Census (2011)*	*NFHS-4 (2015–16)*	*Census (2011)*	*NFHS-4 (2015–16)*
15–19	80.1	83.6	19.5	16.2	0.2	0.0	0.2	0.2
20–24	30.4	33.2	68.5	65.7	0.6	0.3	0.5	0.8
25–29	8.8	8.4	89.1	89.4	1.3	1.1	0.8	1.1
30–34	3.3	2.4	93.2	93.9	2.5	2.2	1.1	1.5
35–39	1.8	1.3	92.7	92.6	4.4	4.5	1.2	1.6
40–44	1.4	1.0	90.0	90.0	7.4	7.3	1.2	1.6
45–49	1.2	0.8	86.8	86.8	10.8	10.9	1.1	1.4
Total	22.2	22.5	73.8	73.4	3.2	3.1	0.8	1.1

Sources: (i) Census of India, Social and Cultural Tables, Table C-2, 2011.
(ii) IIPS, NFHS-4, Table 6.1, p. 164.
Note: * Includes 'Married' but *gauna* not performed.

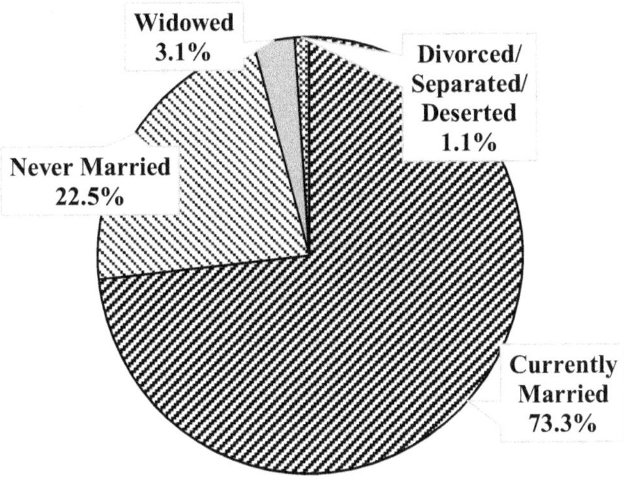

FIGURE 8.1 Marital status of women (age 15–49 years) in India, 2016 (NFHS-4)

Source: Author.

offence according to the amended *Child Marriage Restraint Act* of 1978. Scholars are of the opinion that the practice of child marriage in the country had its origin only in the 7th century. Evidences indicate that the average age at marriage in the country was quite high during the *Vedic* period. Kapadia (1966) suggested that the practice of child marriage in the country began sometime in the 7th century under the influence of religious writings such as *Dharmasutras* and *Smiritis*. These religious texts prescribed for marriage of daughters before they attained puberty. According to these writings 'parents who fail to give their daughters in marriage before puberty are destined to go to hell'. The importance of virginity was also highlighted as the virtue in a woman. Thus, keeping daughters unmarried after they attained puberty increasingly became a matter of anxiety for the parents. Under the influence of such writings, child marriage spread fast and took deeper roots in our society (Kapadia, 1966). It flourished throughout the medieval period and further degenerated during the British period, taking the shape of infant marriage.

Table 8.4 presents the trends in the 'proportion single' women in India in some of the younger age groups viz. 5–9, 10–14, 15–19 and 20–24 years for the period 1891 to 2011. The table also gives the estimates on 'singulate mean age at marriage' (SMAM) for females during the period. As the table reveals, marriage pattern in the country have undergone marked improvement during the last century. The proportion single that was only 49 per cent in the age group 10–14 years at the time of the 1891 census has increased to 97 per cent in 1991. Similarly, while only 13 per cent of the females age 15–19 years were single in 1891, the figure is as high as 80 per cent at the time of the 2011 census. In fact, the proportion single has recorded a continuous increase across all age groups during the period, excepting on the occasion of the 1931 census. In addition, the 1961 census also reported a decline, albeit

TABLE 8.4 Proportion single and singulate mean age at marriage of females in India, 1891–2011

Census Years	*Proportion Single*				*SMAM (years)*
	5–9	*10–14*	*15–19*	*20–24*	
1891	0.87	0.49	0.13	0.03	12.5
1901	0.89	0.54	0.15	0.04	13.1
1911	0.89	0.55	0.16	0.04	13.1
1921	0.91	0.60	0.19	0.05	13.7
1931	0.86	0.49	0.17	0.04	12.7
1941	0.92	0.76	0.25	0.04	14.7
1951	0.95	0.83	0.28	0.04	15.6
1961	*	0.81	0.29	0.06	15.9
1971	*	0.88	0.44	0.10	17.1
1981	*	0.93	0.56	0.14	18.3
1991	*	0.95	0.64	0.17	18.9
2001	*	0.97	0.75	0.23	20.2
2011	*	0.97	0.80	0.30	21.0

* From 1961 onwards all persons below 10 years of age have been treated as never married irrespective of their marital status.

Sources: (i) For the period 1891–1991, Bhagat, 2002, Table 3.1, p. 62.
(ii) Census of India, Social and Cultural Tables, Table C-2, 2001 and 2011.

marginally, in the 'proportion single' in the age group 10–14 years. The decline in the 'proportion single' in all age groups and in SMAM on the eve of the 1931 census can be attributed to the sudden rise in the child marriage rates towards the close of the 1920s. It may be recalled that the British government had passed the Child Marriage Restraint Act in September 1929, which became effective only from April 1930. The intervening period between the passage and enforcement of the Act witnessed large-scale marriages, involving even infants, to escape from the Act. The impact was seen in a decline in SMAM from 13.7 years in 1921 to 12.7 years in 1931. However, thereafter, the SMAM for females has continuously increased from 1941 to 2011. Thus, over a period of 120 years, average age at marriage for females in the country has gone up by 8.5 years. Remarkably, the gain in the proportion single as well as SMAM has been more conspicuous during the post-independence period.

Based on the state-level trends in proportion single women below 15 years of age, Bhagat (2002) mentioned that at the turn of the 20th century, the states of Andhra Pradesh (formerly Hyderabad), combined Bihar and Orissa, West Bengal, combined Maharashtra and Gujarat (formerly Bombay Presidency), Uttar Pradesh (formerly United Provinces) and Madhya Pradesh were marked with significantly higher incidence of child marriages than the nation's average. Rajasthan joined the group in the post–1931 period. Although, the proportion singles is found to have increased across all the states, Andhra Pradesh, Madhya Pradesh, Rajasthan, Uttar

Pradesh and Bihar continued to be on the lower side up to 1971. The incidence of child marriage declined faster thereafter. Nevertheless, the major states like Bihar, Madhya Pradesh, Rajasthan and Uttar Pradesh in the Hindi belt of the north continued to reveal higher incidences of child marriage up to the close of the century. Against this, the southern states of Kerala, Karnataka and Tamil Nadu have occupied the lowest positions in terms of the prevalence of child marriage throughout the period. In fact, early marriage, particularly child marriage, was not common in the whole of south India, except in Andhra Pradesh, even at the close of the 19th century.

Table 8.5 presents state-wise figures on proportion single women separately for the age group 10–14, 15–19, 20–24 and 25–29 for the year 2011, along with singulate mean age at marriage pertaining to 2001 and 2011 censuses. The last two decades have witnessed remarkable change in the marital status of population across the states in India. Despite legal provisions against child marriage, till as recent as 1991, in Rajasthan 13 per cent of the females in the age group 10–14 were returned as 'ever married' (Hassan, 2005:187). The states of Bihar, Madhya Pradesh and Uttar Pradesh were only marginally behind Rajasthan in regard to the incidence of child marriage. Singulate mean age at marriage for females in these states also worked out to be the lowest in the country. Remarkably, in all of them, except Uttar Pradesh, the average age at marriage was well below the prescribed minimum. In Uttar Pradesh also the average was just close to the minimum prescribed for marriage for girls. At the time of the 2011 census, however, only 4 per cent (as compared to 13 per cent in 1991) females in the age group 10–14 years in Rajasthan were counted as 'ever married'. Nevertheless, the actual magnitude of child marriage will definitely be much more than what it appears from the census figures. Remember that the census treats population below 10 years of age as 'never married' irrespective of their marital status. In the age group 15–19, in Rajasthan 71 per cent females were returned as single i.e. 'never married' which implied that another 29 per cent were already married. Remarkably along with Rajasthan, states like West Bengal, Bihar Tripura and Jharkhand also reported at least one-fourth of the girls in age group 15–19 as already married in 2011. It may be recalled that West Bengal ranked very high in terms of the prevalence of child marriage till the early decades of the 20th century. Although the state recorded an impressive increase in the age at marriage in the post-independence period particularly after 1961, it still appears at the lowest rung among other states in terms of SMAM. In addition, in states like Gujarat, Maharashtra, Karnataka and Andhra Pradesh along with Madhya Pradesh and Assam, at least one-fifth of the girls in age group 15–19 were already married. Obviously a significant portion of such marriages must have taken place before the prescribed minimum of 18 years. Remarkably, these states report the lowest SMAM as per the latest estimates based on the 2011 census.

On the other extreme, as revealed in the table, the union territories along with most of the north-eastern states, in general, report higher SMAM than the all India average in 2011. The highest SMAM is 25 years in Nagaland and Manipur. Thus, the gap in singulate mean age at marriage between the highest and the lowest is

TABLE 8.5 Proportion single females in broad age groups and singulate mean age at marriage of females by states in India, 2011

States/Union Territories	*Proportion Single 2011*				*SMAM (years)*	
	Age Groups					
	10–14	*15–19*	*20–24*	*25–29*	*2001*	*2011*
Andhra Pradesh	97.4	79.0	28.1	7.0	19.3	20.5
Arunachal Pradesh	97.4	85.2	43.2	17.1	21.0	22.2
Assam	97.9	77.3	32.5	14.2	21.6	21.0
Bihar	97.1	74.0	16.2	3.3	18.4	19.5
Chhattisgarh	98.3	85.5	29.5	8.3	20.0	21.1
Goa	96.1	87.2	57.7	27.4	24.4	23.4
Gujarat	96.3	79.7	30.9	8.0	20.4	20.7
Haryana	97.2	83.4	31.7	6.3	19.6	20.9
Himachal Pradesh	97.8	90.8	46.7	11.9	21.6	22.4
Jammu and Kashmir	97.9	91.3	60.1	27.2	22.9	24.2
Jharkhand	97.6	74.9	24.0	8.3	19.5	20.1
Karnataka	97.0	79.5	33.2	10.2	20.8	20.9
Kerala	98.3	87.3	41.6	11.9	21.9	21.5
Madhya Pradesh	97.1	78.6	24.4	6.0	18.9	20.3
Maharashtra	95.8	80.1	31.3	9.8	20.6	20.7
Manipur	97.9	89.7	61.3	36.0	25.5	25.0
Meghalaya	97.8	82.0	40.3	18.9	22.1	22.0
Mizoram	98.5	87.5	50.4	27.4	23.3	23.3
Nagaland	98.4	90.6	63.2	36.6	25.5	25.0
Odisha	98.1	85.1	39.1	13.0	21.7	21.8
Punjab	96.9	89.6	48.4	14.0	21.5	22.5
Rajasthan	95.8	71.2	18.8	3.5	18.1	19.4
Sikkim	98.2	83.1	45.5	23.2	21.9	22.3
Tamil Nadu	97.8	84.9	39.6	11.3	21.3	21.6
Tripura	98.1	74.3	29.3	11.5	21.2	20.7
Uttar Pradesh	97.1	83.6	30.1	6.6	19.4	20.8
Uttarakhand	98.3	89.6	39.9	10.0	21.1	21.9
West Bengal	97.4	71.6	23.6	8.7	19.9	19.8
A and N Islands	98.4	84.5	39.2	17.1	21.8	22.1
Chandigarh	98.5	90.8	53.6	17.7	22.0	23.1
Dadra and Nagar Haveli	98.0	76.6	21.9	6.1	19.5	20.0
Daman & Diu	98.3	82.1	29.3	10.5	21.2	20.7
Lakshadweep	97.9	91.8	53.1	19.5	21.7	23.4
NCT of Delhi	98.5	90.2	48.5	15.3	21.5	22.6
Puducherry	98.0	88.5	48.6	15.9	22.0	22.4

Source: Census of India, C Series, Social and Cultural Tables, Table C-2, 2001 and 2011.

as much as 5.6 years. The other prominent states reporting mean age at marriage above the nation's average are Goa, Punjab, Kerala, Tamil Nadu, Himachal Pradesh and Orissa. It should be noted that Kerala reported a somewhat higher age at marriage even when literacy rate among females was not that high. Kerala is the only state in the country which had crossed the pre-puberty cut-off level, i.e. 15 years, as early as in the 19th century. The other southern states of Karnataka and Tamil Nadu achieved this distinction only towards the middle of the 20th century. Punjab was the leading state from the north to have achieved this level in the early decades of the 20th century. Maharashtra and Gujarat, which experienced rapid urbanisation and industrialisation in the post-independence period, rank very low in average age at marriage.

India's population has been marked with a great amount of diversity in its socio-cultural attributes. Hence, there is a marked contrast in marital status between the urban and rural areas and between different social and economic groups. Age at marriage is almost invariably lower in the rural areas and in some social groups than that among others. As a result, proportion single in such populations in some early age groups is always lower in the former than in the latter. Table 8.6 presents percentage distribution of females in the age group 15–29 years by residence and by social groups based on religion and caste in India as per the 2011 census. In the age group 15–29 years, over 60 per cent of the females in rural areas were returned

TABLE 8.6 Differentials in marital status of females (age 15–29 years) in India, 2011

Parameters	*Percentage Distribution of Female Population (Age Group 15–29 Years)*					*SMAM (years)*
	Never Married	*Currently Married*	*Widowed*	*Divorce/ Separated*	*Total*	
	By Residence					
Rural	38.5	60.3	0.7	0.7	100.0	20.3
Urban	46.7	52.2	0.6	0.5	100.0	21.9
	By Religion					
Hindus	40.1	58.8	0.7	0.5	100.0	20.7
Muslims	43.0	55.9	0.6	0.6	100.0	20.9
Christians	56.0	42.6	0.6	0.7	100.0	23.4
Sikhs	51.4	47.7	0.5	0.4	100.0	22.5
Buddhists	45.7	52.5	0.9	0.9	100.0	21.9
Jains	53.4	46.0	0.4	0.2	100.0	23.1
Others	43.8	54.5	0.9	0.8	100.0	21.2
	By Caste/Tribe					
SCs	39.2	59.4	0.8	0.6	100.0	*
STs	40.2	58.2	0.8	0.8	100.0	*
Non-SC/ST	41.7	57.2	0.6	0.4	100.0	*

Source: Census of India, Social and Cultural Tables, C-02 and C-03, 2011.
Note: (i) * Required data not available.

as 'currently married' as against only 52 per cent in the urban areas. Similarly, 38 per cent of females in the age group in rural areas were 'never married' as compared to around 47 per cent in its urban counterpart. The social, cultural and economic conditions in the rural areas in general favour an early marriage. Thus, singulate mean age at marriage has always been lower in rural areas. Census data indicate that the difference in age at marriage between rural and urban areas has continuously declined since 1971. In the year 1971 the difference was of the extent of 2.5 years, which has come down to 1.6 years in 2011. Remarkably, rural areas have recorded a faster increase in age at marriage during the recent past. The difference in rural and urban age at marriage can be seen in all the states of India. It should be noted here that the states reporting a lower age at marriage than the national average also report a higher rural-urban differential. Among the religious groups the Christians report the highest age at marriage followed by the Jains and the Buddhists. Interestingly, SMAM among the Hindus is lower than that among the Muslims albeit marginally. Corresponding differentials can be noticed in the marital status among these religious groups. As data on marital status in required age brackets are not available separately for SCs and STs, SMAM for these groups could not be generated. However, the differentials in percentage distribution among different categories of marital status make it evidently clear that SCs have the lowest age at marriage, followed by STs, in the country.

The regional variations in marital status of population in India based on state-level data conceal more than what they reveal. In fact, the regional variations in the social and cultural attributes affecting marriage patterns are often as great within a state as between the states. For instance, in Uttar Pradesh, which reports a lower mean age at marriage than the nation's average, there are select pockets of distinctly higher age at marriage in its western parts. The coastal areas differ markedly from those in the interior peninsula. Likewise, the peninsular uplands behave differently from the northern plains while the hilly states in the north and north-east appear markedly different in social and cultural attributes from the rest of the country. Map 8.2 presents district-level patterns in singulate female mean age at marriage based on 2011 census data. On an average, the Indian peninsula reports higher mean age at marriage than its northern counterparts although there are significant variations within the region also. A belt of high age at marriage (above 22 years) can be seen in the coastal areas along the Western Ghats from southern Maharashtra up to northern parts of Kerala, in the extreme southern part of the peninsula covering parts of Kerala and Tamil Nadu and in the coastal districts of Tamil Nadu in the east. In addition pockets of high age at marriage can also be seen over the coastal and upland districts in Odisha, southern Chhattisgarh and over bordering areas of Madhya Pradesh and Maharashtra in the central part of the upland plateaus. Pockets of low age at marriage (below 20 years) in the peninsular plateau are scattered over central Maharashtra, northern Karnataka and the bordering areas of present-day Telangana and Andhra Pradesh. In the rest of the peninsula, age at marriage varies from 20 to 22 years. In the north, almost the whole of Jammu and Kashmir and Punjab, along with parts of Himachal Pradesh, report high age at

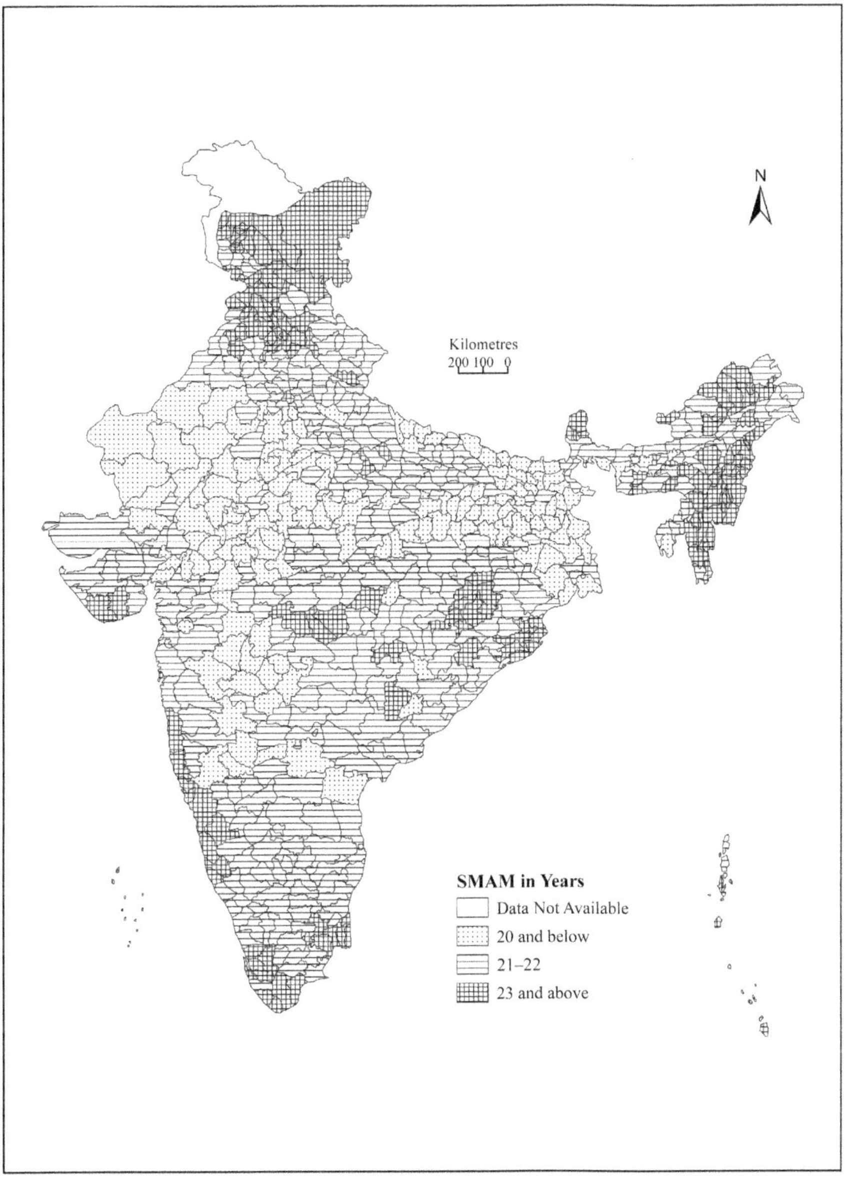

MAP 8.2 Singulate mean age at marriage (SMAM) of females in India, 2011

Source: Census of India, 2011.

marriage. As a contrast, in almost the whole of Rajasthan and its adjacent districts in northern and western Madhya Pradesh along with over a greater part of Bihar plains and Jharkhand, average age at marriage is below 20 years. In the rest of the northern plains, mean age at marriage ranges from 20 to 22 years. Finally as could be seen, the north-eastern states report distinctly higher age at marriage than the

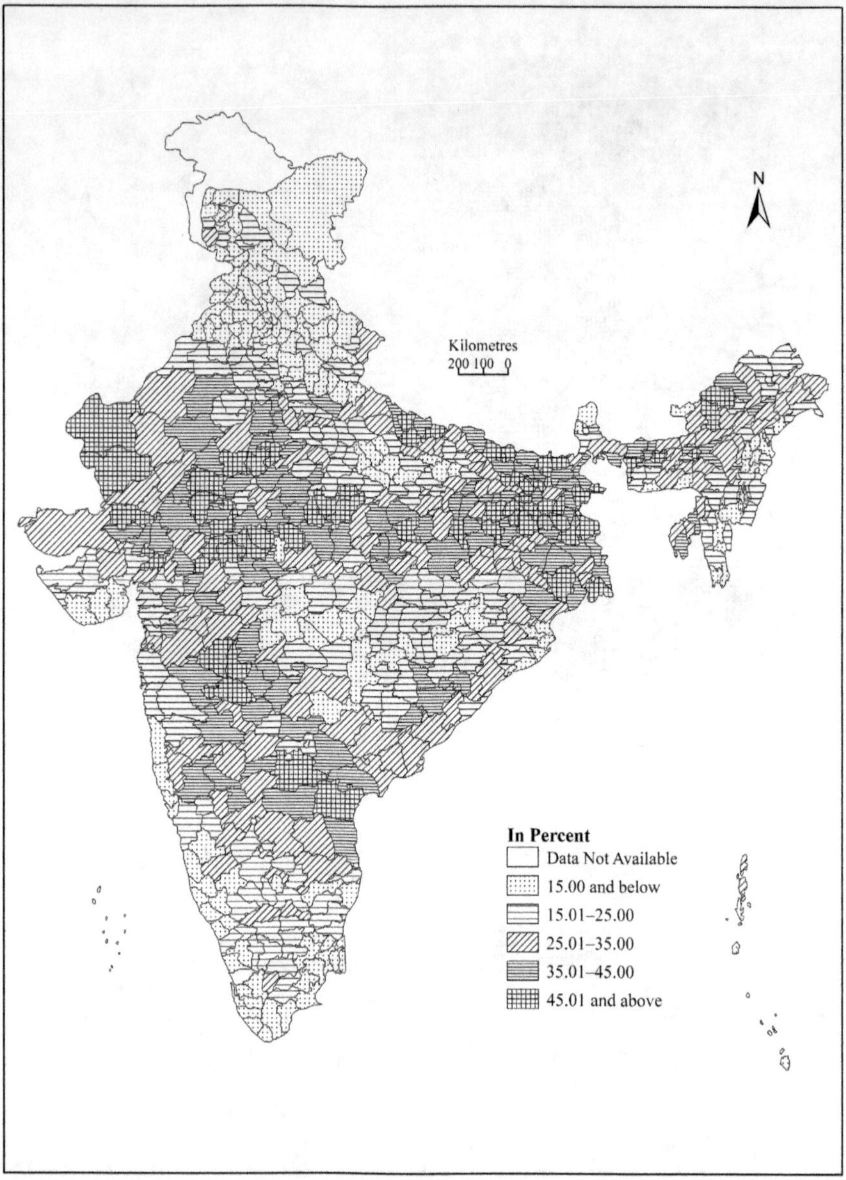

MAP 8.3 Proportion women (age 20–24 years) married before the legal age in India, 2015–16

Source: NFHS-4, 2015-16.

nation's average. In the north-eastern region, age at marriage is particularly high in Nagaland, Manipur and Mizoram.

It may be noted that singulate mean age at marriage for females as per the 2011 census was above the minimum prescribed all over the country barring only two districts – Bhilwara and Chittaurgarh, both in Rajasthan. However, it should not be concluded that child marriage in India is now a matter of the past. Rather evidences indicate that marriages of girls before they attain the legal age of 18 years is still widely prevalent in the country, and the same cannot be captured by mean age at marriage. From census data it is always possible to work out the percentage share of women who were married before age 18. But since this includes women of all age brackets, current status cannot be derived using them. National Family Health Survey Round (NFHS) provides data on the share of women age 20–24 years who were married before attaining 18 years of age. Figures from the latest round, i.e. NFHS-4 conducted during the year 2015–16, provide a very good insight into the spatial dimension of persisting child marriages in India.

According to NFHS-4, as high as 27 per cent of women age 20–24 years were married before the age of 18. The corresponding figure was 47 per cent at the time of NFHS-3 (2005–06), indicating a decline of 20 percentage points in just one decade. Despite this decline some areas in the country are still characterised by prevalence of child marriage of a significant magnitude. Map. 8.3 presents district-wise proportion women age 20–24 years married before the legal age of 18 years. Interestingly, there is a marked correspondence between the patterns that emerge from Maps 8.2 and 8.3. Areas with low singulate mean age at marriage in Rajasthan, parts of Madhya Pradesh, Bihar and West Bengal plains, interior upland plateaus in Maharashtra and Andhra Pradesh report greater child marriage – as much as 40 per cent of the women age 20–24 years are married before 18 years.

9
ECONOMIC COMPOSITION

Patterns in socio-economic characteristics of population have formed the core concern of Population Geography ever since its inception. This includes, among others, a discussion on economically active population and its industrial and occupational structure – broadly defined as economic characteristics of population. In other words, the share of population engaged in economic activities for survival and sustenance, and, its distribution across broadly defined categories of economic activities occupies an important place in the overall scheme of the discipline. While the former refers to what is known as *work participation rate*, the latter subsumes discussion on *occupational* or *workforce structure*.

Labour is an important factor of production and hence the size of labour force is of great importance for level of economic activity in a country. It is generally argued that economic wellbeing of people in a region is dependent upon size of labour force available, and its proportion engaged in economic activities. There is a wide variety of economic activities, each with its own level of real income. Unskilled workers engaged in various activities in primary sectors of economy, for instance, have much lower income levels as compared to skilled and trained workers in secondary and tertiary sectors. Within tertiary sectors also, certain activities which are now grouped under 'quaternary activities', e.g. services rendered by white-collar professionals related to decision making and management, are marked with levels of real income that are much higher than that of others. Thus, a larger share of persons in the workforce alone does not necessarily mean a better standard of living, and it becomes important to look into distribution of the workforce in broad occupational categories also. This division of the workforce in different occupations is called occupational or workforce structure. There is a close relationship between development of an economy, on the one hand, and its occupational structure, on the other, and economic progress is generally associated with certain distinct necessary and predictable changes in occupational structure (Datt and Mahajan, 2016:92). Both work participation and workforce structure of a population are governed by a host of factors like physical settings of the region, its resource endowment, social and culture attributes, historical experiences, demographic situations, stage of economic development, government policies etc. (Clarke, 1972:88). The present chapter concerns itself with a geographical account of economic characteristics of population in terms of work participation rate and occupational or workforce structure of the world in general, and India, in particular.

The size of the workforce or labour force in relation to total population is an important indicator of the economic conditions of a society. The term *workforce* refers to the section of population actually engaged in economic activities. If population looking for work, or available for work, is also included, it is called *labour force.* Thus, labour force refer to the section of population actually engaged as well as available to engage itself in the production of goods and services in a society. Based on this, various measures of *work/labour force participation rates* can be calculated. Some of them are discussed in the following.

$$\text{Crude work participation rate } (\text{CWPR}) = \frac{TW}{TP} \text{ X } 100 \tag{9.1}$$

where TW is total workers in a population at a given time, and TP is total population at that time. It can be worked out separately for male and female, and for rural and urban areas. Since it takes into account total population which also includes children and old age people who are otherwise supposed to be outside the workforce, this is only a crude measure. A refinement is possible if data by age groups are available. If both numerator and denominator in Equation (9.1) are confined to working age group i.e. 15 to 59 years (or 15 to 64 as in developed societies), it gives a better measure of workforce. Consider this:

$$\text{Work participation rate (WPR)} = \frac{\textit{Total Workers aged } 15 - 59 \textit{ years}}{\textit{Total Population aged } 15 - 59 \textit{ years}} \text{ X } 100 \tag{9.2}$$

WPR can also be worked out separately for male and female, and for rural and urban areas. Not only this, it can be worked out for any specific age group of the population if data are so available. In the same manner *labour force participation rate* is:

$$\text{LFPR} = \frac{\textit{Number of persons in Labour Force}}{\textit{Total Population aged } 15 - 59 \textit{ years}} \text{ X } 100 \tag{9.3}$$

LFPR refers to the total number of persons who are actually employed combined with those who are actively looking for work, and is expressed as a percentage of working age population. Thus, LFPR combines incidence of both employment and unemployment in a population at a given time point. While the former includes persons in 'paid' as well as 'self-employment', the latter includes persons in working age groups currently without work but seeking/available for work.

Another important term in analysis of economic characteristics of population is *workforce structure*. Workforce structure of a population refers to percentage distribution of economically active population in different sectors of economy. The economic activities are of various types. They are customarily grouped in three sectors of economy, following the work of Colin Clark (1951), viz. *primary*, *secondary* and *tertiary* sectors (Clarke, 1972:91). Primary sector is related to production of raw materials and basic foods. The activities under this sector include agriculture, mining and quarrying, plantation, animal rearing, forestry, hunting and food gathering and so on. Likewise, the secondary sector includes all activities related to processing of raw materials obtained from the primary sector, manufacturing of goods and construction. Finally the tertiary sector, also known as the *service sector*, includes all other services rendered to the general population. Of late, some activities in the tertiary sector have been isolated and put under the headings of *quaternary* and *quinary* sectors. The quaternary sector represents special types of service work, focussing on professional and administrative services, including financial and health service work, information processing, teaching and government services as well as entertainment activity (Hartshorn and Alexander, 1988:2). Finally, all activities related to high-level decision making in industry, business, education etc. in government as well as private sectors are included in the quinary sector. Research scientists, legal authorities, financial advisors and professional consultants who provide strategic planning and render problem-solving services come under this category (Hartshorn and Alexander, 1988:2). It may, however, be noted that separate data under quaternary and quinary sectors of the economy are generally not available. Therefore, the discussion in the present chapter is based on the traditional three-fold classification of economic activities viz. primary, secondary and tertiary sectors only. The percentage of workers in, say, the primary sector, for instance, can be worked out as under:

$$\text{Share of workers in primary sector} = \frac{\textit{No. of Workers in Primary Activities}}{\textit{Total Workforce}} \times 100 \tag{9.4}$$

It can be seen that proportions across all sectors add up to 100. In the early stage of human history, primary activities engaged the entire workforce. Thereafter, as the economies evolved over time, a variety of non-primary activities came into existence and grew in importance. This process is called *economic diversification* and is accompanied by a gradual decline in share of the workforce in primary activities with a corresponding rise in other sectors. Looked at from this point of view, workforce structure of a population is a very good indicator of the stage of economic development a society has reached. The economies in less developed parts of the world have a relatively higher dependence on primary sectors of the economy while those in more developed parts report a larger share of the workforce in tertiary activities, including quaternary and quinary activities. Based on workforce or labour force participation rate and workforce structure, in the present chapter a geographical account of economic characteristics of population in the world is presented. It may be noted that the concern here is not with economic activities *per se* which forms the subject matter of economic geography. The main purpose is to unravel economic characteristics of population in terms of participation rates and distribution of workforce in different sectors of the economy.

The world scenario

Any discussion on workforce or labour force participation and workforce structure is seriously handicapped by lack of comparable data across countries. International Labour Organisation (ILO), an agency of the United Nations, provides data on employment and unemployment of member countries in its annual publications. ILO sets international standards and promotes social protection and work opportunities for all. The ILO publication provides estimates on 'employment to population ratio' and 'labour force participation rate' for population age 15 years and above. 'Employment to population ratio' is basically work participation rate, and is defined as the proportion of a country's working population that is employed. Labour force participation rate, as already noted earlier, is the proportion of working people as well as those available for work. Based on the ILO estimates, the present section provides the main features of workforce and labour force participation rates in the world.

Table 9.1 presents workforce and labour force participation rates in the world and the major regions for the year 2015. Nearly 59 per cent of the total population age '15 years and above' in the world is employed. If those who are not employed but are available for work are also included, the proportion is well above 62 per cent. The participation rates are much higher in 'low income' regions of the world as compared to 'high income' regions. In less developed parts of the world characterised by subsistence economies, low wage levels necessitate entry into work/labour force at early stages to supplement family income for sustenance. In developed societies, continuation in education and other trainings delays the entry of adult population in work/labour force. Further, the nature of economic activities is also an important determinant of entry into workforce. Most of the activities in the primary sector do not require any formal education or training, and therefore, populations heavily dependent upon primary activities, particularly subsistence in nature, are marked with higher participation rates.

Similarly, the participation rates are higher among males than females. Almost all the societies in the world are based on patriarchal structure wherein bread-earning is the responsibility of the male. Although Western societies are based on more equal gender relations, a higher participation among males than among females is seen across the globe. Nevertheless, the differentials are much smaller in magnitude among the developed regions than elsewhere in the world. Northern America and Europe, for instance, report relatively much smaller gaps in participation rates between males and females. In addition, male-female differentials in low-income regions e.g. is Sub-Saharan Africa, are also much smaller. Obviously, economic compulsions in the region force more females to join the labour force for sustenance. World patterns in 'employment to population' ratio are shown in Map 9.1.

TABLE 9.1 Employment to population ratio and labour force participation rate in the world, 2015

World/ Major regions	*Employment to Population Ratio* (15 years and above)*			*Labour Force Participation Rate (15 years and above)*		
	Total	*Male*	*Female*	*Total*	*Male*	*Female*
World	58.8	71.6	46.0	62.2	75.5	48.8
World: Low income	71.1	77.6	64.9	75.1	81.3	69.2
World: High income	56.3	64.0	48.8	60.3	68.4	52.4
Africa	59.5	68.8	50.4	64.3	73.6	55.2
Northern Africa	41.1	65.1	17.3	46.9	72.1	21.9
Sub-Saharan Africa	64.6	69.8	59.5	69.1	74.0	64.4
Asia and the Pacific#	60.0	74.8	44.8	62.6	78.0	46.7
Eastern Asia	65.6	72.4	58.6	68.6	76.1	61.0
Central and Western Asia	53.9	67.6	41.0	58.9	73.5	45.1
South-eastern Asia and the Pacific#	65.9	77.7	54.4	68.0	80.2	56.0
Southern Asia	51.9	76.4	26.3	54.0	79.2	27.7
Europe and Central Asia	53.6	61.3	46.5	58.5	67.0	50.8
Northern, Southern and Western Europe	51.9	57.8	46.3	57.7	64.2	51.5
Eastern Europe	55.9	63.4	49.4	59.7	68.0	52.6
Latin America and the Caribbean	60.0	73.2	47.3	64.2	77.7	51.4
Northern America	59.0	64.8	53.4	62.4	68.6	56.4

* Proportion of working population that is employed.
# Includes Oceania.
Source: ILO Modelled Estimates 2018 (ILOSTAT. www.ilo.org/ilostat).

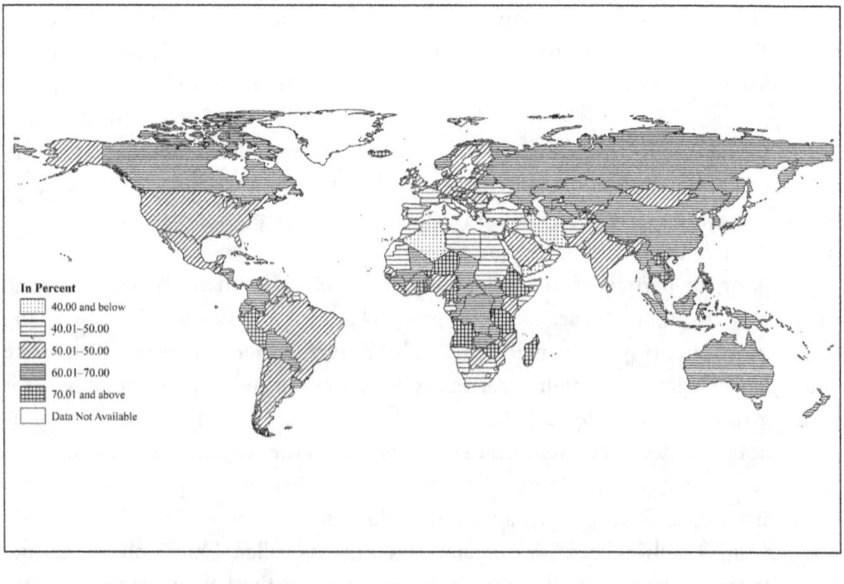

MAP 9.1 Proportion population (age 15 years and above) in employment in the world, 2015

Source: ILO, Modelled Estimates on Employment to Population Ratio 2018.

As noted earlier, in order to get a holistic picture it is necessary to look at percentage distribution of the workforce across different sectors of economy. We have already seen that economic activities are grouped under five sectors but in view of the nature of data available, the present discussion is confined to a three-fold classification. Table 9.2 presents workforce structure of the world population and select major regions in the year 2017. At the aggregate level, agriculture still provides employment to more than one-fourth of the total workers. Industries accommodate another one-fifth while services provide employment to more than half of the total workers in the world (Figure 9.1). A marked contrast in workforce structure can be seen between developed and less developed parts of the world. In high-income regions of the world, nearly three-fourths of the workforce is engaged in services. The corresponding figure for Northern America is 79 per cent. Remarkably in North America, services and industries account for as much as 98 per cent of the total workforce. In the European Union also services and industries account for 72 per cent and 14 per cent of the workforce, thus leaving only 4 per cent in agriculture. Countries like Luxembourg, the Netherlands, the United Kingdom and Sweden in north and north-west Europe, Hong Kong and Singapore in East Asia report more than eight-tenths of their workforce engaged in the service sector alone. Agriculture and its allied activities in these regions account for less than one-tenth of the total employment. Although at the aggregate level 22 per cent of the workforce in the world is engaged in industries, some countries in the Middle East, Northern Africa, Central and Western Asia and adjacent Eastern Europe have more than one-third of their workforce in the industrial sector. On the whole, in as many

TABLE 9.2 Percentage of total employment in agriculture, industries and services in the world and major regions, 2017

World/Major Regions	*Percentage Share of Workers**		
	Agriculture	*Industries*	*Services*
World	26	22	51
High Income	3	23	74
Low Income	68	10	22
Middle East and Northern Africa	18	29	54
Sub-Saharan Africa	57	11	31
South Asia	43	23	34
East Asia and Pacific	21	25	54
Europe and Central Asia	9	25	66
European Union	4	24	72
Latin America and the Caribbean	14	21	64
Northern America	2	19	79
Coefficient of variation#	93.22	45.14	38.40

* ILO Modelled Estimates.

Based on estimates available for 185 countries.

Source: World Bank (https://data.worldbank.org/indicator/SL.AGR.EMP.ZS; accessed on 15–01–2019).

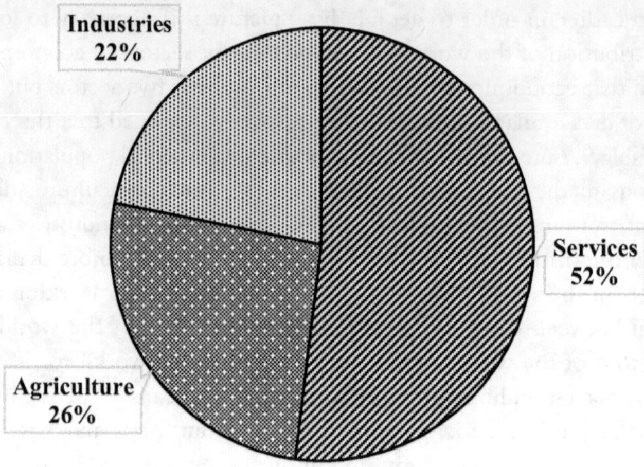

FIGURE 9.1 Percentage employment in agriculture, industries and services in the world, 2017

Source: Author.

as 89 countries out of a total of 185 countries for which data are available, more than nine-tenths of the workforce is outside agriculture. Most of these countries are located in developed realms of the world.

Contrary to the situation in developed parts, a persisting dependence on agriculture for employment in less developed regions is evidently clear (see Map 9.2). In Sub-Saharan Africa agriculture provides employment to as high as 57 per cent workers. Countries like Burundi, Chad, Central African Republic, Malawi, Eritrea, Guinea-Bissau and Congo Democratic Republic are marked with more than 80 per cent of the workforce in agriculture. In South Asia also, agriculture holds a significant place in terms of employment. The only country with at least seven-tenths of the workforce engaged in agriculture outside Africa is Nepal in South Asia. The other country in the region is Afghanistan with above 62 per cent workforce in this sector. India and Pakistan report a little over 40 per cent of workforce in agricultural pursuits.

An interesting feature of the spatial structure of economy across the globe is revealed in values of coefficient of variation of the three sectors of economy (last row in Table 9.2). As seen, per cent workers in agriculture shows the largest range of variation across the world followed by industries and services. The largest range of variation in the case of agriculture should also be viewed in terms of variations in geographical conditions viz. topography, soil types, climatic conditions etc. that determine suitability of an area for agriculture. What is interesting to note is the fact that 'service sector' reveals the lowest range of variation across the globe. In fact, significant rural to urban migration in search of job opportunities in less developed parts of the world and resultant growth of the informal sector in terms of employment reduces the gaps in share of

MAP 9.2 Percentage employment in agriculture in the world, 2017

Source: World Bank, *World Development Indicators, 2018.*

workforce in services between more developed and less developed regions of the world.

Economic characteristics of India's population

Census of India is an important source of data on workers and workforce structure. It classifies population into two broad categories – workers and non-workers. Anyone who has worked or participated in any economically productive activity with or without compensation, wages or profit, anytime during the preceding one year (i.e. reference period) from the date of enumeration is categorised as *workers*. Those who did not work at all are classified as *non-workers* by the census (Bhagat, 2008:4). Workers are further categorised into *main workers* and *marginal workers* depending upon whether or not a person has worked for a major part of the year. If someone has worked for more than 183 days, he or she is classified as a main worker and if less than 183 days he or she is classified as a marginal worker. The later refers to what has been known as *partial unemployment* in the economy (Raj, 1959:258). The concept of work and division into main and marginal workers has remained unchanged since the 1981 census. It may be borne in mind that in terms of CWPR i.e. share of workers in population of all ages, India with barely 40 per cent of its population (main and marginal workers combined) as workers in 2011 ranks one of the lowest in the world. Another characteristic feature of India's population is a very low participation of women in economic activities. Crude participation rate of women for 2011 works out to be as low as 25 per cent. India is a patriarchal society, and women's involvement in jobs outside the four walls of home has traditionally been restricted. However, the recent past has witnessed significant increase in involvement of females in economically gainful activities. As crude activity rates also include children and old age people, they are not an accurate estimate of work participation.

When only adult population is taken into account, participation rate in the country works out to be 65.4 per cent – 87 per cent for males and 43 per cent for females (Table 9.3). It may also be seen that WPR in the country has uninterruptedly increased over time – from 59.5 per cent in 1981 to 65.4 per cent in 2011. This implies that the workforce has managed to grow at a faster pace than growth in population. It is at the same time also true that growth in marginal workers has been much faster than that in main workers particularly in the post–1990s period. There is a sudden jump in the share of marginal workers from 8.7 per cent in 1991 to 21.2 per cent in 2001 and 32.1 per cent in 2011. Interestingly, this increase is more conspicuous in the case of male marginal workers. It is important to note that more than 65 per cent of the net gain in size of the workforce between 1991 and 2011 is contributed by marginal workers. This is indicative of the fact that growth in opportunities for regular employment is not commensurate with growth in the number of job aspirants, leading to more dependence on temporary activities which fall under the 'marginal' category. In other words, the incidence of *underemployment* in the economy has grown at a significant pace. According to Census of India 2011, nearly half of the total marginal workers (about 62 per cent of male marginal workers) are seeking/available for work. Besides, the proportion of non-workers age 15–59 years and seeking or available for work, a proxy indicator of the magnitude of unemployment, also indicates a worsening situation in the post–1991 census period.

In terms of workforce or occupational structure, India's economy is still heavily dependent on primary activities. As per the 2011 census, more than half of the main workforce age 15–59 years is engaged in the primary sector (Table 9.4). As

TABLE 9.3 Trends in work participation, share of marginal workers and proportion non-workers seeking/available for work in India, 1981–2011 (age 15–59 years)

Census Years	*Workers* (% total population)*			*Marginal workers (% total workers)*			*Non-workers Seeking/ Available for work*		
	Total	*Male*	*Female*	*Total*	*Male*	*Female*	*Total*	*Male*	*Female*
1981	59.5	85.3	31.8	8.7	1.6	29.0	-	-	-
1991	60.2	82.8	35.9	8.7	0.9	28.0	4.7	11.0	2.8
2001	61.1	80.7	40.0	21.2	11.7	41.7	17.8	32.2	12.8
2011	65.4	86.6	43.1	32.1	24.8	47.6	18.2	26.9	15.0

Sources: Census of India 1981, *General Economic Tables*, Table B-1Part III-A (i); Census of India 1991, *General Economic Tables*, Table B(S) 1Part-IIIB series; Census of India 2001 and 2011, *General Economic Tables*, Table B-1.

Notes: *. Main and marginal workers put together.

TABLE 9.4 Percentage distribution of main and marginal workers in primary, secondary and tertiary activities in India, 2011

Total/ Rural/ Urban	*Percentage Distribution of Workforce Age 15–59 Years*								
	Persons			*Male*			*Female*		
	Primary	*Secondary*	*Tertiary*	*Primary*	*Secondary*	*Tertiary*	*Primary*	*Secondary*	*Tertiary*
Main Workers									
Total	51.2	17.4	31.4	47.6	19.2	33.3	62.2	12.1	25.7
Rural	72.2	10.8	16.9	69.6	12.1	18.3	79.0	7.7	13.3
Urban	8.8	30.6	60.6	8.3	31.8	59.9	11.2	25.3	63.4
Marginal Workers									
Total	70.7	13.3	16.0	65.1	17.1	17.8	76.1	9.7	14.2
Rural	79.0	10.5	10.4	75.1	13.4	11.5	82.5	8.0	9.5
Urban	19.1	30.5	50.5	17.4	34.5	48.1	21.7	24.1	54.2

Source: Census of India, 2011, *General Economic Tables*, Tables B-4 and B-6.

Note: While primary activities include agriculture and allied activities along with mining and quarrying, secondary activities refer to manufacturing and construction. All other activities are included in tertiary activities.

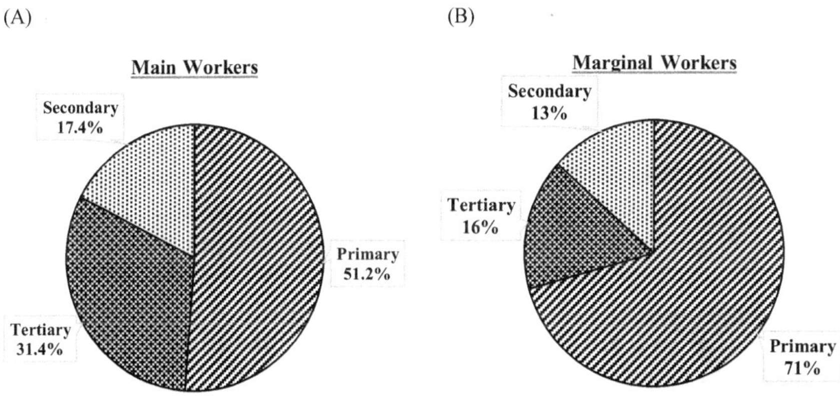

FIGURE 9.2 Per cent distribution of workforce in primary, secondary and tertiary activities in India, 2011

Source: Author.

is expected, the dependence on primary activities is of even a greater magnitude among marginal workforce in the country (see Figure 9.2). Male-female differentials in workforce structure are also on expected lines. The share of female workers is higher in primary activities as compared to male workers in both 'main' and 'marginal' categories. Interestingly, however, in urban areas the share in tertiary activities among female workers is larger than that among its male counterpart. It may be noted that in urban economy secondary activities hold a significant place. In manufacturing-related activities, representation of women is relatively limited as a result of which their share in secondary activities is less than that of males. Further, in the recent past the service sector has witnessed increased involvement of females particularly in low-paid activities. This process is sometimes called as *feminisation* of the workforce.

The occupational structure of population in the country has undergone significant change during the post-independence period. Between 1981 and 2011, proportion adult workers (i.e. age 15–59 years) in the primary sector has come down from 67.6 per cent (excluding Assam where no census was held due to the disturbed situation) to 51 per cent with corresponding increase in the secondary sector from 13.6 per cent to 17.4 per cent, and in the tertiary sector from 18.9 per cent to 31.4 per cent. Obviously, the service sector has been the largest gainer of decline in proportion workers in agriculture and allied activities. This transformation of workforce structure needs to be looked at with caution. In fact, just as elsewhere in less developed parts of the world, a significant part of the labour force shifting from the rural sector to the urban sector ends up in service sectors, mainly in 'informal' and 'unorganised' activities since industries are not quite able to absorb them. This process has been known as *tertiarisation* of economy.

Regional Dimension: Table 9.5 presents a summary of economic characteristics of population based on the 2011 census. A quick glance reveals a wide regional variation across states and union territories. WPR among adult population varies from a high of over 71 per cent in Chhattisgarh to a low of only 42 per cent in Lakshadweep. Chhattisgarh along with Rajasthan and Madhya Pradesh covering a vast stretch of land from the west to north-eastern parts of peninsular plateaus report higher work participation than the nation's average. Besides, the hilly states of Himachal Pradesh in the north, and Sikkim, Mizoram and Nagaland in the east and north-east also report higher work participation rates among adult population. Remarkably, the union territories of Dadra and Nagar Haveli and Daman & Diu also have higher work participation rates. The regional variation in work participation rates becomes still sharper when analysed at district-level data (Map 9.3). In general, higher work participation rates can be seen in the tribal-dominated areas in the interior uplands as well as the hills of the north and north-east with difficult terrain and subsistence agriculture. The arid and semi-arid areas of Rajasthan provide contiguity in the west to the region of high work participation in the central upland plateaus. Apparently economic exigencies in these areas force more and more adults to join the workforce for sustenance. On the other extreme, almost the entire stretch of the northern plains from Punjab in the north to lower reaches of Ganga plain in the east is marked with low participation of its adults in economic activities. The coastal districts, in general, are characterised by lower participation rates than the interior uplands.

It is important to note that both main and marginal workers are included in workforce participation rate. Referring back to Table 9.3, it is seen that marginal workers constitute a little less than one-third of the workforce in India at the aggregate level in 2011. On the whole, barring only Lakshadweep, all the union territories are marked with lower share of marginal workers in the workforce. Needless

TABLE 9.5 Economic characteristics of population (age 15–59 years) in states and union territories in India, 2011

States/ Union Territories	*Work* Participation Rate*	*Marginal Workers as % to Total Workers*	*Percentage Seeking/ Available for Work*		*Percentage Distribution of Main Workers*		
			Marginal Workers	*Non-Workers*	*Primary Sector*	*Secondary Sector*	*Tertiary Sector*
Andhra Pradesh	64.9	15.5	48.2	14.6	58.8	14.7	26.4
Arunachal Pradesh	64.4	17.1	43.7	23.9	57.6	8.9	33.5
Assam	57.1	27.0	48.2	28.9	56.0	11.6	32.4
Bihar	54.5	38.1	55.0	16.0	69.5	8.5	22.0
Chhattisgarh	71.4	31.2	55.0	15.7	68.3	10.0	21.7
Goa	54.4	17.0	47.7	24.8	10.6	24.5	64.9
Gujarat	59.3	17.2	25.5	7.0	47.6	23.4	29.0
Haryana	52.0	20.8	45.7	13.6	41.6	18.6	39.8
Himachal Pradesh	70.3	39.3	47.2	22.2	47.0	15.1	38.0
Jammu and Kashmir	52.6	37.4	52.8	29.0	28.9	12.6	58.5
Jharkhand	62.2	46.9	58.8	18.8	50.6	18.1	31.3
Karnataka	63.9	15.7	26.1	10.9	50.5	18.8	30.7
Kerala	49.4	19.1	52.8	34.5	24.4	28.8	46.8
Madhya Pradesh	66.1	27.4	53.3	14.5	65.9	11.8	22.3
Maharashtra	61.8	10.9	40.9	10.2	50.0	17.5	32.5
Manipur	64.7	24.5	45.9	30.6	53.5	11.4	35.1
Meghalaya	64.5	21.1	38.0	20.7	60.9	7.5	31.6
Mizoram	66.0	13.8	34.0	20.4	56.6	7.2	36.2
Nagaland	70.0	20.3	36.8	24.1	59.9	6.1	34.0
Odisha	60.7	38.4	57.6	23.9	54.5	16.4	29.1
Punjab	49.4	14.0	49.2	15.8	35.9	23.3	40.8
Rajasthan	67.6	28.2	45.1	15.1	59.0	15.0	26.0
Sikkim	68.5	23.2	26.8	19.5	41.5	13.2	45.3
Tamil Nadu	61.6	14.5	35.5	17.1	40.7	25.2	34.1
Tripura	56.9	26.5	71.9	45.6	44.9	16.4	38.7
Uttar Pradesh	50.1	31.7	47.3	13.6	56.3	15.1	28.6
Uttarakhand	56.2	24.4	49.2	15.1	44.1	14.1	41.8
West Bengal	54.1	25.8	69.8	43.5	41.3	22.3	36.3
A and N Islands	54.8	16.9	51.4	30.0	20.1	18.1	61.8
Chandigarh	53.5	4.2	46.1	13.6	1.6	21.8	76.6
Dadra and Nagar Haveli	67.4	16.3	20.5	9.1	21.9	54.6	23.5
Daman & Diu	66.5	3.8	26.3	11.8	8.6	67.2	24.2
Lakshadweep	42.2	42.0	80.8	47.7	6.5	18.4	75.1
NCT of Delhi	47.8	4.8	44.4	10.4	1.3	24.4	74.3
Puducherry	50.3	9.7	39.5	16.0	18.5	23.0	58.5

* Main and marginal workers combined.

Sources: Census of India, 2011, *General Economic Tables*, Tables B-1 and B-4.

Note: While primary activities include agriculture and allied activities along with mining and quarrying, secondary activities refer to manufacturing and construction. All other activities are included in tertiary activities.

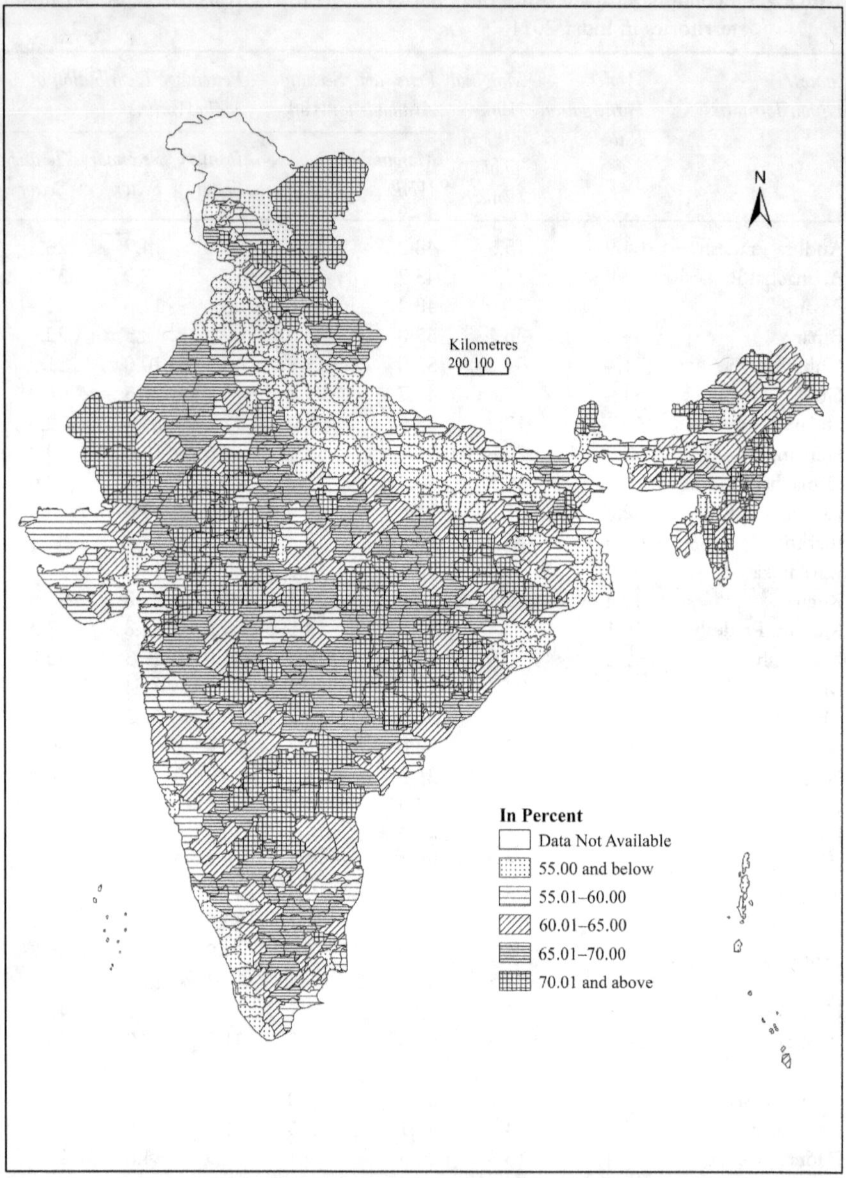

MAP 9.3 Work participation rate (age 15–59 years) in India, 2011 – main and marginal workers combined

Source: Census of India, 2011

to mention that proportion marginal workers in the workforce is indicative of underemployment in an area. Remarkably, the entire southern part of the Indian sub-continent is characterised by a relatively lower magnitude of underemployment. Outside this region, Punjab in the north and Gujarat in the west also report relatively lower share of marginal workers in the workforce. Besides, other two states in north-eastern parts of the country viz. Arunachal Pradesh and Mizoram also report lower share of marginal workers. On the other extreme, in Jharkhand as much as 47 per cent of the workforce comprises marginal workers who on an average find work for less than 6 months in a year only. In other words, a little less than half of the workforce in this state is underemployed. Jharkhand is followed by Himachal Pradesh, Odisha, Bihar and Jammu and Kashmir with respect to the magnitude of 'underemployment' in that order. The magnitude of underemployment is also revealed by the fact that a majority of marginal workers in these states are seeking or are available for work. In Jharkhand as many as 6 out of every 10 marginal workers are reported to be looking for work. Out of a total of 24 districts in Jharkhand, in as many as 22 a majority of marginal workers want some work. Likewise, in 33 districts out of 38 in Bihar, and 25 out of 30 in Odisha, half or more of the marginal workers are reported as 'seeking' or 'available' for work. These three states form a contiguous region in the eastern part of the country. On the whole, there are 262 districts in the country where 50 per cent or more of the marginal workers are reported as seeking or available for work. With only about half of the marginal workers of the country, these districts account for more than 60 per cent of the job seekers in the said category.

The extent of unemployment in India's population is revealed in the fact that a little over 18 per cent of the adult population which is outside the workforce is reported as seeking or available for jobs at the time of the 2011 census. In West Bengal and Tripura more than 40 per cent of non-workers in the adult age group are looking for jobs. Interestingly, of the 25 districts with more than 40 per cent of non-workers seeking jobs, as many as 16 are situated in West Bengal alone. Unemployment of the same magnitude is also seen in Lakshadweep, a union territory. Among the major states Kerala comes next in terms of prevalence of unemployment.

In terms of workforce structure also there is a wide regional variation in the country. As already noted at the aggregate level primary activities provide employment to a major part of the main workforce in the country. The dependence on the primary sector for employment is even of a higher magnitude in states like Bihar, Chhattisgarh and Madhya Pradesh. Among the major states, they are followed by Rajasthan and Uttar Pradesh. The *terai* areas of plains in Bihar and Uttar Pradesh in the north, Chhattisgarh and its adjoining districts in Odisha, and a major part of Madhya Pradesh and adjoining areas in Rajasthan report significantly greater dependence on primary activities (Map 9.4). Agriculture and its allied activities provide employment to more than eight-tenths of the main workforce in many districts in these areas. In addition, interior Maharashtra and parts of Andhra Pradesh and Karnataka also exhibit dominance of primary activities. With difficult terrain, agriculture in these areas, particularly in the central upland plateaus, is largely rain-fed and subsistence in nature. Scheduled tribes form a significant proportion of the population, and a sizeable portion of them sustain on forest resources as a source of livelihood. With very small share of population in urban centres, these areas are characterised by very low level of development.

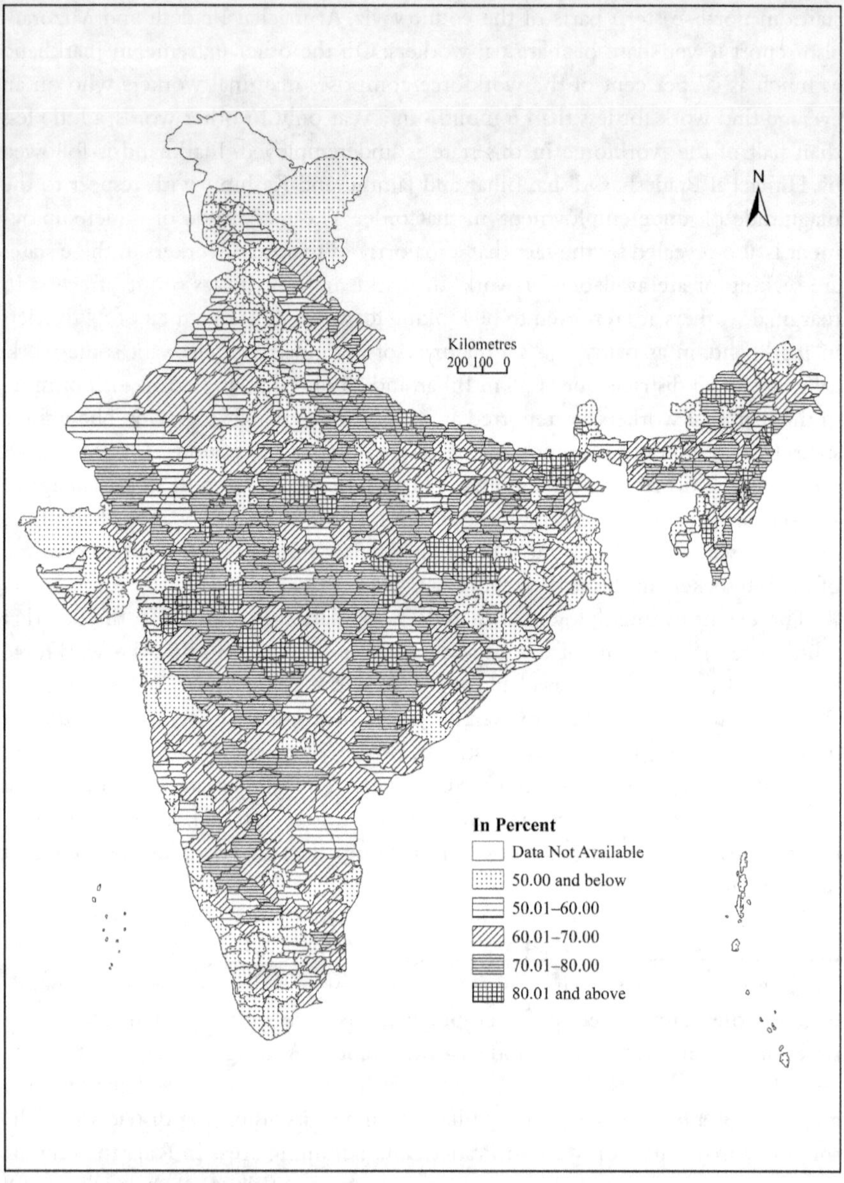

MAP 9.4 Proportion main workforce (age 15–59 years) engaged in primary activities in India, 2011

Source: Census of India, 2011

Secondary activities provide employment to only around 17 per cent of the main workers in India at the aggregate level. However, in the union territories of Dadar & Nagar Haveli and Daman & Diu, which account for a very small share of population in the country, a majority of main workers get employment in activities like manufacturing and construction. Among the states, Kerala with nearly 29 per cent of main workforce in secondary activities tops the list. Kerala is followed by Tamil Nadu and Goa. On the other extreme, in Bihar, one of the least developed states in the country, less than 10 per cent of its workforce is engaged in secondary activities. Chhattisgarh and Madhya Pradesh, the other two backward states, are only marginally ahead of Bihar. Besides, in the hilly states of the north and north-east a very limited contribution of secondary sectors in employment is visible. Although widely located on the Indian sub-continent, districts with a relatively larger share of workforce in secondary activities tend to concentrate in and around major industrial regions of the country. The most prominent of such concentration can be seen in Kerala and adjoining areas of Tamil Nadu; Pune-Mumbai-Ahmedabad belt in the west; Haora-Hugli-Kolkata region in the east; Dhanbad-Bokaro region on the Chhotanagpur plateau; western uplands of Odisha; a major part of Punjab; and NCT of Delhi and its close vicinity. Beyond these regions, pockets of higher share of secondary workforce can be seen scattered elsewhere. Many of these pockets are centred in or near the capital cities like Bangalore, Hyderabad, Bhopal, Lucknow, Jaipur, etc. or industrial centres like Nagpur, Jabalpur, Indore, Kanpur Nagar, Varanasi etc. Besides, a larger share in secondary activities is also over the Kutch peninsula in the west, which largely owes its existence to salt-making activities.

It is generally argued that growth in activities in the secondary sector inherently leads to expansion in the service sector. Going back to Table 9.3, it may be seen that 32 per cent of the main workers in the country are engaged in tertiary activities. A majority of workforce in the service sector in the union territories (barring only Dadar & Nagar Haveli and Daman & Diu), including NCT of Delhi which enjoys a special status of state, is understandable. Among the states Goa tops the list with as much as 65 per cent of its main workforce engaged in services. Goa is followed by Jammu and Kashmir, Kerala, Sikkim and Uttarakhand. It is apparent that tourism as an industry plays an important role in the economy of these states and that explains a relatively larger share of workforce in the service sector. In fact, all the other hilly states in the north and north-east report higher share of workforce in the service sector than the average for India as a whole. Among the major states with a larger share of workforce in the service sector than the national average, mention may be made of Punjab, Haryana, West Bengal and Tamil Nadu. Interestingly, the district-level pattern in share of workers in the tertiary sector is to a great extent identical to the one related to the secondary sector. The only mismatch can be seen in the case of hilly areas where the tourism industry translates into larger share in the tertiary sector while the secondary sector remains negligible in terms of employment. Thus, to conclude it can be said that areas marked with a high level of urbanisation, industrialisation and commercial activities show a relatively larger proportion of workforce in the service sector. It cannot, however, be negated that a part of this workforce, particularly in large urban centres, is engaged in informal and unorganised activities.

10 FERTILITY

Fertility, one of the three components of population dynamics (the others being mortality and migration) holds a very important place in any population study. A positive force in population dynamics, fertility is responsible for biological replacement and continuation of human society. Fertility levels determine the age structure of a population, which in turn governs the social, economic and demographic characteristics of the population. The interest in the study of fertility also arises because it is a very complex phenomenon affected by a host of social, cultural, psychological, economic and political variables. The success of any population programmes, thus, depends upon a proper understanding of interplay between fertility and other variables.

Fertility refers to the number of live births relating to a woman, or a group of women. It is the actual performance and should not be confused with fecundity, which refers to the physiological capacity to reproduce. Since it is not possible to measure the actual reproductive capacity of a woman, fecundity can only be assessed with the help of the maximum levels of fertility (or natural fertility) ever observed in a non-contraceptive population (Misra, 1982:160).

Data on fertility are available mainly from Vital Registration or Civil Registration Systems. Besides, the periodic census counts and sample surveys also provide data on fertility. The data from the vital registration system relate to each calendar year. In the national periodic census, a direct question on 'the number of children ever born' is asked of ever married women, which forms an important source of data on the aspect. In countries where vital or civil registration is not accurate, a question on the number of birth to ever married women during the preceding 12 months is asked during the census enumeration. In India such a question was asked in the 1971 census, and the same has continued in the subsequent censuses also. There are various demographic sample surveys such as National Family Health

Survey (NFHS) which provide data on fertility-related aspects that are not ordinarily available in civil registration or periodic census counts.

Measures of fertility analysis

Fertility measures are devices to quantify the fertility performance of a population over a period of time. These measures are used to compare fertility behaviour of different populations, and to examine the trends in fertility of a population over a period of time. These measures can be grouped into two categories – the direct measures and the indirect measures. While in the former, data on live births are directly used, in the latter an estimate is indirectly arrived at using some other demographic characteristics such as age distribution of population. The latter is a recourse when direct data on number of live births are either inaccurate or unavailable.

Direct measures

Crude Birth Rate (CBR) is one of the most commonly used measures of fertility because of its simplicity in concept and measurement. It is the ratio between the total registered live births in a population during a calendar year and the mid-year population. Crude birth rate is calculated in the following manner:

$$\text{Crude Birth Rate} = \left(B/P\right) K \tag{10.1}$$

where B is the number of live births in a calendar year, P is the mid-year population, and K is a constant which is generally taken as 1,000 in all the measures except otherwise mentioned. CBR is thus the number of live births per 1,000 persons in a calendar year. It is an important measure of fertility as it directly points to the contribution of fertility to the growth rate of population.

However, as the name suggests, CBR is only a crude measure and suffers from various limitations. Since both the numerator and denominator in Equation (10.1) get affected through births, CBR tends to underplay changes in fertility (Ramakumar, 1986:87). Further, in the computation of CBR, total population of an area is taken in the denominator. It is, however, important to note that every individual in the population (of all ages and sexes) is not exposed to the risk of reproduction. *General Fertility Rate* (GFR), an improvement over CBR, therefore, takes into account only female population in the childbearing age groups or *reproductive span* (i.e. 15 to 44 or 49 years). GFR is, thus, defined as the ratio between the total live births and number of women in the reproductive age span. It is calculated as under:

$$\text{General Fertility Rate } \left(\text{GFR}\right) = \left(B \,/\, W_{15-44}\right) K \tag{10.2}$$

where W_{15-44} is the mid-year population of women in the reproductive ages. Necessary modification can be made where the upper limit of the reproductive span is taken as 49 years.

Apart from age, marital status is also a very important differential factor in fertility. In almost all the societies of the world birth is allowed only in a marital bond. It would, therefore, be more appropriate to consider only the currently married women, and not all women, in the reproductive ages. A measure calculated in this manner is termed as *General Marital Fertility Rate* (GMFR) and can be mathematically expressed as:

$$\text{General Marital Fertility Rate (GMFR)} = \left(B / W^{m}_{15-44}\right) K, \qquad (10.3)$$

where W^{m}_{15-44} is the mid-year number of married women in the reproductive ages.

Though a refinement over CBR, GFR also suffers from certain limitations. The measure considers entire the female population in the reproductive ages as a homogenous group, whereas the fecundity of women is not uniform over the period. Thus, GFR is also a crude rate. *Age Specific Fertility Rate* (ASFR) takes care of this problem. ASFR is calculated in the following manner:

$$\text{Age Specific Fertility Rate (ASFR)} = \left({}_{n}B_{x} / {}_{n}W_{x}\right) K, \qquad (10.4)$$

where ${}_{n}B_{x}$ is the number of live births to women in the age group x to x + n, and ${}_{n}W_{x}$ is the mid-year number of women in the age group x to x + n.

Note that this measure can also be worked out with reference to only currently married women in a particular age group. In this case it is termed as the *Age Specific Marital Fertility Rate* (ASMFR) and is expressed as:

$$\text{Age Specific Marital Fertility Rate (ASMFR)} = \left({}_{n}B_{x} / {}_{n}W^{m}{}_{x}\right) / K, \qquad (10.5)$$

where ${}_{n}W^{m}{}_{x}$ is the mid-year number of married women in the age group x to x + n.

Since there is a possibility of a greater incidence of unmarried women in the early age groups, and divorced, separated and widowed women in the older age brackets of the reproductive age span, ASMFR provides a more real picture of fertility levels in a population.

ASFR can be worked out for single-year age data as well as for broad age groups. Usually, the reproductive age span is divided into five-year age groups, numbering six or seven depending upon the upper limit of the reproductive age span. This makes any comparison between two or more populations a cumbersome exercise. *Total Fertility Rate* (TFR), a summary measure of ASFR, facilitates such comparison. This is obtained by multiplying the sum of ASFR by the width of the age group, and then dividing the product by the value of radix (i.e. 1.000). Consider the following:

$$\text{Total Fertility Rate (TFR)} = \{(\Sigma \text{ASFR})\, n\}.\ 1/K \qquad (10.6)$$

where 'n' is the width of the age group, and 'K' is the value of the radix.

TFR, thus, refers to the total number of children a woman will produce during her childbearing age span, if she is subjected to a fertility schedule as prescribed by the age-specific fertility rates. The TFR together with the ASFR can be further used to construct several measures that are useful in the study of fertility changes (Ramakumar, 1986:89).

Another measure that reduces the effects of age structure to its minimum, and hence facilitates comparison of fertility levels of two or more populations, is *Sex Age Adjusted Birth Rate* (SAABR). The United Nations has defined it as 'the number of births per 1000 of a weighted sum of the number of women in various five year age groups from 15 to 44' (UN, 1956:42). The UN has recommended a standard set of weights (1, 7, 7, 6, 4 and 1) corresponding to the six five-year age groups in the reproductive age span from 15 to 44 years. These weights are roughly proportional to the typical relative fertility rates of various age groups. These weights were derived on the basis of a study of 52 nations with varying levels of fertility. The SAABR is calculated as under:

$$\text{SAABR} = \left(\frac{\text{B}}{(1\text{xW1}) + (7\text{xW2}) + (7\text{xW3}) + (6\text{xW4}) + (4\text{xW5}) + (1\text{xW6})} \right) \tag{10.7}$$

where B is the number of live births in a calendar year, and W1, W2 . . . W6 are the number of women in the six five-year age groups in the reproductive age span.

In the calculation of TFR [see Equation (10.6)], if only female births are taken into account, the resultant measure will be known as *Gross Reproduction Rate* (GRR). Gross reproduction rate indicates the number of daughters that every woman is likely to bear during her entire childbearing age span, if she is subjected to a fertility schedule as prescribed by given sex- and age-specific fertility rates. Also considered as *replacement index*, this measure is generally used while comparing the current fertility in different populations. The calculation of GRR requires data on the number of live births by sex along with distribution of women in different age groups in the childbearing age span. In case the same are not available, GRR can also be worked out by simply multiplying the TFR by femininity ratio (i.e. ratio between the number of female babies born and the total live births in a population). In India, for instance there are, on an average, 105 male babies born for every 100 female babies. Thus, femininity ratio works out to be 0.4878 (i.e. 100 / 205). In this case GRR will be worked out using the following formula:

$$\text{Gross Reproduction Rate (GRR)} = \text{TFR} \star \text{Femininity Ratio} \tag{10.8}$$

As in the case of TFR, GRR also assumes that women in the reproductive age group will survive till the end of their childbearing period (Weeks, 2018:228). Gross reproduction rate, thus, indicates the number of daughters a woman is expected to produce, if there is no attrition in the cohort due to mortality (Bhende and Kanitkar, 2011:278). This is, however, not a realistic assumption. *Net Reproduction Rate* (NRR), a refinement over GRR, with a component of mortality built into it, allows for decrease due to deaths among mothers. Thus, NRR is the number of daughters ever born to a woman, if she gives birth according to the given schedule of age-specific fertility rates, and experiences given age-specific mortality rates up to the end of her reproductive span. The NRR, thus, measures the extent to which a woman will replace herself by female babies under predetermined schedules of fertility and mortality and is calculated as under (for details refer to Weeks, 2018):

$$NRR = \sum_{k=15}^{45\,or\,49} \left(ASFR(f).\frac{nLx}{5{,}00{,}000}.\text{n} \right) \qquad (10.9)$$

where *ASFR(f)* is age-specific fertility rate with regard to only female babies born, and *nLx* which is obtained from the life table is the number of years lived by a group of women in the age group 'x' to 'x + n'. The denominator is five times the radix of population i.e. 1, 00,000 in a life table (please refer to Chapter 11 for description of the life table). In other words, if single-year age data are being used for computation of NRR, the denominator will be 1, 00,000 and not 5, 00,000. Finally 'n' is the age interval. NRR is generally less than GRR because all the women do not survive all through their reproductive age span and some may die before reaching the end of the span. However, the gap between GRR and NRR depends on prevailing mortality levels in the population. Thus populations with low mortality rates will have very narrow gaps while the ones with high mortality rates will have wide gaps.

Indirect measures

In addition to the measures discussed previously, there are several indirect measures of fertility, which are useful particularly when data on live births are not readily available or are not reliable. These measures arrive at estimates of fertility indirectly using data on age-sex structure, and marital status cross-classified by age and sex. The *Child Women Ratio* and *Female Mean Age at Marriage* are most commonly used indirect measures.

The Child Women Ratio is defined as the number of children under 5 years of age, per 100 women in the reproductive ages. It is expressed in the following manner:

$$\text{Child Women Ratio (CWR)} = \left(P_{0\text{–}4} / W_{15\text{–}44 \text{ or } 49}\right) K \qquad (10.10)$$

where P_{0-4} is the number of children in the age groups 0–4 years, and $W_{15-44 \text{ or } 49}$ is the number of women in the reproductive ages. K is usually taken in this case as 100. As P_{0-4} is the survivors of the children born over the preceding five years, and not the total births, CWR is affected by infant and child mortality. Hence it is not a very accurate measure of fertility. Nevertheless, it may be used as a relative measure to study the fertility performance of different sections of the same population (Barclay, 1958:172).

Age at marriage is said to have significant bearing on the fertility performance of women in a population. If mean age at marriage is low, women start bearing children at an early age. But when the age at marriage is raised, the reproductive span is reduced, and overall fertility level is low. Mean age at marriage, therefore, is taken as a proximate indicator of fertility levels. Based on data on 'proportion single' in different age groups, the measure is known as singulate mean age at marriage (SMAM) and is worked out in the following manner using Hajnal's method (see Chapter 8 also):

$$\text{SMAM} = [\sum_{i=10}^{50} \text{nSx} - \text{Sk}\ (\text{K})]/1 - \text{Sk} \qquad (10.11)$$

where nSx is the proportion of single women in the age x to x + n, Sk is the proportion of single women at age K (i.e. 50 years) and n is the age interval.

Levels and trends in fertility in the world

Before we embark upon the levels and trends of fertility in the world, it should be noted that reliable and accurate data on birth rates are not available for a greater part of the world, particularly for the less developed, or underdeveloped, countries. It becomes, therefore, necessary to depend upon various estimates. The data for developed countries, on the other hand, are more accurate and are available for a longer time in the past. The discussion in the forthcoming section is based on the data drawn from varied sources including publications of the United Nations.

World patterns

Despite significant decline in the recent past, in terms of fertility levels the world is still neatly divided into two parts (Table 10.1). A gap in the fertility levels has always existed between what we know today as developed, particularly the European realm, and less developed parts of the world. However, prior to the Industrial Revolution in the 18th century, this gap was not that large, although fertility levels in Europe were not as high as those of the rest of the world. Even within Europe there existed a wide gap between the eastern and the western parts of the continent. By the time demographic transition came to an end in the West, a sharp contrast in fertility levels between the developed and less developed world became quite apparent. Fertility transition in less developed parts of the world became visible only in the latter half of the 20th century. Initially the decline was confined to some small countries but later spread to population giants like China and India. In recent decades many countries have experienced major reductions in average family size (UN, 2015:5).

According to available estimates the world average crude birth rate was 37 per thousand persons towards the middle of the last century. After a quarter century i.e.

by 1975–80, it became 28 per thousand, and by the end of the last century it came down to 22 per thousand. Thus, over a period of five decades, CBR declined by 15 points. According to the latest estimates of the Population Reference Bureau, average birth rate of the world is 20 per thousand population (PRB, 2017). Total fertility rate for the world works out to be 2.5 children per woman as against 2.8 at the turn of the century. Almost all the decline in TFR during the recent past has occurred in the less developed parts of the world. It has been argued that the decline in fertility levels in less developed parts of the world has occurred without any prior improvements in economic or living conditions, and therefore, the fertility transition appears to have more to do with cultural factors than to economic factors (Robey et al., 1993 quoted in Norton and Mercier, 2016). Improvement in the education and lives of women along with increased availability and use of modern contraceptive methods had important bearings on fertility decline. Notwithstanding the significant transition in fertility levels, a significant contrast still persists between the developed and less developed world. While the former reports one of the lowest birth rates, the latter, particularly in Africa and parts of Asia, are still characterised by very high birth rates. On an average, the more developed countries report a crude birth rate that is nearly half of those prevailing in the less developed parts of the world (Table 10.1). If we exclude China, the average crude birth rate in the less developed parts of the world works out to be still higher. Likewise, total fertility rate in the less developed countries is more than one and a half times higher than that in the developed countries.

Africa ranks very high in the world in terms of fertility levels, followed by Western and South-central Asia. Latin America and the Caribbean come next (Map 10.1).

TABLE 10.1 Crude birth rate and total fertility rate for the world and major regions, 2003 and 2017

World/Major Regions	*Crude Birth Rate (CBR)*		*Total Fertility Rate (TFR)*	
	2003	*2017*	*2003*	*2017*
Africa	38	35	5.2	4.6
Asia	20	18	2.6	2.2
Europe	10	11	1.4	1.6
Latin America and the Caribbean	23	17	2.7	2.1
North America	14	12	2.0	1.8
Oceania	18	16	2.4	2.3
More developed	11	11	1.5	1.6
Less developed	24	21	3.1	2.6
Less developed (excl. China)	28	24	3.5	2.9
World average	22	20	2.8	2.5

Source: Population Reference Bureau, World Population Data Sheet, 2003 and 2017.

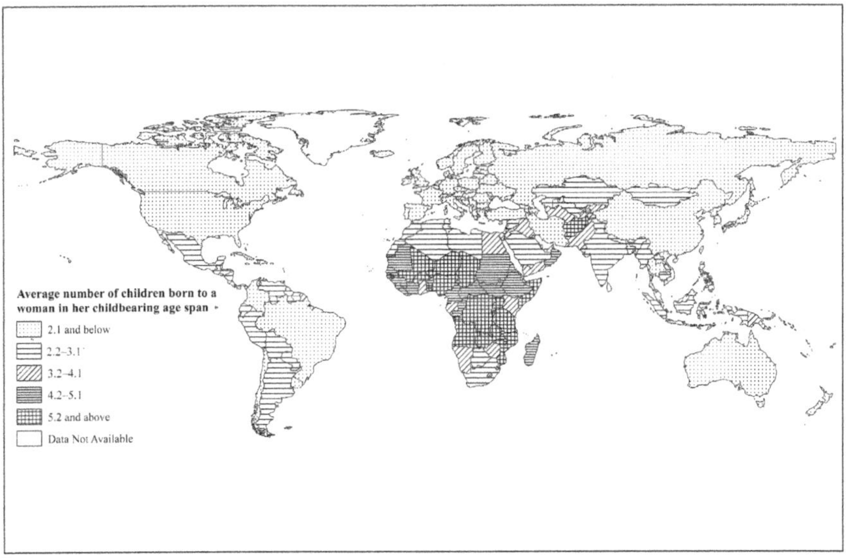

MAP 10.1 Total fertility rate in the world, 2017

Source: Population Reference Bureau, *World Population Data Sheet, 2017*

Within Africa also a wide range of variation can be seen in fertility levels from one part of the continent to the other. On an average, countries in southern and northern parts of the continent fare relatively better than the rest of Africa. The poorest countries located in the western and central parts of Africa report significantly higher birth rates, more than twice as that of the world average. Prominent among them are Niger and Mali in Western Africa, and Angola, Chad and Democratic Republic of Congo in Middle Africa. Total fertility rate in this part of Africa is still more than 6 children per woman. Asia comes next to Africa in terms of fertility levels. The western and south-central parts of the continent are conspicuous with high birth rates. West Asia, mainly the Arab states, which ranked next to African countries till the recent past, have witnessed remarkable improvement. Total fertility rate in the region has come down from an average of 4 in 2003 to 2.8 in 2017. Countries like Saudi Arabia, Yemen, Palestinian Territory and Iraq were marked with TFR of more than 5 children per woman at the turn of the century. In Yemen, TFR was as high as 7 in 2003. Currently, however, only Iraq, Yemen and Palestinian Territory report TFR above 4 and many countries have below replacement-level fertility. Afghanistan, with a total fertility rate of 6 children, a figure quite comparable with countries in Middle Africa, ranks first in the region. The other countries with reasonably high fertility rates in the region are Pakistan, Bhutan and Nepal. The eastern and south-eastern parts of Asia report relatively lower levels of fertility. In East Asia, all the countries have already reached below replacement-level fertility. In Southeast Asia countries like Cambodia, Laos, the Philippines, and Timor-Leste still have a crude birth rate above 20 per thousand. Africa and Asia are followed by Latin America and the Caribbean islands and Oceania. On the other extreme, the whole of Europe, North America (excluding Mexico), Russia, Australia and New Zealand report fertility rates which are below replacement level. Europe, which reports the lowest fertility levels, has experienced a marginal increase in crude birth rate during the recent past. It is remarkable to note that with some exceptions all the Caribbean island countries, and Iran, Sri Lanka, Bhutan, Thailand, Malaysia and Singapore in South and Southeast Asia, have attained replacement-level fertility due to a significant decline in the birth rates in the recent past.

On the basis of current fertility levels, the world is usually categorised in three groups. The first group, representing 'low fertility', is characterised by TFR below replacement level and includes the whole of Europe, North America (minus Mexico), and select countries from low fertility areas from other parts of the world. This group accounts for nearly half of the world population in 2019 (UN, 2019:27). Likewise 'intermediate fertility' accounts for another 40 per cent of the world population. By 2050, this share is expected to be below 30 per cent. TFR in this group ranges from 2.1 to 4, and is represented by countries from different parts of the world – some of the largest being India, Indonesia, Pakistan, Bangladesh, Mexico and the Philippines. And finally, a little more than one-tenth of the world population – down from over one-third in 1990 – is represented by a third group including countries mostly from Sub-Saharan Africa with 'high fertility' i.e. TFR above 4 children per women.

Trends in world fertility

Evidences indicate that world crude birth rates remained very high until the beginning of the 19th century. The world pattern of fertility levels, however, was marked with significant spatial variation even before the process of fertility transition set in. Northern and Western Europe in general had lower birth rates than elsewhere in the world at the turn of the 19th century. For instance, Norway, Sweden, France and the United Kingdom reported birth rates of below 40 per thousand persons even in the 18th century. As against this, the United States, the erstwhile USSR and other European countries reported birth rates well above 40 per thousand towards the end of the 18th century.

The transition from high fertility to low fertility started in north-western Europe in the 19th century. The process, however, did not set in simultaneously in all the countries. There are indications that France was the first country to have experienced a decline in the birth rate (Beaujeu-Garnier, 1978:34; Woods, 1979:136; Bhende and Kanitkar, 2011:299). The process of fertility transition in France is said to have set in during the 1830s. France was followed by Ireland which started experiencing a decline in fertility in the 1840s (Bhende and Kanitkar, 2011:300). Woods (1979) suggests that in France the decline in fertility levels had started as early as in the late 18th century. Fertility transition then gradually spread to other European countries towards the end of the 19th century and the beginning of the 20th century. By the end of the 19th century, crude birth rates had already reached in the range of 20–25 per thousand in countries like France and Ireland. In the

United Kingdom birth rates were somewhat higher but less than 30 per thousand. Within the national boundary of these countries also there were some disparities between urban and rural segments and between different social classes (Woods, 1979:136). The process of fertility transition was somewhat slow in Central and Eastern Europe. Catholic tradition, mainly rural economy and sometimes, as in Italy for example, a Fascist policy in favour of large families, acted against a rapid decline in birth rates (Beaujeu-Garnier, 1978:143). During the period 1900–1904, in countries like Italy, Romania, Bulgaria and the erstwhile USSR, birth rates were as high as 32.6, 39.6, 40.7 and 47.2 per thousand respectively. The conditions, however, changed drastically thereafter. From 1920–24 to 1970 the crude birth rates declined from 30.1 to 16.8 in Italy (a level almost comparable to that in France), 37.6 to 21.1 in Romania, 39.6 to 16.3 in Bulgaria and 38.2 to 17.4 in the erstwhile USSR.

Outside Europe, across the Atlantic in North America also, particularly in the United States and Canada, the fertility transition began only in the latter half of the 19th century. In the United States, for instance, the birth rate, which was as high as 42 to 43 in 1850, recorded a steady decline and reached the mark of 35 by 1878. Between 1930 and 1934 the crude birth rate in the United States was only 17.6. A similar trend was experienced in the case of Australia and New Zealand, which were recently populated by white races. Australia and New Zealand had birth rates between 26 and 27 per thousand at the turn of the 20th century which came down to the neighbourhood of 20 by 1930–34.

The only country in Asia which experienced a similar decline in fertility levels in the first half of the 20th century is Japan. The birth rate in Japan was as high as 35 till 1920–24. But it came down to 18.2 during 1955–59 and 17.2 during 1960–64. This is the best national example of a systematic policy of reducing the birth rate (Beaujeu-Garnier, 1978:143).

This transition from high birth rate to low birth rate in the present-day developed countries was, however, not smooth without any interruptions. Most of these countries experienced reversals in the trend of fertility decline during the period following the two wars. In the north-west European countries, for instance in the United Kingdom, birth rates had recorded an increase even during the 19th century at the time of economic transformation (Beaujeu-Garnier, 1978:145). After a decline in the birth rate during 1915–19 (i.e. the period of the First World War), there was a sudden increase in the birth rates in most of the European countries. This was, however, immediately followed by another declining trend, which continued till the period of economic depression in the 1930s. There was another reversal in the trend during and after the Second World War. Countries outside Europe like the United States, Canada, Australia and New Zealand also experienced this reversal. The extent of the increase in birth rates appears to be related to the differential involvement of the Western countries in the war. The *baby boom*, as the term is used for the upsurge in the birth rates, lasted for a longer period in the United States and Canada than in the European countries (Bhende and Kanitkar, 2011:307). This increase in the birth rates after the Second World War is generally attributed to an increase in marriage rates in the period immediately following the war. The women who were already married but who had postponed having babies during the period of economic depression started having them after the war. Further, demobilisation and return of the military personnel to normal life contributed to the baby boom (Bhende and Kanitkar, 2011:307). The increase in the birth rates was also, in part, the result of a government policy of family encouragement, for instance in France, which had recorded a more conspicuous decline in fertility levels than any other country in the past. Evidences, however, also indicate that the rise in the birth rate was more pronounced among groups which were the first to have experienced the onset of fertility transition and, thus, had already undergone a significant decline in the birth rates (Beaujeu-Garnier, 1978:145). The rising trend in the birth rates after the Second World War did not last long and the birth rates started declining once again to stabilise at a very low level towards the close of the 1970s.

Causes underlying long-term decline in fertility levels in the developed world

Fertility decline during the early phases in the present-day developed world was the outcome of an interplay between a set of social, economic, demographic and motivational factors. These factors were intimately interwoven with each other, and it is very difficult to isolate one from a complex whole.

The process of social and economic transformation, which began with the onset of the Industrial Revolution in the middle of the 18th century, first in England and later throughout Europe and North America, brought about irreversible changes in demographic behaviour. Increased availability of food coupled with innovations and advancement in medical sciences had resulted in a significant decline in the mortality rates, particularly among children and infants, and an increase in longevity. The overall process of social and economic development in the wake of growing industrialisation and urbanisation increased the cost of childrearing. The family gradually lost its functions as an economic unit and became a consumption unit. With the introduction of various welfare measures by the governments in several countries, the role of children as the only source of 'old age security' was minimised. A large number of children, thus, began to be viewed as a burden rather than an economic asset. Further, the spread of education among women and their increasing involvement in gainful employment brought about profound changes in their attitude towards childbearing and childrearing. The process of overall modernisation with the spread of education among the masses led to the growth of rationality, scientific temperament and secularism, which freed them from religious dogmas and facilitated the acceptance of an ideal family size. There was a growing aspiration on the part of the individual to rise in the social scale. A large family began to be perceived as a hindrance in the upward mobility in the social hierarchy. In the early phases the motivation towards a small family size largely operated at the level of individual couples as the social atmosphere was not favourable to birth control, nor were there any effective means of contraception available. The motivation towards limited family size was, however, later facilitated with the development of improved methods of fertility control and their growing use among a larger section of the population. The abortion laws were liberalised and proper facilities were made available to the people in these countries.

Fertility transition in the less developed parts of the world

Fertility decline in the less developed parts of the world did not begin until the second half of the 20th century. Crude birth rates in such countries continued at a very high level, around 45 per thousand, up to 1950–55. The 1960s and the 1970s witnessed some decline, and births came down to 32.9 during 1975–80. While the decline was only marginal in a majority of countries in Africa, Latin America and South Asia, countries in East Asia, mainly China, recorded an impressive decline in birth rate. Along with China other countries which experienced significant declines in the birth rates during the period are Taiwan, Singapore, Hong Kong, Sri Lanka, Mauritius, Indonesia and Malaysia from Asia; and Trinidad and Tobago, Chile, Cuba, and Puerto Rico in Central America. Over a period of nearly three decades birth rates in Singapore declined by about 60 per cent, in Hong Kong and Mauritius by 50 per cent, and in Puerto Rico and Chile by about 40 per cent (Bhende and Kanitkar, 2011:308). All these countries are very small in size. However, in large populations also, for instance in India and Bangladesh, there are clear indications of a decline in birth rates. In India, after the late 1980s, there has been an acceleration in the decline in the birth rate. In some of the less developed countries, the decline in fertility levels is far more rapid than what it was in the West. For instance, it took nearly six decades in the United States (between 1842 and 1900) for total fertility to decline from 6.5 to 3.5 as against only 27, 15, 8 and 7 years for the same level of fertility decline in Indonesia, Columbia, Thailand and China respectively (Bandarage, 1997:146). While in the case of some countries like Sri Lanka and Cuba, the overall development had resulted in a decline in fertility levels, in countries like China and Bangladesh, it is intensified family planning which is the main force behind the decline in the birth rates.

As noted earlier, among African countries fertility levels are still very high. However, demographers are optimistic that the coming future will witness a significant fall in fertility levels in these countries too. In West and South Asia, and Latin America which rank next to Africa, fertility levels are expected to fall rapidly in the coming decades.

Fertility in India

Trends in fertility in India

As already mentioned in Chapter 2, the civil registration system and sample registration system are the main sources of data on vital events in India. Though the civil registration system has a longer history in the country, the quality and coverage of its data is not satisfactory. The sample registration system, which is based on the 'dual report system', provides more reliable and accurate data. This system was, however, introduced only in the late 1960s. Therefore, any attempt to examine the fertility trends in the country becomes a difficult exercise. Nevertheless, several demographers have derived the estimates of birth rates in the past, which are very helpful in identifying the trends of fertility in the country (see for instance, Saxena, 1965; Davis, 1968; Visaria, 1969; Rele and Sinha, 1970, 1973; Adlakha and Kirk, 1974 etc.). These estimates are based on the age-sex distribution of population in the various censuses. The present account of the trends in fertility in India is based on some of these estimates.

Table 10.2 shows the trends in estimated crude birth rates in India since the turn of the last century (please also refer to Figure 10.1). The crude birth rate in India at the turn of the 20th century was in the neighbourhood of 50 per thousand persons. Fertility decline over much of the first half of the century remained only marginal. Over a period of nearly four decades the crude birth rate in the country is said to have declined by only 4 points. In fact, some estimates such as those of the Registrar General of India indicate a slight increase in the birth rate around 1951. During 1951–61, the crude birth rate in the country was around 45 per thousand persons. However, the subsequent decades witnessed a marked dent in fertility levels. During 1961–71, birth rates came down to the neighbourhood of 40 per thousand persons. This 10-point decline since the turn of the 20th century

TABLE 10.2 Estimates of birth rates in India from various sources since 1901

Time Period	*Davis*	*Rele and Sinha*	*Sample Registration System*
1901–11	49.2	-	-
1911–21	48.1	-	-
1921–31	46.4	-	-
1931–41	45.2	-	-
1941–51	39.9	-	-
1951–61	-	45.0	-
1961–71	-	40.0	-
1970	-	-	36.8
1975	-	-	35.2
1980	-	-	33.3
1984	-	-	33.8
1988	-	-	31.5
1995	-	-	28.3
1997	-	-	27.2
1998	-	-	26.5
1999	-	-	26.0
2000	-	-	25.8
2016	-	-	20.4

Sources: Davis, 1968; Rele and Sinha, 1970, 1973; SRS for various years.

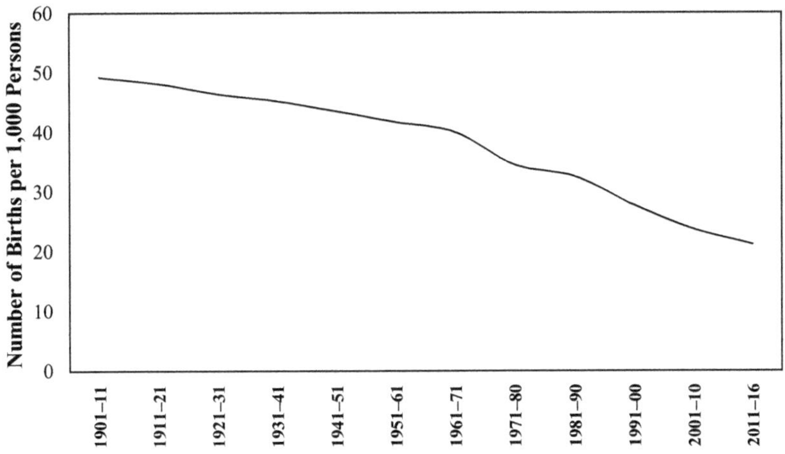

FIGURE 10.1 Trends in crude birth rate in India, 1901–11 to 2011–16

Source: Author.

can partly be attributed to an increase in the age at first marriage among women, though changes in the widowhood rates in the wake of improvement in mortality conditions may have slightly offset the decline in the birth rate. Nonetheless, from the early years of the 1970s, there has been a progressive decline in the birth rates. By the middle of the 1970s when family planning programmes were at its peak, particularly during the emergency period, the crude birth rate in the country, as per SRS estimates, stood at 33 per thousand persons only. This was indeed a remarkable achievement. However, it remained more or less at the same level throughout much of the 1980s. The close of the 1980s nevertheless witnessed another dent in the fertility levels in the country. The crude birth rate came down from 31.5 per thousand in 1988, to 28.3 in 1995 and 25.8 in 2000. The latest figure available from the SRS reveals a crude birth rate of 20.4 per thousand in the year 2016. According to the same source, the total fertility rate in the country has come down from 3.3 during 1996–98 to 2.4 during 2011–13.

Spatial patterns of fertility transition in India

As already discussed previously, fertility levels in India have undergone a marked decline particularly since the middle of the last century. It may, however, be noted that although birth rates have declined throughout India, the onset and pace of decline have not been uniform across states and regions. In general, the southern states of Kerala, Karnataka, Tamil Nadu and Andhra Pradesh were the forerunners in fertility transition, while states from the Hindi belt namely Rajasthan, Madhya Pradesh, Uttar Pradesh and Bihar in the north joined the race much later. Not only this, even the pace of decline in fertility rates also varied a great deal. Based on SRS data, the Office of the Registrar General, India, publishes the *Compendium of*

India's Fertility and Mortality Indicators at regular intervals, which provides state-wise annual estimates on vital rates viz. birth rate, death rate, natural growth rate, infant mortality rate and total fertility rate. The latest such compendium covers the period 1971–2013. Using moving averages of the rates for major states, the forthcoming paragraphs present a summary (Table 10.3) of the spatial patterns of fertility transition in the country.

It may be noted that crude birth rate at the aggregate level in India that was in the neighbourhood of 40 per thousand persons at the time of independence declined to less than 30 not until 1991. As against this, Kerala and Karnataka had achieved this distinction way back in 1973. They were soon joined by Maharashtra in 1974 while the other two southern states, namely Tamil Nadu and Andhra Pradesh, achieved the feat only in the late 1970s and 1980s respectively. By that time the crude birth rate declined to less than 30 in states beyond the southern regime also like Punjab, Gujarat and West Bengal. Interestingly, Odisha, one of the poorest states in the country, achieved the mark in 1990 while Haryana, a very

TABLE 10.3 Cumulative listing of major states with stages of fertility transition

Years	*States*
A: Crude Birth Rate below 30 per 1,000 persons (India reached the stage in 1991)	
1975	Kerala, Karnataka and Maharashtra
1985	Kerala, Karnataka, Maharashtra, *Punjab and Tamil Nadu*
1995	Kerala, Karnataka, Maharashtra, Punjab, Tamil Nadu, *Andhra Pradesh, Gujarat, Haryana, Odisha and West Bengal*
2005	Kerala, Karnataka, Maharashtra, Punjab, Tamil Nadu, Andhra Pradesh, Gujarat, Haryana, Odisha, West Bengal, *Chhattisgarh, Jharkhand, Madhya Pradesh, Rajasthan and Uttarakhand,*
2015	Kerala, Karnataka, Maharashtra, Punjab, Tamil Nadu, Andhra Pradesh, Gujarat, Haryana, Odisha, West Bengal, Chhattisgarh, Jharkhand, Madhya Pradesh, Rajasthan, Uttarakhand, *Bihar, and Uttar Pradesh.*
B: Crude Birth Rate below 20 per 1,000 persons (India yet to reach the stage)	
1990	Kerala
1995	Kerala and *Tamil Nadu*
2000	Kerala, Tamil Nadu and *Uttarakhand*
2005	Kerala, Tamil Nadu, Uttarakhand and *Andhra Pradesh, Maharashtra, Punjab, West Bengal*
2010	Kerala, Tamil Nadu, Uttarakhand, Andhra Pradesh, Maharashtra, Punjab, West Bengal and *Karnataka*
2015	Kerala, Tamil Nadu, Uttarakhand, Andhra Pradesh, Maharashtra, Punjab, West Bengal, Karnataka and *Odisha*

Sources: (i) SRS, *Compendium on India's Fertility and Mortality Indicators*, 1971–2013. (ii) *SRS Bulletin*, 2016.

Notes: (i) Bihar, Gujarat, Haryana, Jharkhand, M.P. Rajasthan and Uttar Pradesh reported CBR above 20 per 1,000 persons in 2015. (ii) From among major states Kerala has the distinction of reaching a CBR level below 10 per 1,000 persons in 2015. (iii) Italicised states refer to states added to the list at each subsequent time point.

developed state, had to wait till 1995. Crude birth rate remained above 30 for a much longer duration in the *BIMARU* states. Bihar and Uttar Pradesh witnessed CBR below 30 not until 2006 and 2007 respectively. Kerala's experience of fertility transition is unique in the country, and currently CBR in the state is well below 10 per thousand. Kerala was the first state to achieve replacement-level fertility i.e. TFR of 2.1 or less in 1988 followed by Tamil Nadu in 1993. The pace of decline in fertility rate in Tamil Nadu also was quite remarkable. TFR in Andhra Pradesh, Karnataka, Maharashtra, Punjab and West Bengal reached replacement level during 2004–06. While Gujarat and Haryana, along with Bihar Jharkhand, Madhya Pradesh, Rajasthan and Uttar Pradesh (part of *BIMARU* states), continue to report CBR above 20, rest of the country including Odisha shows a birth rate below 20 per thousand. Odisha presents yet another instance of fertility transition without corresponding improvements in economic conditions. The state has already achieved replacement-level fertility in 2012 while states like Gujarat and Haryana will take some more years to accomplish the target.

Based on state-level data, it is seen that while some states mainly in the south underwent rapid transition, a major part of the country in the north was marked with only low to moderate decline only (please also see Figure 10.2). In other words, fertility transition in the country has been somewhat more rapid in the south than in the north. Diversity in socio-cultural attributes as well as physical characteristics are sometimes more glaring within the states than between them. Guilmoto and Rajan (2001) have attempted to examine the spatial dimension of fertility transition using district-level estimates of fertility for a period of 40 years from 1951 to 1990. The forthcoming discussion on the regional dimension of fertility transition in the country is based on their study.

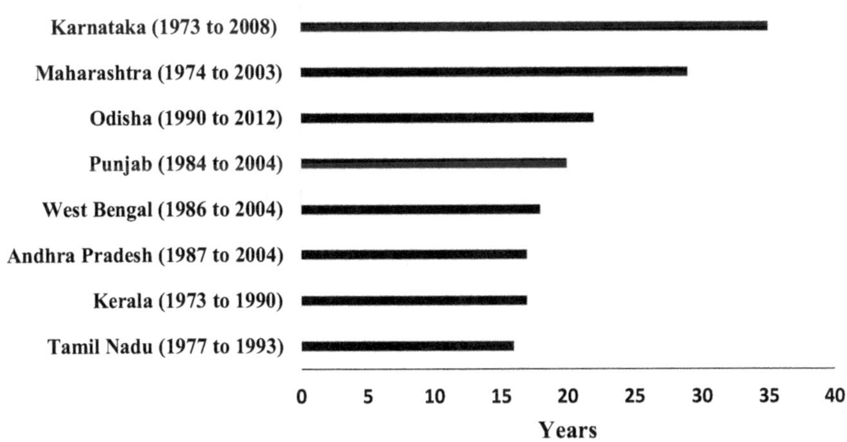

FIGURE 10.2 Duration involved in fertility transition from CBR < 30 to CBR < 20

Source: Author.

Note: CBR is crude birth rate.

Using a suitable standardisation procedure, Guilmoto and Rajan have converted the *Child Women Ratio* (CWR) of the Indian districts into what they call as the *Child Women Index* (CWI), a measure of fertility levels. In order to derive estimates at five-year intervals, they have used a combination of two CWRs using different numerators and denominators. While the one related to children age 0–4 years and women in the age group 15–49, the other took into account children age 5–9 years and women in the age group 20–54. The ratios thus obtained using a particular census data refer to fertility levels of two five-year periods during the preceding decade. The values were then plotted on a series of maps in order to examine the spatial and temporal diffusion of fertility transition in the country.

Their study reveals that during the 1950s there was not much of regional variation in the fertility levels in India. Nevertheless, the north-east exhibited the highest fertility levels. The coastal districts lying in south Kerala and Tamil Nadu, and also the districts in the western Himalayas, reported moderate fertility levels. Remarkably these pockets remained characterised by below-average fertility throughout. Several adjacent districts of Maharashtra and Madhya Pradesh also reported moderate fertility levels in the 1950s. It is interesting to note that the latter half of the decade witnessed a rise in the fertility levels all over India except in the pockets of moderate fertility levels in the south and in the western Himalayas. This rise was especially more conspicuous in western and southern parts of the sub-continent until the 1960s.

The 1960s witnessed fertility decline in several areas, in a more pronounced fashion in southern states along the coasts in Kerala, Tamil Nadu Maharashtra and Andhra Pradesh. The high altitude areas of Himachal Pradesh and Jammu and Kashmir also reported a downward trend in fertility levels during the period. The northern region forming a single contiguous block centred near the border between the three states of Rajasthan, Uttar Pradesh and Madhya Pradesh was marked with high fertility levels. The other pockets with high fertility levels were mainly located in the north-eastern parts particularly in Assam and in the northern part of West Bengal. The other areas in the north-east reported moderate fertility levels.

The 1970s, particularly its second half that is marked with vigorous family planning campaigns, witnessed the spread of fertility decline to other areas. The decline was again more marked in the south. Though the dominance of the pioneering districts in Kerala and Tamil Nadu continued, other areas also picked up in the process of fertility transition. The Punjab plain in the north-western parts of the country experienced a significant decline in fertility. Adjacent Haryana and western Uttar Pradesh, however, still lagged behind. Fertility transition continued in the 1980s and the areas marked with high fertility levels in the north spread over most of Bihar, Madhya Pradesh, Rajasthan and Uttar Pradesh shrunk considerably. In Bihar and Rajasthan, however, the decline was somewhat less conspicuous than that in central Uttar Pradesh. In the north-eastern states also fertility decline was more rapid in Manipur, Nagaland and Tripura as compared to that in Assam, Meghalaya and Arunachal Pradesh. In the former, the transition had set in much earlier and the fertility levels had already reached one of the lowest in the country.

Thus, based on the study of Guilmoto and Rajan, it can be concluded that fertility transition in the country began in the periphery along the coasts in the south particularly in the states of Kerala and Tamil Nadu. It is from here that the transition gradually spread to the rest of the country. Remarkably, the process of diffusion was closely aligned with the coastal stretch of the peninsula. In the north, also, fertility transition seems to have diffused, though at a later stage, from a small pocket spread over the hilly districts of Himachal Pradesh, southern Jammu and Kashmir and northern Punjab. As diffusion proceeded, the high birth rate areas of the north spread over much of Rajasthan, Madhya Pradesh, Uttar Pradesh and Bihar, and forming a contiguous stretch, began undergoing shrink in its spatial extent from sometime in the middle of the 1970s. By the early 1980s, this vast stretch of land with high birth rates got fragmented with further penetration of the diffusion process. This was accompanied by the emergence of several nodes of relatively lower birth rates, which were mainly the state headquarters, or other centres of industrial and commercial activities. They acted as nuclei of diffusion in later stages. Around the same time, much of the peninsula experienced further acceleration in fertility transition. Parts of north Karnataka, eastern Maharashtra and adjacent western parts of Andhra Pradesh in the central Deccan plateau, however, were conspicuous with a slower transition. Geographically, this belt provides contiguity to the high birth rate areas in the north. Much of the extreme southern parts of the Indian peninsula in Kerala and Tamil Nadu, which had taken an early lead in fertility transition, had by the close of the 1980s reached a very low fertility level – almost half of those in the north.

Spatial patterns in fertility levels

Fertility levels in India, as anywhere else, are governed by the prevailing social and economic conditions as well as cultural and religious traditions. With a significant variation in the determinants of fertility behaviour in a vast country like India, there exists a considerable range of variation in the fertility levels from one region to another (Table 10.4). On an average, the Hindi-speaking belt in the north characterised by a patriarchal value system, low level of economic development, predominance of *Brahminical* influence and exclusion of women from education report a generally higher birth rate than the southern states. As already noted, fertility transition in India has been more rapid in the south than in the north. Based on this, a north-south divide is often suggested (see for instance Dyson and Moore, 1983; Malhotra et al., 1995). Till recently, states like Bihar, Madhya Pradesh, Rajasthan and Uttar Pradesh (popularly known as *BIMARU* or sick states) reported crude birth rates that were above 30 per thousand persons. Total fertility rate in these states was 4 or more children (in Madhya Pradesh TFR was just short of 4) per woman in the childbearing age group. Despite a general decline in the recent past, these states continue to rank very high in terms of fertility levels – CBR being nearly 25 per thousand persons. As against this, in Kerala and Tamil Nadu, the crude birth rate is just 15 or below. Kerala, with the lowest birth rate in the country among the major

TABLE 10.4 Crude birth rate, general fertility rate (GFR) and total fertility rate in India and bigger states/UTs, 2016

India/States/UTs	*CBR*	*GFR*	*TFR*
India	20.4	74.4	2.3
Andhra Pradesh	16.4	56.4	1.7
Assam	21.7	78.2	2.3
Bihar	26.8	105.6	3.3
Chhattisgarh	22.8	81.8	2.5
Gujarat	20.1	74.0	2.2
Haryana	20.7	77.5	2.3
Himachal Pradesh	16.0	56.2	1.7
Jammu and Kashmir	15.7	53.5	1.7
Jharkhand	22.9	84.6	2.6
Karnataka	17.6	61.4	1.8
Kerala	14.3	51.1	1.8
Madhya Pradesh	25.1	91.2	2.8
Maharashtra	15.9	58.5	1.8
NCT of Delhi	15.5	55.2	1.6
Orissa	18.6	66.3	2.0
Punjab	14.9	55.2	1.7
Rajasthan	24.3	89.7	2.7
Tamil Nadu	15.0	53.4	1.6
Telangana	17.5	58.8	1.7
Uttar Pradesh	26.2	97.3	3.1
Uttarakhand	16.6	62.9	1.9
West Bengal	15.4	534	1.6

Source: SRS Statistical Report, 2016.

states, has been the pioneering state with respect to fertility transition. Interestingly fertility transition in the state has occurred in the absence of any significant economic development. Scholars have attributed a rapid decline in fertility in the state to widespread female literacy. Tamil Nadu also occupies a unique position in the country for having achieved replacement-level fertility without reaching Kerala's high level of literacy or low level of infant mortality (Guilmoto and Rajan, 2001:715). Total fertility rate in both the states is well below replacement level. The other three major states in the southern peninsula, namely Andhra Pradesh, Karnataka and Maharashtra, report crude birth rates in the range of 15–18 per thousand persons. Outside this demographic regime, Punjab and West Bengal also report crude birth rates of the same level. It is interesting to note that Haryana, a neighbouring state of Punjab, and which occupies a very high position in terms of the levels of economic development in the country, reports a higher crude birth rate than the nation's average. Haryana's crude birth rate is higher than that of even

Orissa, which ranks very low in terms of the levels of economic development. Even Gujarat reports a higher birth rate than that in Orissa. Evidences indicate that the birth rate in Orissa has been on a lower side than the nation's average for quite some time in the past.

Spatial patterns in fertility levels, as revealed by the analysis of state-level figures is, however, not adequate. Because of India's cultural, economic and geographical diversity, the magnitude of regional variations in fertility levels is often as substantial within states as between states (Guilmoto and Rajan, 2001:713). This necessitates an analysis based on district-level estimates on fertility rates. District-level information on births is available from the Civil Registration System but as already remarked they are not reliable. The Sample Registration System provides data only up to state/union territories level. For the first time in the 1981 census, district-level estimates of fertility based on indirect techniques were made available by the Office of the Registrar General of India. This was continued in the 1991 census also. Subsequently, based on the provisional figures of the 2001 census, Guilmoto and Rajan (2002) had derived district-level estimates of fertility in India for 2001. In the earlier edition, the author (Hassan, 2005) had made use of these estimates while analysing the patterns of fertility levels in the country. Using same procedure, Kumar and Sathyanarayana (2012) have derived district-level estimates on the crude birth rate in India based on the 2011 census data. The estimates correspond to the period 2004–10. An analysis of the same reveals a marked regional variation in fertility levels in India with a sharp contrast between the north and the peninsular India (Map 10.2). In general, the Indian peninsula reports lower fertility levels than the rest of the country. Likewise coastal areas fare better than the interior upland. Low fertility levels in the coastal areas extend up to southern Gujarat in the west and lower reaches of the Ganga plains in the east. In the north, areas of low fertility can be seen over Punjab plains and its adjoining hilly areas of Himachal Pradesh and Uttarakhand. Besides patches of low fertility can also be seen in Sikkim, adjoining hilly districts of West Bengal and in north-eastern states. The highest fertility rates i.e. CBR above 25 per thousand persons are over the entire Hindi belt from Rajasthan in the west to Bihar and Jharkhand in the east. In the west a high fertility belt can be seen extending from northern Gujarat along the international boundary with Pakistan in Rajasthan. One branch of this belt extends along the southern boundary districts of Rajasthan and is joined by the high fertility districts of western Madhya Pradesh. The central and northern parts of Madhya Pradesh also reveal high fertility levels. In the northern plains, districts along the foothills of the Himalayas in Uttar Pradesh are also conspicuous with high fertility. In the east, the whole of Bihar, a greater part of Jharkhand and some areas in the north-eastern states are also characterised by high birth rates. Some districts in the high fertility region are exhibiting now signs of a rapid decline in fertility levels, as is the case with Delhi, Kanpur, Gwalior, Indore, and Patna among others. Obviously, these districts are marked with a high degree of urbanisation and non-agricultural workforce. Interestingly,

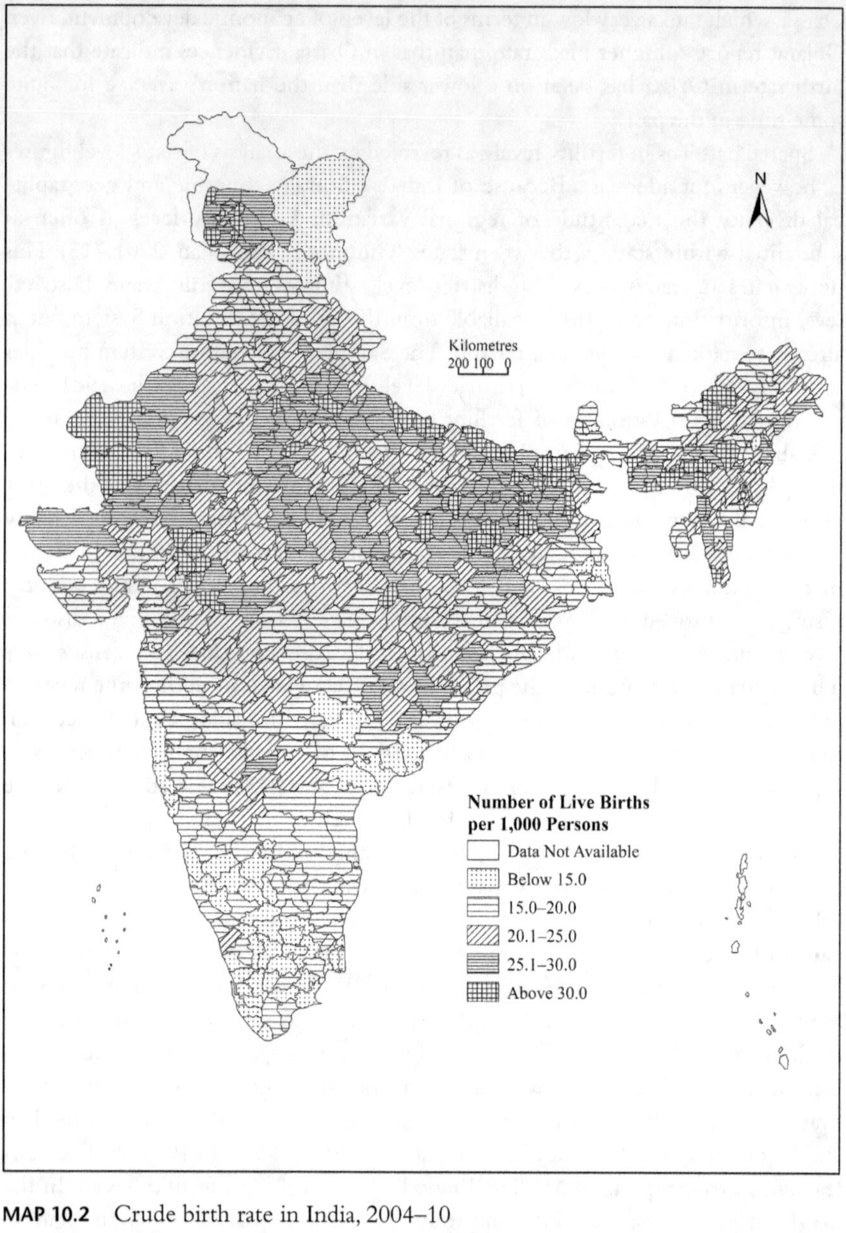

MAP 10.2 Crude birth rate in India, 2004–10

Source: Kumar and Sathyanarayana, 2012

there seems to be a very limited diffusion of fertility transition to the surrounding districts where fertility levels are still very high. It remains to be seen in the coming years whether the profound demographic change in these urbanised districts is able to spread further to accelerate the pace of fertility transition of the otherwise high fertility region.

Fertility differentials

A wide range of social, demographic and economic factors determine the fertility level of a population. These determinants of fertility, however, do not operate independent of each other. They are closely interrelated with each other, and the fertility level in a population is the net result of the interplay between them. The differential effects of these determinants result in considerable variation in the levels of fertility among different groups of the same population. A study of the differentials in fertility levels in various groups of a population, therefore, occupies a significant position in the understanding of the mechanism of fertility decline. This is particularly useful in the implementation of the family planning programmes. These differentials can be viewed in terms of ecological factors like rural-urban residence; social factors like levels of literacy and educational attainment, religion, caste and race; and economic factors like occupation and economic status of the individuals or groups. The forthcoming discussion on fertility differentials is based on the NFHS fourth round (20015–16) data.

It is important to note that fertility performance of a population is determined to a large extent by such demographic characteristics as age and sex composition. It is, therefore, necessary to eliminate their effects while studying the fertility differentials in a population. For this reason, it is suggested to use some standard measure such as total fertility rate and mean number of children ever born to women in the reproductive age span. Table 10.5 presents the same for women with different background characteristics in India.

Residence and fertility

Rural-urban differentials in fertility levels exist in all the countries of the world. In the developed countries of the West, these differentials have narrowed down considerably during the recent past, and it is expected that they would eventually disappear as forces of modernisation impose increasing homogeneity in terms of attitude and life style of people. In many of the European countries, particularly in eastern and southern Europe, rural-urban differentials in fertility rates persisted even during the second half of the 20th century. These differentials arise out of differences in sex composition of population, standard of living, cost of childrearing, occupational status, income levels, levels of educational attainment, female employment and so on.

In India with the decline in fertility levels the rural-urban differentials have sharpened during recent times. The SRS estimates reveal consistently higher fertility rates in the rural areas than in the urban areas. According to the NFHS data, total fertility rate in India was 2.18 children per women in the age group 15–49 years. The corresponding figures for rural and urban areas were 2.41 and 1.75 respectively. On an average a rural woman age 40–49 years produced 1 child more than her counterpart in the urban areas.

TABLE 10.5 Fertility levels by background characteristics of women in India, 2015–16

Background Characteristics	*Total Fertility Rate**	*Mean Number of Children***
Residence		
Urban	1.75	2.74
Rural	2.41	3.50
Schooling		
No schooling	3.07	3.82
< 5 years complete	2.43	3.16
5–7 years complete	2.38	2.97
8–9 years complete	2.19	2.65
10–11 years complete	1.99	2.33
12 or more years complete	1.71	2.01
Religion		
Hindus	2.13	3.13
Muslims	2.62	4.15
Christian	1.99	2.65
Sikh	1.58	2.62
Buddhist/Neo-Buddhist	1.74	2.93
Jain	1.20	2.24
Other	2.57	3.79
Caste/tribe		
Scheduled castes	2.26	3.48
Scheduled tribes	2.48	3.52
Other backward class	2.22	3.28
Others	1.93	2.87
Wealth Index		
Lowest	3.17	4.28
Second	2.45	3.68
Middle	2.07	3.22
Fourth	1.84	2.84
Highest	1.54	2.49
Total	2.18	3.22

* Relates to 3 years preceding the survey. ** Ever born to ever married women age 40–49.

Source: NFHS-4, IIPS, Mumbai, Table 4.2, p. 90.

Education and fertility

Another important aspect of fertility differentials relates to the educational attainment of couples and levels of fertility. The level of literacy and educational attainment, particularly among females, is one of the most important determinants of fertility behaviour. Several studies have confirmed a negative association between the educational attainment of women and fertility rate. This is true for both rural and urban areas. As the NFHS data shows, there is a progressive decline in the total fertility rate with a rise in the educational status of women in India. A woman with no schooling in the childbearing age group gives birth to 1 child more than a woman who has completed at least her high school. This reflects upon the value of education of women in the planning process. Educational attainment of women reduces the fertility rate in two ways. One, their involvement in educational pursuits delays their marriages, reducing the period of exposure to the childbearing process. Second, with a high level of educational attainment, their attitude towards family size undergoes changes, resulting in a greater acceptance of family planning methods.

Religion, castes/tribes and fertility

Religion is another important determinant of fertility in any population. However, it is important to note that religion has more significant influence on fertility behaviour in the less developed or developing countries than the developed countries. A high fertility level in some cases is attributed to religious prohibition of birth control and values about the importance of children. There exists a remarkable difference in fertility levels in different religious groups in India also. The Muslims for instance report higher fertility than any other religious community. They are followed by the Hindus with respect to fertility levels. A higher growth in the population of the Muslims is, therefore, attributed to a generally higher fertility rate. A comparison of NFHS data of the past rounds would show that the fertility differentials among different religious group have significantly narrowed down. With regard to religion and fertility levels in India, there are two popular viewpoints. While the protagonists of *particularised theology* attribute the differentials to the differences in religious doctrine, the advocates of *characteristics hypothesis* argue that the religious differences in fertility are essentially the result of differences in the demographic, social and economic attributes of the members belonging to different religious communities.

Likewise, fertility differentials have been noticed among different caste groups/tribes as well. Several studies have established that fertility levels are generally higher among lower-caste Hindus than the upper-caste Hindus. A comparison of NFHS data shows that fertility rate is the highest among the scheduled castes in the country followed by scheduled tribes and other backward classes.

Economic status and fertility

Among the economic determinants of fertility, the most commonly referred to are economic wellbeing of the couples or group, occupation of the husband, involvement of women in the gainful employment etc. An inverse relationship between economic status of the couple and fertility level is a universal phenomenon. In developed countries, however, this association has undergone substantial changes during the recent past (Bhende and Kanitkar, 2011:323). Occupation of husbands is often considered as an indicator of social and economic status of the family in the society. Studies have highlighted the significant difference in fertility levels by occupation. For example, in Europe, data indicate that women whose husbands were in the agricultural sector reported higher fertility levels than those whose husbands were engaged in non-agricultural occupations (UN, 1976:49). Likewise, there are indications that women who are gainfully employed have a generally lower birth rate than those who are not. Due to the unavailability of suitable data, very few studies have been conducted to examine this association between economic factors and fertility levels in India. Based on NSS data on per capita monthly household expenditure and fertility estimates of the Registrar General of India, scholars have confirmed a negative association between economic status and fertility levels in India. This holds true for urban as well as rural areas. The NFHS data on fertility differentials of women belonging to different economic status groups also reveal a decline in fertility levels with a rise in economic status. On an average, women from the lowest wealth quintile produce 1.6 more children than women in the highest wealth quintile. Mean number of children ever born to a women at the end of the childbearing age span also follows the same pattern.

Evidences indicate that fertility differentials have significantly narrowed down in the developed countries during the recent past. Less developed countries, on the other hand, experienced sharpening of these differentials. Demographers are of the opinion that fertility differentials typically diverge early in the fertility transition, and reconverge though not completely, towards the end of the transition as fertility approaches the replacement level (NFHS, 2000:90). On the basis of trends in fertility differentials of the developed countries, Amos Hawley, in 1950, identified three distinct phases (see Bhende and Kanitkar, 2011:328; Clarke, 1972:116). In the first phase, various social and economic groups exhibit similar fertility levels; the second phase, which began with industrialisation and the resultant overall development in the 19th century, is marked with widening differentials, and finally, the third phase, as in operation in most of the developed countries of the West, there is a positive association between social and economic status and fertility levels. Sweden was the first country in the world to have achieved the third phase, wherein the wealthier people have a higher birth rate (Clarke, 1972:116). India as a whole still has fairly large fertility differentials. Nevertheless, state-wise figures on fertility differentials do show remarkable differences from one state to another.

Theories on fertility

Fertility transition in the past has resulted from the interplay of numerous social, demographic and economic factors. It is indeed very difficult to isolate one factor from the complete whole and determine its impact on the fertility change. It is, therefore, extremely difficult to propose a systemic theory, which is able not only to explain historically observed trends in fertility levels and class differences, but also to provide the bases for predicting the future fertility levels with a fairly good amount of accuracy. Nevertheless, attempts have been made from time to time to propound theories on fertility. These theories are conventionally grouped under three categories – biological theories, cultural theories and economic theories.

The biological theories argue that the law regulating fertility among human beings is the same as that which regulates the growth of plants and other animals. These theories, therefore, emphasise on what is common to all living beings and ignore what is unique or peculiar to human beings. The biological theories believe in the existence of metaphysical will of nature to perpetuate the species.

The cultural theories on fertility, on the other hand, tend to explain fertility in terms of man's psychological attitude, which in turn is determined by prevailing culture. Though culture is defined as 'all which embraces everything materialist or non-materialist', cultural theories do attempt to isolate one or more cultural factors which supposedly shape society's psychological attitude towards reproduction. Thus, while one theory attributes decline in fertility to relative decrease in the pleasure of parenthood as a result of increase in other sources of pleasure, another theory attributes fertility decline to the rational mentality whereby people tend to evaluate carefully the gains and losses of parenthood (Coontz, 1979:16).

Finally, the economic theories are avowedly materialist and stress the importance of economic factors in the overall process of social change, which governs fertility behaviour of a population.

Biological theories

The density principle

Michael Thomas Sadler propounded the density principle in his two-volume work entitled *The Laws of Population* published in 1830. Though much of his work was aimed at refuting the arguments of Malthusians, he did make an attempt to outline a theory of population which he called the true law of population. According to Sadler, fertility varies inversely with density of population. In other words, 'the prolificness of a given number of marriages will, all other circumstances being the same, vary in proportion to the condensation of the population'. With regard to relative condensation of population, Sadler emphasised that space should not be interpreted merely in terms of physical extent but also in qualitative terms. For example, to explain high fertility among the inhabitants of the Maritime Provinces, he included under space at their disposal the vast resources of the sea and, therefore, concluded that density in such areas was in fact low.

Sadler believed that the density principle explained not only differences in rural-urban fertility, but also the low fertility of the upper classes (Coontz, 1979:30). He said that 'man is comparatively sterile when he is wealthy, and he breeds in proportion to his poverty'. According to him, the primitive societies marked with sparse population dependent on hunting and fishing provide the most favourable condition to fertility. As social evolution proceeds, and as humankind passes to the pastoral stage, and to the agricultural stage and finally attains a high level of civilisation, the fertility declines. This progress in social evolution is, according to Sadler, synonymous with increasing density of population.

Sadler cited data from a number of European countries in support of his principle that fertility varies inversely with density. The cases of high-density regions marked with high fertility in the Netherlands, however, created contradictions in Sadler's principle. In order to resolve this apparent contradiction Sadler suggested that apart from density of population, another factor which determines fertility in a population is mortality. Thus emerges his second principle that 'fertility varies directly with mortality' (quoted in Coontz, 1979:29). The second principle, thus, states that 'the prolificness of an equal number of individuals, other circumstances being similar, is greater where the mortality is greater, and on the contrary, smaller where mortality is less'.

It may, however, be noted that in order to resolve the contradiction in his first principle Sadler has shifted his argument from fertility to net increase in population. This shift in the emphasis has exposed a basic difficulty in his law of population. Sadler's second principle states that fertility increases with an increase in mortality. But increasing mortality is itself now attributed to increase in density. According to Sadler's proposition increasing density decreases fertility but increases mortality, which in turn increases fertility. This incompatibility in the arguments attracted severe criticism by scholars later.

The density principle as an explanation to fertility differentials was revived almost a century after the publication of Sadler's work by Raymond Pearl, another biologist, in association with Lowell J. Reid. Pearl, however, maintained that increasing density does not increase mortality, though it reduces fertility. He arrived at this conclusion on the basis of experiments on fruit flies and poultry. With regard to growth in human population, where no such laboratory experiment is possible, Pearl obtained a negative association between density and birth rate with the help of statistical methods. Scholars have, however, questioned the definition of density adopted by Pearl in his explanation.

The diet principle

A decade after the publication of Sadler's work, Thomas A. Doubleday propounded the diet principle in his book entitled *The True Law of Population* in 1841. While experimenting with plants, Doubleday found that an excessive application of manure 'invariably induces sterility in the plant, and if the doses were increased, disease and death'. Pursuing the inquiry, he found that the same principle was applicable to animals also. On the basis of this, he writes that 'whenever a *species* or *genus* is endangered in the wake of lack of food, a corresponding effort is invariably made by nature for its preservation and continuance by an increase of fecundity or fertility'. On the basis of this, he writes that 'whenever a *species* or *genus* is endangered in the wake of lack of food, a corresponding effort is invariably made by nature for its preservation and continuance by an increase of fecundity or fertility' (quoted in Coontz, 1979:43). With this law Doubleday attempted to explain differences in fertility both within and between countries.

Jo Sue de Castro revived Doubleday's principle that fertility is regulated by diet in 1952 in his book entitled *Geography of Hunger*. Castro has contended that the quantity and quality of protein consumption regulate fecundity. As did Doubleday before him, Castro argued that there exists a negative association between crude birth rate and protein consumption. His arguments were based on R. J. Slonaker's experiments on the fertility of rats under varying amounts of protein intake. With regard to human population he cited data pertaining to crude birth rate and protein consumption from selected countries to establish an inverse relation between the two.

Scholars have rejected the theses of both Doubleday and Castro. Even if reproductive capacity is determined by dietary intake, it is very difficult to accept the proposition that it influences the actual performance. There are recent instances of changes in fertility levels, for example decline in birth rates in a number of capitalist countries during the period of economic depression or the baby boom experienced in the post–Second World War period, which cannot be attributed to variation in dietary intake.

Spencer's biological theory

Herbert Spencer in his book *The Principles of Biology*, published in 1880, presented a different biological law governing multiplication of species. According to him, preservation of species is the general biological law governing the growth of all population both human and infrahuman. Spencer's explanation refers to two processes of preservation – individuation and genesis. While the former is defined as the longevity of an individual, the latter relates to the capacity of the species to generate new individuals.

Individuation and genesis are inversely related to each other. Spencer argues that if the fertility level of a species is high its ability to maintain individual life is smaller, and vice versa. Thus, 'while the minutest organisms multiply in their millions, the small compound types next above them multiply in their thousands; the large and more compound type multiply in their hundreds and tens, the largest type do not multiply at all' (quoted in Coontz, 1979:54). According to Spencer, the same principle is applicable to human population also. With regard to fertility differences among different groups Spencer remarked that infertility of the 'upper classes' is attributable to their greater individuation.

Cultural theories

As already mentioned earlier, under the 'cultural theories' we include those explanations which view fertility differentials in terms of factors, both material and non-material, that form part of our cultural milieu. In particular, such theories emphasise mainly the psychological attributes of individuals, which, in turn, are the products of prevailing culture. Though economic considerations are often included in the explanation, they are treated as just one of the several factors affecting psychological attributes.

The theory of social capillarity

In 1890, Arsene Dumont, a French scholar, propounded the theory of 'social capillarity'. According to Dumont, in a civilised community the principle of social capillarity governs the fertility behaviour of population. The principle is based on the recognition that every society is marked with a set of hierarchic social order in which individuals in the upper hierarchy enjoy greater prestige than those belonging to the lower hierarchy. There is a constant effort on the part of the individuals to rise in the hierarchy of social status. A large family is said to be an obstacle in the process of upward social mobility. Dumont, thus, attributed fertility differences among different people to the will of moving up in the social order i.e. social capillarity. This aspiration or will to advance up in the hierarchy of social status is different from the desire to dominate others by power politics or wealth.

Although the principle of social capillarity is manifest in all the societies, it operates more efficiently in communities characterised by great social mobility. On the other hand, in a society where status and caste are rigid factors, social capillarity is very weak. Dumont maintained that poverty is not the cause of high fertility. Citing demographic data from France, he argued that the regions of high fertility are precisely those that are remote from urban centres and are marked with ignorance and poverty. Likewise, he argues that wealth is not the cause of low fertility, for both wealth and low fertility are common products of the will to advance up in the social hierarchy. He claimed that the principle of social capillarity explains fertility differentials not only within a country but also among different countries.

The principle of social capillarity was the first logical attempt of providing an explanation of fertility transition. It had profound influences on the later writings. For instance, Kingsley Davis's theory of change and response concerning fertility also acknowledges the role of the desire to rise in the social scale in declining fertility. The principle holds good even today in explaining the intra- and inter-country differentials in fertility levels. The theory of social capillarity, however, attracted criticism, as it was not backed by sound statistical proof. Nevertheless credit must go to Dumont for underscoring the need of investigating the psychological attributes of individuals in its social context while explaining the fertility levels.

Theory of increasing prosperity

In 1910, L. Brentano presented another explanation of fertility differentials in his theory of increasing prosperity. According to Brentano, the key to fertility differences is rooted in the differences in material prosperity of different peoples. He argues that humans are essentially creatures of pleasure, the sources of which vary from group to group. The poor with an extremely restricted number of alternative pleasures tend to find compensation of this deprivation in sexual indulgence.

This explains high fertility levels among them. On the other hand, the wealthy have a large number of competing pleasures, and in general, their gratification is found outside the home. Brentano suggested that a general decline in fertility levels is the function of technical, scientific, industrial and commercial progress which makes more and more sources of pleasure available to a growing number of people. In order to avail themselves of the facilities of pleasure people must have material means at their disposal. They have to make choices between family size and opportunities of pleasure. It should, however, be noted that according to Brentano, a decline in the birth rate with increasing prosperity 'does not imply an increase in sexual continence' (quoted in Coontz, 1979:68).

Brentano has not been successful in differentiating between sexual enjoyment and the pleasure of parenthood. For the poor, sexual indulgence is identical with the desire of offspring, whereas for the rich the same is not true. Brentano's arguments imply that sexual indulgence is the main pleasure for the poor and lack of information about contraceptive measure leads to high birth rates. But ignorance rather than pleasure then appears to be the main determinant of fertility levels among the poor. On the other hand, among the rich since there is no increase in 'sexual continence', the choice is between parenthood and alternative pleasures.

Growth of rationalism and fertility decline

Roderich von Ungern-Sternberg, in his book, *The Causes of the Decline in the Birth Rate Within the European Sphere of Civilization*, published in 1931, argued that increasing prosperity is not the cause but the goal, and birth control is the means for attaining this goal. He also denies that fertility decline is the result of the changing age structure of population, or decline in the marriage frequency, or decline in infant mortality rates. A generally lower birth rate in the urban centres does not imply a causative association between urbanisation and fertility decline either. In fact, both urbanisation and decline in fertility are the results of a common cause i.e. the development of a capitalist mentality which denotes a 'rationalistic' conception of life in which people weigh all actions carefully including paternity. Ungern-Sternberg made this proposition on the basis of the experience of European countries where a capitalist mentality has permeated all classes of the society.

Economic theories

The economic theories are based on the assumption that fertility behaviour of couples in a population is based on mainly economic considerations. They are, therefore, built within the micro-economic framework. The economic explanations of fertility were developed mostly during the second half of the 20th century. The theories propounded by Harvey Liebenstein, Richard A. Easterlin and J. C. Caldwell are important in this regard.

Incorporating the cost-benefit analysis of children in his theory, Harvey Liebenstein, in 1953, proposed that the fertility decision of a couple is based on the balance between *utilities* and *disutility* of an additional child. According to Liebenstein, there are three types of *utilities* of an additional child viz. as a *consumption good* where a child is considered as a source of pleasure for the parents; as a *productive unit* where a child is expected to contribute to the family income after the child enters into the labour force; and as a *source of security* for the parents in their old age. On the other hand, the *disutility* refers to the direct and indirect costs involved in having an additional child. While the direct costs relate to the conventional expenses involved in the bringing up, the indirect costs are the opportunities, measured in economic terms, foregone in the event of an additional child.

Liebenstein states that a couple makes a 'rough calculation' regarding the balance between the utilities and disutilities before deciding for an additional child. It should be noted here that Liebenstein's emphasis is mainly on the higher-order births. Liebenstein mentioned that the concept of *utility and disutility* is dynamic and is governed by the overall levels of development of the society. The process of economic development operates through income effects, survival effects and occupational distribution effects. The dynamic relationship between economic development and utilities and cost of an additional child is shown in Figure 10.3. It is evident from the figure that with rising income levels, while the *consumption utility* remains unchanged, the other two forms of utilities undergo sharp decline. The costs involved in bringing up the additional child, on the contrary, report a constant rise. On the basis of this, Liebenstein maintained that as economic conditions improve, the number of high-parity children for the representative family has a tendency to decline. It may, however, be noted that Liebenstein's theory has more of an explanatory value than a predictive one.

In an almost identical way Gary S. Becker, in his paper entitled *An Economic Analysis of Fertility* published in 1960, proposed that the micro-consumption theory

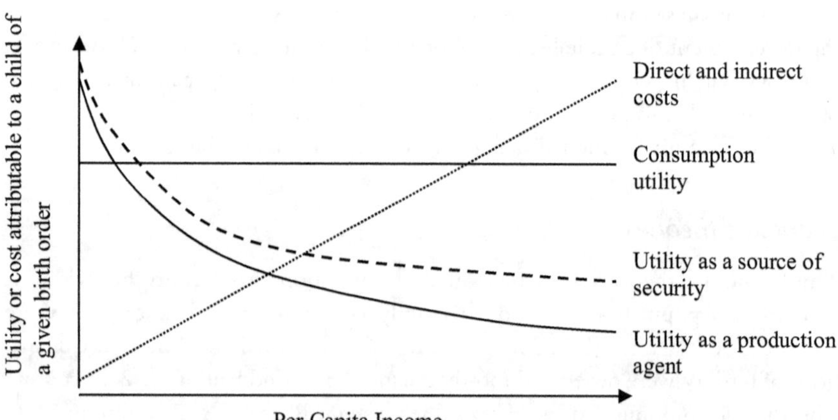

FIGURE 10.3 Liebenstein's Model of Fertility Decline

Source: Based on Bhende and Kanitkar, 2011:336.

in economics is applicable to fertility also. According to him, variations in completed fertility can be understood within the framework used by economists in the analysis of demands of *durable goods*. Just as a consumer with a given taste makes a decision to purchase durable goods after a careful evaluation of its utilities and costs, the household choice of fertility is made after considering the utilities vis-à-vis monetary and opportunity cost of the additional child. Thus, according to Becker's theory both children and household durable goods are identical.

Becker's economic theory of fertility was based on two traditional economic postulates – first, the household behaviour is rational on the basis of changing taste and second, the prices of commodities desired by the representative households remain indifferent to the households' consumption decisions. According to Becker, knowledge about family planning measures is an important factor determining fertility behaviour. He argued that with a uniform knowledge across different income groups there will be a positive association between income and fertility levels because higher income will enable couples to have more children. He attributed the observed inverse relationship between income and fertility levels to differential knowledge of family planning measures in different income groups. He stressed that once the knowledge of birth control measures is evenly spread, a positive association is bound to emerge between fertility and income.

Becker's economic explanations of fertility and income attracted severe criticism later. While some scholars argued that the 'consumer durable' model is not applicable to children and that it cannot predict fertility differentials by income, others, including Easterlin, have argued that tastes cannot be taken as immutable facts, and insisted that tastes change systematically according to one's upbringing.

J. C. Caldwell propounded the *theory of intergenerational wealth flow* to explain the fertility behaviour of people. He argued that the fertility decision of people in any society is rational and is based on the economic worth of the children. He suggested that fertility levels in a society are high if children are economically useful to parents, and on the other hand, low if the children are economic burdens for their parents. In other words, if the flow of wealth is from younger generation to older ones, fertility levels tend to be high. On the contrary, flow of wealth in the opposite direction i.e. from parents to children, results in low fertility levels. Thus, according to Caldwell, it is the direction of intergenerational flow of wealth in terms of goods and services that determines the fertility levels in any society. In all primitive and traditional societies children are useful to parents in several ways, and the flow of wealth in such societies is from the younger generation to the older generation. High fertility among such people is, therefore, economically rational. As against this, in modern societies children are economic liability on parents, and wealth flows from parents to children. This explains a low fertility in such societies.

According to Caldwell a reversal in the direction of flow of wealth is a precondition for any decline in fertility levels. This reversal necessitates emotional and economic nucleation of family. In many developing countries this nucleation of family has already begun under the influence of Westernisation. Caldwell is of the opinion that further strengthening of this process will bring down the birth rates in the less developed parts of the world, thus bringing down overall growth in population in the coming decades.

R. A. Easterlin provided a more comprehensive theory combining sociology and economics of fertility (Bhende and Kanitkar, 2011:340). He has explained the link between fertility transition and modernisation. Easterlin has defined the process of modernisation as 'transformation in economic, social and political organization and in human personality (Easterlin, 1983:563). He argues that although fertility transition has accompanied the process of modernisation, the specific links between the two are not clear. According to him modernisation influences fertility only indirectly. Bongaarts had earlier talked about a set of 'proximate determinants' through which 'modernization' acts upon fertility levels (Bongaarts, 1978:106). These proximate determinants include, for instance, deliberate fertility control, post-partum infecundability, waiting time to conception etc. among others. Easterlin has further added a set of 'intervening variables' between modernisation and 'proximate variables'. These intervening variables are the demand of children, supply of children and costs involved in fertility regulations. While the demand of children refers to the number of surviving children a couple would want if fertility regulations were costless, supply of children is the number of surviving children a couple would have if fertility is not deliberately controlled. The costs of fertility regulations involve both objective and economic costs. Thus, in Easterlin's opinion the process of modernisation directly influences demand, supply and regulation costs, which, in turn, determine the deliberate control. And finally, deliberate measures of fertility control in conjunction with other proximate determinants shape the observed fertility levels in a society.

In a pre-modern society the demand for children is greater because of the nature of the economy and adverse mortality conditions. The individual couples in such societies, however, cannot produce as many children as they want, and demand for children, thus, exceeds supply. In such circumstances, the couples tend to have as many children as possible. In other words, the observed fertility is identical to natural fertility. In due course, the process of modernisation sets in and improving mortality conditions increase the potential supply of children. The regulation costs begin to decline along with a corresponding decline in the demand for children. Since the society lacks deliberate attempts to limit family size, the couples now have more children than they want. Thus, emerges the situation of an excess of supply over demand that generates motivation for family size limitation. The couples then weigh the disadvantages of excess supply against the regulation costs. In the initial stage, since fertility regulation costs are high, natural fertility continues to prevail. As modernisation proceeds, the excess supply over demand further grows and motivation for fertility control becomes still stronger. Since regulation costs have also undergone decline, the motivation for family size control is strong enough to offset the former. The couples begin to take deliberate actions to control fertility, and actual family size falls below potential supply though still exceeding demand. Eventually in the subsequent stages as motivation grows further stronger and regulation costs lower, a point is reached when actual family size corresponds to demand.

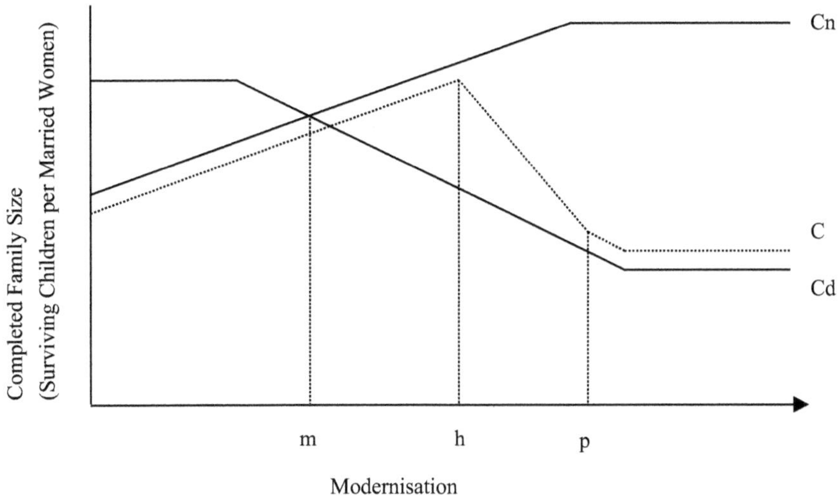

FIGURE 10.4 Easterlin's Model of Modernisation and Family Size

Source: Based on Bhende and Kanitkar, 2011:340).

Easterlin's analysis has been summarised in Figure 10.4 Modernisation has been presented along the horizontal axis, while supply and demand, measured according to the number of surviving children per married woman, have been shown along the vertical axis. As seen, in the initial stage demand for children (Cd) exceeds supply (Cn), and actual family size (C) is equal to supply. As modernisation occurs, a stage is reached (point m) when supply becomes greater than demand generating motivation for controlling family size. As the motivation is not strong enough to offset regulation costs in the initial stages, actual family size continues to correspond to supply. However, with the further inroads of modernisation, motivation becomes stronger and deliberate controls set in (point h) resulting in decline in family size. The process continues and eventually, a point is reached when actual family size falls to a level corresponding to demand (point p).

To conclude, it may be noted that although there are several theories on fertility behaviour none of them is universally acceptable. Fertility levels in a population are governed by a host of socio-economic, demographic and cultural factors including the attitude of parents towards family size. Some of these theories treated fertility behaviour as purely a biological phenomenon, while many others emphasise on socio-cultural and economic attributes. The behavioural or psychological dimension, however, holds a significant place as to why some parents decide for an additional child while others with the same socio-economic background do not.

11

MORTALITY AND LIFE TABLE

Mortality, or the occurrence of death, is another component of population change. Unlike fertility, mortality is more stable and predictable, and is less prone to unique fluctuations. While fertility behaviour of a population depends on a set of social, demographic, psychological and economic factors, mortality is a biological phenomenon. Death control is universally acceptable in all societies of the world. The death rates have, therefore, undergone a more rapid decline than that of the birth rates. It is this decline in the death rates, rather than any increase in the birth rates, which has been responsible for rapid growth in the world population during the recent past. Temporal changes in death rates not only affect the size of a population but also its age composition, which has important bearings on the social, economic and demographic conditions in an area. The study of mortality is, therefore, useful for analysing the current demographic conditions as well as for determining the prospect of potential change in the mortality conditions in the future. The analysis of mortality is of vital importance to planners and policy makers in the provision of basic health care services in any population. The analytical study of mortality can be described as the study of 'the risk of dying' in different populations or different groups in a population.

The meaning of the term 'death' does not involve any ambiguity and, therefore, it facilitates the measurement of mortality. The UN and WHO have defined the term as 'the permanent disappearance of all evidence of life at any time after birth'.

The vital registration or civil registration system provides data on deaths in a country. However, in a country where such registration system is absent or inadequate, statistics on mortality are obtained from periodic censuses and sample surveys. It should, however, be noted that periodic censuses do not provide data on mortality directly. Estimates on mortality are indirectly derived using the age-sex distribution of population of two consecutive censuses. In sample surveys, however, when a direct question on the occurrence on deaths is included estimates on mortality are available.

Measures of mortality

There are several measures employed in the analysis of mortality in any population. *Crude Death Rate* (CDR) is the most commonly used measure as it can be easily calculated. All it requires is the data on number of deaths in a calendar year in an area and its mid-year population. Crude death rate is the number of deaths that occurred during a calendar year per thousand persons. It is computed in the following manner:

$$\text{CDR} = (D / P)K \tag{11.1}$$

where D is the number of deaths registered in a calendar year, P is the mid-year population, and K is a constant, which is usually taken as 1,000.

In populations marked with sharp fluctuations, from one year to another, in the number of deaths due to some specific reasons, it is suggested to take an average of deaths over, say three years, in the numerator, and mid-year population relating to the year falling in the centre of the duration in the denominator. The modified formulae is as follows:

$$\text{CDR} = \{1 / 3\ (D_1 + D_2 + D_3)\} / P_2 \tag{11.2}$$

where D is the number of deaths, P is total mid-year population of year 2, and subscripts 1, 2 and 3 indicate the years.

As noted in the case of crude birth rates, CDR also suffers from some limitations. First, it treats the mid-year population as a homogenous group, and ignores the age structure of population. It is obvious that the risk of death is not uniform across different age groups. Second, the denominator in the formulae gets affected by births, and in a fast-growing population due to high birth rates and declining death rates, CDR tends to underestimate the situation (Ramakumar, 1986:46).

As the relative frequency of deaths varies with age, it is more appropriate to calculate the rates separately for each age group. Death rates specific for different age groups are known as *Age-Specific Death Rate* (ASDR) and can be calculated as under:

$$\text{ASDR or } M_x = (D_x / P_x)K \tag{11.3}$$

where M_x is the age-specific death rate at age x, D_x is the number of deaths at age x, and P_x is the mid-year population at age x.

In case the age interval is more than one year, the symbols will be:

$$\text{ASDR or } {}_nM_x = ({}_nD_x / {}_nP_x)K \tag{11.4}$$

where ${}_nD_x$ refers to the number of deaths registered in the age group x to (x + n), and ${}_nP_x$ is the mid-year population in the age group x to (x + n).

These rates are usually worked out separately for the two sexes, where the measure is known as *Age- and Sex-Specific Death Rate* (ASSDR). The rates if plotted on a graph usually present a 'U' shaped curve, the two sides of which represent usually high mortality rates during the infancy and old ages (Misra, 1982:135). The experiences of developed countries reveal that the risk of mortality reduces first in the early ages of life producing a nearly 'J' shaped curve. The base of the curve widens with improvement in the mortality conditions reflecting increase in the span of life. The curve for female ASDR in developed countries is lower than that of males in all ages. As against this, in the less developed parts of the world, for instance in India, the curve for female ASDR is higher than that of males during both early and reproductive ages. In the old ages, however, the situation gets reversed.

Another very precise measure of mortality is what is known as *Maternal Mortality Ratio* (MMR). Maternal mortality refers to the occurrence of death of women during the childbearing process. Maternal mortality ratio is defined as the number of maternal deaths per hundred thousand (or, in some cases per ten thousand) live births in a calendar year. Numerically, it is expressed in the following manner:

$$\text{MMR} = \left(D_m \,/\, B\right)K \tag{11.5}$$

where MMR is maternal mortality ratio, D_m is the number of maternal deaths, B is the number of live births and K is a constant. If the denominator in the equation is mid-year population of married women in the reproductive age group instead of live births in a calendar year the measure is termed as *maternal mortality rate*. In the developed countries, maternal mortality rate/ratio is generally very low, while in the less developed parts of the world, due to poverty, lack of adequate health care facilities and ignorance, maternal mortality rates/ratios are very high. India reports one of the highest maternal mortality ratios in the world.

Infant Mortality Rate (IMR) is a measure of mortality among infants. Infants include babies who are less than one year of age. Infant mortality rate is defined as the ratio between the infant deaths in a calendar year and the number of live births recorded in that year. This rate is computed in the following manner:

$$\text{IMR} = \left(D_0 \,/\, B\right)K \qquad 11.6)$$

where D_0 is the number of infant deaths during a calendar year, B is the total live births recorded in that year and K is 1,000.

Infant mortality rate is one of the most sensitive indicators of medical and health care facilities in a population. In fact it is a very good indicator of the levels of social and economic development of a population. Several empirical studies have indicated a positive relationship between IMR and birth rates in different populations, and hence IMR is taken as an important parameter to understand the mechanism of fertility change in a population (Misra, 1982:141). However, it may be noted that IMR does not refer to the risk of death of a cohort of babies born during a particular time. This is because some of the infant deaths included in the numerator might relate to the birth cohort of the previous year, and some infant deaths of the birth cohort in question (i.e. the denominator) might occur in the following year. Therefore, the measure is not a proper rate but a ratio (Srinivasan, 1998:89). Infant deaths attributable to some external factors like accidents or infections are called *exogenous infant mortality*. Likewise, the occurrence of deaths among infants due to some congenial malformation and birth trauma is called *endogenous infant mortality*. Infant mortality is further grouped into *neonatal mortality* and *post-neonatal mortality* depending upon the time of the occurrence of death. While the former refers to infant deaths within the first month or 28 days of birth, the latter is a term used for deaths occurring after the first month but before one year of life. Thus, while working out neonatal and post-neonatal mortality rates only the numerator in Equation (11.6) is adjusted, and therefore, the sum of the two rates is equal to IMR.

Analysis of mortality by causes of death holds a very important place in any health-related programme. One important aspect of the study of mortality, therefore, covers the causes of death. Based on the manual of WHO several broad groups of causes of deaths have been identified and used for computing *Cause-specific Death Rate* and *Ratio*. They are calculated as under:

$$\text{Cause-Specific Death Rate} = \left(D_c / P\right)K \tag{11.7}$$

$$\text{and, Cause-Specific Death Ratio} = \left(D_c / D\right)K \tag{11.8}$$

where D_c is the number of deaths in a calendar year due to cause 'c', and P and D are mid-year population and total deaths in that year respectively. The value of K is normally taken as 100 in this case. In other words, while the former relates to deaths due to a particular cause per 100 persons, the latter provides an estimate on the relative share of a particular cause in the total deaths in a population. It has been observed that with changing levels of social and economic development, the relative dominance of various causes undergoes significant changes.

Life Expectancy at Birth, derived from a life table (to be discussed in the following section) is also a very important measure of the levels of mortality in any population. Life expectancy at birth is the average number of years a cohort of new-born babies is expected to survive for, with a given risk of death at each age according to the prevailing age-specific death rates. Since, it is not affected by the age structure of a population, the measure gives a very accurate account of the prevailing mortality conditions. Though it involves a complicated method of computation, life expectancy at birth is easily understood, and is widely used in comparing mortality levels in different populations.

Life table

Mortality experience of a population is best represented by a life table. A life table is the life history of a hypothetical cohort of persons, which over a period of time gets depleted systematically because of death of its members till such time when all the persons are dead. In other words, a life table can be defined as 'a summary presentation of the death history of a cohort'. The credit of preparing the first life table goes to John Graunt who published a rudimentary life table based on the analysis of the 'Bills of Mortality' in 1662. Thereafter, several scholars have contributed towards its improvement.

The concept of a life table is very simple. Let us take a cohort of newly born babies born at a particular time to be P_0. This group will experience depletion due to death of its members at various ages until all of them have died. Thus, at the end of each successive year, the size of the cohort will get reduced to P_1, P_2, P_3 . . . and finally $P\omega$, where ω is the maximum length of life, and $P\omega$ is equal to zero. This sequence P_1, P_2, P_3, . . . $P\omega$ describes the attrition in a cohort. A life table is the summary of this gradual process of attrition in a cohort over time. A life table so constructed is called *a cohort or generation life table*. However, in a real life situation, in view of the length of the life span of a cohort, it is not possible to obtain the actual sequence corresponding to P_1, P_2, P_3, . . . $P\omega$. A solution to this problem is to take a hypothetical cohort and subject it to the age-specific death rates prevailing in a population at a particular time. Such a life table is known as a *current life table or period life table*.

Thus, life tables can be grouped in two categories – a current or period life table, and a cohort or generation life table. While a current or period life table is based on current mortality experience, a cohort or generation life table depicts the actual mortality experience of a birth cohort. The construction of a cohort or generation life table requires collection of data over a very long period. The collection of such data is almost impossible in real life situations, and this restricts the utility such life tables. The current life table is, therefore, more commonly used in any population analysis. The present discussion is confined to current life table only. Life tables can further be grouped under *complete life table* and *abridged life table*. A life table based on single-year age data is called a *complete life table*. Obviously, a complete life table becomes very clumsy and unmanageable. On the other hand, a life table based on broad age groups, say for instance 5- or 10-year interval data, is more precise, easier to construct and is the most commonly used life table in any population analysis. Such a life table is called an *abridged life table*. As the mortality experience of males and females in a population differ from each other, separate life tables are usually constructed for the two sexes.

The construction of a life table is based on certain assumptions. A life table is customarily constructed for a hypothetical cohort of 1,00,000 new-born babies. This is called the *radix* of the life table. The radix is assumed to be closed to migration. It gets depleted only through death of its members. A life table population, thus, resembles a stationary population where births and deaths are equal. The members of the cohort die according to a given schedule of age-specific death rates, and there is no periodic fluctuation in the death schedule due to random factors. A life table is, therefore, a deterministic model. And finally, the number of deaths, barring the few early years, is supposed to be uniformly spread over a year.

Columns of a life table

As the name suggests, a life table is usually presented in a tabular form consisting of different columns. The readers will note that all these columns are interrelated, and once a crucial column is known the rest of the columns can be generated from it. A brief account of these columns and their functional relations is given next (see Table 11.1):

Column 1: Age x to x+n: The first column of a life table relates to age represented by x. Age here means 'exact age'. In an abridged life table it is expressed as 'x to x+n', where n is the age interval.

Column 2: '${}_nq_x$' is the probability of dying of a person between the age group 'x to x+n'. When the age interval is 1 year it is denoted as q_x. In a current life table this is the crucial column. The values of this column are obtained from the age-specific death rates of the population.

Column 3: '${}_np_x$' is the probability of survival of a person between the age 'x to x+n'. A person will either survive or die, hence '${}_np_x$' is equal to 1-'${}_nq_x$'. Since '${}_np_x$' is not required in the generation of other columns, it is generally not included in most of the life tables.

TABLE 11.1 Period abridged life table for females, India, 2012–16

Age	${}_nq_x$	${}_np_x$	${}_nd_x$	l_x	${}_nL_x$	T_x	e_x
1	*2*	*3*	*4*	*5*	*6*	*7*	*8*
0	0.04137	0.95863	4137	100000	96584	7018127	70.2
1–4	0.00919	0.99081	881	95863	381214	6921543	72.2
5–9	0.00394	0.99606	374	94983	473978	6540329	68.9
10–14	0.00295	0.99705	279	94608	472345	6066351	64.1
15–19	0.00489	0.99511	461	94330	470569	5594006	59.3
20–24	0.00638	0.99362	599	93868	467882	5123437	54.6
25–29	0.00668	0.99332	623	93270	464809	4655555	49.9
30–34	0.00742	0.99258	687	92647	461567	4190746	45.2
35–39	0.00980	0.99020	901	91959	457654	3729179	40.6
40–44	0.01376	0.98624	1253	91057	452318	3271525	35.9
45–49	0.01879	0.98121	1687	89804	445134	2819207	31.4
50–54	0.03609	0.96391	3180	88117	433241	2374073	26.9
55–59	0.04957	0.95043	4210	84937	414798	1940832	22.9
60–64	0.08078	0.91922	6521	80727	388378	1526034	18.9
65–69	0.12197	0.87803	9051	74206	349591	1137656	15.3
70–74	0.18581	0.81419	12106	65155	296650	788065	12.1
75–79	0.26625	0.73375	14124	53049	231019	491415	9.3
80–84	0.42664	0.57336	16607	38925	152735	260396	6.7
85+	1	0	22318	22318	107661	107661	4.8

Source: Based on SRS *Abridged Life Tables, 2012–16*, Office of the Registrar General of India, New Delhi.

Column 4: 'l_x' is the number of persons surviving at the beginning of age x. This column starts with l_0, the size of the birth cohort, and undergoes decline through deaths at each subsequent age of life. The value of l_x is obtained by subtracting the number of deaths in the previous age group from its corresponding l_x. In other words,

$$l_{x+n} = l_x - {}_n d_x. \tag{11.9}$$

$$\text{or } .l_{x+n} = l_x \cdot {}_n p_n \tag{11.10}$$

In case of a cohort or generation life table, this column is already known and the rest of the columns are generated from it.

Column 5: '${}_n d_x$' is the number of deaths in the age group 'x to x+n'. It is obtained in the following manner:

$$'{}_n d_x' = l_x \cdot {}_n q_x \cdot. \tag{11.11}$$

Column 6: '${}_n L_x$' is the person years lived by l_x persons in the age group 'x to x+n'. This column is the equivalent to the population and hence it is called the *life table population.*

Column 7: T_x is the total number of years lived by the cohort after exact age x, and is obtained by cumulating the ${}_n L_x$ column upward from the last row.

Column 8: e_x is the end product of a life table. It is the average number of years a person age x years is expected to live. This column is worked out in the following manner:

$$e_x = T_x \ / \ l_x. \tag{11.12}$$

Life expectancy at birth is, thus, denoted by e^0. It is a summary measure of mortality conditions in a population as a whole. It has been found that life expectancy, except for the early age groups in a life table, tends to decline with increase in age. With a somewhat greater risk of deaths at age 0, life expectancy is lower at this age than that at age 1.

As noted earlier, in the construction of a life table ${}_n q_x$ is the crucial column, and once this column is known, columns corresponding to ${}_n d_x$ and l_x can be generated. It has also been noted that the values of ${}_n q_x$ are approximated from age-specific death rates. Thus, all that is needed for the construction of a life table is the data on age-specific death rates in the population concerned. It should be noted that while age-specific death rates relate to mid-year population [see Equation (11.3)], ${}_n q_x$ as probability relates to the population at the beginning of the age interval. Under the assumption of a linear distribution of deaths over the age interval, ${}_n q_x$ is calculated as under:

$${}_n q_x = 2\text{n} \cdot {}_n m_x \ / \ 2 \ + \ \text{n} \cdot {}_n m_x. \tag{11.13}$$

where ${}_n m_x$ is the age-specific death rate in the age group 'x to x + n', and n is the age interval. This formula can be used for all age groups including 1–4 years age group (see Woods, 1979). For probability of dying at age '0' i.e. q_0, however, the suggested formula is:

$$q_0 = 2.m_0 / 2 + m_0. \tag{11.14}$$

In the last row of the column, since all the survivors at the beginning of the age group will die in due course of time, the value of probability of dying is equal to 1. Once the probability of dying has been obtained, l_x and $_nd_x$ can be systematically generated from top to bottom using Equations (11.9) and (11.11) respectively. Under the assumption of a uniform distribution of deaths over the age interval, L_x is the mid-year population [i.e. $(L_x + L_{x+1}) /2$] in a life table based on single-year data. However, the assumption of uniform mortality is not applicable to the first year in life. Therefore, a variety of 'separation factors' are employed to weight what could normally be the average of L_0 and L_1. The suggested formula is:

$$L_0 = 0.3l_0 + 0.7l_1, \text{ and} \tag{11.15}$$

it should, however, be noted that these weights are not applicable universally. Keeping in mind the mortality experiences, different weights are suggested for different populations. For the age groups beyond the first year of life, a uniform weight of 0.5 is generally used in the case of a complete life table. In an abridged life table, the value of subsequent '$_nL_x$' is obtained in the following manner:

$$_nL_x = n / 2(l_x + l_{x+n}) \tag{11.16}$$

Note that this is similar to the weight of 0.5 used in the case of a complete life table. As noted earlier, a life table generally terminates with open-ended interval, for instance 70+ or 80+. The $_nL_x$ value corresponding to the last row, for say '70 years and above', can be approximated in the following manner:

$$_\infty L_{70} = _\infty d_{70} / _\infty m_{70}. \tag{11.17}$$

where $_\infty d_{70}$ is the number of deaths in the age group 70 and above, and $_\infty m_{70}$ is the age-specific death rate of the age group.

And finally, expectancy of life (e_x), the last column of the life table, can be generated using Equation (11.11). Table 11.1 shows a life table of females in India based on the age-specific death rates by sex for the year 2012–16.

The previously discussed procedure for the construction of a life table is based on the assumption of linearity in the distribution of deaths. This assumption is, however, not always empirically acceptable. For the construction of a life table, scholars have, therefore, suggested several alternate procedures. It should, however, be noted that all of them suffer from one or the other defects (Ramakumar, 1986:85). We limit our discussion to two of them, which give better results, and are widely used in construction of life tables. Reed and Merrell proposed a method in 1939, which is simple to calculate and gives fairly accurate results. They suggested the following formula to arrive at ${}_nq_x$ values:

$$ {}_nq_x = 1 - \exp\left[-n.{}_nm_x - a \,.\, n^3.{}_nm_x{}^2\right] \tag{11.18}$$

where the value of 'a' is taken as 0.008 which gives a good fit for age interval 1 to 10 and for ages 0 to 80. Reed and Marrell also constructed a series of tables for ${}_nq_x$ values corresponding to different values of 'n' and age-specific death rates (see Shryock and Siegel, 1976).

For the values of ${}_nL_x$, Reed and Marrell suggested the following equation:

$$L_0 = 0.276l_0 + 0.724l_1, \tag{11.19}$$

$${}_1L_4 = 0.034l_0 + 1.184l_1 + 2.782l_5 \tag{11.20}$$

$$\text{and, } {}_5L_5 = -0.003l_0 + 2.242l_5 + 2.761\, l_{10} \tag{11.21}$$

For ages beyond 10, they suggested calculating T_x directly using the following equation:

$$T_x = -0.20833l_{x-5} + 2.5l_x + 0.20833l_{x+5} + 5\Sigma_{i=1}{}^{\infty} l_x + 5_i \tag{11.22}$$

In 1943, Greville suggested a method which involves fitting a smooth curve to the relationship between ${}_nm_x$ and age (see Srinivasan, 1998b). Greville derived ${}_nq_x$ values in the following manner:

$$ {}_nqx = {}_n m_x / [1/n + {}_n m_x \{1/2 + [n/12.({}_nm_x - \log_e{}^c]\}]. \tag{11.23}$$

where the value of $\log_e{}^c$ is 0.095 which gives the best fit. Greville suggested the following formula for obtaining ${}_nL_x$ values:

$${}_1L_0 = 0.276\,.l_0 + (1 - 0.276)l_1. \tag{11.24}$$

It may be noted that Equation (11.23) is similar to the equation suggested by Reed and Merrell [Equation (11.19)].

Similarly,

$${}_4L_1 = 1.6l_1 + 2.4l_4. \tag{11.25}$$

$${}_5L_x = (l_x + l_{x+5})\ 2.5 \tag{11.26}$$

$$\text{and } L_{70+} = (d_{70+} / m_{70+}) \tag{11.27}$$

Levels and trends in world mortality

Trends in world mortality

Data on mortality rates are generally not available for a distant past, even in the case of developed countries. However, it can safely be argued that world death rates remained very high and fluctuating throughout much of human history. There are indications that death rates occasionally exceeded birth rates causing shrink in human population. A high death rate in the past is generally attributed to frequent famines and shortage of food, poor sanitary conditions and recurrent epidemics, and wars. According to the estimates of Ralp Thomilson, world average life span that was as low as 31 years during the pre-Greek period in 3500 BC increased only marginally to around 40 years in 1750 AD (Bhende and Kanitkar, 2011:211). According to another estimate, average life span in most of the currently developed countries of the West was hardly more than 40 years even during the middle of the 19th century. Thereafter, however, world mortality conditions underwent significant progress, resulting in tremendous rise in average life span.

It was in north-western Europe that the death rates first began to decline in the late 18th and early 19th century (Beaujeu-Garnier, 1978:87). The average crude death rates in West Europe declined from 30 per thousand at the turn of the 19th century to 18 per thousand towards the close of the century. The average life span of Denmark, England and Wales, France, Norway and Sweden in north-west Europe (and the state of Massachusetts in the United States) increased from 41.5 years in the year 1850 to 50.5 years in the year 1900 (UN, 1973:111). The improvement was, however, more conspicuous towards the last quarter of the 19th century.

Based on the analysis of abridged cohort and period life tables prepared by Case et al. (1962) for England and Wales for the period 1841 to 1970, Woods (1979) concludes that the initial decline in death rates, and rise in life expectancy, were mainly due to reduction in death rates in childhood and young adult ages particularly among females. A reduction in infant mortality and mortality among middle and old-aged persons during the subsequent decades further accelerated improvement in overall mortality conditions. According to Woods, other north-west European countries are also likely to have undergone a similar trend.

The causes of the improvements in mortality conditions are to be found in a set of events that began taking place in Europe from sometime in the middle of the 18th century. They include an increased availability of food, overall improvement in the standards of living, and medical discoveries. With the Agricultural Revolution in Europe there was a drastic change in food availability, both in terms of quantity and quality. A better diet was probably the main cause of decline in death rates from diseases such as tuberculosis.

Overall social and economic development and advances in medical technologies brought about significant changes in the living conditions of the people. Sanitary reforms coupled with development of, and discoveries in, medical science led to an increased control over deaths due to epidemics and infectious and communicable diseases. Towards the close of the 18th century, the development and spread of the vaccination against smallpox (which had been responsible for nearly 10 per cent of all deaths and more that 30 per cent of deaths among children up to the age of 4 years) was a major development in the fight against deaths. This was followed by great advancements in anatomical studies. Introduction of anaesthesia and antiseptic surgery at the beginning of the 18th century was another significant achievement, which helped a great deal in the fight against deaths. The fight against deaths was further facilitated by rapid development in the fields of education and transportation.

In the initial stages of industrialisation and urbanisation, however, the west European countries had experienced a rise in death rates, a symptom of the profound misery of the proletariat and appearance of occupational diseases (Beaujeu-Garnier, 1978:89). This had occurred first in the United Kingdom, and a little later in Germany, during the first half of the 19th century. With the introduction of various reforms by the governments, things improved for the better, and the mortality rates started declining again towards the close of the century. These reforms included laws protecting workers from exploitation, wage regulation and regulation of child labour and women workers.

Once mortality conditions began improving in Western Europe, the rest of Europe and other countries inhabited by the white population such as the United States and Canada in North America, Australia and New Zealand in Oceania, and the erstwhile USSR, followed suit. However, the lead of north-western Europe in the reduction in mortality rates over the rest of Europe persisted till the beginning of the 20th century. During the period 1906–1909, high crude death rates were still observed in Romania (26.3), Yugoslavia (24.9), Spain (24.3), Bulgaria (24.0), Hungary (24.0) and Poland (22.9). On the other hand, the north-west European countries reported death rates ranging from 10 to 20 per thousand persons. Countries like Denmark, Norway, Sweden, the United Kingdom and the Netherlands were on the lower side of the range, while Finland, Iceland, Belgium, East and West Germany, France and Switzerland were on the higher side. Outside Europe, Australia, New Zealand and the United States of America also reported crude death rates in the range of 10 to 20 per thousand persons.

This disparity in death rates among the developed countries narrowed down drastically by the middle of the 20th century. Japan, the only country from Asia, experienced an unprecedented decline in mortality rates during the second quarter of the 20th century. Crude death rates in Japan declined from 23.0 per thousand persons during 1920–25 to 9.4 in 1950–54, a decline which took more than a century in most of the north-west European countries.

The closing decades of the 20th century, however, have witnessed still another rising trend in the death rates among the developed countries, which is largely attributed to age structure of the population. The populations of these countries have grown older with a long-term decline in fertility rates. Earlier during the century also most of these countries had recorded an increase in death rates, though temporarily, during the war periods, the extent of which depended upon their differential involvement in wars. Some countries, for instance Sweden, experienced disruption in the decreasing trend due to specific reasons such as the influenza pandemic of 1918 and the economic depression of the 1930s (Woods, 1979:65).

Mortality decline that once began in the developed countries gradually spread to the less developed parts of the world towards the beginning of the 20th century. However, improvement in mortality conditions in the less developed countries became perceptible only towards the middle of the century. Innovations and discoveries in medical sciences were grafted in this part of the world, and the resultant effects were a somewhat faster decline in mortality rates. Though unavailability of reliable data does not permit us to construct an accurate trend, it can be safely argued that the latter half of the 20th century did witness an impressive decline in death rates, much faster than what had happened in the West. As a result of this, the levels of death rates among many of these countries are now similar to those in the developed countries. In some cases death rates are even lower than those prevailing in the latter.

Some of the developing countries, which had reasonably high death rates at least up to the middle of the 1940s, and which experienced significant decline thereafter, are Mauritius, Mexico, Singapore, Chile and Sri Lanka. Countries like Jamaica, Puerto Rico, and Trinidad and Tobago in the Caribbean started experiencing decline in mortality rates a little earlier in the century. In Sri Lanka death rates, which remained above 20 per thousand persons up to 1940–45, declined to less than 10 by 1960–64, thanks to a vigorous campaign against malaria in the country. India also witnessed a perceptible decline in death rates since the 1930s.

Causes underlying high mortality in the past

High mortality rates throughout much of the past can mainly be attributed to famines and shortages of food, recurrent epidemics in the wake of poor sanitary conditions and frequent wars. However, as society progressed, humankind gradually developed control over these factors, and mortality rates began declining. This development first occurred in the developed realm of the world and gradually spread to the rest of the globe.

The Agricultural Revolution and subsequent changes in the agricultural practices drastically improved food supply leading to disappearance of deaths caused by food scarcity. Further, improvement in nutritional intake enhanced man's resistance to several diseases, which used to take a heavy toll of life in the past. Improvements in the mode of transportation enabled movement of food from areas of surplus to areas of scarcity, thus, neutralising the effects of local famines. Improvement in overall living standards helped people in several ways by protecting them from the vagaries of nature.

The Agricultural Revolution was followed by the Industrial Revolution in Europe in the middle of the 18th century. With the emergence of large industrial centres marked with extreme congestion, poor hygienic and sanitary conditions, and adverse working conditions in the factories, the Industrial Revolution had initially led to an increase in mortality rates in some countries in Europe. However, during the subsequent period, once improvement in sanitary conditions and health measures began, mortality rates once again started declining. Sanitary reform included measures such as provision of safe drinking water and introduction of sewage disposal systems. These measures played a crucial role in eliminating the environmental conditions that were previously favourable to the spread of communicable diseases. The process of disinfecting water by chlorinating brought many waterborne communicable diseases like cholera, diarrhoea and dysentery under control. Simultaneously, social reform measures like improvement in working conditions in factories, introduction of a social security system covering old-age pension benefits, health insurance and medical care etc. were initiated in several countries in Europe. All these had profound effects on mortality levels.

Personal hygiene and community cleanliness gradually occupied a central position in the hygiene movement all over Europe. Growing literacy in the wake of overall improvement in living conditions generated awareness among people regarding the importance of personal and social hygiene. Medical advances including expansion of hospitals, changes in health education and improvements in medicines and treatment further provided a boost to the fight against death. In the late 19th century, the development of asepsis and antisepsis helped a great deal in arresting mortality rates. This was followed by development of vaccines against several diseases like smallpox, chickenpox, sheep anthrax, hydrophobia, diphtheria etc. among others. Prophylactic antitoxins were developed later to control diseases like typhoid, yellow fever, scarlet fever, influenza, measles, whooping cough etc. Plague, the largest killer, had already disappeared from Europe since long back. The incidence of tuberculosis, another deadly killer, was brought under control with the introduction of antibiotics by the middle of the 20th century. The control of polio by vaccination around the same time is also a milestone in the medical advancement of humankind.

These measures were later grafted in the less developed countries, which resulted in a drastic decline in mortality rates since the middle of the 20th century. Scientific communication and international co-operation have made it possible for the less developed countries to import techniques from the developed countries and apply them in 'mass health programmes' at a relatively lower cost. The World Health Organisation (WHO) has played a crucial role in death control programmes in these countries. However, as most of the sanitary reforms are very costly, many of the less developed countries continue to struggle with high mortality rates.

World patterns in mortality rates

Table 11.2 presents the latest estimates on select indicators of mortality rates in the world and its major areas. It is important to note that CDR in the more developed world has almost remained unchanged over the past decade and a half, but the same in less developed parts has further declined. Consequently the gap between them has drastically widened. Low mortality rates in the less developed world, however,

TABLE 11.2 Estimates of mortality and life expectancy in the world and major areas, 2017

World/ Major Areas	*Crude Death Rate*	*Infant Mortality Rate*	*Life Expectancy at Birth (years)*	
			Male	*Female*
Africa	9	51	61	64
Asia	7	28	71	74
Europe	11	4	75	81
Latin America and the Caribbean	5	19	73	79
North America	8	6	77	81
Oceania	7	20	75	79
More developed	10	5	76	82
Less developed	7	35	69	72
Less developed (excl. China)	7	39	67	71
World Average	8	32	70	74

Source: Population Reference Bureau, *World Population Data Sheet*, 2017.

does not mean better mortality conditions than those among the more developed countries. The less developed parts of the world have undergone a more rapid decline in death rates during the recent past than what had earlier happened in the developed West at this level of economic development. As noted already, the developed countries of the world experienced an increase in the death rate due to its typical age structure in the latter half of the last century. The populations of these countries have grown older in the wake of a very low level of birth rates over a very long time in the past. A significantly larger proportion of population in the higher age brackets, which have a greater probability of dying, inevitably results in a higher level of general mortality rate. This phenomenon is more prominent among countries in Europe. The death rates in some of these countries are, in fact, higher than the birth rates. As a result of this, such countries are experiencing gradual shrink in their populations. Till some recent past, Russia had a significant gap between its death rate and birth rate resulting in annual deficit of 0.95 million persons. However, the situation in Russia has of late changed with a slight rise in birth rate accompanied by a similar decline in death rate. Bulgaria and Ukraine report the largest gap between birth and death rates. The population of Ukraine is losing about 0.34 million people each year because of more deaths than births. Currently as many as 10 other countries in Europe namely Serbia, Lithuania, Hungary, Croatia, Greece, Portugal, Estonia, Latvia, Belarus, and Romania are characterised by more deaths than births (PRB, 2017). Japan, the only country outside Europe, joined the group recently with more deaths than births.

At the macro-level, ignoring Europe which has witnessed a rise in death rates during recent times, Africa still reports the highest death rate in the world. The highest death rate above 10 per thousand can be seen in western and middle Africa

(Map 11.1). Starting from west to east, Mali, Nigeria, Chad, South Sudan and Somali are some of the prominent countries in Africa where death rates are very high. Barring Europe and Russia, nowhere else in the world is there such a high level of death rate. The northern parts of the continent along the Mediterranean Sea comprising Morocco, Algeria, Libya and Egypt, along with some countries in the eastern and southern parts like Ethiopia, Kenya, Tanzania and Botswana, show a low death rate (below 7 per thousand). In the rest of the countries in Africa, death rates vary between 7 and 10 per thousand. By contrast, countries in Latin and Central America along with the Caribbean islands report far better mortality conditions. The crude death rate in none of the countries in the continent exceeds a level of 7 per thousand except Argentina and Uruguay. Interestingly, the crude death rate in Argentina has remained unchanged at this level since the mid-1990s, while Uruguay has reported a rather slow decline in CDR during the recent past. In the less developed realm, Asia occupies a position somewhere in between these two extremes. Till recent past, in some countries like Afghanistan, Iraq, Yemen, Kazakhstan, Nepal, Pakistan, Cambodia, Laos, Myanmar and South Korea, death rates were between 10 and 20 per thousand persons. Mortality conditions have undergone significant transformation, and it is only in Georgia, Japan and Timor-Leste where CDR exceeds 10 per thousand. Japan's case is similar to any European country. The demographic situation in Georgia, located on the eastern side of Black Sea in West Asia, is also more like the European realm. CDR in the country has reportedly gone up from 10 in 1995 to 14 in 2017. Timor-Leste, also known as East Timor, is a small country in Southeast Asia occupying the eastern part of Timor Island. In the rest of the countries in Asia,

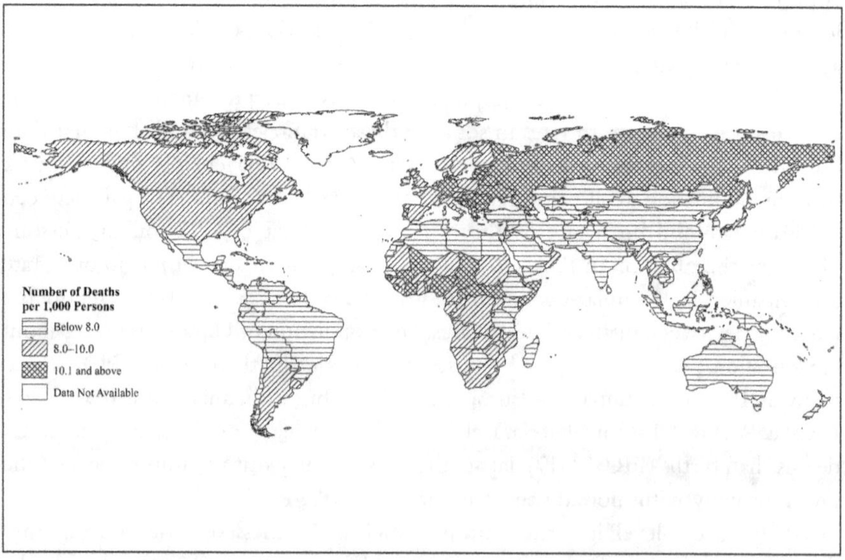

MAP 11.1 Crude death rate in the world, 2017

Source: Population Reference Bureau, *World Population Data Sheet, 2017*

death rates have come down to less than 10. Further, barring only a few countries like Myanmar, Thailand and North Korea in south-eastern parts and Armenia in western parts, the whole of the continent reports CDR below 7 per thousand persons. It is interesting to note that crude death rates in by and large the whole of Asia along with Latin and Central America including the Caribbean islands are identical to those prevailing in the developed countries prior to the recent rise in death rates.

As noted earlier in the chapter, *infant mortality rate* provides a better picture of mortality conditions in a population. In other words, the infant mortality rate (IMR) reveals a closer correspondence with levels of social and economic development achieved in a population. Infant mortality rate refers to the number of infant deaths per thousand live births in an area. The infant mortality rate for the world as a whole works out to be 32 in 2017 down from 55 in 2003. This means that 1 out of every 31 babies dies before attaining the age of 1 year. Unlike the death rate, in case of IMR one comes across a stark contrast between the developed and less developed parts of the world. In the developed parts of the world, 1 in every 200 newly born babies is at the risk of dying before attaining the age of 1 year, while in the less developed countries excluding China, 1 in every 25 newly born babies does not survive up to the age of 1 year.

The estimates on the infant mortality rate reveal a grim picture for the newborn babies among the poorest countries of the world, mainly in Africa. Just as in the case of crude death rates, countries in Africa, particularly in its western and central parts, report unusually higher infant mortality rates (Map 11.2). Evidences indicate that infant mortality in these regions has undergone drastic decline during the last half a century. Surveys conducted during the late 1950s and early 1960s had revealed that infant mortality rates above 200 were quite common in this part of the world (Bhende and Kanitkar, 2011:192). Mozambique in the eastern part of the continent reported an infant mortality rate above 200 till as early as 2003. The diffusion of medical technologies from the developed countries of the world has resulted in significant reduction of infant mortality rates in Africa. Nevertheless, the risk of death in the early stage of life is still higher here than that in any other parts of the world. Among the countries reporting an infant mortality rate of still over 55, mention may be made of Sierra Leone, Mauritania, Guinea-Bissau, Nigeria, Benin, Burkina Faso, Côte d'Ivoire, Niger, Guinea and Mali from Western Africa, Somalia, South Sudan and Mozambique from Eastern Africa and Central African Republic, Chad, Democratic Republic of Congo, and Equatorial Guinea. In some of them IMR is even more than 85 per thousand live births. Outside Africa, the only countries having an equally higher level of infant mortality are Afghanistan and Pakistan in south Asia. Countries in Central and South America fare far better in terms of infant mortality rates also. In fact, a large number of countries in Central and South America have infant mortality rates below 10, a level almost at par with those prevailing in the developed world. Countries in Europe report less than 8 deaths among infants per thousand live births. On an average countries in Eastern Europe report slightly higher infant mortality rate than the rest of the continent. The same level of infant mortality exists in North America. Countries like Japan,

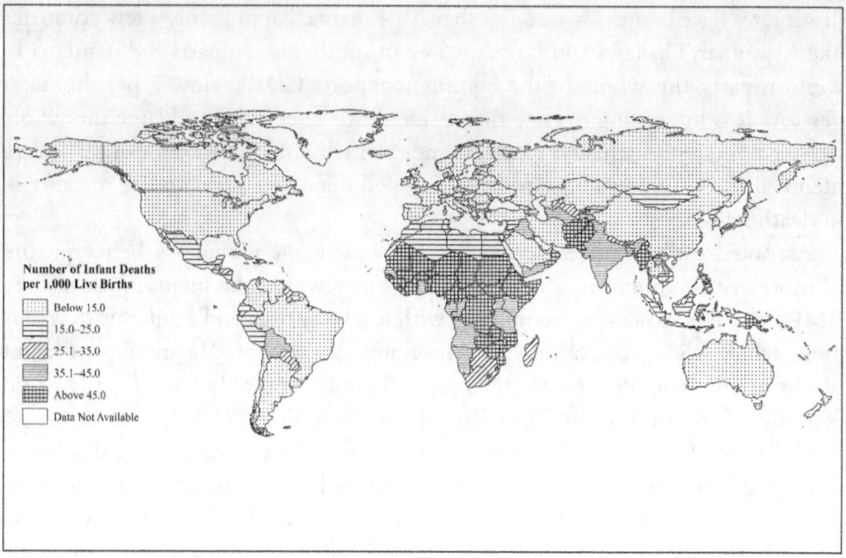

MAP 11.2 Infant mortality rate in the world, 2017

Source: Population Reference Bureau, *World Population Data Sheet, 2017*

South Korea and Taiwan also have an infant mortality rate below 5 per thousand live births. It is remarkable to note that many countries in western parts of Asia, including Bahrain, Cyprus, Qatar, Kuwait, Lebanon, Oman and United Arab Emirates, also report very low infant mortality rates – below 10. In general, it may be argued that the low level of infant mortality rate in these areas is associated with a low level of general mortality rates.

Infant deaths are grouped under two categories depending upon the exact age of the baby at death. If death occurs during the first month i.e. within four weeks of birth, it is called as *neonatal mortality*. Similarly, if the baby dies after four weeks but before attaining the age of 1 year it is termed as *post-neonatal mortality*. While factors leading to neonatal mortality are largely biological in nature, the post-neonatal mortality is mainly caused by a set of social and economic and or environmental factors. Post-neonatal mortality can be attributed to various epidemics caused by communicable diseases, both of the digestive systems such as diarrhoea and enteritis, and of the respiratory system such as bronchitis and pneumonia as well as some faulty feeding system and poor hygiene (Bhende and Kanitkar, 2011:195). All these factors reflect upon the extent of poverty and ignorance in the society. High infant mortality rates among the poorest countries of the world can thus be attributed to incidences such as exposure to infectious and parasitic diseases, poor conditions of hygiene, adverse social circumstances and lack of proper health care facilities. Since these factors operate differently among different groups within the same country, significant differentials in infant mortality rates can be seen at lower levels. Such differentials are a universal phenomenon and can be seen even among the developed countries. In the United States, for instance, evidences indicate a sharp contrast in infant mortality rates of different social groups. African-Americans, as well as other ethnic minorities, both in the urban and the rural areas, report infant mortality rates that are twice as high as the national average (Knox and Marston, 1998:122). The point is that the global patterns based on national-level estimates tend to obscure many of the regional and local variations in mortality conditions.

Like infant mortality, life expectancy at birth also reveals a true picture of the level of social and economic development a society has attained. Life expectancy, therefore, varies a great deal from country to country, region to region and group to group within the same country (see Maps 11.3 and 11.4). Since life expectancy is worked out using the age-specific death rates, the measure provides a more accurate estimate of mortality condition in a population. With overall improvement in mortality conditions, average world life expectancy at birth has undergone significant improvement during the recent past.

A baby born now in the world, on average, is expected to live to the age of around 72 years. A female baby, in general, is expected to live longer than a male baby. A higher life expectancy for females is a universal phenomenon. However, the gap between female and male life expectancy is somewhat larger in the case of more developed countries. Females are physiologically superior to males and, thus, they are less prone to various diseases. In the less developed parts of the world, the effect of this biological advantage is partly offset by a survival disadvantage during childhood and childbearing age groups. This occurs due to prevalent gender inequality, differentials in treatment of sons and daughters, extreme poverty, ignorance and lack of adequate health care facilities.

MAP 11.3 Life expectancy of males at birth in the world, 2017

Source: Population Reference Bureau, *World Population Data Sheet, 2017*

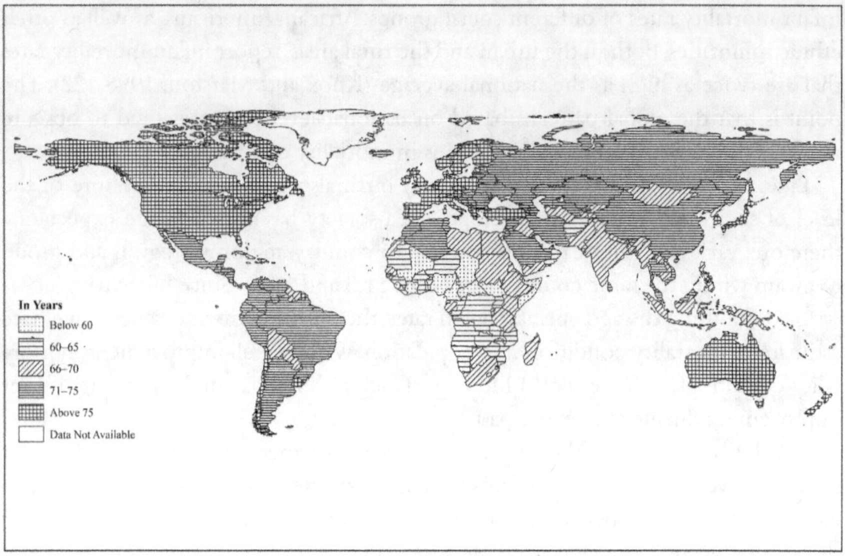

MAP 11.4 Life expectancy of females at birth in the world, 2017

Source: Population Reference Bureau, *World Population Data Sheet, 2017*

On an average, a new-born baby in the more developed countries is expected to survive up to the age of 79 years – higher by almost 10 years than those in the less developed countries. At the continent level, Africa reports a very low level of life expectancy. This is despite the fact that the largest gains in life expectancy during the recent past have been witnessed in Sub-Saharan Africa (UN, 2019:28). As one would expect, the eastern and central parts, which are characterised by a very adverse mortality condition, reveal even a lower life expectancy (Maps 11.3 and 11.4). A large number of countries spread over the whole of Africa barring its northern parts report 'low' to 'very low' life expectancy. The most prominent among them are Sierra Leone, Côte d'Ivoire, Nigeria, Guinea Bissau, Mali, Somalia, Burundi, Chad and Equatorial Guinea. A low level of life expectancy in such countries can mainly be attributed to a very high infant mortality rate. In addition, decades-long civil war and the resultant social and economic disruptions in some countries can also be responsible for adverse mortality conditions and resultant lower life expectancy. Outside Africa, low life expectancy is seen in Turkmenistan, Afghanistan and Pakistan in South Central Asia, and Myanmar in Southeast Asia. Afghanistan has been marked with political turmoil for over two decades with its devastating effects on economy and mortality conditions. On the whole, Asia occupies the second position with a value close to the world average. Latin America and the Caribbean countries, however, report higher life expectancy than the world average. The whole of North America (including Mexico), western, northern and southern Europe, Australia and New Zealand have very high life expectancy – more than 75 years. Some of the Asian countries like Cyprus, Georgia, Israel and Kuwait in the west, and Japan, Singapore, South Korea and Taiwan in the east also exhibit a very high level of life expectancy. Interestingly, Caribbean countries like Cuba, Jamaica and Puerto Rica and Costa Rica in Central America have also reached this category. In addition, countries like Chile, French Guiana and Uruguay in South America also have very high levels of life expectancy.

Health transition

For much of human history until the time of the Industrial Revolution in Europe, death rates remained at a very high level, and average life expectancy generally did not exceed 30 years. Early deaths were commonplace and nearly half of the children did not survive till five years of age. Early deaths were primarily due to widespread communicable diseases. Increased food availability accompanied by improvement in hygiene, public health and discoveries in medical sciences resulted in a decline in deaths due to communicable diseases. Beginning in north-western Europe, the decline in death rates gradually spread to other parts of the world. Improvement in survival meant growing concentration of population in higher age brackets, and this brought about a significant transformation in morbidity pattern and age distribution of deaths. Communicable or infectious diseases gradually gave way to degenerative or non-communicable diseases, a phenomenon often called as *epidemiological transition*. Epidemiological transition is generally described as 'a shift from the predominance of infectious and parasitic diseases to that of chronic and degenerative diseases of adulthood as the main cause of death' (Radkar et al., 2010:23). Of late, the term *health transition* is preferred to epidemiological transition as it is concerned more with health and survival rather than death (Phillips, 1994:72). It may be noted that epidemiological or health transition and demographic transition (demographic transition as an actual experience of world population has been discussed in Chapters 5, 'Population Growth', and as a model in Chapter 13, 'Population Theories') overlap and both result from the processes of socio-economic development and modernisation. The more developed regions of the world are characterised by more deaths due to non-communicable diseases and vice versa. As the timing of demographic transition varied over space depending upon social and economic conditions, the nature and pace of health transition also varies from one country to another. This is reflected in the varying mix of disease burden – communicable and non-communicable – across the world (Table 11.3).

Diseases caused by bacteria such as tuberculosis, pneumonia and the plague, or virus such as influenza, chicken pox and measles, or protozoa such as malaria, diarrhoea and cholera are known as communicable diseases. Until recently, communicable diseases were the major cause of deaths across the world. Although significant progress has been made in eradication of some of the worst communicable diseases, the less developed countries continue to grapple with some of the deadliest communicable diseases. Measles and tuberculosis for instance continue to be a major challenge in Sub-Saharan Africa (Weeks, 2018; Newbold, 2012). Based on the estimates of WHO, Weeks (2018:161) indicated that in the year 2011, out of the 10 major causes of deaths, as many as 8 were communicable diseases among the low

TABLE 11.3 Estimated deaths by causes in the world, 2016

Regions/World*	*Communicable Disease*		*Non-communicable Diseases*		*Injuries*		*All Causes*	
	Deaths (thousands)	*% of Total Deaths*	*Deaths (thousands)*	*% of Total Deaths*	*Deaths (thousands)*	*% of Total Deaths*	*Deaths (thousands)*	*% of Total Deaths*
Low income countries	2804	52.3	1970	36.8	584	10.9	5357	100.0
Lower middle income countries	6537	29.5	13439	60.7	2158	9.8	22134	100.0
Upper middle income countries	1418	7.4	16118	84.4	1570	8.2	19106	100.0
High income countries	687	6.7	9019	87.8	571	5.6	10277	100.0
World	11445	20.1	40545	71.3	4883	8.6	56874	100.0

* Based on World Bank Income Groups 2010–15

Source: Based on World Health Organisation, 2018.

income countries. On the contrary, 9 out of 10 major causes of death in high income countries are non-communicable or degenerative diseases. Non-communicable diseases include heart disease or cardio-vascular problems, cancer, diabetes, hypertension, Alzheimer's disease, etc. It may be noted that the pace of mortality transition in less developed parts of the world was much faster than what had earlier happened in the developed world. Further, the decline in death rates in these parts began without sufficient progress on social and economic fronts. As a result, the age structure of population in these regions underwent a change, leading to a gradual rise in deaths due to degenerative diseases while communicable diseases were yet to be completely eradicated.

Despite successful eradication of some of the deadliest communicable diseases like smallpox, the plague, cholera etc., the last few decades have seen the emergence of new forms of old infectious and parasitic diseases. Examples of drug-resistant malaria, tuberculosis, new forms of cholera etc. can be cited here. The rise of some new infectious and parasitic diseases like Ebola, HIV/AIDS, H1N1, Nipah etc. have posed additional challenges to the world community. The virus for Ebola, a deadly disease for which there is no known cure, was identified for the first time in 1976 in tropical Africa. Since then there have been several outbreaks of Ebola from different parts of Africa claiming thousands of lives. Ebola was soon followed by another deadly infectious disease known as HIV/AIDS.

Appearing for the first time in the early 1980s, HIV/AIDS soon acquired the nature of a pandemic disease. According to UNAIDS, as many as 37.9 million people were living with HIV/AIDS in 2018 (Table 11.4). This number is up from 35 million people in 2012 (Weeks, 2018:162). The rise in the number, however, should not mean that the disease is spreading faster now than before. Rather, it is the availability

TABLE 11.4 Persons living with HIV/AIDS, number of new cases and deaths due to AIDS in the world and major regions, 2018

World Regions	*Adults and Children Living with HIV (millions)*	*Adults and Children Newly Infected with HIV (thousands)*	*Adult and Child Deaths Due to AIDS (thousands)*
Eastern and Southern Africa	20.6	800	310
Western and Central Africa	5.0	280	160
Middle and North Africa	0.24	20	8.4
Asia and the Pacific	5.9	310	200
Latin America	1.9	100	35
Caribbean	0.34	16	6.7
Eastern Europe and Central Asia	1.7	150	38
Western and Central Europe and North America	2.2	68	13
World Total	37.9	1700	770

Source: Based on *UNAIDS Data, 2019*, p. 20.

of new treatments that keep HIV-affected people alive for a longer period after the virus was contracted. If anything, the number of deaths due to AIDS-related illness as well as the number of new cases has come down during the recent past. In 2018, a total of 0.77 million deaths in the world were reported due to HIV/AIDS (UNAIDS, 2019) as compared to 1.6 million in 2012 (Weeks, 2018:163). At the same time the number of new infections has also come down from 2.3 million in 2012 to 1.7 million in 2018. However, a reduction of this magnitude still leaves the world far off the 2020 target of below 0.5 million new infections (UNAIDS, 2019:7). The poorest countries Sub-Saharan Africa report the highest prevalence rate as cases of new infections which had reversed the rising trend in life expectancy since the time the virus exploded in the region. Eastern and southern Africa alone account for over half of the world population living with HIV. Simple preventive measures like use of condoms and discouraging used syringes etc. have been quite successful in controlling the spread of HIV/AIDS in the developed West. However, the Sub-Saharan countries have been slow in simply recognising the existence of the virus and in adopting HIV/AIDS awareness programmes (Newbold, 2012:110). Elsewhere in the world although the HIV prevalence rate is low, drug addicts using injections, visitors to prostitutes, people engaged in sex with multiple partners, gays etc. are at a much higher risk of getting infected. The respective governments have to be really alert and respond to the risk of transmission of the virus.

The virus of Ebola as well as HIV/AIDS spreads through direct contact with body fluids of affected persons. Similarly, the Nipah virus is transmitted from animals to human. The first outbreak of the virus was reported from Malaysia among pig farmers in 1991. This was followed by the outbreak of the disease in Bangladesh and since then it is reoccurring in the country almost every year. The evidences of the virus have been reported periodically from eastern India. The virus was transmitted to humans from unprotected exposure to secretions from the pigs or tissues of a sick animal. In Bangladesh and India, consumption of fruit products contaminated with urine or saliva from infected fruit bats is said to be the source of transmission of the virus to humans. Thereafter, the virus spread from one person to another through close contact with the secretions and excretions of the affected person. Birds are also the source of many new viral diseases that spread fast among humans through contact. In 2003, a new strain of virus H5N1 (called *bird flu*) was reported in Asia that originated from poultry and spread through migratory birds. This was soon followed by a new virus H1N1 in 2009, causing symptoms of flu, known as *swine flu*, and it rapidly took the form of an epidemic. The virus is contagious and spreads from one affected person to another.

Mortality in India

Trends in mortality rates

As anywhere else in the less developed parts of the world, mortality transition in India is a phenomenon of the 20th century. However, India has the distinction of having experienced one of the earliest declines in mortality among the less developed countries. The less developed countries, in general, began experiencing declines in mortality levels only towards the middle of the 20th century. As against this, in India the decline is found to have set in as early as in the 1920s. Prior to that, death rates were usually very high, often exceeding birth rates in the wake of famines and epidemics. This excess of deaths over births occasionally resulted in the shrink in the population size of the country. The decade 1911–21, for instance, had witnessed a negative growth in population due to heavy loss of life in the wake of the influenza epidemic that struck several areas in north India. It is, therefore, rightly remarked that the history of population growth in the country prior to 1921 is the history of a great fight against death.

It may be recalled that accurate estimates on trends in mortality in the country for much of the past, when death rates were very high and fluctuating, are not available. Although the civil registration system has a longer history, its estimates are not reliable. The sample registration system, which is based on the principle of the *dual report system* and which provides more reliable estimates, was introduced in the country only in the late 1960s. Scholars have, however, derived estimated on trends in mortality in the country using some indirect measures. The present account of trends in mortality rates in the country is largely based on those estimates. Table 11.5 presents the average annual death rate and life expectancy in India over a period of roughly 100 years.

Till 1921 crude death rates in the country remained very high. The decade 1911–21, in fact, witnessed a drastic increase in the death rate as compared to the

TABLE 11.5 Trends in average annual death rates and life expectancy in India, 1901–11 to 2015–17

Average Annual Crude Death Rate		*Average Life Expectancy*	
Period	*No. of Deaths per 1,000 persons*	*Period*	*In Years*
1901–11	42.6	1901–10	22.6
1911–21	48.6	1911–20	20.1
1921–31	36.3	1921–30	26.8
1931–41	31.2	1931–40	31.8
1941–51	27.4	1941–50	32.1
1951–61	22.8	1951–60	41.3
1961–71	18.9	1961–70	46.4
1986–88	11.0	1976–80	52.3
1996–98	9.0	1981–86	56.0
2005–07	7.5	1990–91	58.6
2015–17	6.5	2010–14	67.9

Sources: (i) Bhende and Kanitkar, 2011:225, 227 (ii) RGI, *Compendium on India's Fertility and Mortality, 2013–17* and (iii) *SRS Bulletin*, Vol. 50, No. 1–2, 2016 and 2017, and (iv) SRS, Office of the Registrar General, India (obtained from NITI, Ayog website, https://niti.gov.in/content/life-expectancy).

previous decade due to the disastrous influenza epidemic of the year 1918, which claimed the lives of 15 million persons. The death rate was indeed the highest ever known in the history of India's population. Thereafter, the rates have declined continuously over the period. The first major decline occurred during the decade 1921–31 when it came down to 36 per thousand persons. Thereafter, decline in death rates continued during each of the subsequent decades, and by the end of 1980s it was close to 10 per thousand persons. The latest SRS estimate for the years 2015–16 indicates a death rate of 6.5. It may be noted that over a period of only 80 years, the death rate in the country declined by a margin that had earlier taken more than 170 years in the developed West. Obviously, the decline in India, as also in other less developed countries, has been much faster than that in the developed countries.

One of the main reasons of the high mortality rates in the past was a significantly higher incidence of deaths among infants and children. Although firm data on trends on mortality among infants and children are not available, it is understood that infant mortality rates in India during the early parts of the 20th century were abnormally high. According to one estimate, infant mortality rates during the decade 1901–11 were as high as 290.0 for males and 284.6 for females. As a result, average life expectancy at the turn of the last century was one of the lowest in the recorded history of humankind. During much of the first half the century, the average life expectancy remained below 30 years. Nevertheless, with improvements in general mortality conditions, life expectancy has recorded an increase in each successive decade. Though infant mortality has undergone an impressive decline during the last century, the percentage decline in it has been smaller than that in the general mortality rates. The current level of infant mortality is still higher than the world average. While the general mortality rate has responded to community health measures such as control of infectious and parasitic diseases, much is still desired for the improvement in mortality conditions among infants in the country.

Despite significant decline, the death rate still remains higher than many of the less developed countries in Asia, e.g. Sri Lanka, Maldives, Indonesia, Malaysia and the Philippines. The gap becomes wider if one compares the estimates on the infant mortality rate. India still reports an IMR of 34 per thousand live births as against less than 20 in all the countries in Western Asia barring only Iraq and Yemen. Some of the neighbouring countries in South and Southeast Asia like Sri Lanka, Malaysia and Maldives report IMR below 10. Similar is the case of the differences in life expectancy. It can be argued that though mortality conditions in the country are far better now than before, there is still a lot of scope for further improvement to ensure a speedy social and economic progress. The rural areas report a 23 per cent higher crude death rate than that in the urban areas (Table 11.6). Similarly, population in the rural areas exhibits a 40 per cent higher IMR than its counterpart in the urban areas. Remember that a little less than 70 per cent of the country's population still resides in the villages. Thus, the health care measures have to be extended farther to the rural areas, particularly among the weaker sections of the society, where mortality conditions are far worse despite significant strides made at the aggregate national level.

TABLE 11.6 SRS estimates on select mortality indicators in India, 2016

Mortality Indicators	*Total*	*Rural*	*Urban*
Crude Death Rate	6.4	6.9	5.4
Infant Mortality Rate	34	38	23
Neonatal Mortality Rate[1]	24	27	14
Early Neonatal Mortality	18	21	11
Late Neonatal Mortality Rate	5	6	3
Post-Neonatal Mortality Rate[2]	11	11	9
Child Mortality Rate	9.4	10.7	6.0
Under-five Mortality Rate	39	43	25
Maternal Mortality Ratio[3]	130	N.A.	N.A.

Sources: (i) Registrar General of India, *SRS Statistical Report*, 2016. (ii) Registrar General of India, *Special Bulletin on Maternal Mortality in India*, 2014–16

Notes:

1. Infant deaths that occur within four weeks i.e. one month of birth. If the death occurs within the first week it is termed as early neonatal mortality and beyond the first week but within 28 days it is termed as late neonatal mortality.
2. Infant deaths beyond occurring after one month but before 1 year of life.
3. Relates to the period 2014–16.

India has experienced a remarkable improvement in infant and child survival during the recent past. IMR that was as high as 84 per thousand live births in 1990 came down to 47 in 2011 and 34 in 2016. Similarly 'Under-five' mortality rate has come down from 118 per thousand live births in 1990 to 39 in 2016. However, with respect to infant and child mortality rates, the conditions are still alarmingly worse compared to those in other countries with similar socio-economic conditions. More than one in 30 children die within the first year of life, and more than one in 25 die before reaching the age of five. According to UNICEF, India contributes about 21 per cent of the global burden of child deaths (quoted by Jain et al., 2013:348). Another area of major concern for health care planners and policy makers relates to an extremely high incidence of maternal mortality. WHO defines maternal deaths as 'the death of a woman while pregnant or within 42 days of termination of pregnancy, irrespective of the duration and site of the pregnancy, from any cause related to or aggravated by the pregnancy or its management, but not from accidental or incidental causes' (WHO). Despite significant improvements during the last two decades, India continues to have one of the highest maternal mortality rates in the world.

A host of socio-economic factors including income levels, educational status, housing conditions, availability and access to health care facilities, exposure to media, socio-cultural practices, family structure etc. determine mortality conditions in any region. Although the decline in mortality levels during the recent past has occurred across regions, and across different socio-economic groups in India, there still exist significant mortality differentials. An understanding of these differentials is of immense value for the health care planners and policy makers in a country like India. Availability of data, however, is a serious constraint in attempts to analyse the differentials at the national level. The present discussion is confined to data on indicators of early childhood mortality by background characteristics of family. It may be noted that despite significant reduction in early childhood mortality rates across the board, there still exists a wide range of variation in the same across different social and economic groups.

The association between mortality levels and socio-economic factors is very complex. Education is often identified as a key determinant of mortality rates. It is argued that an increase in levels of education leads to improvement in the ability of the people to use health care services in a more effective manner. In this regard, educational attainment of mothers, particularly, is considered as the most powerful determinant. The findings of the NFHS-4 indicate an inverse relationship between length of mother's schooling and all indicators of early childhood mortality rates in India (Table 11.7). Rates of early childhood mortality among children born to

TABLE 11.7 Social and economic differentials in infant and child mortality in India, 2015–16

Background Characteristics	*Neonatal Mortality*	*Post-neonatal Mortality*	*Infant Mortality*	*Child Mortality*	*Under-five Mortality*
Schooling					
No schooling	37.2	16.0	53.2	15.1	67.5
< 5 years complete	37.6	13.6	51.2	11.0	61.7
5–7 years complete	33.0	10.3	43.3	8.9	51.8
8–9 years complete	28.9	10.9	39.8	6.1	45.6
10–11 years complete	19.8	8.0	27.9	4.1	31.8
12 or more years complete	17.9	5.6	23.5	3.0	26.5
Religion					
Hindus	30.5	11.1	41.6	9.3	50.5
Muslim	27.8	12.2	40.0	10.3	49.9
Christian	15.1	9.9	25.0	7.4	32.2
Sikh	20.9	8.8	29.7	5.4	34.9
Buddhist/ Neo-Buddhist	17.7	12.4	30.0	4.3	34.4
Other	29.4	11.6	41.0	16.8	57.1
Caste/tribe					
Scheduled caste	33.0	12.2	45.2	11.1	55.9
Scheduled tribe	31.3	13.1	44.4	13.4	57.2
Other backward class	30.5	11.6	42.1	9.0	50.8
Others	23.2	8.9	32.1	6.6	38.5
Wealth index					
Lowest	40.7	15.6	56.3	16.3	71.7
Second	34.2	13.0	47.2	10.6	57.3
Middle	28.0	11.1	39.2	7.3	46.2
Fourth	21.6	8.1	29.6	5.4	34.9
Highest	14.6	5.2	19.8	2.8	22.6

Source: National Family Health Survey (NFHS-4), 2015–16: India. Mumbai: IIPS. 2017, Table 7.2, p. 193.

women with 'no schooling' are many times greater than those among children born to women with 12 or more years of schooling. Similarly, children born to women belonging to scheduled castes and scheduled tribes have a significantly higher probability of dying during infancy and childhood. Needless to mention that the scheduled castes and scheduled tribes occupy the lowest rung of the society in terms of social and economic development. Infant mortality and 'under-five mortality' rates among households having the lowest standard of living are almost thrice as high as those of the highest standard of living. More striking difference is found to exist in the case of the child mortality rate. Households with the lowest standard of living have five times as high child mortality rates as those among households with the highest standard of living. Interestingly, similar pattern of the differentials exist in the rural and urban areas separately (IIPS, 2017:191–2). Obviously, child survival programmes need to be further intensified among specific social and economic groups in order to achieve further improvement in mortality conditions. This will go a long way in bringing down fertility rates in the country.

Spatial patterns

Table 11.8 presents the estimates on crude death rate and infant mortality rate in states and union territories for the year 2016. The table provides estimates for rural and urban separately. Mortality rates vary a great deal across states, particularly in the case of the infant mortality rate. It is significant to note that the magnitude of regional variation in mortality rates is of a greater magnitude in rural segments than its urban counterpart. The crude death rate in the country varies from a high of 7.8 in Odisha to a low of 4 in NCT of Delhi. In fact, Odisha, which appears at par with some of the most developed states in India in terms of fertility levels, has reported the highest death rate in the country for quite some time now. Odisha is perhaps the only instance of such a mismatch between fertility and mortality transition in the country. A high death rate in the state can largely be attributed to a very high incidence of mortality among infants and children. The other major states with higher crude death rates than the nation's average are Uttar Pradesh, Madhya Pradesh, Assam, Andhra Pradesh and Bihar. It can be recalled that the states of Bihar, Madhya Pradesh, Rajasthan and Uttar Pradesh are also marked with very high birth rates. Thus, any improvement in mortality conditions in the future in these states would mean a further rise in the natural rate of growth in the population. Taken together these states account for a little less than one-fourth of the country's population. The future prospect of India's demographic transition will continue to depend on the performance of vital transition in these states.

Among the smaller states, Chhattisgarhi, Jharkhand and Meghalaya report a higher crude death rate than the nation's average. The first two were formerly parts of undivided Madhya Pradesh and Bihar respectively. A high crude birth rate in these states is, therefore, understandable. But what is more striking is a relatively higher death rate in Meghalaya. Among the north-eastern states, Meghalaya appears conspicuous with a very high death rate. Strikingly, in terms of crude birth rate also,

TABLE 11.8 Estimates on mortality rates in states and union territories, 2016

States/Union Territories	*Death Rates*			*Infant Mortality Rate*		
	Total	*Rural*	*Urban*	*Total*	*Rural*	*Urban*
Andhra Pradesh	6.8	7.7	4.9	34	38	24
Arunachal Pradesh	6.2	6.5	4.5	36	38	23
Assam	6.7	7.1	4.9	44	46	22
Bihar	6.0	6.1	5.5	38	39	29
Chhattisgarh	7.4	7.8	6.2	39	41	31
Goa	6.7	7.6	6.1	8	10	7
Gujarat	6.1	6.5	5.5	30	38	19
Haryana	5.9	6.3	5.1	33	35	27
Himachal Pradesh	6.8	7.0	4.3	25	25	19
Jammu and Kashmir	5.0	5.2	4.4	24	25	23
Jharkhand	5.5	5.8	4.7	29	31	21
Karnataka	6.7	7.9	4.9	24	27	19
Kerala	7.6	7.3	7.8	10	10	10
Madhya Pradesh	7.1	7.6	5.7	47	50	33
Maharashtra	5.9	6.9	4.6	19	24	13
Manipur	4.5	4.4	4.8	11	12	10
Meghalaya	6.6	7.0	5.0	39	40	26
Mizoram	4.2	4.4	4.1	27	35	14
Nagaland	4.5	5.6	2.8	12	11	14
Odisha	7.8	8.1	6.1	44	46	34
Punjab	6.0	6.6	5.1	21	23	18
Rajasthan	6.1	6.4	5.2	41	45	30
Sikkim	4.7	5.5	3.4	16	18	13
Tamil Nadu	6.4	7.1	5.7	17	20	14
Telangana	6.1	7.1	4.6	31	35	24
Tripura	5.5	5.2	6.1	24	21	32
Uttar Pradesh	6.9	7.3	5.5	43	46	34
Uttarakhand	7.7	7.0	5.9	38	41	29
West Bengal	5.8	5.7	6.1	25	25	22
A and N Islands	5.2	5.7	4.6	16	12	22
Chandigarh	4.5	1.6	4.6	14	6	14
D and N Haveli	4.0	5.0	3.2	17	24	12
Daman & Diu	4.6	6.1	4.2	19	18	19
Delhi	4.0	4.5	4.0	18	24	17
Lakshadweep	6.0	7.9	5.5	19	16	20
Pondicherry	7.2	7.8	6.9	10	16	8
Coefficient of Variation	17.7	20.4	19.3	42.2	43.2	35.9

Source: *SRS Bulletin*, Volume 51, No. 1, September 2017.

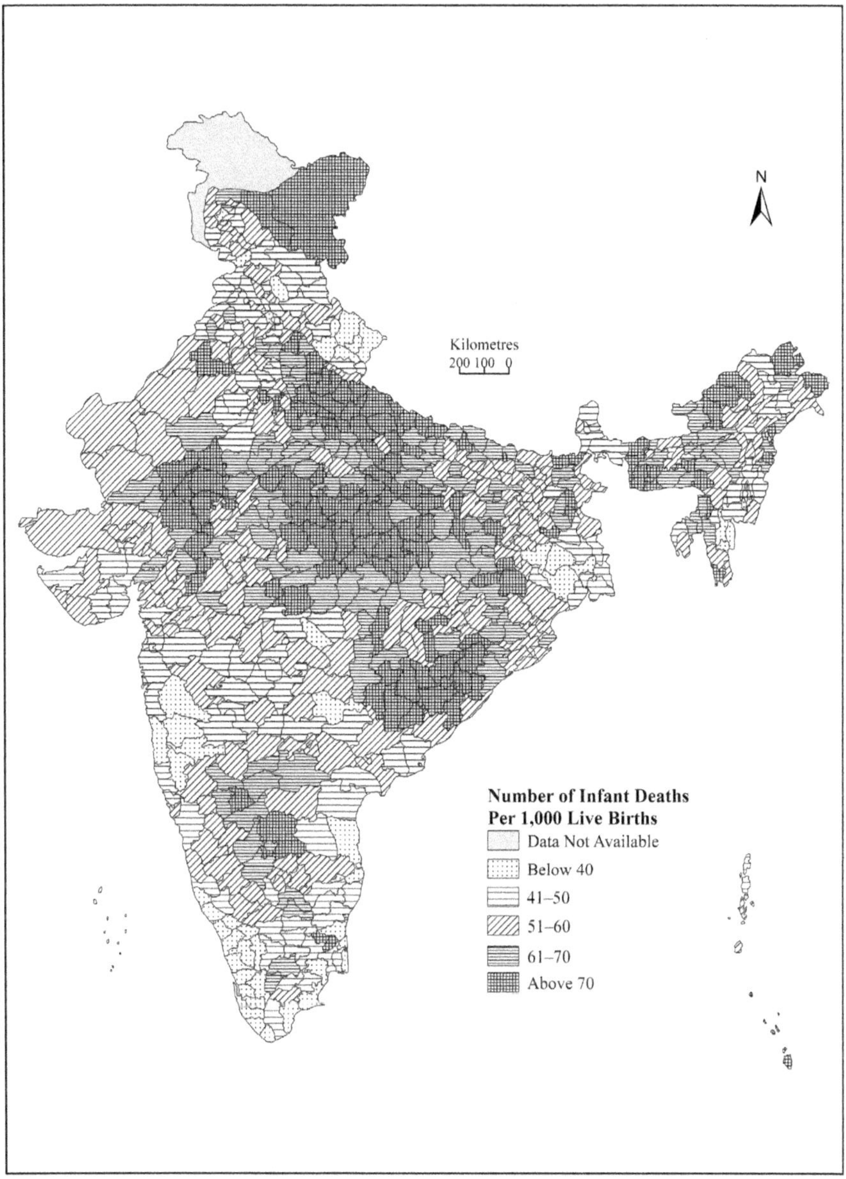

MAP 11.5 Infant mortality rate in India, 2011

Source: Ministry of Health and Family Welfare, NHSRC Estimates Based on 2011 Census

the state stands quite distinct from its neighbouring states. The southern states, in general, report a lower death rate – the lowest being in the case of NCT of Delhi and union territory of Dadar & Nagar Haveli. It is interesting to note that the union territories, in general, report lower crude death rates than most of the states in the country. Dadar & Nagar Haveli is closely followed by Chandigarh. Among

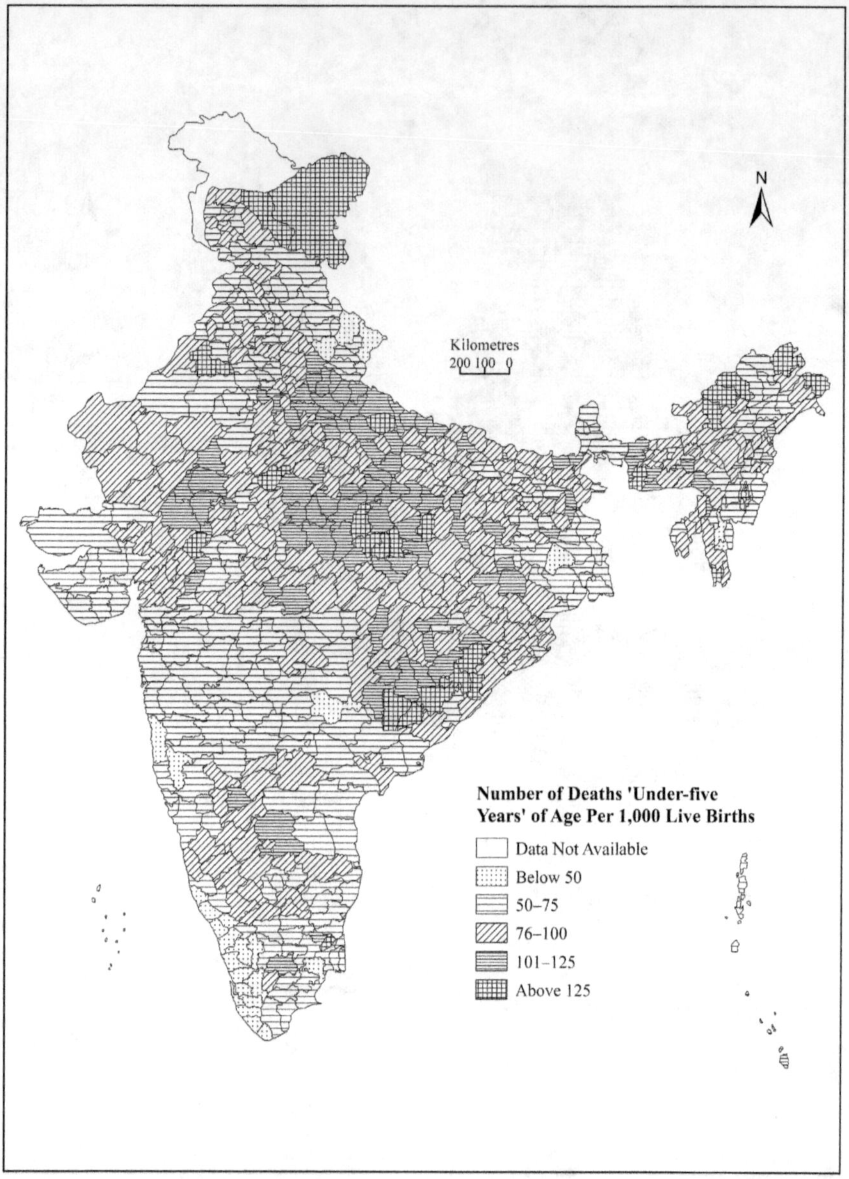

MAP 11.6 Under-five mortality rate in India, 2011

Source: Ministry of Health and Family Welfare, NHSRC Estimates Based on 2011 Census

the union territories, the highest crude death rate is noticed in Puducherry followed by Lakshadweep. Kerala, which reported one of the lowest death rates among the major states till some recent past, has experienced a rise in crude death rates perhaps because of its age structure. Goa, a smaller state in the south, also shows a lower death rate than the nation's average. One comes across more or less similar patterns with regard to the levels of infant mortality rates also.

India is a vast country with a great amount of variation in the determinants of mortality levels from one region to another. More often than not this regional variation turns out to be as great within states as between them. State-level patterns, thus, often mask regional variation at local levels. This necessitates a district-level analysis of mortality levels. However, district-level estimates of vital rates, as mentioned already, are not generally available. The Office of the Registrar General of India, and also some independent authors (e.g. see RGI, 1988, 2001; Rajan and Mohanachandran, 1998; Rajan et al., 2008 among others), have attempted to derive indirect estimates of mortality rates at district level from time to time. These estimates have served an extremely useful purpose in monitoring the trends of early childhood mortality for health care planning. One such estimate based on latest data of the 2011 census is by the National Health System Resource Centre (NHSRC) of the Ministry of Health and Family Welfare, Government of India. Based on data on the number of children ever born and number of children surviving, it provides estimates on infant and under-five mortality rates at district level. Maps 11.5 and 11.6 present the same. A marked correspondence can be seen between the patterns in infant mortality and under-five mortality. In general, both infant and under-five mortality rates are relatively lower in the southern states as compared to the rest of the country. In addition, the Bengal plains, the hilly states of Uttarakhand and Himachal Pradesh along with parts of Punjab in the north also report lower rates of infant and under-five mortality. The interior upland districts of southern Odisha and adjoining districts of Chhattisgarh, northern parts of Madhya Pradesh, western Uttar Pradesh and south-eastern parts of Rajasthan and its bordering districts in western Madhya Pradesh, on the other hand, report high mortality rates. Patches of high infant and under-five mortality rates are also seen scattered in the northern plains, upland plateaus and in the north-eastern parts of the country.

12 MIGRATION

Migration is the third component of population change, the other two being fertility and mortality. The nature of migration as a component of population change is, however, different from fertility and mortality. Though a set of social, economic, political and cultural factors determine the fertility and mortality levels in a population, these components largely operate within the biological framework. Unlike this, migratory movements are basically a product of social, cultural, economic and political and/or physical circumstances in which individuals or groups find themselves (Bhende and Kanitkar, 2011:362). Furthermore, unlike the other two components, the concept of migration is somewhat less easily understood. The meaning of the term *migration*, as used in its technical sense, is different from the common usage. In population studies migration implies a permanent, or at least a semi-permanent, change in the place of residence of individuals from one location to another. The *United Nations Multilingual Demographic Dictionary* defines migration as 'a form of geographical or spatial mobility between one geographic unit and another, generally involving a change in residence from the place of origin or departure, to the place of destination or arrival'. Thus, migration is different from other forms of mobility such as temporary movement of tourists, or frequent trips of people in business, or constant movements of nomads, or movement of students for the purpose of studies, or daily movement of commuters to place of work. These movements do not involve any permanent or semi-permanent change in the place of residence to qualify as migration.

The study of migration occupies an important place in population studies, as together with fertility and mortality, migration determines the size, distribution and growth of population along with its composition and characteristics. As compared with the other two components, migration has been a more popular subject of interest for population geographers. Interestingly, demographers have paid very little attention to this component of population change. Population geographers have since long been concerned with the relationships between movement of people, distance and interacting areas (Woods, 1979:165). Along with its various demographic, social and economic effects, population geographers have also been concerned with the environmental influences upon migration streams and consequences in areas of departure and destination (Clarke, 1972:130).

Mobility and migration: general terms and concepts

As noted previously, migration refers to permanent or semi-permanent change in the place of residence of an individual or a group of individuals from one location to another. Hence, it is different from the more general term *mobility*, which refers to all types of movements of people (Rubenstein and Bacon, 1990:75). Thus, the term *mobility* includes both permanent (and semi-permanent) and temporary movements of people over the earth. With regard to temporary movements, the examples of which have already been cited, a distinction is generally made between a *cyclic* and a *periodic* movement. A cyclic movement includes short duration trips to place of work (i.e. *commuting*), or frequent business trips of people in business, or movement of nomads, which is comparatively irregular in timing. A periodic movement, on the other hand, involves a longer period of residence away from home base than that in the cyclic movement (Blij and Muller, 1986:103). Periodic movement includes the movement of students away to other locations for the purpose of studies, or the movements of military personnel to military bases, training schools or combat zones. The movement of migrant labourers and their families is also periodic movement, although it is more cyclic than that of students or military personnel. Still another form of periodic movement is what is commonly known as *transhumance*, a system of pastoral farming in the mountainous areas wherein people keep changing their abodes along with their livestock between high slopes in the summer and lower valleys in the winter.

Migration, a permanent move, involves crossing over of the boundary of an administrative unit. When the national boundary of a country is involved, such movements are called *international migration*. Similarly, if migration takes place within the national boundary of a country, it is termed as *internal migration*. In the case of international migration the departure of an individual or a group from a country is termed as *emigration*, while arrival or entry into a country is known as *immigration*. The equivalent terms in respect to internal migration are *out-migration* and *in-migration*. In fact each movement is simultaneously emigration (or out-migration) for the place of origin or departure, and immigration (or in-migration) for the place of destination.

Gross migration refers to the total number of migrants moving into and moving out of a place, region or country, while *net migration* is the balance between the number of migrants coming into and moving out of a place, region or country. In other words, net migration is the gain or loss in the total population of an area as a result of migration. *Migration stream* is a term used for spatial mobility in which the migrants have a common place of origin and common place of destination.

A variety of factors can cause migration of individuals. While the factors leading to migration can be classified into several categories, in general terms people take decisions to migrate based on push and pull factors. *Push factors* are events and conditions that force individuals to move to other locations. They include a variety of motives from the idiosyncratic, such as an individual's dissatisfaction with the facilities at home, to the dramatic, such as war, economic dislocation or ecological deterioration (Knox and Marston, 1998:127). On the other hand, *pull factors* are those conditions that attract people to move to a particular new location. It is, however, important to note that both push and pull factors operate simultaneously in any migration, though with varying magnitude.

Further, migration can be either voluntary or forced. While *voluntary migration* involves the choice of an individual or a group, *forced migration* involves a perception of compulsion against the will or choice of concerned individuals. People forced to move are usually compelled by political factors, whereas voluntary migration is usually for economic reasons (Rubenstein and Bacon, 1990:86).

Migration indices

Just as in the case of fertility and mortality, experts suggest a number of rates/ratios that can be worked out when data are available (see for instance Weeks, 2018). The most commonly used measure is what is known as *Crude or gross rate of in-migration*. It is worked out in the following manner:

$$\text{Crude or gross rate of in-migration} = \frac{\text{IM}}{p} \star 1000 \qquad (12.1)$$

where *IM* is the total number of in-migrants in a region during a given year and p is the mid-year population.

It may be noted that the measure is a little misleading as the mid-year population taken in the denominator in its entirety is not at the risk of moving. However, the measure provides a quick idea about the impact of in-migration in a region. Sometimes the measure is also called *rate of mobility*. Given the nature of data provided by Census of India, we generally divide the number of migrants in a region by its total population, and express it in percentage terms.

Similarly, we can also derive a rate of out-migration when it can be called as *crude or gross rate of out-migration* in the following manner:

$$\text{Crude or gross rate of out-migration} = \frac{\text{OM}}{p} \star 1000 \qquad (12.2)$$

where *OM* is the number of persons who out-migrate from a region during a year and the other notation is same as that in Equation (12.1). This measure can also be called as *out-migration ratio*.

As already noted, the difference between the volume of in-migration and out-migration with reference to a particular region is called net migration. In the same way, the total volume of in-migration and out-migration is called gross migration.

Thus, crude net migration rate and crude gross migration rate can we worked out as under:

$$\text{Crude net migration rate} = \frac{NM}{p} \star 1000 \tag{12.3}$$

and,

$$\text{Gross migration rate} = \frac{GM}{p} \star 1000 \tag{12.4}$$

where *NM* and *GM* are the volume of net migration and gross migration in a region respectively.

It may be noted that if volume of in-migration and out-migration are the same, net migration rate will be zero, even if at the aggregate level lot population redistribution has been substantial. Likewise, if more people have moved out than people who have moved in the region, net migration rate is negative and positive in a reverse situation. Related to in-migration rate and out-migration rate is the concept of *migration effectiveness*. Migration effectiveness is basically a ratio between net-migration rate and gross migration rate expressed as percentage. It is, thus, worked out in the following manner:

$$\text{Migration Effectiveness} = \frac{\text{Net Migration Rate}}{\text{Gross Migration Rate}} \star 100 \tag{12.5}$$

It can be seen that migration effectiveness is 100 per cent when there is only in-migration and no out-migration from a region. Likewise, if net migration rate is negative i.e. the volume of out-migration is larger than in-migration, the ratio is negative. And finally, when net migration is zero i.e. volumes of in-migration and out-migration are the same, migration effectiveness works out to be zero.

In the case of fertility and mortality analysis we have measures like total fertility rate and life expectancy which provide an overall idea about fertility/mortality levels in the population. In the case of migration analysis, however, we do not have a corresponding summary measure. As an alternative, experts (Weeks, 2018) suggest *migration ratio* which is very easy to work out:

$$\text{Migration Ratio} = \frac{\text{Net Migration Rate}}{\text{Natural Increase}} \tag{12.6}$$

Natural increase is simply the difference between the number of births and the number of deaths (i.e. births minus deaths) in the population during the period. Thus, if the volume of net migration is larger than the natural increase, the ratio is greater than unity and vice versa. Same way, the share of net migration in overall growth or increase in population over a period of time can be calculated by replacing the denominator in Equation (12.6) by net gain population during the period. This is as under:

$$\text{Contribution of Net Migration} = \frac{\text{Net Migration Rate}}{\text{Net Increase in Population}} \star 100 \tag{12.7}$$

The preceding measures can be worked out with reference to total population as well as its rural and urban segments separately. Similarly, calculations can be done for male and female separately depending upon the availability of data. Migration data are generally given by duration of residence. It is, thus, possible to calculate the share of inter-censal migrants in the total lifetime migrants of an area.

General theories on migration

Migration is a very complex phenomenon. Apart from a set of social, economic, political and environmental factors, migration of population in any region is determined, to large extent, by the perception and behaviour of the individuals concerned. Therefore, there is no comprehensive theory of migration, although attempts have been made, from time to time, to integrate migration into economic and social theory, spatial analysis and behavioural theory (Johnston et al., 1981:218). The attempts on *generalisation* of migration flows have generally followed two approaches. While the first approach views migration as adjustment to existing conditions, mainly economic, in terms of *push* and *pull* factors, the second tends to arrive at empirical *regularities* in the migration flows, and the characteristics of migrants.

Regional economic inequalities and differentials in employment opportunities have provoked many migration flows in the past. In the present time also they are potent forces of migration, both at the international and inter-regional levels. Among the other push and pull factors, as already mentioned earlier, there are several non-economic factors which provoke migration of people. Though the 'push and pull' approach is extremely useful in explaining many of the migration flows, it does not by itself lead to any theory on migration (Bhende and Kanitkar, 2011:390). Evidences indicate that in many cases migration occurs due to either of the two factors alone. In the less developed economies, rural-urban migration occurs not because of any 'pull' factor operating in the urban areas as such, but because of strong 'push' factors in the rural economies in the form of appalling poverty, acute unemployment etc. Todaro has rightly remarked that much of the urban-ward migration in the poor countries is due to the expectation of better opportunities in the large urban centres (Hassan, 2005:285). Likewise, with regard to the immigration in Britain from the West Indies in the period before restrictions were imposed in 1962, 'pull' factors were more prominent than 'push' factors (Woods, 1979:192). Another problem with the 'push and pull' approach relates to its inadequacy in explaining as to why some people under the same conditions choose to migrate, while others do not.

Ravenstein's Laws of Migration

The first attempt to spell out the 'laws of migration' was made by E. G. Ravenstein as early as in 1885. Using the birthplace data, Ravenstein identified a set of generalisations, which he called as 'Laws of Migration' concerning inter-county migration in Britain in the 19th century. Most of these generalisations hold good even today. These generalisations can be listed as follows (see Grigg, 1977:42; Johnston et al., 1981:218):

(a) There is an inverse relation between distance and volume of migration. The majority of migrants move to a short distance only. Migrants going a long distance generally go by preference to the large centres of commerce and industry.
(b) Migration proceeds step by step. The inhabitants of the countryside flock into the nearby rapidly growing towns. The gap created by this out-migration in the countryside is filled up by in-migration from the still remoter countryside. The inhabitants of the town then move to the nearby urban centre up in the hierarchy.
(c) Every migration current produces a counter-current.
(d) The natives of the rural areas are more mobile than their counterparts in the urban areas, and the major direction of migration is from agricultural areas to the centres of industry and commerce.
(e) Females are more mobile than males in the country of birth, but males more frequently venture beyond.
(f) Migration is highly age-selective where adults in the working age groups display a greater propensity to migrate.
(g) The volume of migration increases with the process of diversification of the economy and improvements in transport facilities.
(h) Migration occurs mainly due to economic reasons.

That migration tends to decline with increasing distance is almost a universal fact. Evidences also indicate that there are generally currents and counter-currents in the migration process (Woods, 1979:191). It has also been established that development and modernisation promote internal migration. Several studies have proved that migration is highly age-selective. However, doubts have been raised concerning some of the other generalisations. That migration occurs in different steps is rather difficult to be established. Similarly, though, the rural population in the less developed parts of the world is more mobile than its counterpart in the urban areas, and migration in the economically developed countries is more likely to be urban to rural than in the opposite direction.

Gravity Model

One of the most important contributions of geography in the field of migration analysis is with respect to the relationship between distance and migration. A clear and persistent inverse relationship between the two has been established in several studies (Woods, 1979:183). The Gravity Model based on Newton's law of gravitation goes one step further and states that the volume of migration between any two interacting centres is the function of not only distance between them but also their population size. In other words, migration is directly proportional to the product of their population size and inversely proportional to the square of the distance separating them. The model was initially proposed by the exponents of *social physics* in the 19th century and was later revived in the middle of the 20th century (Johnston et al., 1981:141). The index of migration between two centres according to this model can be expressed as follows:

$$MI_{ij} = \frac{P_i \, P_j}{d^2_{ij}} \star K \tag{12.8}$$

where MI_{ij} is the volume of migration between the centres *i* and *j*, P_i and P_j are population size of the two centres, d_{ij} is the distance between them. Finally, 'K' is a constant.

Besides in the area of migration analysis, the model has been used to account for a wide variety of flow patterns in human geography like telephone traffic, passenger movements, commodity flows etc. It was W. J. Reilley who had first applied the law of gravitation in 1929 to the retail trade of a city centre (Srivastava, 1994:169). Known as *Reilley's Law of Retail Gravitation*, the model states that a city attracts retail trade from an individual customer located in its hinterland in proportion to its size and in inverse proportion to the square of the distance separating the individual from the city centre. John Q. Stewart, an American astrophysicist, in 1947 also pointed that there exists an isomorphic relationship between these concepts and Newton's law of gravitation (James and Martin, 1981:413). In 1949, G. K. Zipf, an American linguist, used this empirical generalisation in his *Principle of Least Effort* in human behaviour while explaining the movement of people between two centres.

Later, using the basic principles of the gravity model, Stewart and Warnz developed the concept of population potential. Population potential of an urban centre is the potential exerted on it by a series of centres in the region. It is worked out in the following manner:

$$PP_i = \sum_{j=I}^{K-1} P_j \,/\, D_{ij} \qquad {}_j\neq i \tag{12.9}$$

where PP_i is the population potential of a centre *i*, P_j is the population of *j*th centre, and D_{ij} is the distance separating *i* from *j*. Thus population potential exerted on point *i* equals the sum of the ratios of the population of points *j* to K-1, to the distance between point *i* and all the points *j* to K-1. The concept of population potential depicts the average access to population and as such summarises very simply the changing gravity of a population distribution (Woods, 1979:182).

The gravity model later attracted severe criticism. Doubts have been raised regarding the validity of population size as a potential force for attraction. Use of simple linear distance, rather than distance measured in terms of transport routes and facilities, frequency of movement and cost of transport, is another weak point of the model. Further, the model treats all the migrants as one homogeneous group and fails to explain the age and sex selectivity of migration. It has, therefore, been suggested that the model is too simple to account for a complex phenomenon like migration. According to P. J. Taylor, the model is based on a crude analogy with Newton's law of gravitation having no theoretical bases in social sciences (quoted in Chandna, 2002:255). Subsequently, the model has been modified for maximum applicability to the study of various forms of flow patterns. These modifications relate to the introduction of some weights to the population size and use of distance in social and economic, rather than geometric, terms. Stouffer introduced one such modification in 1940.

Stouffer's Theory of Mobility

S.A. Stouffer, an American sociologist, introduced one such modification in the Gravity Model. Stouffer formulated his *Intervening Opportunity Model*, published in 1940, and claimed that there is no necessary relationship between mobility and distance (Stouffer, 1940:846). Instead the observed decline in the volume of migration is due to an increase in the number of intervening opportunities with increasing distance. Stouffer's model suggests that the number of migrants from an origin to a destination is directly proportional to the number of opportunities at that destination, and inversely proportional to the number of intervening opportunities between the origin and the destination. Stouffer's formulation can be mathematically expressed as follows:

$$Y = \frac{\nabla x}{x} \star k \tag{12.10}$$

where Y is the expected number of migrants; ∇x is the number of opportunities at the destination; x is the number of intervening opportunities; and k is a constant.

Stouffer modified his theory of migration and intervening opportunities in the mid-1950s and added the concept of competing migrants in his model. His modified Theory of Mobility was published in 1960. The revised model proposes that during a given time interval, the number of migrants from city 1 to city 2 is the direct function of the number of opportunities in city 2, and an inverse function of the number of opportunities intervening between city 1 and city 2, and the number of other migrants for the opportunities in city 2. Thus, the revised formulation would read as under (Galle and Taeuber, 1966:6):

$$Y = \left(X_1 / X_B X_C\right) k \tag{12.11}$$

where Y is the number of migrants moving from city 1 to city 2; X_1 is the number of opportunities in city 2; X_B is the number of opportunities intervening between city 1 and city 2; X_C is the number of migrants competing for opportunities in city 2; and k is a constant.

It may be realised here that the volume of migration from one city to another is the function of as much the attraction of one city as the repulsion from the other. Hence, another component as a measure of disadvantages that push people from city 1 is introduced in the numerator. The final formulation may be expressed as under:

$$Y = \left(X_0 X^a{}_1 / X^b{}_B X^c{}_C\right) k \tag{12.12}$$

where X_0 is the number of out-migrants from city 1; a, b and c are parameters to be determined empirically; and other notations are as before.

In Stouffer's model the measure of 'disadvantages' or 'push' factors in city 1 (X_0) is defined as the total out-migrants from the city. Likewise, the measure of number of opportunities in city 2 (X_1) is defined as the total in-migrants in city 2, whereas the measure of intervening opportunities between city 1 and city 2 (X_B) is defined as the total number of in-migrants in a circle centred mid-way between city 1 and city 2, and having a diameter equal to the distance between the two cities. And finally the measure of competing migrants (X_C) is defined as the total number of out-migrants from a circle centred on city 2 with the distance between the two cities as its radius.

Lee's Theory

Everett Lee proposed another comprehensive theory of migration in 1966. He begins his formulations with factors, which lead to spatial mobility of population in any area. These factors are:

(i) factors associated with the place of origin,
(ii) factors associated with the place of destination,
(iii) intervening obstacles, and
(iv) personal factors.

According to Lee, each place possesses a set of positive and negative factors. While positive factors are the circumstances that act to hold people within it, or attract people from other areas, negative factors tend to repel them (Lee, 1975:191). In addition to these, there are factors which remain neutral, and to which people are essentially indifferent. While some of these factors affect most of the people in the area, others tend to have differential effects. Migration in any area is the net result of the interplay between these factors. Lee suggests that individuals involved in migration have near-perfect assessment of factors in the place of origin due to their long association. However, the same is not necessarily true for that of the area of destination. There is always some element of ignorance and uncertainty with regard to reception of migrants in the new area (Lee, 1975:192). Another important point is that the perceived difference between the areas of origin and destination is related to the stage of the life cycle of an individual. A long association of an individual with a place may result in an over-evaluation of positive factors and under-evaluation of negative factors in the area of origin. At the same time, the perceived difficulties may lead to an inaccurate evaluation of positive and negative factors in the area of destination.

The final decision to move does not depend merely upon the balance of positive and negative factors at the places of origin and destination. The balance in favour of the move must be enough to overcome the natural inertia and intervening obstacles. Distance separating the places of origin and destination has been more frequently referred to in this context by authors, but according to Lee, distance while omnipresent, is by no means the most important factor (Lee, 1975:193). Furthermore, the effect of these intervening obstacles varies from individual to individual.

Apart from the factors associated with places of origin and destination, and the intervening obstacles, there are many personal factors which promote or retard migration in any area. Some of these are more or less constant throughout the life span of an individual, while others tend to vary in effect with the stages in the life cycle. It may be noted that the real situation prevailing at the places of origin and destination are not as important in affecting migration as individual's perception of these factors. The process of perception depends, to a large extent, on personal factors like awareness, intelligence, contacts and the cultural milieu of the individual.

The decision to migrate is the net result of the interplay among all these factors. Lee pointed out that the decision to migrate is, however, never completely rational. Also important to note here is the fact that not all persons who migrate do so on their own decision. Children and wives move with the family where their decisions are not necessarily involved.

After outlining the factors at origin and destination, and the intervening obstacles and personal factors, Lee moves on to formulate a set of hypotheses concerning the volume of migration, streams and counter-streams, and the characteristics of migrants. With regard to the volume of migration, Lee proposed the following set of hypotheses:

1. The volume of migration within a given territory varies with the degree of diversity of the areas included in that territory.
2. The volume of migration varies with the diversity of the people in that territory.
3. The volume of migration is related to the difficulty of surmounting the intervening obstacles. In other words, the greater the intervening obstacles, the less is the volume of migration.
4. The volume of migration varies with the fluctuation in the economy.
5. Unless severe checks are imposed, both volume and rate of migration tend to increase over time.
6. The rate and volume of migration vary with the state of progress in a county or area.

Likewise, with respect to the development of streams and counter-streams of migration, Lee suggested the following six hypotheses:

1. Migration tends to take place largely within well-defined streams.
2. For every major migration stream a counter-stream develops.
3. The efficiency of a stream (measured in terms of a ratio between stream and counter-stream, or the net redistribution of population affected by opposite

flows) is high if negative factors at the place of origin were more prominent in the development of a stream.

4 The efficiency of a stream and counter-stream tends to be low if the origin and destination are similar.
5 The efficiency of a migration stream will be high if the intervening obstacles are great.
6 The efficiency of a migration stream varies with the economic conditions. In other words, it is high in the time of prosperity and vice versa.

And finally, Lee outlined the following hypotheses relating to the characteristics of the migrants.

1 Migration is selective in nature. Due to differences in personal factors, the conditions at the places of origin and destination and intervening obstacles are responded to differently by different individuals. The selectivity could be both positive and negative. It is positive when there is a selection of migrants of high quality and negative when the selection is of low quality.
2 Migrants responding to positive factors at the destination tend to be positively selected.
3 Migrants responding to negative factors at the origin tend to be negatively selected.
4 Taking all migrants together, selection tends to be bimodal.
5 The degree of positive selection increases with the difficulty of intervening obstacles.
6 The heightened propensity to migrate at certain stages of the life cycle is important in the selection of migration.
7 The characteristics of migrants tend to be intermediate between the characteristics of populations at the places of origin and the place of destination.

Zelinsky's Mobility Transition Model

As societies evolve over time, the processes of social and economic development bring about significant changes in the demographic behaviour. The demographic transition model is a very good summary of temporal changes in birth and death rates as a response to changing socio-economic conditions. Zelinsky believed that the factors that lead to demographic transition are also responsible for temporal change in the nature of migration over time. Recognising the linkages between stages of development and characteristics of spatial mobility of population, Zelinsky proposed his Mobility Transition Model in 1971. Thus, Zelinsky's model of mobility transition is closely linked with demographic transition model.

Zelinsky proposed five stages or phases in the process of modernisation, each marked with particular set of migration characteristics. These stages/phases along with characteristics of migration are shown in Table 12.1.

TABLE 12.1 Temporal change in migration characteristics: Zelinsky's Model of Mobility Transition

Phases	*Migration Characteristics*
PHASE I Pre-modern Traditional Society	• Little migration in the true sense of the term • Limited circulation related to customary practices in land utilisation, social visits, commerce, warfare, or religious observances
PHASE II Early Transitional Society	• Massive internal migration from rural to urban areas • Significant movement to colonised frontiers and emigration to attractive foreign destinations • Immigration of skilled workers from more developed parts of the world • Significant growth in general forms of mobility
PHASE III Late Transition Society	• Slackening, but still major, migration from countryside to urban areas • Decline in migration to colonisation frontiers • Urban to urban migration accelerates • Decline in emigration
PHASE IV Advanced Society	• Urban to urban migration i.e. movement from city to city and within individual urban agglomerations becomes dominant • Decline in significance of rural to urban migration (although continues to occur) in absolute and relative terms • Significant net immigration of unskilled and semi-skilled labourers from other countries
PHASE V Future Super Advanced Society	• Almost all internal migration is of inter-urban or intra-urban type • Immigration of unskilled labourers likely to continue

Source: Based on Zelinsky, 1971:23–31.

A Pre-modern Society (i.e. Phase I) represents the characteristics of the pre-urbanisation stage and is parallel to the *high stationary stage* of demographic transition with high birth rates and high and fluctuating death rates. In the long-term perspective, the size of population remains almost stagnant in this stage, and there is very limited scope of migration although other forms of general mobility e.g. nomadism are quite prevalent. With the onset of decline in death rates, the society graduates to the second stage (i.e. Phase II). Zelinsky called it an Early Transitional Society. This stage corresponds to the *early expanding stage* of demographic transition characterised by continuing high birth rates but rapidly declining death rates resulting in high rates of natural increase. As the society experiences the process of modernisation, this stage is characterised by massive internal migration from countryside to newly emerging urban centres of industrial and commercial activities. Along with this a significant overseas migration also characterises this stage. However, towards the end, both rural to urban migration as well as overseas migration witness significant decline, and the society enters into the next stage (i.e. Phase III) which corresponds to the *late expanding stage* of the demographic transition model. Because of declining birth rates, the rate of natural increase slows down in the stage. Growing urbanisation and industrialisation result in more of intra-urban migration than 'rural to urban', although the latter continues to be significant numerically. At the same time, there is more of immigration than emigration, resulting in net gain through international migration. As the society further advances on the path of modernisation, birth rates and death rates finally settle at a low level with no or very low rate of growth in population in the next stage (i.e. Phase IV). This stage corresponds to the *low stationary stage* of demographic transition. Urban to urban migration becomes more conspicuous with vigorous migration from city to city and within individual urban agglomerations. In addition, migration of both skilled and unskilled workers from less developed parts to more developed parts of the globe is an important characteristic of this phase. Finally, Phase V which Zelinsky called as the *Future Super Advanced Society* is marked with continuing low birth rates and death rates but the birth rate is expected to fall below replacement level leading to shrink in the size of population. Almost all internal migration is 'urban to urban' type, and selective immigration continues.

Zelinsky's Model of Mobility Transition is a useful summary of temporal changes in migration characteristics. However, it has invited criticism on the ground that it envisages a fixed idealised sequence of transition and ignores global processes and unique events taking place in a country that affect redistribution of population in a significant way.

Other views

It may be noted that the second half of the last century witnessed massive migration from rural areas to urban areas in the less developed parts of the world. In fact this rural to urban migration forms an integral feature of internal migration in such countries. Redistribution of population of almost a similar nature was witnessed earlier in the developed countries particularly in Europe in the post–Industrial Revolution period. Several economists in their theories of development have indirectly talked about this shift of population from rural areas to towns/cities. One of the earliest attempts in this regard was made by W. Arthur Lewis in 1954. In his classic theory of development he elaborated upon the shift of surplus population from the farm sector to the industrial sector. His ideas were later modified and extended by Gustav Ranis and John C. H. Fei in 1961. In 1969, M. P. Todaro, later jointly with J. Harris in 1970, presented a framework of rural-urban migration. These scholars have propounded their theories of economic growth in the context of dual economy, and in that course have reflected upon migration of population from countryside to urban and industrial centres. A brief description of their reflections on rural-urban migration is presented now.

In his theory of economic development with unlimited supply of labour, Lewis propounded that the economy of an underdeveloped region is dual in nature with the presence of two sectors – a modern or capitalist sector and an agricultural or subsistence sector. In the wake of rapid growth of population, unemployment and disguised unemployment are rampant in such economies. The subsistence agricultural sector is marked with abundant labour, part of which may have zero or negative marginal productivity. The capitalist sector takes advantage of this abundant labour supply. A shift of labours from the subsistence agricultural sector to the capitalist industrial sector, thus, sets in. The industrial sector grows with this unlimited supply of labour. The process of shift of labour from the subsistence agricultural sector to the capitalist industrial sector continues till the entire surplus labour is absorbed in the industrial sector. The marginal productivity of labours in agriculture is no longer zero. Any further shift of labour from the agricultural sector will result in loss in agricultural production because land resources are not optimally utilised in the wake of adverse man-land ratio.

Ranis and Fei explained their theory of development in three phases. According to them, in the first phase workers with negative marginal productivity in the farm sector tend to migrate to the urban/industrial sector. They are followed, in the second phase, by workers who are contributing to overall agricultural production but at a diminishing marginal return. If the process of shift of labour from agriculture to industrial sector continues, a stage comes when the farm sector is no longer having any surplus labour, and marginal labour productivity is higher than the institutional wage. This is the third stage of development when migration from the farm sector comes to a halt. Development to them consists of re-allocation of surplus labour whose contribution to output may have been zero or negligible, to industry where they become productive members of the labour force (Ranis and Fei, 1961:534).

Yet another economic interpretation of rural to urban migration was provided by Harris and Todaro in 1970. Initially proposed by Todaro in 1969 and later restated by Harris and Todaro in 1970, the model became a classic method of migration analysis in less developed countries (Petrov, 2007:185). According to the model migration from the underdeveloped sector (rural) to the developed sector (urban) is dependent upon the 'expected' wage differentials between the two. Minimum wages in the farm sector are much lower than that in the urban areas. A prospective rural migrant who is assumed to be perfectly informed and pragmatic compares his existing income level with expected income in the urban sector. If the later outweighs the former, he chooses to migrate. Here, expected income is the function of wage differentials between urban and rural sectors and probability of obtaining a job in the urban sector. Not all those who migrate to urban areas get a job and many of them get absorbed in the informal sector where the wage rate may even be lower than that in the farm sector. Thus, unemployment and disguised unemployment shift from the farm sector to the urban sector. According to Harris and Todaro, migration from the rural sector to the urban sector persists despite high unemployment in the latter, as long as expectations of finding a job with higher wages continue.

To conclude, it might be suggested that although there are numerous studies on migration, most of them are empirical in nature and lack generalisations. The few attempts on generalisations that are available have mainly adopted two different approaches – one focussed on the contextual circumstances revolving around 'push-and-pull' factors, and the other aimed at generalisations regarding patterns of migration often in the form of mathematical models. The 'push-and-pull' approach, although providing some convincing explanations, is not adequate as it does not by itself lead to any theory of migration. The fact that under similar circumstances why some people to choose to migrate while others don't leads us to the motivational factors which are highly subjective in nature.

International migrations

Man has been a mobile creature ever since his emergence on the earth. Movement of people on the earth surface has continued unceasingly for thousands of years and the present distribution of human population over the globe owes much to this mobility of humankind. During the early periods any long-distance migration was fraught with a great amount of dangers, and migratory movements were largely controlled by physical factors. There used to be high casualty in the process of movement. Many of those who could finally make it did not survive in the unfamiliar geographic conditions of the new home. However, as time went, improvements in transport and communication gave a new direction to the long-distance migratory movements. The world has witnessed a population transfer on an unprecedented scale during the last five centuries. Of late, however, almost all the countries of the world have adopted policies to regulate international migration. They have made their frontiers a barrier as a result of which international migration is of much smaller magnitude in modern times and its spontaneous character has tended to disappear (Beaujeu-Garnier, 1978:179).

Among the greatest international and intercontinental human migration in the history of humankind are the flow of people from Europe, South Asia and Africa. From Europe, emigration took place to the Americas across the Atlantic Ocean, to Africa and to Australia and New Zealand. The European emigration has no counterpart in modern world history in terms of size and numbers involved (Blij and Muller, 1986:106). Also significant in terms of volume was the emigration of Africans to Central America, which had begun during the 16th century and continued up to much of the 18th century. And, finally considerable redistribution of population occurred in South and Southeast Asia with emigration from China and India. Some of these migratory movements were instances of forced migration, while the rest were voluntary in nature.

Forced international migration

The best example of forced international migration is served by the slave trade from Africa. The earliest instance of the slave trade could be seen in the first half of the 15th century when the Portuguese sought blacks from Africa to meet the labour requirements of the Iberian Peninsula (Beaujeu-Garnier, 1978:180). In the 16th century, the Portuguese, and also the Spanish, began deporting slaves to South

America and the Caribbean islands. The British, Dutch and French later joined them in the trade. Millions of Africans, particularly from West Africa, were captured and deported to the Western Hemisphere to work in the sugar plantations. The slave trade continued for more than three centuries, and though officially abolished in 1807, it continued until after 1850 (Beaujeu-Garnier, 1978:180). From 1620 onwards, the British became the largest 'salve hunters'. The infamous *Triangular Slave Trade* (Map 12.1) initiated by the British saw millions of Africans being uprooted from their homeland. In this trade, the British ships carried slaves and gold from Africa to the Caribbean islands. The same ships then carried sugar, molasses and coin from the Caribbean to the North American colonies. And finally, the triangle was completed when the ships returned to Africa with iron bars, used as currency in Africa, and rum (Rubenstein and Bacon, 1990:83). The slave trade remained integral to European economic expansion for over three centuries. The exact number of slaves deported to the West will perhaps never be known. Estimates vary from 10 to 30 million. Two-thirds of the displacement took place during the 18th century alone. The Caribbean islands were the destination of nearly half of the slaves deported from Africa, while another 45 per cent were taken to Central and South America. The rest constituting nearly 5 per cent ended up in the United States.

Another example of forced migration at the international level is the large-scale displacement of population due to political reasons in the 20th century. The two wars provoked forced migration of millions of people, mainly in Europe. Approximately 6 million people were reportedly forced to leave their country as a result

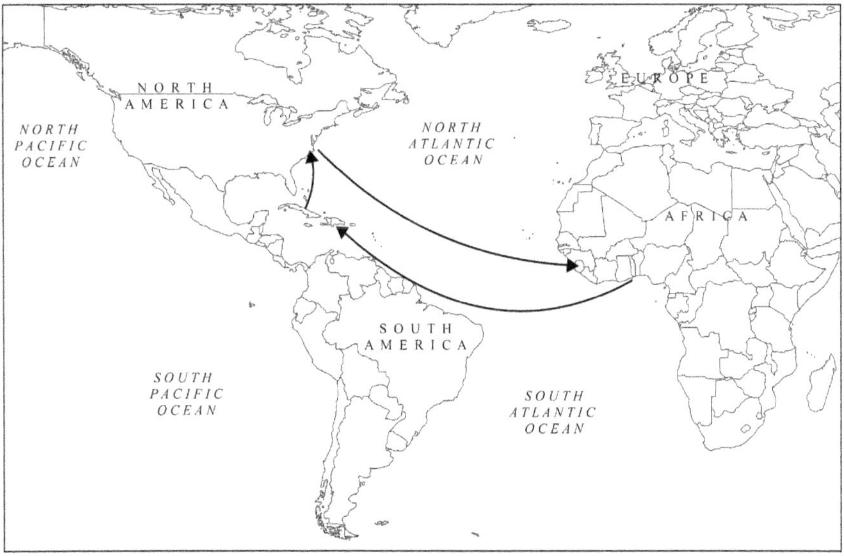

MAP 12.1 Triangular Slave Trade initiated by the British

Source: Adapted from Rubenstein, 1990.

of the First World War (Rubenstein and Bacon, 1990:84). The Second World War produced forced migration on a much larger scale. Estimates indicate that nearly 45 million people were uprooted from their homeland during the 1930s and 1940s. This massive displacement occurred in the form of several streams and counter-streams of exchange, deportation, expulsion and evacuation in the wake of war-related events. During the war period alone approximately 27 million Europeans were forced to migrate, in the wake of first, the German military expansion, and later by the Russian army advances (Rubenstein and Bacon, 1990:84).

The under-developed parts of the world, particularly African and Asian countries, also witnessed large-scale forced migration due to internal disturbances and wars during more recent times. It is estimated that in Africa alone millions of people have been forced to seek refuge in other countries due to political instability caused by inter-tribal and international wars. As a result refugees can be found throughout Africa. Prolonged war in the Southeast Asian countries of Vietnam, Cambodia and Laos in the early decades of the second half of the 20th century resulted in large-scale international migration. Another instance of forced migration due to political strife is seen in Sri Lanka, where Tamil-Sinhalese conflict during the last two decades produced a large number of refugees, many of whom had escaped to India. Elsewhere in the world, the proliferation of totalitarian governments resulted in large-scale forced migration of people because of disagreement with the political ideology in their home country. For instance, several thousand Cubans have escaped to the United States after Fidel Castro came to power in 1959.

In Asia, the end of colonial rule and partition of India into two states – India and Pakistan – in 1947 provoked migration of nearly 17 million people on the basis of religion. Pakistan consisted of two non-contiguous parts – West Pakistan and East Pakistan. Nearly 6.5 million Muslims are reported to have emigrated from India to West Pakistan, while nearly 1 million left India for East Pakistan (present-day Bangladesh after it got separated and gained independence in 1971). In return nearly 10 million Hindus immigrated to India from Pakistan. During the same time, in West Asia, the creation of Israel as an independent state for the Jews in 1948 led to massive redistribution of population in the region. While thousands of Jews from all over the world came to Israel – many of whom were in fact forced to emigrate from other countries, several thousand Arabs also fled from the territory of the newly created state as a result of Arab-Israel conflict. These Palestinian refugees still live in camps close to Israel's borders in Gaza, Jordan, Syria and Lebanon. Many of these camps are multi-generational dating back to 1948.

Voluntary international migrations

Not all international migrations are forced. The last few centuries have witnessed large-scale migration of people from one country to another and from one continent to another (Map 12.2). These migrations are termed 'voluntary international migrations' not because there were no 'pressures' to move but because the people

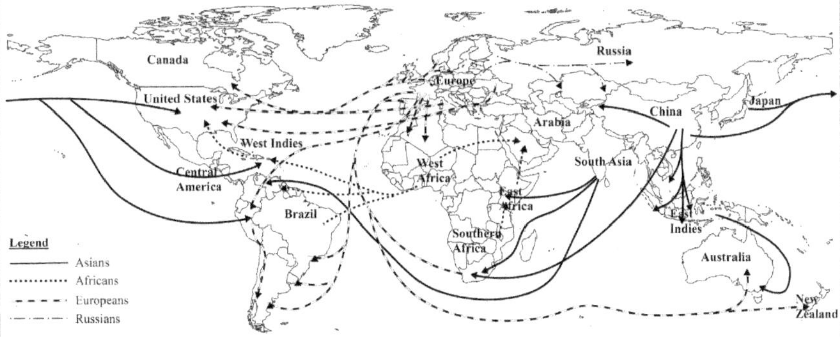

MAP 12.2 Major human migrations in modern times, 1500–1900

Source: Adapted from Norton and Mereier, 2016, Figure 5.14, p.166.

who migrated chose to do so on their own. A variety of reasons have been put forward for this voluntary migrations including economic advancement, family unity, political preferences and group cohesion.

European migration

Perhaps the most important example of voluntary international migration in the history of humankind is the large-scale exodus of Europeans during the last one and a half-century. A total of at least 50 to 60 million are estimated to have emigrated from Europe (Beaujeu-Garnier, 1978:186). Even if those who returned later are taken into account the figure still stands above 50 million. This large-scale emigration from Europe was, however, not a sudden phenomenon. A slow infiltration of people from France, England, Portugal and the Netherlands into the West Indies and the coastlands of America, South Africa and India has been taking place since the turn of the 16th century (Beaujeu-Garnier, 1978:186). The sudden intensification of emigration from Europe in the middle of the 19th century was in fact related to rapid demographic expansion as a result of decline in mortality rates due to improvements in food supply, public health and medicine. The other factors that contributed to the intensification of emigration from Europe were development in the means of transport and aspiration for a better economic opportunity overseas.

The north-western parts of Europe, mainly the British Isles, Scandinavia, Belgium and the Netherlands, were the first to have experienced the exodus of its people. Other countries such as Germany and Italy joined the group towards the close of the 19th century. Central and Eastern Europe began sending their people across the ocean only from the beginning of the 20th century.

It is remarkable to note that since the middle of the last century, emigration from Europe has declined appreciably though not ceased completely. At the same time some European countries like France and the United Kingdom received a considerable influx of immigrants after the end of the Second World War, mainly from their former colonies. In fact in France, immigration had been taking place from other European countries earlier during the intervening period of the two wars. Post–Second World War, however, saw significant immigration from outside Europe, mainly North African countries like Algeria, Morocco and Tunisia, apart from other French-speaking territories in Africa. In the United Kingdom migrants mainly came from the West Indies, Australia, New Zealand, Canada, South Africa and Asia. The main reason of this emigration into Europe during the 20th century was labour requirements in the host countries (Beaujeu-Garnier, 1978:190).

Emigration from Asia

Some of the Asian countries enjoying specific location close to sea coasts, like China, Japan, India, Syria and Lebanon, have long been experiencing emigration of their people. Chinese, though found in almost all the big cities of the world, constitute a significant proportion of population in Singapore, Malaya and Thailand. People of Chinese origin are also found in Indonesia, the Philippines, Vietnam and Myanmar. Similarly, Syrians and Lebanese can be found in many towns of North Africa. They, and also the Chinese, basically act as small traders and middlemen in the host countries.

The spread of people of Indian origin to other parts of the world has a different origin. Emigration from India during the British period owes much to the colonial rule. In order to meet the labour requirements in their other colonies, the British transplanted them in countries like South Africa, Malaya, Guyana and West Indies.

The emigration from Japan, which started in the latter half of the 19th century, was marked with two distinct streams – one headed to the Americas and the other to Japan's adjacent countries with growing influence of Japanese imperialism. Japanese emigration to the United States was met with stiff opposition when the US government adopted restrictive measures. This led to diversion of the flow towards the Latin American countries.

Immigration to the United States

More than half of the total emigrants from Europe landed in the United States of America. Until much of the first half of the 19th century, immigration into the United States was very slow. Thereafter, however, the volume of immigrants increased manifold. Initially north-western Europe was the main source of immigrants, but later countries from other parts of Europe also started joining the migration wave.

Immigration into the Unites States from Europe did not continue unabated. As the conditions improved and Europe became a better place to live, emigration from Europe started declining. This decline became more perceptible towards the beginning of the 20th century. Migration waves from Europe were, thus, replaced by immigration from the underdeveloped parts of the world (Brock and Webb, 1978:430). In the 1920s immigration laws were passed to regulate immigration into the country, which provided for a quota system determined on the basis of national origin of the total white population as per the 1920 census. The economic depression of the 1930s and events related to the Second World War during much of the 1940s disrupted the flow pattern. The contribution of net migration to the growth of population in the country declined sharply from 18.1 per cent during 1920–30 to 1.2 per cent during 1930–40.

In 1965, the immigration policy was revised, and the quota system was abolished. As a result, there was a marked shift in the origin of immigrants. Latin America occupied the first position in terms of volume of immigrants followed by Europe. At the same time there was significant immigration from Asian countries, mainly the Philippines, China, India and Korea, as well. Many of these migrants were professionals and technical personnel, the emigration of whom is generally known as *Asian Brain Drain* (Brock and Webb, 1978:431). It may be noted that the US immigration policy favours people with technical skills. In addition to these official immigrants, there are several thousand illegal immigrants in the US who live mainly in the large cities by concealing their identity. These illegal migrants are mainly males in the working age groups. Mexico is the single largest source of these illegal migrants. However, a good number of such migrants also come from the Caribbean islands.

International migration in recent times

An international migrant is defined as a person who is 'living in a country other than his own country of birth' (UN, 2017:3). According to the latest UN estimates, there are nearly 258 million (up from 173 million in 2000) international migrants worldwide. High income countries of the world alone host almost two-thirds of the total international migrants. Middle income and low income countries account for another 32 per cent and 4 per cent respectively. Absolute size of international migrants has grown uninterruptedly in the past despite increasing restrictions in almost every country. However, if looked at in terms of share in population, international migrants account for a little over 3 per cent only, up from 2.8 per cent in 2000. It is important to note that the annual rate of growth in the volume of international migrants has undergone a decline since 2010. Evidently, in the wake of the economic slow-down of the late 2010s, high income countries, particularly the United States, have changed their policies to the deterrence of the prospective immigrants.

Not all these migrants are voluntary migrants. According to the UN estimates, a little over 10 per cent of these international migrants were forced to migrate across the boundary of their home country. The size of forced migrants at the global level continues to rise. Importantly, a big majority of them (over 85 per cent) is hosted by less developed parts of the world (UNDP, 2016:35). Turkey with nearly 3.1 million refugees of late has become the largest host followed by Jordon, Palestine, Lebanon, Pakistan, Germany and Uganda in that order with more than 1 million in each. It may be noted that Turkey, which occupied only a sixth position among the largest hosts till 2014, received a huge number of Syrian refugees since then. Lebanon, which has hosted Palestine refugees for decades, has also received a huge influx of displaced Syrians (Samers and Collyer, 2017:26). Displaced population from Syria constitutes a significant portion of refugees in Jordon also. In fact, the Syrian crisis over the last six to seven years has seen displacement of nearly half of its population, and Syrian refugees constitute over one-fourth of the total refugees in the world. Pakistan has hosted Afghani refugees for quite some time now. In view of the size of refugees in the developing countries, there is an urgent need for sharing the burden and responsibility of hosting and caring for refugees more equitably (UN, 2017:8).

Table 12.2 presents distribution of international migrants in major areas or geographical regions of the world for the years 2000 and 2017. It is evident that Asia alone hosts over three-tenths of the world international migrants closely followed by Europe. Taken together Asia and Europe account for over 60 per cent of the total international migrants in the world. Northern America i.e. the United States and Canada host a little over 22 per cent. Deceleration in the pace of growth in the number of international migrants in the high income countries is clearly visible in the changing shares between 2000 and 2017.

TABLE 12.2 Distribution of international migrants in the world, 2000 and 2017

Major Regions / World	*International Migrants*			
	2000		*2017*	
	Absolute Size (millions)	*As % to World Total*	*Absolute Size (millions)*	*As % to World Total*
Asia	49.2	28.49	79.6	30.88
Europe	56.3	32.60	77.9	30.22
Northern America	40.4	23.39	57.7	22.38
Africa	14.8	8.57	24.7	9.58
Latin America and the Caribbean	6.6	3.82	9.5	3.69
Oceania	5.4	3.13	8.4	3.26
High income countries	100.4	58.3	164.8	64.1
Middle income countries	64.0	37.2	81.4	31.7
Low income countries	7.7	4.5	10.9	4.2
World Total	172.7	100.00	257.8	100.00

Source: Based on United Nations, *International Migration Report: Highlights, 2017*, Figure 12.2, p. 5.

The unevenness in the distribution of international migrants becomes evident when analysed at a further lower level. It may be noted that at present only 20 countries of the world account for more than 67 per cent of the international migrants, and more than 51 per cent of the migrants live in just 10 countries (Table 12.3). The United States is the largest host with a little less than one-fifth of the total international migrants in the world followed by Saudi Arabia, Germany, the Russian Federation and the United Kingdom among others. It may be noted that of the 20 largest countries of destination of international migrants worldwide, nine are located in Asia, seven in Europe. Among the other two countries viz. the United States and Canada come from Northern America, while Africa and Oceania contribute one each – South Africa and Australia respectively.

A perusal of Map 12.3 reveals a wide range of variation in the share of international migrants in population across the globe. In countries like UAE, Kuwait and

TABLE 12.3 Top 20 countries hosting the largest number of international migrants, 2000 and 2017

2000				*2017*			
Countries	*Absolute Number (millions)*	*As Percentage to*		*Countries*	*Absolute Number (millions)*	*As Percentage to*	
		World Total	*Popu-lation*			*World Total*	*Popu-lation*
United States	34.8	20.2	12.3	United States	49.8	19.3	15.3
Russian Federation	11.9	6.9	8.1	Saudi Arabia	12.2	4.7	37.0
Germany	9.0	5.2	11.0	Germany	12.2	4.7	14.8
India	6.4	3.7	0.6	Russian Federation	11.7	4.5	8.1
France	6.3	3.7	10.5	United Kingdom	8.8	3.4	13.4
Ukraine	5.5	3.2	11.3	UAE	8.3	3.2	88.4
Canada	5.5	3.2	17.9	France	7.9	3.1	12.2
Saudi Arabia	5.3	3.1	25.3	Canada	7.9	3.1	21.5
United Kingdom	4.7	2.7	8.0	Australia	7.0	2.7	28.8
Australia	4.4	2.5	23.0	Spain	5.9	2.3	12.8
Pakistan	4.2	2.4	3.0	Italy	5.9	2.3	10.0
Kazakhstan	2.9	1.7	19.1	India	5.2	2.0	0.4
Iran	2.8	1.6	4.2	Ukraine	5.0	1.9	11.2
China, H.K. SAR	2.7	1.6	40.1	Turkey	4.9	1.9	6.0
UAE	2.4	1.4	77.6	South Africa	4.0	1.6	7.1
Italy	2.1	1.2	3.7	Kazakhstan	3.6	1.4	20.0
Côte d'Ivoire	2.0	1.2	12.0	Thailand	3.6	1.4	5.2
Jordon	1.9	1.1	37.8	Pakistan	3.4	1.3	1.7
Israel	1.9	1.1	30.8	Jordon	3.2	1.2	33.3
Japan	1.7	1.0	1.3	Kuwait	3.1	1.2	75.5

Source: Based on United Nations, *International Migration Report, 2017: Highlights*, Annex, pp. 25–31.

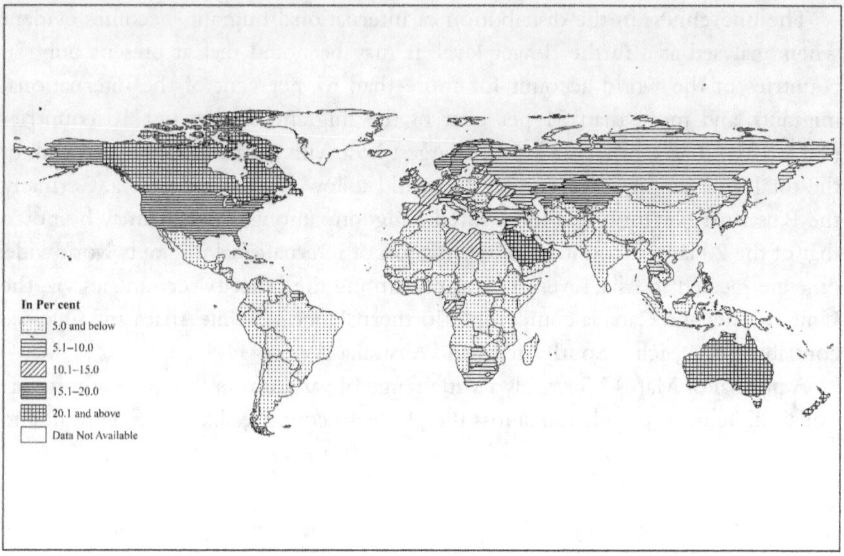

MAP 12.3 International migrants as percentage of total population in the world, 2017

Source: United Nations, Department of Economic and Social Affairs, *International Migration Report, 2017*

Qatar in West Asia, international migrants constitute more than half of the population as against less than 1 per cent in a large number of countries elsewhere in the world. Australia and New Zealand, along with many island countries of Micronesia and Polynesia with a sizeable proportion of people from European origin, report larger shares of international migrants. The same level of concentration of international migrants is seen in Northern America i.e. mainly in the United States and Canada, and Europe. A greater part of Latin and South America, Africa and Asia report less than 5 per cent international migrants in their population.

The UN report on international migration reveals that nearly two-thirds of the international migrants were born in Asia and Europe – individual contributions being 41 per cent and 24 per cent respectively. Northern America contributes less than 2 per cent. Latin America and the Caribbean countries contribute another 14 per cent each. However, if compared with their share in world population, Europe and Latin America and the Caribbean appear to be contributing disproportionately larger shares of international migrants than others (Table 12.4).

Nearly half of the international migrants in 2017 had their origin in 20 countries while more than one-third came from 10 countries only. Table 12.5 provides a list of the 10 largest countries with their share in world population and volume of international migrants having origin within their boundaries in 2017. It may be noted that among the 10 countries of largest origin of international migrants, as many as six are located in Asia alone. India, which occupied fourth position in the world in 2000, is now the largest source of international migrants. India is followed by Mexico, Russia, China and Bangladesh among others in that order. However,

TABLE 12.4 World distribution of population and international migrants by regions of their origin, 2017

Regions of Origin	*Total Population*		*Number of International Migrants*	
	Absolute (millions)	*% Share in World Total*	*Absolute (millions)*	*% Share in World Total*
Africa	1,256.3	16.6	36.3	14.1
Asia	4,504.4	59.7	105.7	41.0
Europe	742.1	9.8	61.2	23.7
Latin America and the Caribbean	645.6	8.6	37.7	14.6
Northern America	361.2	4.8	4.4	1.7
Oceania	40.7	0.5	1.9	0.7
Unknown	-	-	10.6	4.1
World Total	7,550.3	100.0	257.7	100.0

Source: United Nations, *International Migration Report: Highlights, 2017*, p. 9.

TABLE 12.5 Ten largest countries of origin of international migrants, 2017

Country	*Total Population*		*Total Emigrants*	
	Absolute (millions)	*% Share in World Total*	*Absolute (millions)*	*% Share in World Total*
India	1352.6	17.9	16.6	6.4
Mexico	129.2	1.7	13.0	5.0
Russian Federation	146.8	1.9	10.6	4.1
China	1386.8	18.4	10.0	3.9
Bangladesh	164.7	2.2	7.5	2.9
Syria	18.3	0.2	6.9	2.7
Pakistan	199.3	2.6	6.0	2.3
Ukraine	42.3	0.6	5.9	2.3
Philippines	105.0	1.4	5.7	2.2
United Kingdom	66.2	0.9	4.9	1.9
Total	3611.2	47.9	87.1	33.8

Source: Based on United Nations, *International Migration Report: Highlights, 2017I*, Figure 12.7, p. 13.

in comparison to its share in world population, India contributes a much smaller share of international migrants. The same is true with China, the largest populous country of the world. As against this, the contribution from Mexico, Russia, Syria, Ukraine and the United Kingdom etc. to international migrants is larger than their share in world population.

Internal migrations

Internal migration refers to the process of population redistribution within the national boundary of a country. Such movements often involve significant population shift even though the migrants do not cross any international boundary. Evidences indicate a continuous shift of population within a country in response to various social, economic and demographic factors in both developed and less developed parts of the world. Apart from specific migration waves in different countries, the process of industrialisation and urbanisation has provoked a significant shift of people from rural to urban areas. In the less developed parts of the world, another factor that has contributed to this rural-urban migration is the gap in the levels of development between the two areas. In more recent times, the world has witnessed a series of forced internal migration, particularly in Africa, as a result of civil war, ethnic conflict, famine, deteriorating economic conditions and political repression. These instances of internal migration have had significant bearings on the population geography of the individual countries. In the present section, an account of the levels and nature of internal migration in India is presented.

Internal migration in India

Though information on migrants' characteristics has been collected in a number of large-scale and localised sample surveys, the census remains the single most comprehensive source of migration data at regular intervals in the country. Migration data based on 'birth place' have been available right from the 1881 census. According to this, any person who is enumerated at a place other than his 'place of birth' is classified as migrant. The 1961 census, for the first time, classified migration data into 'rural and urban' and into different distance categories viz. intra-district, inter-district and inter-state. Information on duration of residence at the place of enumeration was also collected for the first time in the 1961 census. In the 1971 census, a question on 'place of last residence' was also included for gathering data on migration. Further, yet another question on 'reasons of migration' was included in the schedule in 1981. Indian census provides data on migration in the country by sex and by different streams and distance categories right up to the district level. The following account of internal migration in the country is based on census data for various years.

India's population has been largely immobile, and despite an increase in the rate of mobility during the last two decades, only 37 of its total population was classified as migrants in 2011 (Table 12.6). The population living in the urban areas is more mobile than its counterpart in the rural areas. Further, female population in the country is almost three times more mobile than male population. This sex differential in mobility can be seen consistently in both rural and urban areas. However, much of this mobility among females is basically marriage-induced. Ours is a *patrilocal* society in which brides move to the grooms' place after marriage. This explains a higher mobility rate among females in the country.

TABLE 12.6 Internal migrants as percentage to total population in India, 1961 to 2011

Census Years	*Criteria*	*All Areas*			*Rural*			*Urban*		
		Total	*Male*	*Female*	*Total*	*Male*	*Female*	*Total*	*Male*	*Female*
1961	POB	33.0	20.8	46.0	30.4	15.4	46.0	44.8	43.7	46.1
1971	POB	28.9	17.2	41.1	27.1	12.9	41.9	35.3	33.6	37.4
	PLR	29.1	17.5	41.7	27.2	12.9	42.2	36.9	35.0	39.2
1981	POB	29.4	16.6	43.1	27.4	11.5	44.1	35.8	32.4	39.7
	PLR	30.3	17.2	44.3	28.3	12.0	45.3	36.8	33.2	40.8
1991	POB	26.5	13.8	40.3	25.1	9.4	41.9	30.6	26.0	35.7
	PLR	26.9	14.0	40.8	25.6	9.7	39.8	30.9	26.3	36.1
2001	POB	29.3	16.4	43.1	27.2	10.5	44.8	34.7	31.2	38.5
	PLR	30.1	17.0	44.1	28.0	11.1	45.8	35.5	32.0	39.4
2011	POB	36.5	22.5	51.3	32.5	14.5	51.4	45.4	40.0	51.1
	PLR	37.2	23.0	52.2	33.0	14.9	52.2.	46.3	40.9	52.1

Source: Census of India, *Migration Tables*, Tables D-1 and D-2 for various years.

Notes: (i) POB and PLR refer to 'place of birth' and 'place of last residence' respectively.
(ii) Excluding Assam in 1981 and Jammu and Kashmir in 1991, where the respective censuses were not held.

Table 12.6 reveals a continuous decline in the mobility of population in the country at least up to 1991. Kingsley Davis, a famous demographer, had earlier attributed a low rate of mobility in the country to the prevalence of the caste system, joint families, the practice of early marriage, diversity of language and culture, lack of education and predominance of agriculture in the economy (Kundu and Gupta, 2002:260). It is generally suggested that a society bound by caste, family system and traditional values often acts as a deterrent to mobility of population. The post-independence period witnessed a remarkable progress in the form of the spread of literacy and education, growth of industries and diversification of the economy, and modernisation of norms and social values in the wake of rapid urbanisation. Accordingly, one would have expected a rise in the population mobility. Interestingly, however, this did not happen at least up to 1991. The decline in population mobility in the early decades of independence was viewed in terms of growth in transport facilities, which made commuting to a workplace increasingly easier over the period. Kundu and Gupta attributed the deceleration in population mobility during the 1980s to social and political factors constraining mobility in the country (Kundu and Gupta, 2002:264). However, the post-reform period is marked with a reversal in the trends in mobility rate. This reversal in population mobility has to be viewed in terms of 'push and pull' factors generated in the wake of economic reforms introduced in the early 1990s (Hassan and Daspattanayak, 2007:75).

Census data on migration enable us to examine the spatial mobility of population by different streams and distance categories. Based on that, Table 12.7 presents the percentage distribution of internal migrants in various streams and distance categories for the 2011 census. The 'rural to rural' stream constitutes the largest proportion of internal migrants in the country. Of the total internal migrants in the country, this stream alone accounts for nearly 55 per cent in 2011. With almost three-fourths of the total population still residing in the countryside, this is rather not surprising. The 'rural to urban' and 'urban to urban' streams explain nearly one-fifth of all internal migration each. The remaining 7 per cent of the internal migration in the country is found to have taken in the form of 'urban to rural' migration. Although separate figures for males and females follow a similar pattern, a greater predominance of mobility within rural areas in case of females is worth attention. Likewise, migration from countryside to towns or cities is more conspicuous in the case of male migrants. This reflects upon sex differentials in the nature and determinants of internal migration in the country. Migration among males is almost always induced by economic reasons. Forced by economic compulsions, more males who are almost invariably the bread earner of the family move out to urban centres in search of job opportunities.

Geographers have traditionally been interested in the inter-relation between volume of migration and distance. It is generally found that migration declines with increasing distance. Census of India does not provide migration data by exact distance. The data are instead classified into three categories on the basis of administrative boundaries crossed by migrants. These are intra-district, inter-district and inter-state, roughly corresponding to increasing distance. Since intra-district migration occurs within the district boundary, it represents 'short distance' migration. On the other hand, inter-state migration, which occurs between one state and another, is called 'long distance' migration. Likewise, inter-district migration takes place between one district to another but within the boundary of the same state and represents medium distance migration. Intra-district and inter-district migrations taken together are called 'intra-state' migration. This scheme has a serious limitation as migration within a district may involve a distance that is greater than that in inter-state migration between two places closely located on either side of a state boundary. Although it does not truly correspond to increasing distance, the scheme is widely used while analysing internal migration by distance in the country.

A majority of internal migrants in the country move only a short distance (Table 12.7), and as distance increases the propensity to migrate declines sharply. This is consistent among both male and female migrants. However, as anywhere else, distance appears to be a stronger deterrent to female than male migrants. A significantly larger proportion of female migrants in the 'short distance' category than that among males is indicative of this phenomenon.

Information on *reasons of migration* began to be collected from the 1981 census onwards. At the time of the 1981 census, 'employment', 'education', 'family moved' and 'marriage' were taken as reasons of migration while factors other than these were included under the heading 'others'. Subsequently, in the 1991 census two more reasons viz. 'business' and 'natural calamity' were added in the list. The 2001 census partly modified the reasons of migration by dropping 'natural calamity' from the list and replacing 'family moved' with two separate factors such as 'moved after birth' and 'moved with household'. This has continued in the 2011 census also. The data on reasons of migration hold a very important place in understanding the

TABLE 12.7 Distribution of internal migrants by streams and distance categories in India, 2011 (as per place of last residence criterion)

Migration Streams/ Distance Categories	*Percentage of Lifetime Internal Migrants*		
	Total	*Male*	*Female*
Migration streams			
Rural-rural	53.8	31.3	63.3
Rural-urban	19.7	30.1	15.3
Urban-urban	19.7	29.9	15.4
Urban-rural	6.8	8.6	6.0
Distance categories			
Intra-state	87.9	83.4	90.1
Intra-district	61.7	57.8	63.5
Inter-district	26.3	25.5	26.6
Inter-state	12.1	16.6	9.9

Sources: Census of India, *Migration Tables D-2*, 2011.

motivational factors behind internal migration in the country. The data are based on 'place of last residence' criterion and pertain to all migrants in different streams and distance categories by sex irrespective of duration of stay at the place of enumeration. The reasons are classified into seven categories viz. 'work/employment', 'business', 'education', 'marriage', 'moved after birth', 'moved with household', and 'others' which included movement due to displacement, retirement etc.

The analysis of migration data by reasons clearly establishes the fact that 'work/employment' remains the single most important reason of male migration in the country (Table 12.8) if 'others', which includes a variety of circumstances under which an individual chooses or is forced to move, is ignored. This is more so in the case of 'rural to urban' migration in the country. As is expected, the importance of 'employment' as a reason of migration grows as one moves up in the distance categories. Unlike this, among females 'marriage' explains a major part of migration. Interestingly enough, 'work/employment' becomes more important with increase in distance among females also. An associated factor like 'moved with household' emerges as the second most important reason among both males as well as females. As revealed in the table, 'moved after birth' appears as the next important reason for males but not for females. It may be noted that in Indian customs and traditions, for delivery of the first baby an expecting mother generally moves to her parents' place, and joins back her husband only after a time lag. As a result on return such babies acquire the status of migrants both on the basis of 'birth place' as well as 'place of last residence' criteria. 'Moved after birth' was added to capture these instances of migrants. It is interesting to note that for girls 'moved after birth' becomes redundant after marriage, while for boys it continues to hold true for the rest of their life if they choose not to move to new locations. That explains the sex differentials in

TABLE 12.8 Reasons of migration by streams and distance categories in India, 2011

Migration Types	*Percentage Share of Total Internal Migrants*							
	Work/ Employment	*Business*	*Education*	*Marriage*	*Moved After Birth*	*Moved with Household*	*Others*	*Total*
Male								
Total	24.8	1.87	2.3	3.7	13.9	20.0	34.2	100.0
Intra-district	13.7	1.2	2.0	4.2	16.3	17.9	44.6	100.0
Inter-district	32.5	2.4	3.0	3.7	13.5	23.5	21.4	100.0
Inter-state	47.2	3.0	2.1	1.8	6.2	21.9	17.8	100.0
Female								
Total	2.1	0.3	0.7	66.7	4.5	11.5	14.2	100.0
Intra-district	1.4	0.2	0.6	68.7	4.7	8.2	16.1	100.0
Inter-district	2.8	0.4	0.8	66.7	4.2	14.2	10.9	100.0
Inter-state	4.3	0.5	0.8	54.1	3.4	25.8	11.1	100.0
Male								
Rural-rural	17.2	1.1	2.5	9.4	23.2	21.8	24.8	100.0
Rural-urban	45.4	3.0	3.2	2.1	7.3	23.8	15.1	100.0
Urban-urban	28.2	2.7	2.4	1.7	12.0	26.1	26.8	100.0
Urban-rural	12.7	1.0	2.0	2.7	34.5	17.3	26.7	100.0
Female								
Rural-rural	1.2	0.2	0.4	83.8	3.0	4.6	6.7	100.0
Rural-urban	4.3	0.5	1.5	52.1	4.1	28.0	9.5	100.0
Urban-urban	3.8	0.7	1.3	41.2	7.2	27.2	18.5	100.00
Urban-rural	2.0	0.3	0.8	53.4	17.2	12.1	14.6	100.0

Sources: Census of India, 2011, *Migration Tables, D-3*.

relative significance of 'moved after birth' as a reason of migration. And last but not the least, 'others' reasons account for a significant proportion of internal migration in the country particularly among males. However, with growing distance its relative importance undergoes a sharp decline.

Spatial Patterns: Barring some exceptions, the developed states have continuously gained in their populations through inter-state migration while the backward states have recorded loss due to more out-migration than in-migration. So far as regional variation in migration rates in the country is concerned, it can be seen that the developed states like Goa, Maharashtra, NCT of Delhi, Gujarat, Punjab etc. report much higher rate of migration than the nation's average. In the hilly states of Himachal Pradesh and Uttarakhand also mobility rates are very high. The only exception to this can be seen in Tamil Nadu and West Bengal, which otherwise rank higher than average in terms of social and economic development. A low rate of migration has long been the characteristic feature of Tamil Nadu. In West Bengal, the migration rate that was higher than the nation's average till 1971 has undergone a drastic decline thereafter. The backward states, on the other hand, generally report a very low percentage of migrants in the population. For instance, Bihar and Uttar Pradesh among major states have reported much lower migration rates than the nation's average. A notable exception among major states in this case is Madhya Pradesh. The state has reported a consistently higher share of inter-state migrants, which could possibly be explained in terms of massive public sector investments in the early years resulting in creation of job opportunities. Local population could not take advantage of these developments due to their low level of literacy and skill, leaving the door wide open for the migrants from other states (Kundu and Gupta, 2002:266). The other backward states like Orissa and Rajasthan, however, report mobility rates that are very close to the nation's average (for spatial pattern of population mobility based on district-level data in the country, see Map 12.4).

Net impact of migration on population growth at regional levels is an important aspect for discussion. Census data on migration enable us to derive estimates on net migration for states and union territories. Based on birth-place data scholars have identified the 'gaining' or 'losing' states in the country during individual decades in the post-independence period. A perusal of the findings suggest that although the pattern of gaining and losing states underwent minor changes from one decade to another, on the whole states like Maharashtra and Gujarat consistently appeared as the gaining states while Uttar Pradesh, Bihar and Andhra Pradesh have lost population throughout the period (Bhende and Kanitkar, 2011:386–7). Based on 'place of last residence' data on lifetime migrants of the 2011 census, Table 12.9 presents net migration in states and union territories in India. As is seen in the table, all the union territories excepting only Lakshadweep have gained in their populations through internal migration. Mention may be made of Chandigarh where net migration accounts for as much as 25 per cent of its population in 2011. Likewise, in National Capital Territory of Delhi which enjoys a special status of 'state', net gain through internal migration contributed nearly one-tenth of its population. Among the major states Chhattisgarh, Gujarat, Haryana, Jharkhand, Karnataka, Maharashtra and Punjab have recorded net gain through internal migration. In terms of absolute net gain Maharashtra occupies the first place in the country followed by NCT of Delhi, Gujarat and Haryana. Although migrants from all over India can be seen in Maharashtra, the largest contributors are Uttar Pradesh, Gujarat, Madhya Pradesh, Andhra Pradesh, Rajasthan and Bihar. Remarkably, all the states gaining in population through internal migration, excepting Chhattisgarh and Jharkhand, are relatively developed ones. Early development activities or projects initiated in these states after independence had attracted sizeable numbers of migrants from other states. The case of net gain in population of these states should be seen in the light of the same. On the other extreme, Uttar Pradesh, Bihar, Rajasthan and Odisha which have characteristically been out-migrating states have lost sizeable population through migration. Net loss to population in Uttar Pradesh and Bihar is of the order of 8.25 million and 6.34 million respectively. Among the southern states Kerala, Tamil Nadu and Andhra Pradesh which otherwise rank better in terms of development have also been losing population through more out-migration than in-migration for quite some time. Kerala has been known as a source of a large number

TABLE 12.9 Rate of migration and inter-state migration in India and states/union territories, 2011 (based on 'place of last residence' concept)

States/Union Territories	*Internal Migrants as % to Total Population*	*Inter-state Migrants*				
		as % to Total Internal Migrants	*Total in-migrants*	*Total out-migrants*	*Net Migrants*	*Out-migrants/ In-migrants Ratio*
Andhra Pradesh	45.18	4.17	1591890	2030004	–438114	1.28
Arunachal Pradesh	44.79	21.95	136010	37368	98642	0.27
Assam	33.75	4.71	495699	659694	–163995	1.33
Bihar	25.78	4.14	1111954	7453803	–6341849	6.70
Chhattisgarh	34.54	14.37	1267668	693632	574036	0.55
Goa	76.99	24.02	269689	106196	163493	0.39
Gujarat	44.14	14.68	3916075	1571862	2344213	0.40
Haryana	41.12	34.79	3626318	2315915	1310403	0.64
Himachal Pradesh	37.58	15.33	395504	535823	–140319	1.35
Jammu and Kashmir	22.12	5.60	155187	328919	–173732	2.12
Jharkhand	29.18	22.81	2195521	1704827	490694	0.78
Karnataka	43.13	12.32	3247660	2502956	744704	0.77
Kerala	53.01	3.70	654423	1291325	–636902	1.97
Madhya Pradesh	33.93	11.14	2744332	2979492	–235160	1.09
Maharashtra	50.73	15.94	9087380	3068231	6019149	0.34
Manipur	23.96	2.94	20100	75751	–55651	3.77
Meghalaya	25.34	14.36	107915	70268	37647	0.65
Mizoram	33.90	11.12	41380	30365	11015	0.73
Nagaland	27.45	19.89	108020	45734	62286	0.42
NCT of Delhi	41.74	90.34	6330065	1556308	4773757	0.25
Orissa	36.55	5.57	855096	1271121	–416025	1.49
Punjab	48.50	18.49	2488299	1740877	747422	0.70
Rajasthan	31.87	11.92	2604298	3756716	–1152418	1.44
Sikkim	37.39	26.79	61163	21459	39704	0.35
Tamil Nadu	42.97	5.32	1650771	1985157	–334386	1.20
Tripura	29.31	8.11	87378	85862	1516	0.98
Uttar Pradesh	28.06	7.25	4061933	12319592	–8257659	3.03
Uttarakhand	41.97	29.54	1250575	993570	257005	0.79
West Bengal	34.44	7.57	2381045	2405522	–24477	1.01
A and N Islands	55.81	38.26	81267	20700	60567	0.25
Chandigarh	62.98	95.38	633966	265645	368321	0.42
D and N Haveli	53.10	74.29	135602	16635	118967	0.12
Daman & Diu	60.21	85.03	124522	18906	105616	0.15
Lakshadweep	31.40	30.01	6077	15680	–9603	2.58
Puducherry	56.60	48.13	339967	288834	51133	0.85

Source: Census of India, 2011, *Migration Tables (D-2)*.

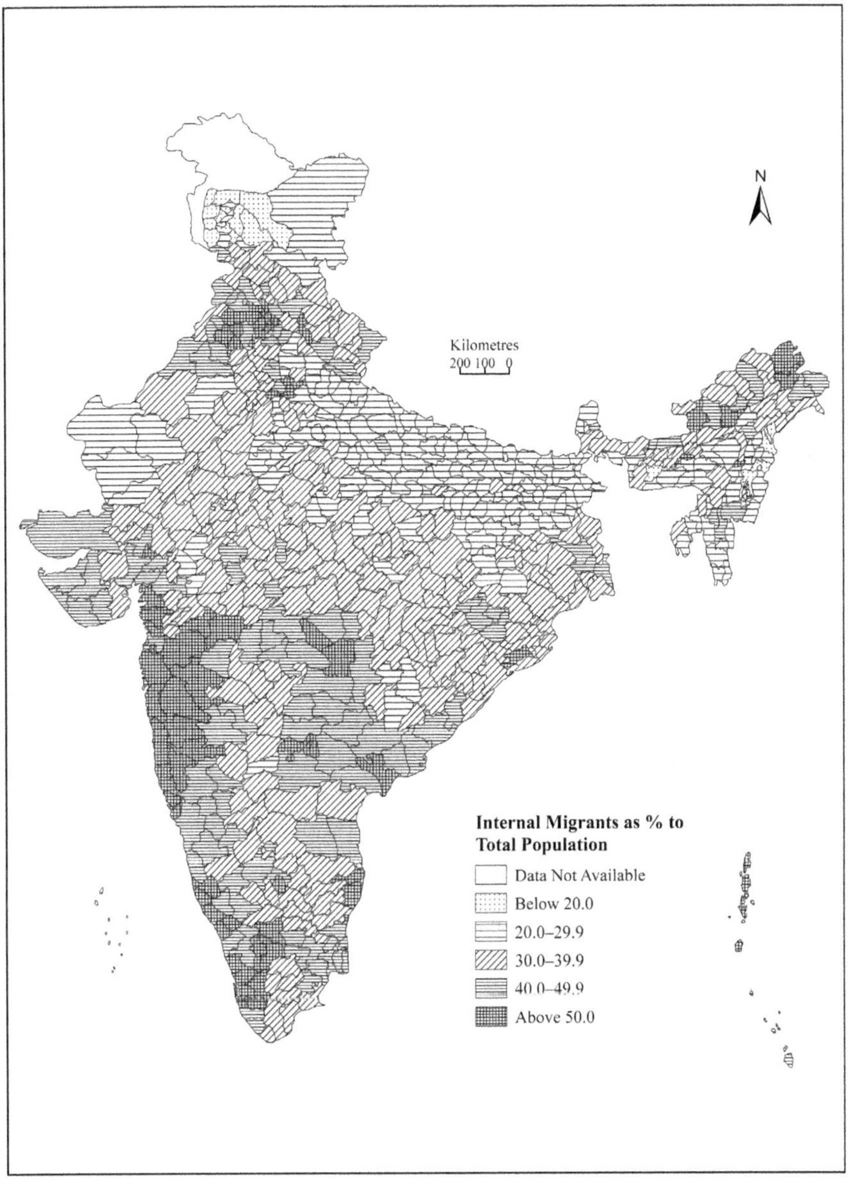

MAP 12.4 Population mobility in India, 2001

Source: Census of India, 2011

of emigrants to the Gulf countries. In the context of internal migration also, the out-migration/in-migration ratio in Kerala is next only to Uttar Pradesh and Bihar among the major states. Karnataka, Maharashtra and Tamil Nadu alone house over two-thirds of out-migrants from Kerala. Almost similar is the case of Tamil Nadu for which Maharashtra, Karnataka and Kerala are the largest hosts for out-migrants.

13 POPULATION THEORIES

Population size and change therein play such an important role that they have been the subjects of theorising since time immemorial. Most of the religious doctrines either directly or indirectly have something or other to say on population issues. Many of the ancient philosophers and thinkers expressed concern over size, growth and quality of population. In modern times, population-related issues have occupied a central position in the politico-economic theories of mercantilism and physiocrats; in the formulation of classical economists like Adam Smith, David Ricardo and others; in the romantic and utopian ideas; in the Malthusian and neo-Malthusian formulations and in Marxists and Socialist views. However, in the true sense of the term, a scientific theory of population is said to have emerged only towards the end of the 18th century, when Thomas Robert Malthus published his much-debated and controversial *Essay on Population* in 1798. Malthus's formulation on population was a landmark in the history of population theories, and, therefore, for all times to come, population theories and generalisations began to be categorised with reference to Malthusian theory.

By a 'theory of population' is generally understood an attempt to explain the major factor or factors determining growth in population (Coontz, 1979:13). Although all the three components of population change viz. fertility, mortality and migration determine the dynamics of population, the first of the three has been accorded a central position in most of the theories. In the chapter on fertility, an account of theories on fertility was presented. Likewise, various models and theories of migration have also been presented in the chapter on migration. In the present chapter, therefore, some of the important theories that account for wider social, economic and political determinants of population change are being presented.

Population theories in antiquity

The survival of ancient societies despite a very high level of mortality implies that all societies that persisted were successful in maintaining high fertility levels. Most of the ancient thinkers and philosophers were pro-natalist in approach. The doctrines of the great Chinese philosopher Confucius and his followers on marriage, family and procreation were essentially in favour of a large and expanding population. However, at the same time, the Chinese thinkers were also conscious of the possible checks on population growth, and the interrelations between population size, on the one hand, and availability of agricultural land and other resources, on the other.

In ancient Greece also there were explicit policies that encouraged growth in population. The interest in growing number among the Greeks was essentially rooted in military and political concern rather than any economic consideration. An individual in the political life of ancient Greece was subordinate to the state, and marriage and procreation were to be determined by the needs of the state. A growth in population was favoured as it provided the state with adequate people for recruitment in the army. Marriage was compulsory among the Spartans, and the law prohibited celibacy. In Athens also, though rules governing procreation were less stringent, and frequent childbearing was invariably encouraged. Nonetheless, quality of population was also accorded a very high priority in the policies. Babies born with deformities were always eliminated. The ancient Greek philosophers at the same time also advocated measures for fertility control in order to avoid the situation of overpopulation. Plato (427–347 BC) suggested a figure of 5,040 households with a population of 50,000 as the ideal size of his city-state. Although Plato did not mention the bases on which he arrived at this figure, his concern with population size was both qualitative as well as quantitative (Overbeek, 1974:24). He was of the opinion that only the able-bodied citizens should be allowed to reproduce. With regard to the size of population, Plato mentioned that a minimum number of citizens was necessary for a proper division of labour. If population crosses the ideal size, Plato suggested measures to limit procreation. Emigration and colonisation were other options to tackle such a situation. Likewise, in the event of population deficit, Plato recommended various incentives for increasing the number of births and for immigration.

Aristotle also held a similar view regarding population size. In his opinion, a very small size of population is not viable from both economic and military points of view. He argued that population size beyond a certain limit would adversely affect the distribution of wealth (mainly land) leading to political instability. In order to keep the size within a desirable limit, Aristotle recommended abortion and infanticide through exposure of newly born babies (particularly of deformed babies).

The early Romans were also pro-natalist in approach. They apparently did not fear the problem of overpopulation. From Connius to Varro, all the early Roman writers were characterised by the fertility cult and claimed that the main function of marriage was to provide citizens (Premi, 2003:201). The Romans needed an expanding population as it provided the state with adequate numbers of soldiers that it needed to fulfil its destiny. In order to achieve the set objectives, a system of reward and punishment was in vogue among the ancient Romans to encourage procreation. The unmarried and childless couples were punished through additional taxes and loss of the right of inheritance. On the other hand, those who were married and had children enjoyed certain privileges in the form of priority for high offices and exemption from certain taxes.

Pro-natalist approaches can also be seen in the doctrines of most of the religions of the world. Interestingly, the traditions of Christianity on the subject of population issues have been mixed. Initially, population was viewed from the moral and ethical perspectives, and celibacy was considered as a sacred virtue. Marriage and procreation were, thus, regarded as necessary evils. Later, however, the emphasis underwent a significant change. Marriage became desirable and high fertility began to be encouraged. The religious tradition prescribed strict opposition to birth control.

In Hinduism marriage and procreation have always been considered sacred and necessary in the life of an individual. In an agrarian economy a large family has been desirable among the Hindus. Even in modern times, marriage is a universal phenomenon, and newly married brides are often blessed by elders to be prolific. Kautilya, a contemporary of Plato, had written in his *Arthashastra* that 'a large population is a source of political, economic and military strength of a nation' (Premi, 2003:201). Like Plato, Kautilya also suggested an ideal size of a village and was of the opinion that a population smaller than the ideal size was a greater evil.

Likewise, the Islamic texts have also favoured an expanding population. The prime objective of the establishment of a family in Islam is perpetuation of the human species. The 14th-century Arab historian Ibn Khaldin (1332–1460) accorded a very high priority to demographic factors in his theory of the 'rise and fall' of empires. He stated that a dense population was conducive to a higher standard of living through a greater division of labour and an optimum utilisation of resources. A small size of population, on the other hand, necessitates immigration for administration and defence purposes, which in turn, creates economic and political instability. Thus, Ibn Khaldin regarded growth of dense population as generally favourable to the maintenance and increase of imperial power (Encyclopaedia Britannica, 1993:1039).

Importantly, however, contrary to the generally held view, in Islamic tradition, measures to control birth rates have also been promoted since long back. According to a *Hadith*, it is better to leave your children rich than poor like beggars. This clearly implies that if a father is not in a position to ensure a better future for his offspring, better he does not beget them. Thus, family planning measures are permitted in Islamic tradition for certain reasons such as to keep away from illegal income, protecting the health of the wife and to provide the offspring with all material and spiritual needs (Bhagat, 1998:77). Contraceptive was an acceptable practice in Islam from the days of the Prophet, and the great physicians of the Islamic world during the Middle Ages gave extensive attention to contraceptive methods. However, abortion and foeticide have been forbidden by common consent in Islam, except otherwise when it becomes necessary for protecting the life of the mother.

In Judaism also, the sacred books have emphasised a pro-natalist approach. To the Jews, the injunction to Adam and Eve by the Almighty to 'be fruitful and multiply, and replenish the earth' has been a guiding principle for their attitude towards marriage and procreation. Childlessness has always been considered as a 'misfortune' and prolificness was regarded as a virtue.

Pre-Malthusian theories

The period from the beginning of the 16th century witnessed revolutionary changes in several aspects of life. A series of scientific discoveries were made, new routes to India were explored, and America was discovered. All these developments had profound effects on the arts and on science as well as on manufacturing, trade and commerce across wider areas of the globe. The old feudal system of medieval Europe collapsed and gave way to capitalism. These developments saw the emergence of several powerful states in Europe like England, France, Spain and Portugal, and culminated in a new direction to the thinking on power, economy and population.

One such change in the economic thought that dominated the policies all over Europe from the 16th through the 18th century was *mercantilism*. Mercantilism as a philosophy was designed to guarantee and increase the power and wealth of the rulers and to enhance the prosperity of mercantile classes. The principal means of increasing the wealth was the expansion of trade and development of manufacturing (UN, 1973:35). To the mercantilists, a favourable trade i.e. excess of exports over imports meant more wealth in the form of precious metals. A large and expanding population suited the economic philosophy of mercantilism. A large population meant a greater supply of labour (and hence a low labour cost), larger markets and larger and more powerful armies for defence and for foreign expansion. Since the mercantilist policies often resulted in rivalry between nations, a large and powerful army was an absolute necessity. As one scholar has pointed out, there was 'an almost frantic desire to increase population' in all the countries pursuing the mercantilist policy (Heckscher, 1935:158).

Mercantilism dominated the politico-economic thought of many of the European countries including Prussia, Germany, France, Italy and Spain for almost three centuries. For the mercantilists, the goal of economic activity was not the welfare of the individuals but the glory and power of the empire. Man was, thus, a means and not an end. Accelerating the growth of population by encouraging procreation and immigration and by prohibiting emigration formed the central part of the mercantilist philosophy. In France emigration was completely prohibited. In certain other countries, measures were taken to discourage celibacy and childlessness. Bachelors were denied government jobs. In Spain a law was passed granting certain tax exemptions to those who were married before reaching the age of 25.

The mercantilists were confident that growing population will create its own subsistence and had no worries concerning the adverse effects of an extremely large size of population. Mercantilist writers were, in fact, influenced by the obvious prosperity of certain countries, e.g. the Netherlands, which were relatively densely populated. They, thus, concluded a positive association between density and economic prosperity without going into the details of the inter-linkages between the two. Mercantilism was also influenced by the religious climate of that time. In its early phases, mercantilism coincided with *Reformation*, which marked a return to the *Bible* promoting the ethos of a high fertility of the *Old Testament*.

Two of the most important mercantilist writers were Niccolo Macchiavelli (1469–1527) and Giovanni Botero (1540–1617). Although both Macchiavelli and Botero shared the pro-natalist views, they sounded a caution that population growth cannot continue for an indefinite period. According to them, population growth in an area is ultimately halted by the inroads of physical or natural factors or by human intervention in the form of emigration and/or abstinence from marriage. According to them, the amount of land available and its productivity act as constraints and set the limit to which a country's population can grow. Thus, both Macchiavelli and Botero can be considered as precursors of Malthus (Bhende and Kanitkar, 2011:111).

Mercantilism was designed to promote the interest of the ruling elite and merchants, and the members of the working classes were only the means to achieve the goals (Overbeek, 1974:32). In order to compete in the international markets, the mercantilists adopted strict measures to keep the cost of the finished products at the lowest possible level. These measure included depressing wage levels and wheat prices. An obvious consequence of such measures was the worsening conditions of the agricultural economy and the members of the working classes. Poverty became widespread resulting in heavy toll of life. Towards the second half of the 18th century, therefore, writers began criticising mercantilist philosophy. The critics stressed the need for improving the agricultural practices, which had remained hitherto completely neglected under the influence of mercantilism. This development culminated in the emergence of the *physiocratic* school of thought. The physiocratic school of thought, mainly a reaction to the mercantilist ideas, evolved in France. Quesney (1694–1774) was the founder of the school. Mirabeau (1715–1789) was another French thinker who contributed to the growth of physiocratic ideas. Both of them argued that population growth should not be encouraged beyond a point where impoverishment becomes inevitable. In the opinion of the physiocrats, land was the source of all wealth, and hence, they emphasised the importance of agriculture and internal tax reforms. They argued for a minimum living standard for the people and advocated disassociating economic theory from practical policies. They argued in favour of the policy of *laissez-faire*. They refused to accept the shortsighted nationalism of the mercantilists and favoured a somewhat more open-minded attitude towards other countries. The physiocrats believed that increase in population should be permitted only if it was possible to expand agricultural production. Since the pro-natalist approaches of the mercantilists had ultimately resulted in a shrink in population size through poverty and deaths, as for instance in Spain, physiocrats remained moderate populationists.

The physiocrats had some broad and important effects upon the thinking of the classical economists such as Adam Smith, especially with the respect to role of free markets unregulated by state. The classical economists expressed little interest on the issue of population, and whenever they did so, they tended to see it as an effect, rather than a cause, of economic prosperity. Although the pro-natalist approach of mercantilism began to be rejected towards the second half of the 18th century, it got a lease on life in what is known as *utopian* viewpoints. The development of these romantic viewpoints, as they are sometimes called, had its origin in the French Revolution. The utopian ideas were based on the idea of human progress and perfectibility. It argued that once a society attains the stage of complete perfection, there would be no need of coercive institutions like politics, criminal law, property ownership and family. In a perfect society, according to this viewpoint, progress is consistent with any level of population since population size is the main determinant of the amount of resources. Such resources will be held in common by all persons, and, if needed, a limit to population size will automatically set in as a result of the normal functioning of the society.

The main proponents of the utopian ideas were Condorcet and William Godwin. Condorcet, an ardent French revolutionary, while hiding in a student boarding house, wrote his famous treatise on the history of human progress from its beginning to its imminent culmination in human perfection (Bhende and Kanitkar, 2011:113). He outlined 10 stages of human civilisation, where the last stage was characterised by universal brotherhood of all the people of the world, liberated from inequalities of race, gender and class (Rao, 1994:51). William Godwin, a British writer, in his book *Enquiry Concerning Political Justice*, published in 1793, had proposed that all the problems of humankind would disappear from the earth if the evils of political and social institutions are successfully removed. He argued that if national income were distributed more equitably, poverty would disappear, and even with limited working hours a reasonable level of prosperity would become possible in such a society. It is interesting to note that Daniel Malthus, the father of Thomas Malthus, was so impressed by these ideas that he gave the works of Condorcet and Godwin to his son for reading. Remarkably, however, the younger Malthus developed his own thesis in refutation to the romantic ideas of Condorcet and Godwin.

Malthus and his essay

In 1798, Malthus published his first Essay on population. The title of his work read as *An Essay on the Principle of Population as It Affects the Future Improvement of Society, with Remarks on the Speculations of Mr. Godwin, M. Condorcet and Other Writers*. As the title suggests, it was in the first place a reaction to the *utopian* ideas concerning a perfect society. Malthus echoed a view similar to that of Robert Wallace who, in his book *Various Prospects of Mankind, Nature and Providence*, published in 1761, had suggested that 'the perfection of society carried with it the seeds of its own destruction' (Encyclopaedia Britannica, 1993:1040). Malthus's first essay was very poorly drafted without any support of empirical evidence. He soon revised his arguments and published the second edition in 1803. Subsequently, another four editions of his Essay appeared in his lifetime. The seventh edition of his Essay was published posthumously in 1872. The revised editions were more meticulously drafted and were based on extensive study of works on related topics. However, the essence of his arguments remained the same in all the editions. Malthus based his arguments on two basic propositions:

- that food is necessary for human existence, and
- that the passion between sexes is necessary and would continue in the present state.

Having set these propositions, he proceeded to suggest that in all the societies there exists an equilibrium between population size and subsistence level i.e. food supply. However, he argued that population has a superior power to grow over the means of subsistence. According to him, population increases at a rate akin to *geometric progression* (1,2,3,4,8,16,32 . . .), thus doubling every 25 years. Growth in the means of subsistence, on the other hand, can at best follow an *arithmetic progression* (1,2,3,4,5,6, . . .). Over a period of 200 years, the population of an area would be to the means of subsistence as 256 to 9. In the opinion of Malthus, the passion between the sexes, a psychological factor, underlies the geometric progression of population growth, whereas the diminishing returns from the land leads to arithmetic progression in the case of increase in the means of subsistence. It follows, therefore, that population will continue to grow as long as food remains available. Further, if unchecked, population has a tendency to outstrip the limit set by subsistence level. Once this happens, the equilibrium between population and subsistence is disturbed, and further population growth is halted by a set of checks. This brings about decline in numbers and eventually results in the restoration of equilibrium between population and subsistence level. Malthus grouped these checks into two categories – *positive* and *preventive* checks. Positive checks resulting from both human action (wars and increased exposure of individuals to dangerous occupations) and natural factors (famines, epidemics and other natural calamities) tend to shorten the length of life span in the form of rise in death rates. The preventive checks, the result of exclusively human action, tend to reduce birth rates through, for instance, delay in and abstinence from marriage. Note that Malthus was a clergyman, and therefore, he was strongly opposed to artificial measures of birth control.

Malthus argued that the positive and preventive checks are inversely related to each other. In other words, where positive checks are very effective, the preventive checks are relatively less effective and vice versa. However, in all the societies, some of these checks are in constant operation, although in varying magnitude of effectiveness. Malthus believed that despite these checks, the inability of the increased food supply to keep abreast of population increase always results in some kind of a situation of overpopulation.

Another topic that was very close to the heart of Malthus was *Poor Law*. At the time of Malthus, in England, *Poor Law* was in practice, under which the responsibility of the maintenance of the poor and disabled rested with the local community called *parish*. The charity to the poor and disabled used to be given out of the fund generated in the form of taxes collected from the general public. According to Malthus, the law did more harm than good to the society. He was convinced that the law led to early marriage and high birth rates among the poor resulting in further worsening of the food-population balance. He, therefore, strongly opposed the law and argued for its complete abolition. In place of charity to the poor, he recommended free use of yet uncultivated small tracts of land. He was, thus, instrumental in the passage of the Reform Bill in 1834, which finally abolished the law (Rao, 1994:41).

Malthus's essay provoked a great deal of debate and controversy. Although his followers hailed his essay as one of the most important contributions on population-economy interrelations, others discussed it threadbare and criticised it on various counts. Some scholars even challenged the originality in his ideas. As noted, the mercantilist writers like Macchiavelli and Botero had already suggested that population grows faster than food supply. Others like James Steuart (1713–1780) had earlier echoed the concern that 'population was always pressing against food, and was ready to start off at a faster rate than at which food was actually increasing'. However, as pointed out later by a scholar, Malthus had himself admitted that his was not an original doctrine (Stangeland, 1904:355). It can, therefore, be suggested that although others had already proposed some of the postulates, Malthus deserves the credit for presenting a comprehensive account of the interrelation between population growth, on the one hand, and politico-economic development, on the other.

Malthus has also been criticised for according too much emphasis on agriculture and ignoring the non-agricultural sectors of the economy. However, at the time of Malthus, it may be recalled, a substantially greater proportion of the commodities consumed had their origin in plant and animals. Nonetheless, critics are correct in pointing out that Malthus had completely failed in forecasting the revolutionary changes that later took place in agricultural practices. The gloomy picture sketched by Malthus, thus, did not come true at all. The strongest denunciation of all came from the Marxist and Socialist writers. These writers have severely criticised Malthus for his attitude towards the poor and underprivileged sections in the society. They have pointed out that Malthus was against any reform in the system. Throughout his essay, he seems to have defended the interests of the ruling elite and landed gentry by proposing that poverty is the result of *natural law* i.e. disequilibrium between population and food supply and not due to any lack of distributive justice. Malthus in his second essay had written this infamous passage, which was dropped from the subsequent editions in the wake of strong criticism:

> A man who is born into the world already possessed, if he can not get subsistence from his parents on whom he has just demand, and if the society do not

> want his labour, has no right to the smallest portion of food, and in fact, has no business to be where he is.
>
> *(quoted in Foster, 1999:7)*

One of the reasons of the immediate popularity of the Malthusian thesis, as his followers argue, was its foundation on the two ratios of progression. Critics have, however, called these ratios as the weakest point in his thesis. As pointed out later by Kenneth Smith, the concept of these ratios was based on a very slender foundation, which could never be proved empirically. In fact, Malthus had based his entire argument of geometric progression of population growth on the basis of the experience of the United States, which was undergoing a rapid growth in population mainly through immigration from European countries. Ignoring this factor completely, Malthus arrived at a conclusion that if unchecked population would double every 25 years. Although reinforced later in the *law of diminishing returns*, the arithmetic progression of subsistence also proved to be untenable in the wake of massive strides made in agricultural technology in the later years.

Malthusian doctrine has also been criticised with regard to his scheme of positive and preventive checks. The critics have argued that contrary to Malthusian arguments, the positive and preventive checks are mutually not exclusive. Scholars have also criticised Malthus for his injunctions against artificial measures of birth control, which later became a very powerful preventive check in the developed countries of the world. Malthus in his essay had called these measures as *immoral*. He was of the opinion that if people could limit their family size by choice, there would be no incentive for working hard towards improving their living condition.

Despite these criticisms, Malthusian thesis gained widespread currency during his lifetime. The success of Malthus's ideas owes much to the social and political conditions prevailing in Europe at that time. The French Revolution had disillusioned intellectuals, and though the idea of the perfectibility of society was not given up completely, people had begun looking for some realistic solution to the prevailing situation of uncertainty. The ruling classes saw in Malthus their ideologue and their prophet, who had scientifically proved by the *eternal law of nature* that poverty was inevitable and not the product of any unjust social and political institutions. His ideas had profound effects on public policies (e.g. the case of Poor Law as noted earlier); on the classical and neoclassical economists; on demographers and evolutionary biologists led by Charles Darwin. The later-day followers of Malthus – the neo-Malthusian – perpetuated the basic ideas of Malthus, although rejecting his ideas on artificial measures of birth control.

Population issues and classical and neoclassical economic thought

Ideas concerning population and its interface with economic wellbeing continued to engage the attention of classical and neoclassical economists from the early years of the 19th century to the end of the First World War. The opinion of the scholars, however, remained mixed. Initially, the Malthusian viewpoint dominated the debate culminating in the development of the *principle of diminishing returns* in the second decade of the 19th century. The principle envisaged a declining marginal productivity with increasing labour inputs. The controversy over the exact nature of interrelations, nonetheless, remained largely unresolved at both empirical and theoretical levels. As time went on, empirical evidences increasingly established the fact that population growth and improvement in the wellbeing of the people can go hand in hand. This became possible mainly due to advancement in production technologies. At the theoretical level, some of the classical and neoclassical economists even argued that population growth acts as a powerful motivating force for economic progress. Some neoclassical economists like Marshall emphatically pointed out that the 'law of diminishing returns' was applicable to the agricultural sector alone. For the industrial sector, which offered a much greater opportunity for division of labour, increasing population would instead enhance production. At the same time there was a growing realisation that the interrelation between population growth and economic prosperity should be viewed in totality and not in isolation. In other words, an inquiry based on population alone would not reveal an accurate association. Other factors such as resources, labour, capital and technology must also be incorporated along with population factor in the analysis. For a proper assessment, thus, the role of population must be viewed in the framework of a total economic system.

Importantly, however, towards the end of 19th century, the population factor began to lose focus in the economic thought of the neoclassical economists. This change in the thinking on population can be attributed to the fact that in the Western world, economic growth had successfully kept pace with the growing population. Some of the neoclassical economists, however, continued to consider population growth as a threat to overall economic prosperity in the long run.

Two of the most often cited direct statements on population growth and its net impact on the economy were those from David Ricardo and John Stuart Mill. Ricardo, who wrote after Malthus, echoed a similar concern to that of the latter. He had also argued that population continues to grow at least as long as capital is being accumulated. At the time of Ricardo, the Corn Law was in practice in England, which put a series of restrictions on imports of grain from other countries. The law was aimed at encouraging tillage within the country. Ricardo was concerned with the adverse effects of the Corn Law on the economy in the long run.

In his theory on *land rent*, Ricardo said that with a limited amount of land available and with exclusion of foreign grain, as was the situation in England at that time, growing numbers would make the agricultural output on the most fertile land insufficient. Once this happens, cultivation on the next grade land, hitherto left uncultivated, becomes inevitable. When the next grade land is brought under cultivation, the tenants on the most fertile land who were earlier paying no rent are now are required to pay rent to the landlords. The rent is in proportion to the advantage they enjoy over next grade land. According to Ricardo, the peasants on the most marginal land are not required to pay any rent. But when cultivation on further marginal land sets in due to growth in population, they, too, are required to pay rent to their landlords. Since land rent on better-off lands is always determined by the advantage the peasants enjoy over the most marginal land, colonisation of new land at every stage would mean increase in the rent on the better-off lands. In other words, the wealth of landlords will increase at every stage of expansion of cultivation, while the tillers would be left with smaller and smaller profit. As the tillers are left with same profit irrespective of the quality of land they cultivate, a continuous growth in population ultimately results in a situation where net profit for the tillers equals zero. At this stage, there will not be any possibility to save, as a result of which capital accumulation would cease. Since demand of labour is also dependent upon capital accumulation, the same eventually becomes stationary (Overbeek, 1974:50). The positive checks then become operative restricting further growth in population. Thus, economic growth and also population growth come to an end.

As a solution to these problems, Ricardo suggested the abolition of the Corn Law and argued for free trade in grain. Like Malthus, he also talked about some deliberate measures of population control. He said that 'it is a truth which admits no doubt, that the comforts and well-being of the poor cannot be permanently secured without some regard on their part, or some effort on the part of the legislature, to regulate the increase in their numbers, and to render less frequent among them early and improvident marriages' (quoted in Overbeek, 1974:50).

In agreement to the views of scholars of his time, J. S. Mill also suggested that population increase up to a certain level is desirable in order to avail the benefits of division of labour and economies of scale. But with the fixed supply of land and its limited productivity, the net increase in aggregate output, beyond a given limit, has a tendency to become smaller and smaller. With regards to the situation in Europe and more so in England, Mill was of the opinion that the point of diminishing returns had long been crossed. He, however, conceded that improvement in technology and skill can fend off, and sometimes even counterbalance, diminishing returns. Nevertheless, Mill deviated considerably from his predecessors, mainly Malthus, in arguing that a population can remain permanently below the extreme degree of overpopulation, and the standard of living can even be improved. The success in this regard, he suggested, lies in the extent to which the prolific low-income groups can be convinced to adopt measures of birth control. Technical progress and additional capital stock should, of course, accompany this. He, thus, enunciated a far more optimistic view of man's future than many of his contemporaries.

Optimum population theory

The idea that population growth up to a certain point is desirable, and that once this point is reached, further growth results in diminishing returns, was finally incorporated in the *Optimum Population Theory* during the early decades of the 20th century. Edwin Cannan, a British economist, is said to have propounded the idea of *optimum population*. But before him, Karl Winkelblech had already laid the foundation of the concept when he classified the countries of the world into three categories on the basis of the size of population. These categories represented – underpopulated countries, overpopulated countries and countries which had an ideal population size, which resulted in the greatest possible productivity level. Cannan later coined the term 'optimum' for population considered as ideal by Winkelblech. He later clarified that 'at any given time, the population which can exist on a given extent of land, consistent with the greater productiveness of industry at that time is definite' (quoted in Bhende and Kanitkar, 2011:124).

Initially, the concept of optimum population was only in relation to economic indicator i.e. per capita income or productivity. Considering the concept too restrictive, later writers argued for the inclusion of some other social indicators to make it reflective of the complete wellbeing of the people. Thus, indicators on health, longevity of nation, ideal family size, conservation of natural resources, power, defence and other spiritual, cultural and aesthetic factors were also included in the definition of optimum population (Bhende and Kanitkar, 2011:125). Mukerjee, a distinguished Indian economist and demographer, while criticising the narrow definition of optimum population in 1933 had suggested that the most suitable criterion in the definition of optimum population should be the average life span of people. According to him, the ultimate end of an ideal population-resource balance is reflected in life expectancy of people. Later writers have, however, questioned the practical applicability of the concept in view of the difficulties involved in working out the optimum size of population in any area. It has been remarked that the concept of optimum population is essentially static and ignores the dynamics of technology, resources, social structure and trade etc.

Marxist and Socialist writers on population issues

Even prior to Marx, several Socialist writers had argued that widespread poverty and misery of the working people were due, not to an eternal law of nature as propounded by Malthus, but to the misconceived organisation of society. They felt that distress in the form of overpopulation and unemployment has been thrust upon men by the working of the system. They were of the opinion that if certain reforms were introduced, the problems including overpopulation and unemployment would be solved. Karl Heinrich Marx, a well-known German philosopher and founder of modern Communist theory, went one step further and argued that the prevailing poverty and misery among the working class was created by the system of class rule and class exploitation.

Although sharing many of the views of classical economists, Marx was very critical of the Malthusian postulates. It may be recalled that Malthus had believed his principle to be universally applicable. Marx, rejecting this claim, argued that the 'eternal laws' of classical economists are applicable to specific economic systems. According to him there could not be a universal law of population, rather every mode of production has its own specific population principles that are valid only within its limits. The problems of overpopulation and limits to resources, as enunciated by Malthus, are inherent and inevitable features associated with the capitalist system of production. Though differing on many counts from the 'utopian ideas' he agreed that any size of population could be supported by a properly organised society.

It should be noted that Marx did not propound any theory of population *per se*, and all one finds in Marx's works on the issue of population are some scattered statements. He merely defined the population principle peculiar to capitalist society characterised by large-scale replacement of labour by machinery. He called this the 'law of relative surplus population'. Marx's explanation implied that the relative surplus of population associated with the capitalist mode of production would disappear when capitalism is replaced by some kind of a collective mode of production. Marx believed that the surplus product of labour, previously appropriated by the capitalists, would be returned to its natural owners – the workers, thereby eliminating poverty. With rise in income and improvement in standards of living, the death rate would decline. The birth rate would also, in the long run, begin declining with the rise in living standards and the end of the exploitation of children.

All the later Socialist writers attributed the problems of overpopulation and poverty to the inherent defects in the capitalist social order. Engels, in addition, maintained that the problem of surplus population was always associated with surplus capital, and the same can be overcome only with revolutionary reorganisation of the social order. Engels argued that the productivity of labour is essentially unlimited, as application of capital and improved techniques could significantly increase the same under any situation of stress.

The later Socialist writers also emphasised the importance of improving the status of women in the society. They argued that a superior status of women, an inherent feature of socialism, would inevitably result in a bourgeois society. They continued their opposition to the practice of contraception as an independent means of controlling population growth. They held the view that in a Socialist society reproductive behaviour would automatically develop a harmony between the individual and the society. For instance, although in 1920 Lenin legalised abortion in the Soviet Union as a right of every woman to control her body, he opposed the practice of contraception for the purpose of regulating population growth. His successor, Joseph Stalin, adopted a pro-natalist policy that was intensively followed during the 1930s when the threat of war intensified in Europe. Although contraception later became a widespread practice in most of the Socialist states, the traditional Marxist writers continue to call the birth control drives in the less developed parts of the world as shabby Malthusianism.

Logistic law of population growth

The early 19th century witnessed the development of several mathematical techniques that encouraged attempts to formulate mathematical laws of population growth. The credit for the earliest attempt in this regard goes to Quetlet, a Belgian astronomer. In 1835, he had suggested that 'demographic evolution progresses at an accelerated rate up to a certain point, and beyond that point the pace of growth in population has a tendency to slow down'. He argued that the resistance or the sum of the obstacles opposed to the unlimited growth in population increases in proportion to the square of velocity with which population tends to increase (Premi, 2003:215). Thus, in the absence of any change in the underlying conditions, a population tends to grow more and more slowly after a certain point is reached. The most important among the mathematical explanations to population growth is the theory of *logistic population growth*. The theory treats the rate of growth in population as a linearly decreasing function of population size, producing an S-shaped curve (please see Figure 13.1) with population size gradually approaching an asymptotic value (Wilson, 1985:130). If P_{max} is this asymptote and a and b are constants, the population at time t, Pt is given by:

$$P_t = P_{max} / 1 + e^{a-bt}$$

Verhulst first proposed the application of the logistic curve as a model of population growth in 1838. The early works on mathematical explanations of population growth in the form of the theory of 'logistic growth' remained forgotten for almost a century until it was revived independently by two American demographers Pearl and Reed in 1920. According to them, the growth of population occurs in cycles, and 'within the cycle and in a specially limited area or universe, growth in the first half of the cycle starts slowly, but the absolute movement per unit of time increases steadily until the mid-point of the cycle is reached. After this point, the increment per unit of time becomes steadily smaller until the end of the cycle' (UN, 1973:52).

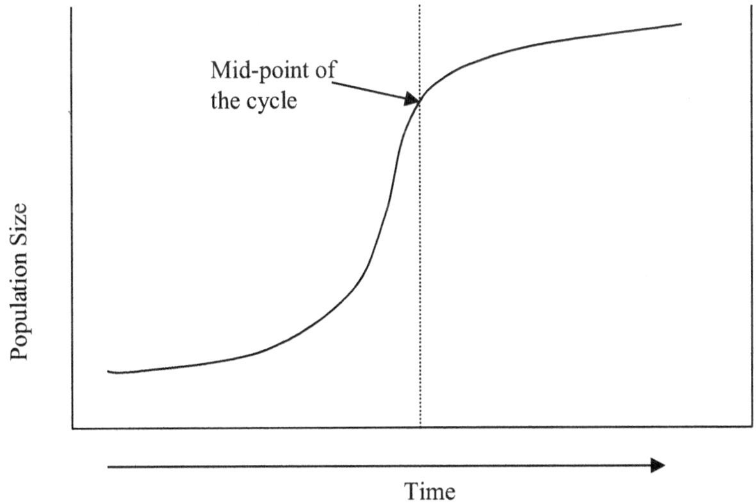

FIGURE 13.1 Logistic Law of Population Growth

Source: Author.

The 'logistic law' of population growth and the mathematical equation proposed for deriving the curve commanded a great deal of attention and popularity up to the middle of the 20th century. Later on, however, its usefulness for estimating and projecting future population size began to be questioned (Bhende and Kanitkar, 2011:127). It has been argued that the theory does not take into account changes in those traits which permit a population to exploit its resources effectively, nor does it anticipate changes in aspirations and tastes, and hence in reproductive behaviour, brought about by such factors.

The Darwinian tradition

Charles Darwin with his book *Origin of Species* in 1859 once again reinforced some of the Malthusian views on population. Darwin has acknowledged an intellectual debt to Malthus in the development of his theory of *natural selection*. Although Darwin himself was not much involved in the debate on human population, many of his followers revived Malthusian arguments in the guise of *Social Darwinism* and *Eugenic Movement*.

Darwin's ideas on 'struggle for the existence', 'survival of the fittest' and 'natural selection' were taken by his followers with great enthusiasm and applied to the social and economic spheres of life. This led to the rise of 'Social Darwinism', which explained the dominance of certain class, race, or nations in terms of 'natural selection' and 'survival of the fittest'. The followers of eugenic movement, on the other hand, were concerned with the differential fertility levels among different groups. According to them fertility levels among those they considered superior stock (mainly the rich nations) was far lower than that among the so-called biologically inferior stock (which invariably constituted the poor). This differential resulted in a gradual decline in the share of biologically superior human stock. This, to them, meant a decline in the overall quality of the population. To some of the eugenics, a low fertility level among the so-called superior stock was the result of deliberate attempt to limit family size, while for others it was an evidence of biological deterioration. Some of the hard-core eugenics, therefore, advocated strict measures of control on the growth in the number of 'inferior', while at the same time arguing for encouraging breeding among the superior. The eugenic movement remained a dominant ideology in the 1920s and 1930s in both Europe and the United States. By the 1940s, however, eugenics began losing acceptance, first with the discovery of the theory of mutation, and later in the wake of the German Holocaust during the Second World War. However, one natural consequence of the concern regarding differential fertility levels led to a growing interest among scholars in the socio-economic and cultural factors that governed fertility decline in the developed countries. This resulted in the development of demographic transition theory in the early decades of the 20th century.

Theory of demographic transition

The classic explanation of changing demographic behaviour in Europe, which later came to be known as *demographic transition*, was attempted in the early decades of the 20th century. Thus, unlike many other theories on population, demographic transition theory was based on the actual experience of the European countries. These countries had experienced a transition in their demographic behaviour from a stage of high birth rate and high death rate to a stage of low birth rate and low death rate. The theory is in fact a generalisation of the historical sequence of changes in vital rates i.e. birth and death rates, and is not truly a scientific theory offering predictive and testable hypotheses. The theory has its origin in some of the early works of Landry and Thompson. It was later developed by Notestein and Blacker in the mid-1940s. The theory gained a much broader interpretation when its applicability to the less developed parts also was realised. Until the 1970s, the demographic transition theory was widely accepted as a complete explanation of changes in demographic behaviour, although its conclusions had never been tested empirically. However, some recent researches on European historical experiences have forced a reappraisal and refinement of the theory.

Landry was perhaps the first scholar who made an attempt in 1909 to identify different demographic regimes related with productivity (Premi, 2003:216). He identified three distinct regimes – the primitive, the intermediate and the modern. Under the *primitive regime*, the birth rates, though not necessarily at its biological maximum, remain stable at a very high level and free from the influences of any social and economic factors. In the *intermediate regime*, however, economic factors begin affecting fertility levels mainly through delay in marriage as people become conscious of certain standards of living and tend to maintain it. Finally, in the *modern regime* decline in the birth rate continues independent of economic factors and becomes a general practice as a result of changes in the aspirations and attitudes of people towards their living standards.

Similarly, in 1929, Warren Thompson made an attempt to construct a typology to describe the process of transition from a stage of high fertility and mortality rates to a stage of low fertility and mortality rates. He suggested the following three categories of countries roughly representing three stages of transition in the demographic behaviour (Premi, 2003:217).

1 In the first category he put those countries where fertility and mortality rates were very high and less controlled. The mortality rates showed evidence of coming under control at a rate faster than fertility rates, indicating a rapid growth in the future.
2 In the second category he put those countries where fertility and mortality rates had begun declining, particularly among some select groups. The decline in mortality was, however, faster than that in the fertility rates, indicating the persistence of acceleration in the pace of population growth.
3 Finally, the third category consisted of countries with rapidly declining birth rates, indicating a slowing down in the pace of population growth.

In 1945, Notestein presented a very comprehensive account of the transition with explanations for changes in birth and death rates, which no other demographer had earlier attempted. It is with his contributions that different groups came to be identified as different stages of transition. Notestein is, therefore, generally credited for propounding the theory of demographic transition in a mature form. He identified three stages in the transition.

In the first stage, he included most of the countries of Asia, Africa and Latin America where transition had not yet begun. In such populations the death rate was high and variable, and was the main factor of population growth. Birth rate, too, was very high with no tendency to decline. This meant a very high growth potential as mortality rate was expected to undergo a rapid decline with technical advancements. In the second stage, Notestein included the populations of the Soviet Union, Japan and some countries in Latin America. These countries were marked with *transitional growth*. Though birth and death rates were still high, the former revealed a definite dent in it. As of now, most of these countries have already completed the transition process. And, in the final stage, Notestein included the United States, most of Europe, Australia and New Zealand. Populations in this stage of *incipient decline* were marked with birth rates fast approaching replacement level. Birth rates in some of these countries had even gone below replacement level.

Notestein's work was soon followed by another attempt by C. P. Blacker in 1947. Blacker explained the transition in five stages (Premi, 2003:217; Bhende and Kanitkar, 2011:130):

I 'high stationary stage' characterised by high birth and death rates,
II 'early expanding stage' with high birth rate but declining death rate,
III 'late expanding stage' with declining birth rate but rapidly declining death rate,
IV 'low stationary stage' with low birth and death rates, and
V 'declining stage' with both birth and death rates at low levels but the latter exceeding the former.

Among the later demographers who further elaborated upon the role of development and modernisation in the process of transition in demographic behaviour, mention may be made of Coale and Hoover. In 1958, these two demographers examined the changes in birth and death rates as typically associated with the process of economic development.

A society characterised by peasant economy is marked with very high birth and death rates. Death rates are high because of lack of adequate food, primitive sanitary conditions and absence of any preventive and curative measures of control over diseases. Death rates remain fluctuating in response to variations in food supply, and occasional famines and epidemics. A high birth rate, on the other hand, is a functional response to high death rates particularly among infants and children. Although there is occasional decline in numbers when death rates exceed birth rates, in terms of its long-term effects, population size remains static. This situation is represented by stage 1 in Figure 13.2. In due course of time, however, the peasant economy begins undergoing change. Improvement in agricultural techniques and practices results in growing availability of food. With this death rates begin to decline, while birth rates continue to remain at a very high level. In fact, according

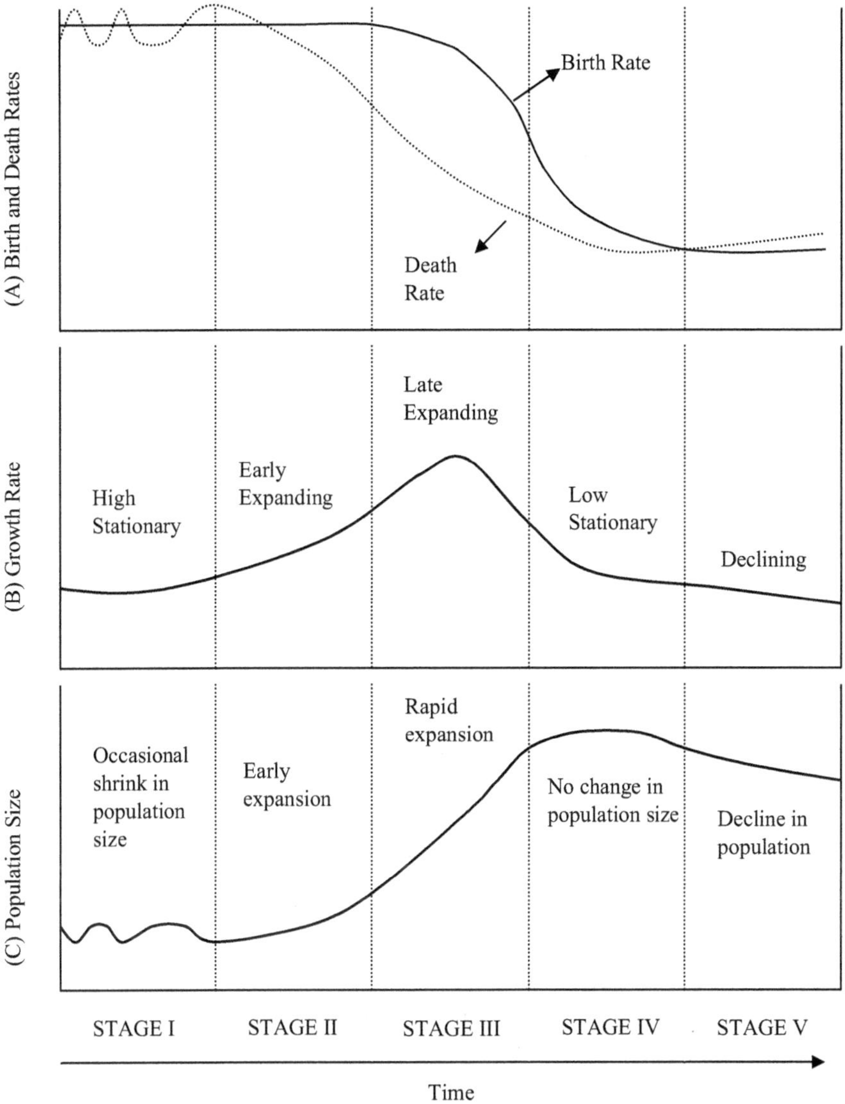

FIGURE 13.2 Demographic Transition Model. Trends in birth and death rates (A), growth rate in population (B) and population size (C)

Source: Author.

to the model, there is always some time lag between the onset of decline in death rates and birth rates because decline in birth rates begins only when sufficient changes occur in the long-standing pro-natalist attitude of the people.

With the onset of decline in death rates, which marks the entry into the second stage of transition, population size that remained static so far begins to expand rapidly. As time goes on, with further improvement in farming practices, surplus production becomes a permanent feature of the economy. With this emerges the process of urbanisation and industrialisation. Improved living conditions and development in medical and health care facilities accompanied by improved hygienic and sanitary conditions result in further control over diseases. Death rates, thus, continue to decline. In the meanwhile, a gradual change begins to occur in the attitude of the people towards size of the family. With the process of development and modernisation, rearing of children becomes increasingly costlier, as a result of which people tend to have fewer children. A decline in birth rates, thus, sets in marking the entry of the population in the third stage of transition. Initially, this decline is rather slow and confined to select people in the urban areas occupying the higher strata in the income scale. Therefore, population continues to grow at an increasing pace. Decline in birth rates later gradually spreads to other income groups in the urban areas and eventually to the rural communities. This marks acceleration in the pace of decline in birth rates, and consequently, in the rate of population growth as well. As social and economic conditions further undergo progress, birth rates decline and become stable at a low level. By this time, death rates are already stable at a low level, and further decline in it is not possible. This stage representing stage 4 in Figure 13.2, is, thus, marked with a very slow growth in population. Finally towards the end of this stage, a long-term decline in birth rates brings about perceptible change in the age structure of the population. This change in the age structure ultimately leads to a rise in death rates, which finally exceeds over birth rates. Although birth rates also occasionally rise in response to voluntary decisions of the individual couples, in terms of its long-term effect, societies in this stage once again witness decline in population size.

The demographic transition theory has been widely used as a generalised description of the evolutionary process. Even at present times, the theory is frequently accepted as a useful tool in describing the demographic history of a country. However, since the close of the 1970s, availability of improved sets of data on both historical and contemporary populations has revealed several weaknesses in the classical formulation of demographic transition theory. Many of the weaknesses have come to light with the availability of new data on European populations. Scholars have pointed out that the theory is merely a broad generalisation of the experiences of the Western countries. According to the critics, even within Europe the sequence of change in demographic behaviour, and its relationship with the process of economic development, has not been identical among different countries. Some of the recent findings indicate that in some countries, e.g. in Spain and elsewhere in Southern and Eastern Europe, the decline in birth rates began even when death rates were reasonably higher. The theory envisages a decline in birth rates primarily as a consequence of the process of industrialisation and urbanisation. But France demonstrated widespread control of fertility even at a low level of industrial, urban and social development. France had, as pointed out by critics, registered a decline in birth and death rates more or less simultaneously. As against this, Britain experienced a decline in birth rates only after it had attained a reasonably high level of development. Critics have, therefore, argued that fertility transition, a dominant force in the evolutionary process, had indeed occurred under extremely diverse conditions among the European countries. Moreover, even within individual countries, regional cultural factors such as religion and language appear to have contributed more in fertility change in many cases than the economic variables. The critics, therefore, argue that the theory does not provide a fundamental explanation of fertility decline, nor does it identify the crucial variables involved in the process of fertility decline. It, therefore, does not have any predictive value. In addition, it is also argued that the theory does not provide a time frame for a country to move from one stage to another. Critics insist that in the first place it cannot be called a theory. Finally, the theory does not hold good for the developing countries of the world, which have recently experienced unprecedented growth in population due to a drastic decline in death rates.

14

POPULATION–DEVELOPMENT–ENVIRONMENT INTERRELATIONS

The fact that size, growth and age structure of population have significant bearings on the material prosperity of people has been recognised since time immemorial. It has also been widely acknowledged that the process of economic development too impacts upon the demographic situations of a country. Indeed, there exists a bi-directional relationship between population and its various attributes, on the one hand, and economic development, on the other. In Chapter 13, the influence of the process of economic development on size and growth of population was discussed in connection with the *demographic transition theory*. The effect of population growth on the process of economic development, however, has been a matter of intense debate and controversy. Scholars hold divergent views regarding the impact of population growth on the economy of an area. There exists a vast literature on the subject by demographers, economists, sociologists, development planners and other social scientists. What emerges from the existing literature is the fact that the impact of population growth on economic development is itself governed by a host of other social, economic and political factors, and that it is almost impossible to arrive at any generalisation at the global level. The net impact of an expanding population varies a great deal from country to country, from region to region and from one group of people to another.

For much of the past, up to the middle of the 18th century, a large and expanding population was generally considered as a source of wealth and power of a nation. Towards the second half of 18th century, the idea that an indefinite growth in population ultimately retards the process of economic development started getting a wider currency. The publication of Malthus's *Essay on the Principle of Population* in 1798 was a turning point in the evolution of people's thinking on the effects of population growth on economic prosperity. It began to be argued that an indefinite growth in population causes scarcity and poverty. The present-day proponents of Malthusianism virtually attribute all the problems of human civilisation to rapid growth in population. In support of their argument, they point to the correlation between high birth rates and low standards of living in the less developed countries. It is argued that rapid growth in population in low income countries, marked with inelastic supply of capital, forces diversion of investments to duplicate existing facilities, leaving very little to spend on improving the productivity of each labour. A rapidly growing population through a high birth rate is marked with an adverse dependency ratio, which, in turn, retards savings and capital formation, and arrests economic growth. Thus, population growth leads to growing incidence of poverty, hunger, unemployment and other forms of social and economic evils in such countries. In a developed economy, on the other hand, with an elastic supply of capital, a growth in population acts as a stimulus to economic growth. While earlier debates on the issue concerning adverse effects of population growth centred mainly on scarcity and possible exhaustion of basic raw materials, the recent past has witnessed a major thrust on environmental quality. Environment is being perceived as the key finite resource in the wake of rapid growth in world population. The neo-Malthusian commentators, therefore, advocate population control as the single most important measure in rescuing the world from an imminent collapse.

The idea that growth in population has led to the prevailing social and economic crises in the less developed parts of the world has strongly been contested by some scholars. On the basis of evidences, it has been argued that the main reason underlying the crises lies in the social, economic and political institutions, and not in growth in population. According to this perspective, just as poverty, a rapid growth in population is a symptom, and not a cause, of the crises. In the context of the adverse effects of population growth on economic development, one topic that has attracted the widest attention relates to the growing scarcity of food in the wake of expanding population. Of late, degradation in environmental quality has begun to be viewed as a direct consequence of a rapid growth in the world population. The forthcoming sections attempt to examine the alarmist views with respect to food supply and environmental degradation. For the sake of clarity of ideas, a political economy of the alarmist viewpoint has also been presented.

Population growth and food supply

Humankind began domestication of plants and animals some 10,000 years ago when sedentary life was possible. This switchover from a food-gathering stage to a food-growing stage, one of the most crucial developments in human life, is commonly known as the *Neolithic Revolution*. Some of the earliest sites of Neolithic Revolution are in the Dead Sea region of the Middle East, and it is from the eastern end of the Mediterranean that the agricultural innovations spread gradually to Europe and Asia (Weeks, 2018:447). This transformation brought about a drastic change in human-environment relations, in general, and per capita food availability, in particular

Ever since Malthus published his first essay in 1798, the idea that growing population leads to scarcity of food has engaged the attention of academia the world over. Malthus had postulated that 'food production was losing the race with population growth', and that 'some forms of terrible disasters were inevitable in the wake of growing imbalance between population and food supply' (Sen, 1999:205). The last few decades have witnessed a widespread revival of the concern regarding population growth and worsening food situations in the world. Most of the concerns in this regard were raised during the 1960s and 1970s when a large number of African countries were facing serious food shortages. Remarkably, it was during the 1960s that the rate of growth in world population had reached an all-time high. The problem of food scarcity was instantly blamed on rapid growth in population. In the year 1968, Paul Ehrlich, a noted population biologist, claimed in his book *The Population Bomb* that 'the battle to feed all humanity is over'. In 1990, again Ehrlich in his co-authored book entitled *The Population Explosion* warned the world community of the pressing problem of food supply in the wake of growing population. In the same vein the Washington-based Environmental Fund remarked that 'world food production cannot keep pace with the galloping growth of population' (quoted in Hartmann, 1995:15). These alarmist views were based on a very simplistic generalisation. To the proponents of the view, more mouths to feed meant less food per person. This would indeed be true if the food supply remains inelastic and somewhat unaffected by growing demand in the wake of an expanding population. But the reality is quite contrary – food supply never remains fixed, and it can be affected by growing demand in a positive way. This is so not only because population growth provides more hands to work but also because it acts as a motivating force for technological and institutional innovations in farming practices for meeting a growing demand of food. Expanding population pressure is said to have forced changes in the pattern and techniques of agriculture throughout its history (Hassan, 1998:293). Among the most common responses to growing population pressure are the expansion of cultivated area, more frequent cropping of the existing arable lands, increasing labour and other inputs, substituting higher-yielding crops and a switchover to a new system of cropping (Grigg, 1976). Colin Clark, a noted economist, argued that growing population pressure in the long run results in a beneficial counter-pressure, which, in turn, promotes economic growth. With regard to frequent occurrence of food scarcity and hunger in certain parts of the world, he commented that 'the fact *that* so many people fall short of satisfactory livelihood must be blamed entirely upon human shortcomings *and* not upon the inadequacies of nature' (quoted in Overbeek, 1974:189). Likewise, Boserup (1965) also regarded growing population pressure as a powerful motivational force behind technological change in farming practices. Like Clark, she also argues that economic development can come about as a result of an adjustment process to growing population pressure.

Empirical evidences also indicate that growth in food production in the world has successfully kept pace with growth in population. Barring some bad years, the last quarter of the 20th century saw a faster growth in food production than that in population especially in the developing countries (Shrivastava, 1992; Hartmann, 1995). The data by Tim Dyson had earlier revealed that per capita cereal output did not decline in Western Europe and Asia where two-thirds of world population lives (Hartmann, 1995:16). The fact that growth in food output in the world successfully outpaced growth in population throughout the last quarter of the 20th century was also highlighted by Sen (1999) based on indices of per capita food production for the world as a whole and for some of the major regions. The indices were based on statistics from the Food and Agricultural Organisation (FAO) of the United Nations, and related to three-year averages. It was evident that not only there was no decline in per capita food output in the world, but also some of the fastest increases in per capita food output occurred in the more densely populated areas of the Third World, particularly in Asia including India and China. Similar statistics for some more recent times are given in Table 14.1. Remarkably Asia has recorded the fastest increase in per capita food production index since the onset of the present century. It is only in Africa that one comes across a marginal decline in per capita gross food production between 2009–11 and 2014–16. On the whole the huge increase in population over the last two centuries has been associated with an equally gigantic rise in food production (Weeks, 2018:447).

Dereze and Sen (1989) have, therefore, argued that 'it seems unlikely that the real danger in the near future can lie in the prospect of food output falling short of the growth of population'. Thus, the claims of Malthusian commentators like Lester Brown of World Watch Institute that 'per capita cereal production has declined in all the major regions of the world' owing mainly to growing population is grossly misplaced. Decline in per capita output in food production, notably in Africa, has got more to do with institutional constraints, unfavourable grain prices and changing cropping pattern than to growth in population. According to Dereze and Sen, in the 1980s the decline in per capita output of food grain had occurred in areas outside Africa also, but the deficit was successfully met by import of the same from other countries. Africa, however, was not able to do this, because the non-food sectors were underdeveloped and there were no sufficient earnings for the import of food grains. What may, therefore, appear to be the problem of scarcity of food in the

TABLE 14.1 Gross per capita food production (2004–06 = 100) in the world by regions

Regions/World	*1999–2001*	*2004–06*	*2009–11*	*2014–16*
Africa	93.0	100.0	102.2	101.2
Asia	91.4	100.0	112.5	120.5
Caribbean	103.6	100.0	103.0	111.1
Central America	93.4	100.0	100.7	106.6
Europe	98.2	100.0	102.6	108.1
North America	99.2	100.0	101.3	105.3
South America	87.6	100.0	111.7	120.2
Oceania	102.0	100.0	92.5	93.6
World	94.4	100.0	107.0	112.0

Source: FAOSTAT, Production Indices (www.fao.org/faostat/en/#data Q1; accessed on 17–04–2019.

wake of rapid growth in population in Africa is actually a reflection of the general economic crisis that plagues the continent. The problem of hunger for instance at the time of famines is a function of peoples' access to food rather than absolute scarcity of food. In India, we have food surpluses, and yet hunger and malnutrition are common features in some areas because people are not having enough money to buy food.

A majority of population in many parts of the less developed countries resides in the rural areas, whose economy is overwhelmingly dependent upon agriculture and its allied activities. Distribution of land in such areas is highly uneven, forcing a substantial portion of the population to live at the mere margin of survival. As has been revealed in several studies, people in such areas go hungry because of the lack of access to food, rather than because of shortage of food at aggregate level. The main problem, therefore, is not that there are too many people and too little food, but that resources are not evenly distributed. Even famines have more to do with poor peoples' inability to command access to food than its actual scarcity (Hartmann, 1995:17). For instance, in the Sahelian countries at the time of famines in the 1960s and 1970s, there was enough food (and export of agricultural produce had actually recorded an increase during the period) but people lacked access to it due to insufficient efforts on the part of the government. Many of the famines in the African continent are reported to be the outcome of a complete breakdown of economic and political institutions and not because of population growth *per se*. Recent famines in Ethiopia and Somalia, for instance, were largely caused by the ravages of civil war, aided and abetted by the Cold War policies of the United States and the erstwhile USSR, and not by incessant population growth or any form of natural disaster. Another apparent reason of frequent occurrence of food crisis in many African countries has been the dominance of cash crops for export for quite some time now. The government policies often at the behest of foreign agribusiness corporations have throughout favoured cash cropping at the cost of food crops, resulting in frequent food crisis. Cash crops invariably occupy the best available lands while food crops are forced to the marginal lands in terms of soil fertility. The globalisation of the world economy and the related structural adjustment programmes have only exacerbated the crisis in several areas of the underdeveloped world during the recent past.

The proponents of the alarmist views have of late begun arguing that even if it is possible to maintain a favourable balance between population and food supply, it can only be achieved at the cost of environmental quality. A large-scale irrigation practice, for instance, is said to have caused significant amount of land degradation through water logging and salinisation. Growing demand of food in the wake of rapid growth in population, as is generally suggested, is pushing agriculture into ecologically marginal areas. Elsewhere, intensive application of modern inputs of farming is said to be taking a heavy environmental toll. Most of the environmental issues raised by the neo-Malthusians in this regard are in fact real and they need immediate attention. But the extent to which these environmental problems are related with population growth needs a careful investigation. As will be seen in the forthcoming paragraphs, although at the surface population growth appears to be an important factor, it is not certainly the primary force behind the crises. Moreover, so far as the adverse environmental consequences of the Green Revolution are concerned, it should be noted that the technologies for further agricultural expansion are not going to be the same for all time to come. Already in several parts of the world the problems of water depletion and land degradation have successfully been taken care off by such practices as trickle (or drip) irrigation, water harvesting and multiple cropping. Further, the rates of growth in population have already begun slowing down in many parts of the less developed countries. The deceleration in the pace of growth, it is expected, would soon spread to the hitherto demographically vulnerable areas also. The good news is that the current number of undernourished humans has come down to 842 million as compared to 1 billion in the 1990s (Weeks, 2018:446). There has been an impressive reduction in the prevalence of undernourishment in areas with large and dense population (Table 14.2).

There is no denying the fact that earth's capacity to support humans is fixed at a given technology, and that improvements in technology can have serious repercussions for earth as an ecosystem. Needless to mention that the earth cannot support even the 7 billion population if the average diet of an individual becomes similar to that of an average American. The world should not aim for the average American diet but rather a better and decent diet that is not wasteful. According to Vaclav Smil (2000), a Canadian geographer, improved agricultural practices accompanied by reduced waste and a healthier diet (with limited fat, especially meat, intake) can lead to dramatic improvement in efficiency of food production without bringing in any additional land under cultivation (quoted in Weeks, 2018:458).

Population growth and environmental quality

With the onset of mortality decline in European countries sometime in the middle of the 18th century, the world population began growing at an unprecedented rate. By the time the demographic transition was accomplished in the developed

TABLE 14.2 Prevalence of undernourishment (per cent) in the world and major regions

Regions/World	*1990–92*	*2014–16*
Africa	27.6	19.8
Asia	23.6	12.1
Latin America and the Caribbean	14.7	5.5
Oceania	15.7	14.2
Developed countries	< 5.0	< 5.0
Developing countries	23.3	12.9
World	13.6	10.8

Source: UN, FAO, *Statistical Pocketbook* World Food and Agriculture, 2015:14

world towards the beginning of the 20th century, the less developed countries began experiencing a similar change. Mortality decline in this part of the world was strikingly more rapid than what had earlier happened in the developed world. Since more than three-fourths of the world humanity lives in the less developed countries, world population began growing at a rate unknown in entire human history. The rate of growth reached an all-time high during the 1960s, which provoked the revival of Malthusian prescription once again. It began to be argued that an incessant growth in population not only causes scarcity and poverty in the underdeveloped countries but also leads to environmental degradation the world over. The ecological movement received a widespread currency in the West, particularly in North America. Perhaps the most influential work in the environmental movement was by Ehrlich (1968) who warned the world of the imminent demographic catastrophe. These views were further reiterated in his later (co-authored) work in 1990. In the meanwhile the *Limits to Growth*, a report of the Club of Rome in 1972, reinforced the concern regarding impending ecological crisis in the wake of expanding population. Limits to Growth, a computer-based simulation of the interaction between population growth and resource depletion underscored the fact that 'the critical point in population growth is fast approaching, if it has not already been reached' (Findlay, 1995:161). The updated version, *Beyond the Limit* published in 1990, once again reiterated the concern regarding the ecological consequences in the wake of growing population.

Among the environmental issues that have widely been discussed are global warming, depletion of the ozone layer, acid rain, deforestation, soil degradation, desertification, and depletion and pollution of water resources. Most of these environmental problems, it is argued, owe their origin in the growth of world population. Although there is no doubt that over the recent past, the environmental quality has undergone an alarming deterioration, it remains debatable as to whether population growth lies at the back of these crises. Most of the environmental crises are intrinsically linked with the process of reckless extraction and processing of natural resources, and the resultant generation of waste products. There exists a glaring inequality in per capita resource consumption across the globe. The industrialised countries of the West, with barely one-fourth of the world population, consume 75 per cent of its raw materials and energy resources. They account for two-thirds of greenhouse gases, mainly carbon dioxide and methane, and nine-tenths of the CFCs which damage the lifesaving ozone layer (Bandarage, 1997; Hassan, 1997). 'A typical resident of the industrialised fourth of the world uses 15 times as much paper, 10 times as much steel and 12 times as much fuel as a resident of the developing world' (Durning quoted in Bandarage, 1997:232). Among the industrialised countries, the United States alone does more harm to the ecosystem than any other nation. With less than 5 per cent of the world population, the United States consumes as much as one-fourth of the fossil fuel, one-fifth of metals and one-third of paper, and contributes more than seven-tenths of the world hazardous products (Ashford, 1995:30) (see Table 14.3). According to the World Development Report (1995) per capita consumption of energy resources in the United States is some

TABLE 14.3 Percentage share in population, hazardous waste production and consumption of natural resources – developed vs. less developed world

	Percentage Share in the World Total				
World Regions	*Population*	*Hazardous Waste Production*	*Consumption*		
			Fossil Fuel	*Metals*	*Paper*
United States	5	72	25	20	33
Other developed countries	17	18	35	60	42
Total DCs	22	90	60	80	75
Developing countries	78	10	40	20	25

Source: Ashford, 1995:30.

32 times as high as that in India. UNICEF in its report on *The State of the World Children – 1994* commented that 'the impact of an average American citizen on environment is approximately 3 times that of an average Italian, 13 times that of an average Brazilian, 35 times that of an average Indian, 140 times that of an average Bangladeshi and more than 250 times that of a citizen born into one of the least developed nations of Sub-Saharan Africa' (quoted in Bandarage, 1997:233).

It is often argued that shift in agricultural practices for feeding the growing world population has led to increased emission of greenhouse gases, causing climate change during the recent past. Furthermore, according to the 2014 IPCC report, between now and 2050, this could be one of the fastest-growing sources of emission of greenhouse gases. However, it is also true that 'much of this is due to increase in methane gas associated with the increasingly industrialized methods of raising animals for food' (Weeks, 2018:461).

A somewhat similar contrast in per capita resource consumption exists in the LDCs between the rich and the poor. Remarkably, it is the poor who live on bare subsistence level and who are rapidly growing in number. The proponents of the alarmist views ignore this inequality, and attribute the prevalent crises to that part of the population which is growing the fastest but which happens to consume the least both at the aggregate as well as at per capita levels (Rao, 1994:50). While most of the growth in the world population during the last few decades came from the less developed parts, much of the damage to the environment has been undertaken either by or for the populations in the developed world. This, however, does not imply that environmental problems do not exist in the less developed countries or that population growth in such countries does not deserve any serious attention. There are problems of environmental degradation in these countries also, but the nature of the problem differs markedly from that in the developed countries. While in the North, affluence and overindulgence have caused irreparable damage to the world as an ecosystem, it is the abject poverty and lack of access to resources for a majority of people that are the main factors underlying environmental degradation in the South. It needs to be recognised that both poverty and environmental problems are the symptoms of faulty social, economic and political systems. Many of the LDCs depend heavily on export of forest and agro-based products apart from a host of minerals like copper, iron ore etc. (Miller, 1995:25). The oppressive debt burden accompanied by uneven terms of trade and declining international prices of export goods force these countries to maximise their earnings through exploitation of more and more natural resources, including forests, at the cost of ecological balance (Hassan, 1997:60). A rapid depletion of forest cover is often attributed to population growth. The reality, however, indicates a different picture. According to an international forestry expert, although at surface population growth appears to be a dominant factor, it is neither a decisive nor an important factor behind forest depletion. Rather, there are other more important factors than population growth such as social mores, political expedients, national and global economies and ideological conflicts (Shrivastava, 1992:3034). Even in a country like India the commercial exploitation of forest resources in the Himalayas or elsewhere could hardly be attributed to population growth. Large-scale commercial exploitation of tropical forest in the world during the last half a century or so has been undertaken by big international companies and the benefit of the same has largely been accrued to the developed West. The developed countries alone consume a major part of the forest products. In some cases, the developed countries have indirectly contributed to the depletion of the tropical forest. The spread of large-scale commercial livestock production in some of the Latin American countries like Brazil and Costa Rica, at the cost of the low-profit food sector, to meet the growing demand of meat in the developed countries has forced poor peasants to undertake cultivation in the ecologically marginal areas for survival. This has led to mass destruction of the tropical forest (Findlay, 1995:167).

The rationale behind the alarmist views is that 'more people would consume more resources, and, therefore, would cause more harm to the environment'. Logically it sounds valid, but what is more important here to note is the fact that some people have far greater impact on the ecosystem than others by dint of a closer access to resources. This access to resource endowments of the ecosystem operates through a set of social, economic and political factors. The world economy has grown manifold during the recent past, but the people in the less developed parts who are growing the fastest have a strikingly limited access to it, and on a per capita basis, they are far less consumptive and polluting than those in the developed parts (Table 14.4).

This brings us to the concept of what is called as *ecological footprint*. The United Nations defines ecological footprint as the land and water area required to support indefinitely the material standard of living of a given human or human population using prevailing technology (Weeks, 2018:464). In simpler words, ecological footprint refers to the actual pressure on the ecosystem an individual (or a group of individuals) exerts (or exert) in day-to-day life by consuming ecological resources. In general, prior to the Industrial Revolution and rapid urbanisation that accompanied it, human population in different parts of the world, by and large, did not influence the life outside its region in any significant manner in terms of

TABLE 14.4 Carbon dioxide emission and per capita energy use in the world and regions

World/ Regions	*Carbon Dioxide Emission, 2010 (million metric tons)*	*Per Capita Energy Use, 2011 (kilograms of oil equivalent)*
World	33,615.4	1890
Low income	222.9	359
Middle income	16554.9	1280
High income	14901.7	4877
East Asia and Pacific	9570.5	1671
Europe and Central Asia	1416.7	2080
Latin America and Caribbean	1553.7	1292
Middle East and North Africa	1277.9	1376
South Asia	2252.6	555
Sub-Saharan Africa	703.8	681

Source: World Bank, *World Development Indicators*, 2015, p. 70.

their resource consumption. However, industrialisation and urbanisation drastically altered the balance in the form of growing dependence on resources from far-off areas and increased spread of the wastes in multiple directions beyond its boundary. Needless to mention that rich countries of the world consume more than their carrying capacity by borrowing ecological resources from other parts of the globe, particularly the less developed regions, and hence they are marked with ecological deficit (Table 14.5).

From the foregoing discussion, it appears that population growth is not the primary source of prevailing social and economic crises, although it might have exacerbated it in certain parts of the world. Thus, by reducing the rate of growth in population in the South, which forms the central idea of the neo-Malthusian propaganda, hardly any resource can be generated. Nor can it help arrest the process of environmental degradation in any significant manner. The questions that arise, therefore, are – how genuine is the concern of the developed world over the prevailing crises and the future of the earth as an ecosystem? Why is that even though evidences indicate to the contrary, the proponents of the alarmist views insist on blaming the crises on population growth? Are there some other hidden agendas behind the concern regarding population growth? The following section attempts to discuss some of the political-economic aspects of the population control movement.

The politics of population control movement

The social crises as well as the population dilemma result from the contradiction within the twin forces of modern technology and social relations of capitalism (Bandarage, 1997:15). The proponents of neo-Malthusianism, however, insist that

TABLE 14.5 WWF estimates on average per capita ecological footprints of the world and select countries, 2008

World/ Regions/ Countries	*Ecological Footprint*	*Available Bio-capacity*	*Ecological Reserves or Deficit*
World	2.70	1.78	–0.92
High income countries	5.60	3.05	–2.55
Middle income countries	1.92	1.72	–0.20
Low income countries	1.14	1.14	0.00
United States	7.19	3.86	–3.33
Canada	6.43	14.92	8.49
United Kingdom	4.71	1.34	–3.37
Germany	4.57	1.95	–2.62
Japan	4.17	0.59	–3.58
India	0.87	0.48	–0.39
Indonesia	1.13	1.32	0.19

Source: Weeks, 2018:465–5.

population control in the South will help alleviate the social and economic crises including poverty and environmental degradation.

The developed countries with barely one-fourth of the global population appropriate a disproportionately larger share of world income. Evidences also indicate that despite decades of development, the economic gap between the two worlds has steadily widened over time. At the same time, the underdeveloped regions have witnessed a continuous increase in their share in the world population, and it is estimated that by the year 2025, nearly 85 per cent of the world's population will reside in the underdeveloped regions. The developed nations of the North view this widening disparity between demographic and economic power as a threat to their hegemony in the world. It is feared that unequal population dynamics could shift the geo-political balance in the world to the detriment of Western countries (Bandarage, 1997:49–50). The concern of the developed world over rapid growth in population in the South, therefore, needs to be viewed in this context.

It is the global economic inequality that forms the main issue of the present time. The development of the North has historically been built upon the economic exploitation of the South. Economic surpluses and profits continue to flow from the *periphery* to the *core* even at present. International trade has been an important mechanism for perpetuating the gap between the 'core and periphery'. Contrary to what the alarmist views emphasise, rapid growth in population is just a symptom and not a cause of socio-economic crises. Thus, by focussing on population growth the neo-Malthusians tend to divert attention from the real issues – the issues of unequal access to economic and political resources across different regions. Malthusian ideas were invoked to explain poverty in India even at a time (i.e. as early as the 19th century during the colonial period) when there was hardly any growth in population, and poverty was undoubtedly the consequence of the plunder and economic exploitation of India by the British (Rao, 1994:48). The exploitative colonial economic policies were, thus, absolved from the blame of creating conditions of poverty in India.

The process of globalisation and structural adjustment programmes under the directive of the World Bank and IMF in the Third World countries have further worsened poverty and have increased vulnerability of the people at the lowest rung of the economic strata. The fact that the benefits of globalisation have been unequally shared was admitted even in the UNDP Human Development Report of 1999 (Sacher, 2000:30). Increasing concentration of global economic power in the hands of powerful business enterprises, commonly known as Transnational Corporations (TNCs) underlies the problem of increasing global inequality. The TNCs based in the developed countries of the West, particularly in the United States, play a central economic role in the countries in which they operate. The TNCs control over 70 per cent of the world trade, 80 per cent of the foreign investment and 30 per cent of the world GDP. All the commercial enterprises undertaken by the TNCs have direct bearings on environmental quality, whether it is large-scale exploitation of natural resources (e.g. oil in tropical Latin American countries, or lumbering in the tropical rainforest), or modern industries (e.g. chemical, iron and steel, petroleum and paper), or large-scale mono-cropping (e.g. in Brazil where TNCs own more lands than the indigenous peasants taken together). The TNCs are able to influence the policies of the developed countries as well, and the alarmists deliberately choose to ignore this dimension.

The developed countries, as already seen earlier, cause more harms to the environment both at the aggregate and per capita levels. They are also involved in the trade and dumping of hazardous and toxic wastes in the underdeveloped world. The alarmist views only help them hide their role in the ongoing ecological crises. The overindulgence and consumerism are fast spreading among the affluent class in the South despite the general agreement reached at the Rio Earth Summit in 1992 to reduce overconsumption. The globalisation of the world economy has only facilitated the spread of consumerism. Media advertising plays a significant role in widening the market of consumer goods. The West sets the standard for global consumerism, and there is a mad rush among the rich in the South for the same goods and comforts that are projected through the media. Overindulgence and consumerism, the inherent attributes of the capitalist market economy, cause more harms to the environment than population growth among the poor. The hidden agenda of the alarmists is to obscure this fundamental fact.

Much of the resource consumption in the North is met by imports from the South (see for instance Barrat-Brown, 1976; Michael Meacher, 1976; Tanzer, 1980). Some Western scholars (e.g. Rees, 1985), however, emphasise that though developed countries import resources from the underdeveloped world, they themselves remain the main source of their consumption. They argue that imports from the underdeveloped countries constitute only a small portion of their total consumption. This may be true in the case of some of the mineral resources, but the fact remains that these countries consume world resources far in excess of their own production. The reverse is true for the underdeveloped world. On the whole, the developed countries consume much more than their carrying capacity by importing the same from the less developed parts of the world. The transfer of resources is facilitated by unequal economic and political power. The concern of the developed world with population growth is guided by the objective of maintaining their access to resources in the less developed parts of the world. The DCs, therefore, want to prevent a growing Third World from using up resources and waste sinks that they are used to regarding as theirs (Miller, 1995:24).

Concluding remarks

The neo-Malthusians believe that a rapid growth in population is the primary cause of social and economic crises in the Third World. More people mean fewer resources, and more poverty, hunger, environmental degradation, social and political unrest etc. The argument is, however, based on unconvincing conceptual and methodological foundations. That people do not have equal access to resources needs hardly any evidence. The neo-Malthusian paradigm is class-biased and is committed to preserving the status quo. It diverts attention from the real causes of poverty (and hence, population growth) such as global economic inequality, overconsumption in the North (and also among the affluent in the South), arms trade, trade of hazardous and toxic wastes, and dumping of the same in the Third World. The alarmist perspective provides a very narrow and compartmentalised view isolating population growth from all other issues having vital bearings on the current crises. Yet the central idea of the alarmist gets widespread acceptance among people not only in the North but also in the Third World countries. Despite the flimsy conceptual foundations, the argument is received by scholars and policy makers in the Third World countries even with a greater zeal, indicating that the social barriers are often stronger than the bond of nationality. So pervasive are the assumptions of the alarmist views that many of us seem to have internalised them even without realising it. Just as the ideas of Malthusianism are invoked by the developed West from time to time to explain the socio-economic crises in the Third World, the ruling elite of the latter tend to hide their failure in challenging the unequal distribution of wealth and power by blaming population growth among the poor. The national elite in these countries, who tend to identify themselves more with their counterparts in the West than with their own people, view a growing population of the poor as a threat to their supremacy. They project population control as a substitute to basic reforms and broad-based development through land redistribution, creation of employment opportunities, provision of mass education and health care, particularly for women and children, and empowerment of women. It goes without saying that these reforms will not only remove poverty and hunger but also control growth in population.

15

POPULATION POLICY

The term 'population policy' refers to a set of government actions – legislative and administrative – which intend to influence, alter or modify some aspects of population (Chaubey, 2001:9). The United Nations has defined population policy as 'measures and programmes designed to the achievement of economic, social, demographic, political and other collective goals through affecting critical demographic variables'. In addition to the specifically designed measures, population policy also includes those aspects of overall public policy of a country that affect its demographic attributes. Thus, population policy embraces both direct as well as indirect measures that influence demographic variables for the achievement of desired national goals. In many cases, a population policy is not explicitly stated, but is found contained in programmes launched by the government, or in legislative measures, which are adopted by it (Chaubey, 2001:9). Important to note that in most of the cases, when it is explicitly stated, attention is focussed upon regulating the size of population. Nevertheless, concern regarding the composition and geographical distribution of population also forms a crucial part in a population policy. The desired national social, economic and political goals of a country can be achieved through one or more of the three components of population change – fertility, mortality and migration. Needless to say that through these components, not only the size and numbers but also the composition and geographic distribution of population in a country can be regulated in a desired direction.

Government concern over population issues is not a phenomenon of modern times alone. Even during the ancient periods, state interventions in the form of laws or decrees governing size and growth of population existed in some of the earliest civilisations in the world. Ancient Greeks, for instance, were particularly concerned with the size and quality of their populations. Similarly, early Romans, characterised by a fertility cult, had state-sponsored provisions of a number of privileges to married couples with children, and additional financial burdens in the form of taxes to childless couples and unmarried persons. These provisions were aimed at encouraging procreation. Later, under the influence of mercantilism, which equated power and prosperity with large size of population, most of the European countries adopted measures encouraging marriage and procreation. While immigration was always encouraged, emigration was completely banned under the state law. The pro-natalist population policy reached a climax in some of the European countries like Germany and Italy during the intervening period between the two world wars. Closely linked with the political and territorial ambitions, the populationist policies were implemented in the form of certain rewards and incentives to the families with a large number of children while birth control measures were almost suppressed. A similar policy existed in Japan also during the period. All the measures reflected the drive for large native and racially 'pure' populations.

In countries like France and Austria also strict measures were taken to encourage growth in population, although the pro-natalist approaches were backed by a different rationale. These countries were experiencing an excess of deaths over births, which posed an imminent threat of population decline. Thus, unlike the case of Germany and Italy, the policy measures in France and Austria were not expansionist in the imperialist sense. Similar pro-natalist policies existed in the erstwhile USSR and some East European countries also. The expansionist policies in these countries stemmed from the works of Marx and other Socialist writers, who strongly argued that the problem of 'overpopulation' is a unique and inevitable feature associated with the capitalist mode of production.

In the post–Second World War period, with the emergence of a large number of independent nations marked with mass poverty and underdevelopment, population policies representing a different point of view began to evolve. All the newly emerging nations, which were earlier colonies of one or the other European power, were characterised by mass poverty and underdevelopment. In such countries death rates had begun declining rapidly in the wake of the spread of large-scale preventive measures developed in the West while birth rates continued at a very high level leading to rapid population growth at rates unknown in entire human history. It was increasingly being realised that all efforts to raise the standard of living would be jeopardised if rapid increases in population were not checked. Policies favouring stable or declining population begun to evolve in some of the most densely populated countries including India.

Elements of a population policy

The formulation of an ideal population policy is a multi-stage exercise. It begins with an assessment of the past and present demographic trends and their determinants in a country. This is followed by an appraisal of the future demographic change if the present trends continue, and its social and economic consequences. Accordingly appropriate measures are designed to regulate the future demographic change in the desired direction. Demographic trends in a society are the net result of interplay between the three components of population change. Policy makers are, therefore, concerned with factors affecting these components, both at the aggregate level and among different socio-economic segments in order to regulate them in the desired direction. However, most of the population policies, as is commonly noticed, are directed at influencing fertility, although trends and effects of migration and mortality also form important parts of a population policy.

Migration

As far as international migration is concerned, most of the countries today have now well-defined policies regulating immigration – both regular flows as well as migration of refugees, asylum seekers or illegal immigrants – from across their boundaries. Although immigration of highly skilled professionals is encouraged, such policies prescribe for strict quota for different source regions. A number of countries at the same time impose restrictions on *emigration* of skilled and professionals in order to curb 'brain drain' from their country. In 2013, 73 per cent of the countries reported policies to maintain the current level of immigration while another 15 per cent had policies to reduce it (Chamie, 2016:46). Of late more and more countries have framed policies encouraging return migration of their citizens. In addition to these national policies, the UN and other intergovernmental agencies propose conventions from time to time addressing issues related to international migrants and their rights (Chamie, 2016:47).

Insofar as *internal migration* is concerned, most of the countries offer liberty to their citizens to move freely within their boundaries on their choice. In the event of a restricted international migration, as it exists today, internal migration is the only recourse to the problem of population-resource imbalance in the least developed countries of the world. Much of such internal migrations in the world is unplanned and unguided. The most important of such migration is the one that takes place between the rural and urban centres, particularly among the less developed countries. The problems of congestion and slums have become integral features of the urban landscape in such countries. Efforts to tackle these problems can be seen in the form of measures related to city planning, urban renewal and relocation of industry apart from various aid/incentives to the agricultural sector. In such countries, the efficacy of development programmes depends, in part, on the success with which they are able to regulate internal migration. Instances of some successful internal migration affecting policies can be seen in Indonesia and Malaysia. Elsewhere, including India, measures aimed at regulating internal migration form part of the overall public policies of development strategies. The indirect measures regulating internal migration are various tax incentives and disincentives in the location of industries, subsidies to industries located in certain areas, investments in public services and utilities, decentralisation of government services, location of administrative headquarters in certain locations etc. Problems, however, arise when such measures come in conflict with the economic goals of a country. More often than not, under economic compulsion, economic goals take precedence over measures aimed at regulating internal migration.

Mortality

Ever since their emergence on the earth, humans have been relentlessly making efforts to improve mortality conditions, and to enhance longevity. It is logical, therefore, that policies aimed at reducing the incidence of death have been an integral feature of human societies throughout its history. Broadly defined, policies pertaining to mortality do not merely aim at reduction in mortality rates, but also include measures for improvement in the health conditions of people. In the industrialised countries of the West, death rates have already reached the lowest possible level, and any further decline in it is very difficult to attain. In such countries, therefore, population policies, as such, do not place much of an emphasis on reduction in mortality rates. Rather, other aspects of welfare policies such as the health insurance scheme get precedence over mortality reduction. In some of the less developed countries, on the other hand, where mortality rates continue to be very high, control over morbidity and mortality has been accorded a very high priority in the overall population policies, even though it means a further rise in the rate of growth in population. The concept of public policy as recommended by the WHO, which reads as 'a state of complete physical, mental and social wellbeing, and not merely the absence of diseases or infirmity' (quoted in Hassan, 2005:371), now forms part of the national policy in all the countries of the world. Death rates in many of the less developed countries have undergone significant decline during the recent times in the wake of the spread of heath care measures. International organisations like WHO have played a major role in the eradication of some of the 'killer' diseases from these countries.

Fertility

Insofar as fertility as an element in population policy is concerned, two distinct approaches – pro-natalist and anti-natalist – can easily be distinguished. The low-fertility level countries, in general, adopt pro-natalist approach in order to stimulate growth in population. As against this, for the high-fertility countries it becomes imperative to adopt the anti-natalist approach in order to restrain growth in their populations.

As noted already, the pro-natalist policy has been adopted throughout much of the past in order to cope with high death rates. Presently, most of the European countries marked with a very slow growth, and even decline in their populations, provide examples of pro-natalist population policy. Prominent among them are Sweden, France, Romania and Hungary.

Sweden has a highly developed population policy that is geared around sustaining growth in population. Remarkably, however, the consideration of individual welfare and personal freedom takes precedence over the national expansionist policy in the event of any conflict between the two. On the basis of the recommendations of the Population Commission set up in 1935 and 1941, the Swedish government has made provisions for various welfare measures aimed at voluntary parenthood and child welfare. In order to ensure voluntary parenthood, contraceptives are made available to the people, and laws against induced abortion have been relaxed. Sex education has been made a regular part of teaching in schools. Thus, Swedish population is truly a welfare policy designed to improve the quality of population rather than being an 'expansionist' in the true sense of the term.

France offers another example of pro-natalist policy in modern times encouraging family formation and childbearing in order to overcome the problems of ageing and decline in population. Financial aid for marriage and childbearing, and measures restricting contraceptive and induced abortion, form part of the policy in France. Although distribution of contraceptives was later legalised in 1967, restrictions against advertisement of the same continued to exist. Families get monthly allowances at an increasing rate depending upon the number of children under 15 years of age (in some special cases 20 years of age). Similarly, families having a single bread-earner are also entitled for a monthly allowance, the rate of which varies depending upon the number of children. In addition, prenatal and maternity allowances are available to all women. Further, additional incentives are provided to married couples in the form of government loans for various purposes, tax reduction and certain rebates on the public services etc.

In Asia, Japan is, perhaps, the only country with a pro-natalist policy. Japan's fertility affecting policy has been unique in the world. During the intervening periods of the two wars, Japan had adopted an intensive populationist policy under the influence of the 'eugenic movement' designed for encouraging growth of a racially 'pure' population. Soon after the end of the Second World War, the country switched over to anti-natalist population policy, which continued up to the 1960s. By the end of the 1960s, it was increasingly realised that a sustained low birth rate was resulting in ageing of the population and decline in the young labour force. Therefore, in 1969, the Population Problems Advisory Council recommended a moderate populationist approach. The emerging demographic trends compelled the country once again to revert back to pro-natalist policy. Family planning programmes came to be identified as measures enabling married couples to have as many children as they desired. The pro-natalist drives were further intensified with the introduction of the Child Allowance Scheme, although presented in the form of a welfare scheme rather than a pro-natalist measure.

To the contrary, high-fertility less developed countries are invariably marked with anti-natalist population policies. Anti-natalist population policies in such countries were necessitated by a phenomenal growth in population during the recent past. Most of these countries including India (a detailed account of India's population policies will be presented next) have, therefore, incorporated a series of measures to control the birth rate. These anti-natalist policies include both direct and indirect measures for fertility control. While the direct measures include provision of contraceptives, liberalisation of laws regulating abortions, increase in age at marriage etc., the indirect measures tend to reduce fertility levels indirectly through some other proximate variables. They include measures aimed at improving the status of women; strengthening health care services for mothers, infants and children;

providing social security; popularising population education at school and college levels etc. They are included in various developmental programmes undertaken by the government. In addition to these measures, various incentives and disincentives aimed at controlling the birth rate also figure among the indirect anti-natalist measures.

India's population policy

Pre-independence scenario

From the middle of the 20th century onwards, a growing concern regarding the adverse effects of population growth on development and prosperity was witnessed in the less developed parts of the world. India was the first country to have awakened to the need of a firm policy of population control. However, the concern regarding population problems in India dates back to the pre-independence period. Although the British rulers had shown their reluctance to interfere with the controversial issue of birth control, some intellectuals had begun expressing their concern on population issues as early as in the beginning of the 20th century. In 1916, one P. K. Wattal published a book entitled *The Population Problems in India*, in which he discussed population issues in health and socio-economic perspectives. According to him, population growth was the main factor behind a widespread poverty and ill health. He, therefore, strongly recommended measures for population control. Although his work did not evoke much of a response, it was perhaps the first well-known public advocacy for family planning in India. Soon after this, some enlightened scholars like Prof. N. S. Phadke and G. D Kulkarni formed 'Birth Control Leagues' in the cities of Bombay and Pune (Premi, 2003:244). In 1925, a 'birth control' clinic was opened in Bombay. The credit for this goes to R. D. Karve, a lecturer in mathematics in a college run by Christian missionaries. In 1921, he published books such as *Birth Control and Venereal Diseases* and started a contraceptive centre in the then Bombay (Srinivasan, 2017:3). Karve had to lose his job for this bold initiative in the wake of stiff opposition from his orthodox employers.

In 1930, the world's first government-sponsored 'birth control' clinic was opened in Mysore at the behest of the Maharaja. Similar clinics were opened in the state hospitals in Madras in 1933. Growing concern with population issues ultimately got incorporated in the programme of the national movement for independence. In 1935, the Indian National Congress set up a National Planning Committee under the chairmanship of Jawaharlal Nehru. The deliberation of one of the sub-committees chaired by Radhakamal Mukherjee was exclusively devoted to the problems of rapid growth in population in the country. The committee in its report identified the size of India's population as a basic issue in national economic planning, and recommended measures for the spread of the knowledge of cheap and safe methods of population control and increase in age at marriage. Remarkably, some of its recommendations, particularly the one on sterilisation of persons suffering from certain diseases, were influenced by the *eugenic movement*. In 1938

Radhakamal Mukherjee published a book, *Food Planning for Four Hundred Millions* (Premi, 2003:244), highlighting the impending scarcity of food in the wake of the rapidly growing population in the country.

Towards the close of the 1930s, the arguments in favour of population control got further momentum, and several 'birth control' clinics were opened in the northern states. These developments prompted the British government to take active interest in population-related issues. In 1945, the government set up a Health Survey and Development Committee under the chairmanship of Sir Joseph Bhore. The committee suggested measures for strengthening birth-control services for promoting the health of mothers and children (Bhende and Kanitkar, 2011:511). Mahatma Gandhi, the leader of the masses, also shared the concern regarding the adverse social and economic effects of the rapidly growing population. However, he strongly differed on the methods of birth control. He was of the opinion that on moral and ethical grounds measures such as *brahmacharya* and abstinence from marriage, and not any artificial measure of contraception, should be encouraged for population control.

Initially, the issue of birth control remained the concern of a small group of intellectuals, and the actual practice of birth control was confined to the select Westernised urban elite. The overall social atmosphere in the country remained hostile to the propagation of the artificial measures of birth control. Some other intellectuals and public figures, to whom foreign dominance, and not population growth, was the main factor responsible for underdevelopment and poverty in the country, also opposed the move. The outbreak of the Second World War in 1939, for the time being, diverted the attention of the people from population issues. The war ended in 1945, and two years later India got independence. With this began the era of concerted efforts by the government towards improving the socio-economic conditions of its people. The government accorded a very high priority to the population issues in its overall policy of economic development.

Post-independence development

Soon after independence, the government of India set up the Planning Commission in 1950 to assess the country's need of material capital and human resources so as to formulate a plan for their balanced and effective utilisation. Thus, the country embarked upon the era of planning, and the First Five-year Plan was launched in 1950–51. This was followed by a series of five-year plans, apart from some annual plans in between. It may be noted that the Planning Commission was replaced by NITI Aayog in 2014 when the BJP-led government came to power. A review of the development plans evidently indicates that population-related issues have always occupied a prominent position in Indian planning.

Considering population as a strategic component of the development plan, the Draft Outline of the First Plan itself devoted a whole section on the problems of population pressure. It recognised the urgent need of a population policy in the overall planning for development in the country. Although a policy was formally not announced, the government initiated the family planning programme – the first such official programme in the world – in the country in 1952 itself. China, the largest populous country in the world, followed suit only in 1956. In the Draft Outline of each successive five-year plan in the country, population issues have occupied a very high priority. The growing importance of population issues is also reflected in the budget allocation, at least in absolute terms, for family planning programmes during different five-year plans.

Family planning programme in India

Ever since its inception in 1952, family planning programmes have undergone several changes. Since India was the first country in the world to implement a nation-wide family planning programme, the planners heavily depended on the experiences of developed countries of the West concerning their Planned Parenthood Organisations. Under the Planned Parenthood Organisation, family planning clinics were set up, and the couples who needed family planning services visited those clinics. A similar approach often termed as the *clinic approach*, was initially adopted in India as well. Obviously, 'clinic approach' had its own limitations. Under the socio-economic and psychological atmosphere that prevailed in the country, the approach could reach only a small fraction of the population. The clinic approach was, therefore, replaced later in the early 1960s by the *extension approach*.

The extension approach involved the adoption of an educational approach in bringing about changes in knowledge, attitude and behaviour of the people with regard to family planning. It also meant a change in the focus from individuals or couples to the group. This change in focus stemmed from the growing realisation that 'the power inherent in a group itself to bring about change in deeply rooted practices is greater than influence of individual instruction by outsiders' (Bhende and Kanitkar, 2011:520). The approach, thus, meant identifying some influential formal or informal leaders in each group, and then encouraging them to acquire knowledge concerning population-related problems. These prominent leaders were expected to popularise small family norms among the people of their respective groups. This extension approach also called for associating the local bodies such as *Panchayat Samitis*, Village Development Committee and the like in family planning programmes. Due emphasis was also placed on the supply side of family planning measures. Thus, the underlying principles of the extension approach were group acceptance, knowledge about family planning and easy availability of supplies and services.

Although since its inception family planning programmes concerned itself primarily with birth control, issues related with maternal and child health care were also given its due attention. But it was not until the Fifth Five-year Plan that an explicit commitment in this regard was seen. In order to achieve a wider acceptance of family planning measures among the people, the approach in the Fifth Five-year Plan treated 'maternal and child health and nutrition services' as an integral part of family planning programmes. This was necessitated by the fact that in the event of a persisting high death rate among infants and children in the country, it was very difficult to achieve the targets of birth control. Such an approach, it was believed, would provide a wider credibility to the services related to family planning. This *integrated approach* has continued up to the present time. The broadened scope of family planning operations, thus, included:

- immunisation of infants and pre-school children against DPT,
- immunisation of expectant mothers against tetanus,
- prophylaxis against nutritional anaemia among mothers and children, and
- prophylaxis against blindness caused in children by the deficiency of vitamin A.

The significance of these welfare measures can be seen in the proportion of budget outlay for family planning earmarked for these health care measures in successive plans. In order to meet the requirement of a comprehensive health and family planning care, the Fifth Five-year Plan provided for the Multipurpose Workers Scheme. The multipurpose workers were trained personnel to provide first aid and treatment for minor ailments, in addition to health and family planning care and nutritional education. Care was taken to ensure the presence of female members in the multipurpose workers in order to have a greater access to, and acceptability among, people particularly in the rural areas. Another feature of the integrated approach was the opening of post-partum centres in medical colleges, district hospitals and maternity hospitals in subsequent periods. It was realised that when women visit hospitals for maternity care, they are in a positive frame of mind to receive family planning education. The objective of the post-partum clinics was to take advantage of this situation in extending family planning services.

In the meanwhile, by the early 1970s mass vasectomy as a measure of birth control suddenly got widespread prominence in family planning programmes. Mass vasectomy camps were organised in the Ernakulum district of Kerala in 1970 and 1971, where over 78 thousand vasectomies were performed within a period of barely six months. Encouraged by this success, various state governments were persuaded to organise such camps. Known as the *camp approach* it required a tremendous organisation and inter-departmental co-ordination. This often meant a diversion of manpower and resources from other developmental activities. The massive drive on mass vasectomy, thus, resulted in the neglect of other family planning programmes. The success of such camps heavily depended upon top-notch medical care, and a minor neglect on the part of the medical personnel could mean a disastrous result. Several instances of deaths were reported from different parts of the country, caused by tetanus. In addition, instances of some or the other kind of coercion were also reported from different parts of the country. Thus, the camp approach soon lost its credibility and the number of vasectomies performed underwent a sharp decline. However, some states continued to organise camps on a smaller scale where they were known as *mini camps*.

Development since the mid-1970s

Towards the middle of the 1970s, family planning programmes in India entered a new phase. A state of National Internal Emergency was promulgated in June 1975, and it continued up to February 1977. Family planning programmes were pursued vigorously all over the country, often in association with state-sponsored coercion. In the year 1976, the first National Population Policy was announced which aimed at making a 'frontal attack on problems of population' (Srinivasan, 2017:33). But some other events that preceded this development also shaped future policy on population control programmes. The 1971 census revealed a still higher rate of growth in population than the previous decades which frustrated the policy makers who were rather anticipating a decline in it. The other event that influenced family planning programmes in the country was the deliberations at the World Population Conference at Bucharest in 1974.

Representatives from many developed and developing countries attended the UN World Population Conference held at Bucharest. Although the conference was originally meant for evolving a general consensus among the world community on population control, the deliberations ended with an atmosphere of de-emphasis on population control and an increased concern for rapid social and economic progress in the developing countries. India played a leading role in the move of the developing world in asserting that economic development and removal of poverty constitute the best contraceptive. The representatives from the developing countries argued that an equitable social and economic development at the global level was the answer to the perceived demographic threat. It was, thus, perhaps for the first time that a political-economic perspective of the population problem was raised at the world forum.

Dr. Karan Singh, the leader of the Indian delegate and the then Minister of Health and Family Planning, had later remarked that family planning programmes would not work unless the conditions of people living below the poverty line improved. India's commitment towards population problems, however, remained intact. In the meanwhile in June 1975, internal emergency was clamped in the country. The approach to family planning took a swift turn. The Union Minister of Health and Family Planning, contrary to his earlier stand, suggested the need of 'some elements of compulsion' in the matter of family planning in one of his official notes to the then prime minister. The period was marked with some other rapid developments. The 20-point programme of the prime minister, announced soon after the promulgation of emergency was revised to include the issue of population control in its framework. Till that time a population programme was under the legal jurisdiction of the state governments. The constitution was amended to include the subject in the concurrent list, which provided an upper hand to the central government in the event of any conflict between the state and the centre. A sudden change in the approach came with a major dependence on compulsion. The then prime minister remarked in January 1976 that 'we must now act decisively and bring down birth rate. We should not hesitate to take steps, which might be described, as drastic' (Shah Commission of Enquiry quoted in Chaubey, 2001:88). The government soon began a vigorous implementation of the birth control programme. In April 1976, the first National Population Policy was announced. Prior to that population policy in the country was generally equated with family planning policy.

National Population Policy of 1976

The first formal policy document *National Population Policy: A Statement* was announced by the central government on April 16, 1976. The statement of the population policy took into account a broader perspective of India's population problem as it related with social, economic and political aspects. It was emphasised that the country cannot wait for education and economic development to bring about decline in the birth rate. The policy statement prescribed for a direct assault on fertility in the form of a set of incentives as well as a certain degree of compulsion or coercion. Each state was given the option to frame its own legislation in this regard, which was to be uniformly applicable to all the people without any regard to caste, creed or religion. Although many of the features of the statement policy were already existing, the element of compulsion was for the first time incorporated in the population control programme.

The broad features of the policy statement were as follows:

- raising the minimum age at marriage from 15 to 18 years for girls, and 18 to 21 years for boys,
- emphasis on female education (at least up to middle level), and child nutrition programme,
- freezing the representations in the *Lok Sabha* and the state legislatures on the basis of the 1971 census up to 2001,
- allocation of central assistance to the state plans, the devolution of taxes, duties and grants-in-aid on the basis of the 1971 census up to 2001,
- provision for 8 per cent of central assistance to state plans against the performance in the field of family planning.

In addition, the policy statement emphasised that concerted efforts should be taken to create awareness among people regarding the virtue of small family norms. This was to be achieved through educational channels. Monetary compensations were proposed for the acceptors of sterilisation, the rate of which was to be decided on the basis of number of children. Special attention was focussed on research in reproductive biology and contraception. The support of voluntary organisations in the family planning programme was emphasised and donations to the organisations were exempted from taxes. The policy statement proposed for a new multi-media motivational strategy with rural orientation for use in the spread of small family size norms. The policy had remarked that public opinion, in general, was in favour of a somewhat more stringent measure for family planning.

For quick results, government machinery was let loose for compulsory tactics. Several deaths were blamed on the unsanitary conditions in the camps organised for mass sterilisation. There was an overall resentment among the people. Elections were held in March 1977, and Congress was voted out of power. One of the reasons for this was said to be the excesses committed in the family planning programme. Within a month of coming to power, the new government led by the Janata Party announced a new policy document entitled 'Family Welfare Programme – A Statement of Policy'. The term *family planning* was replaced by *family welfare*. It was emphasised that the population control programme would continue purely on a voluntary basis as an integral part of a comprehensive policy package covering education, health, maternity and child care, and women's rights and nutrition. Although many of the features of the Population Policy of 1976 were retained, the revised statement completely ruled out the element of any form of compulsion and coercion.

Family planning programmes, however, suffered a serious setback in terms of number of acceptors during the period immediately after the emergency was lifted. This created a great amount of anxiety among policy makers. Experts attributed this development to the mistrust and suspicion generated during the emergency period. Although measures were initiated to revive the population control programme in the country, not much could be done as the Janata government fell, and general elections were announced in the end of 1979. The Congress came back to power in January 1980. Attempts were made afresh to revive family planning programmes. The family planning programme was made the *people's programme* where acceptance was to be on a voluntary basis without any element of coercion. With special emphasis on health care for women and children, the *welfare approach* continued to dominate the strategy. The revised strategy particularly focussed on the provision of family planning services at the doorsteps of the people. In addition, emphasis on research on bio-medical aspects and contraception, as enunciated in the first population policy, was continued in the modified strategy. Without much change, these features of the family welfare programme continued throughout the 1980s. Towards the end of the decade, however, it was realised that the country needed a fresh statement on population policy which could take a broader view of the problem.

The 1990s witnessed a marked shift in the approach of family planning programmes in the country. The early years of the decade had seen an intensification of the women's movement, both within and outside the country, in reaction to the overwhelming responsibilities imposed on women in family planning programmes for achieving fertility reduction. The proponents of the movement were very critical of the approach, and regarded the prevalent methods of birth control as an infringement on women's fundamental rights. It was in this background that an expert group under the chairmanship of Dr. M. S. Swaminathan was appointed in August 1993 to prepare a draft of a new population policy. The committee submitted its report in May 1994. In the meanwhile another event that shaped India's future policy orientation was the UN-sponsored *International Conference on Population and Development* (ICPD) held at Cairo during September 5–13, 1994. In addition to the official nominees of different countries, representatives of a large number of NGOs from across the world attended the conference. The conference was unique in many ways as compared to the earlier international conferences. A wide range of issues concerning population and development were addressed, and a new approach to population policy was recommended in the Programme of Action adopted at the conference (Rao, 2000:4317). According to the Programme of Action, of which India was also one of the signatories, the population policy of a country must incorporate activities aimed at women's development and rights, women's reproductive health, poverty alleviation and sustainable development. It was strongly argued at the conference that 'population policies dominated by macro demographic targets unnecessarily and unevenly burden women with the task of regulating fertility behaviour'. It was, therefore, decided that henceforth population policies should be guided primarily by the considerations of reproductive health, reproductive right and gender equity, rather than solely by the concern of fertility control as hitherto practised (Maharatna, 2002:975). The Joint Mission of the Government of India and the World Bank, set up in 1994, recommended the *Reproductive and Child Health* (RCH) approach in its report submitted in 1995. Subsequently, the Government of India adopted the RCH approach in the family planning and population stabilisation programmes, and on February 1, 1996, the *method-specific-target-based* approach was withdrawn from the entire country. Reproductive health has been defined by the WHO as 'a state of complete physical, mental and social wellbeing, and not merely the absence of diseases or infirmity, in all matters pertaining to the reproductive system and its functions and processes'.

The Programme of Action adopted at the ICPD was a turning point in the evolution of world opinion on population problems and its bearings on development. In the words of the then Executive Director of the United Nations Population Fund (UNFPA), 'the adoption of Programme of Action clearly marks a new era of commitment and willingness on the part of the government, the international community, the non-government sector and concerned organisations and individuals to truly integrate population concern into all aspects of economic and social activity, in order to achieve a better quality life for all individuals as well as future generations' (UN, 1995:1). The population debates till ICPD had been marked with two contrasting views – one which viewed unequal development as the main agenda argued for eradication of poverty, and the other which viewed birth control as the key to the solution of social and economic problems. The Cairo conference put the debate to rest and placed the population problem in the development context focussing on individual need rather than demographic targets. The salient influences of the Cairo conference on India's population programme can be listed as follows (Bhende and Kanitkar, 2011:560):

- The emphasis shifted from demographic goals to meeting individual needs for improving the quality of life.
- The Reproductive and Child Health Approach to the Family Welfare Programme was adopted, with a package of essential services offered for meeting the needs of individuals.

- The method-specific target approach was withdrawn and the 'community need based approach' was adopted for determining the path to be followed.
- Incentives for acceptors for family planning and their motivators were withdrawn.
- Intensive efforts for improving the quality of services offered in the family welfare programme continue to receive serious attention.
- The focus is now on achieving horizontal integration of services for historical convergence of services at the users' level rather than the Reproductive and Child Health Programme being a vertical one.

National Population Policy (NPP) 2000

In 1991, the National Development Council appointed a committee on population under the chairmanship of Shri Karunakaran. The committee in its report submitted in 1993 proposed the formulation of a National Population Policy taking a holistic view of population-development inter-linkages. Subsequently, an Expert Group headed by Dr. M. S. Swaminathan was appointed for preparing the draft of a National Population Policy. The committee submitted its report in 1994, which was then circulated among the members of the parliament and various agencies of central and state governments. In 1997, the cabinet approved the draft, but the same could not be placed before the parliament in the wake of the dissolution of the *Lok Sabha*. In 1998, when the new government was formed, a fresh round of consultations was held. After a detailed discussion and deliberation another draft was finalised and placed before the cabinet in March 1999. The cabinet appointed a group of ministers headed by the chairman of the Planning Commission to examine the draft policy. Suggestions were invited from people belonging to various walks of life. The draft population policy as finalised by the Group of Ministers after modification was placed before the cabinet for discussion on November 19, 1999. On the basis of the deliberations, a final draft was approved, and in February 2000, the Government of India announced its second population policy. Subsequently, in the month of May, a National Commission on Population headed by the Prime Minister was set up. The new policy affirmed the 'commitment of the government towards voluntary and informed choice and consent of citizens while availing of reproductive health care services, and continuation of target free approach in administering family planning services' (GoI, 2000:2). It may be recalled that earlier as per the policy statement of NPP 1976, the number of seats in the *Lok Sabha* and the state legislatures were frozen on the basis of 1971 census up to 2001. In 2001, this constitutional freeze of seats was extended up to 2021 on the recommendations of NPP 2000 (Srinivasan, 2017:63).

The policy statement underscores the fact that stabilising population is an essential requirement for sustainable development with more equitable distribution. At the same time, it also concedes that a stable population is 'as much a function of making reproductive health care accessible and affordable for all, as of increasing provision and outreach of primary and secondary education, extending basic amenities including sanitation, safe drinking water and housing, besides empowering women and enhancing their employment opportunities, and providing transport and communication'.

The objectives of the NPP 2000 have been classified as under:

- Immediate objective: To address the unmet needs of contraception, health infrastructure and health personnel as well as to provide integrated service delivery for basic reproductive and child health care.
- Medium term objective: To bring the total fertility rate (TFR) to replacement level by 2010, through vigorous implementation of inter-sectoral operation strategies.
- Long term objective: To achieve a stable population by 2045 at a level consistent with the requirement of sustainable economic growth, social development and environmental protection.

In pursuance of these objectives, the policy document outlines 14 national socio-demographic goals to be achieved by 2010. These goals relate to the following:

- making school education free and compulsory up to the age 14 and reducing the dropout rate to less than 20 per cent;
- reducing IMR to below 30 per 1,000 and maternal mortality rate to less than 100 per 100,000 live births;
- achieving universal immunisation of children against all vaccine preventable diseases;
- promoting delayed marriage for girls;
- achieving 80 per cent institutional deliveries and 100 per cent deliveries under the care of trained persons;
- universal access to information and counselling, and services for contraception with a wide basket of choices;
- achieving 100 per cent registration of vital events including pregnancy; and
- prevention and control of communicable diseases especially AIDS.

The policy document hopes that if NPP 2000 is fully implemented, India's population would be 1107.0 million as against 1162.3 million as projected by the Technical Group on Population Projections. In other words, the absolute population would be lower by over 55 million if TFR is brought down to replacement level by 2010. The policy document further identifies a set of strategic themes, which are to be pursued vigorously in order to achieve national socio-demographic goals within the stipulated time framework. These themes are:

- decentralised planning and implementation through *panchayati raj* institutions;
- convergence of health services at the village level;
- empowering women for improved health and nutrition;
- child health and survival;

- diverse health care providers;
- strengthening information, education and communication (IEC) component;
- increased collaboration with NGOs and private sector;
- mainstreaming Indian System of Medicine and Homeopathy; and finally
- contraceptive technology and research on reproductive and child health.

In addition, the document states a special strategic theme for under-served populations. This includes the slum population, tribal communities, hill area population, displaced and migrant population, and adolescents. With improved life expectancy, the absolute number as well as proportion of people age 60 and above in the country has grown rapidly during the recent past. The number is anticipated to nearly double during 1996–2016, from 62.3 million to 112.9 million. In view of the increasing weakening of the traditional support system, the aged persons are becoming more and more vulnerable. They need proper care and protection. The NPP 2000 has, therefore, identified a separate strategic theme for the aged persons, which is expected to reduce incentives for a large family in the coming future.

The new population policy is to be implemented largely at the *panchayat* and *nagarpalika* levels with the support of the administration of respective states/union territories. This will necessitate a proper co-ordination in the activities of various departments. The NPP 2000, therefore, proposes to set up a National Commission on Population (already done in May 2000) with the Prime Minister as its Chairman to oversee and review the implementation of the policy. Likewise, there is also a proposal to set up a similar body in each state and union territory with the Chief Minister of the respective states or union territories as its Chairman. In addition, the NPP has proposed a Coordination Cell to be set up in the Planning Commission for inter-sectoral co-ordination between ministries for enhancing performance, particularly in states or union territories needing special attention on account of adverse demographic and human development indicators. And last but not least, a Technology Mission in the Department of Family Welfare has been proposed to provide technology support in respect of design monitoring of projects and programmes for reproductive and child health as well as for IEC campaigns.

Post-NPP 2000 developments

Among the developments that have important bearings on population issues and family planning services mention should be made of the National Health Policy (NHP) which was announced in 2002. NHP 2002 was aimed at achieving an acceptable standard of good health of population in the country through increased public spending on health, involvement of the private sector in provision of health care services, a more equitable access to health services across social groups and geographical regions and increased access to tried systems of traditional medicine. It may be noted that issues pertaining to prevention and control of communicable diseases; priority to the containment of HIV/AIDS infection; universal immunisation of children against all major preventable diseases; unmet needs for basic and reproductive health services; and augmentation of infrastructure were common to both NPP-2000 and NHP-2002. Therefore, a synchronised implementation of these two policies is the first condition for achieving goals pertaining to health standards in the country.

Status of health plays a significant role in the process of social and economic development of a country. Nearly seven-tenths of India's population still resides in rural areas, and hence a special focus on health-related issues of the rural segment is a prime necessity. Recognising this, the Government of India launched the National Rural Health Mission (NRHM), a flagship programme in 2005. The plan of action included increasing public spending on health, eradicating regional inequality in health infrastructure and optimisation of health personnel among others. The mission aimed at increased availability of, and access to, quality health care by people particularly the poor, women and children in rural areas of 18 'Special Focus States'. These states include Empowered Action Group (EAG) states, states of the north-eastern parts, Jammu and Kashmir and Himachal Pradesh (Sharma, 2014:288). To cater to the need of the urban poor, particularly slum dwellers and other marginalised groups, a similar mission for the urban segment i.e. National Urban Health Mission (NUHM) was initiated in 2013, and both NRHM and NUHM were brought under one umbrella called the National Health Mission (NHM). NUHM envisaged to cover all state capitals, district headquarters and cities/towns with a population of more than 50,000 persons. The mission envisaged a key role for the central government in designing national health programmes with the active participation of state governments (Srinivasan, 2017).

Maternal and child health has been the core of concern for planners and policy makers for quite some time. There was a growing realisation that the problems of maternal and child health cannot be addressed in isolation, and independent, of the health status in other age segments or stages of life. For instance, the health of an adolescent girl impacts pregnancy while the health of a pregnant woman impacts the health of the new-born and the child (GoI, 2013). This demands interventions at various stages of the life cycle which are mutually linked. In order to provide a cohesive approach for managing issues related to child and maternal health care, the RCH programme was renamed as Reproductive, Maternal, New-born, and Adolescent Health (RMNCH+A) in 2013. The new approach was essentially designed to address the major causes of mortality among women and children as well as delays in accessing and utilising health care and services with a particular focus on vulnerable and underserved sections of the population (GoI, 2013).

Summing up

India has the distinction of being the first country in the developing world to have launched a government-sponsored population control programme way back in 1952. Ironically enough, the family planning programme (or family welfare programme as it came to be known later) failed to deliver desired results at least till recently. Much of the failure, as is generally suggested, can be attributed to a deep-rooted contradiction and confusion among the decision makers regarding the potential of family planning in reducing fertility levels. For quite some time the political leaders and policy makers remained apparently afflicted by confusion as to whether economic development by itself would take care of the population problems, or the population control programme for its success deserves a special priority, not only on paper but also in action. The fact that the policy makers remained hesitant in their approach is also manifest in the mismatch between expressions of priority and the actual outlays of expenditure throughout the past. Although in absolute terms budget allocation has increased from one plan to another, its percentage share in the total budget outlay has remained miserably low – less than 2 per cent. Ironically enough, a substantial portion of the budget allocation on the family planning programme remained unutilised in every plan.

The history of family planning in the country is the history of successive changes in the approach from time to time. The clinic approach, which dominated the family planning programme up to the end of the Second Five-year Plan, was a complete failure. The very fact that the clinic approach was adopted at a time when the literacy rate in the country was very low, the transport network was very poor and mortality rates, particularly among infants and children were very high, shows the immaturity of the official understanding and perception of the issue. The clinic approach was replaced by the extension-education approach in 1962. However, demographic goals and targets soon overwhelmed the family planning programme in the country. With this, emphasis on publicity and motivational efforts for demand creation lost its focus. The target approach dominated the thinking for over three decades before it was finally abolished in 1996. The approach ultimately culminated in mass sterilisation camps in the 1970s, particularly during the emergency. This was quite contrary to the official stand taken at the Bucharest conference in 1974. A massive and occasionally indiscriminate sterilisation campaign accompanied by state-sponsored coercion became synonymous with family planning programmes. The coercive methods adopted in family planning programmes only resulted in increased suspicion and mistrust among the people, leading to a serious setback to the population control programme in the country.

India's population control programme, as also in other less developed countries, has for a long time been marked with overwhelming responsibilities imposed on women for decline in fertility levels. Critics have regarded this as a serious infringement on women's fundamental rights. They have argued that the bias in the family planning approach has caused a great amount of suffering of women. Towards the middle of the 1990s, therefore, the Reproductive and Child Health (RCH) approach was adopted in the country, and the method-specific-target-based approach was completely withdrawn. The policy document of NPP-2000 further reiterated the necessity of population stabilisation with more equitable distribution. The shift from population control to population stabilisation i.e. from coercion to cooperation, was taken as a great move towards a qualitative change in the government's approach to population issues. However, according to critics 'a large number of studies by women's groups and feminist researchers document that not much has changed in India's population policy except the rhetoric' (Prasad, 2011:30). Scholars also expressed their apprehension about the efficiency of the newly introduced approach. It is argued that since the package of the programme under RCH requires a much-enlarged budget, 'the emphasis on contraceptive services will get diluted when budgets are not adequately increased to cover the wider goals of RCH programme' (Srinivasan, 1998a:14–15). Some scholars have even expressed their apprehension that emphasis on RCH would amount to the neglect of primary health care. Further it is also argued that with abolition of demographic targets, the family planning performance is likely to suffer a setback at least in the initial phases. The scope of RCH was in 2013 broadened by bringing in components on other stages of the life cycle which are mutually linked with issues concerning maternal and child health. Apart from these developments, implementation of NRHM (later changed into NHM including the urban component) also marked the paradigm shift in our approach to population issues at the turn of the present century. Experts have reiterated the necessity to strengthen the primary health care system for an effective way to attain goals of the health mission.

GLOSSARY

abortion: The termination of pregnancy before the foetus has become capable of sustaining an independent extra-uterine life i.e. while the foetus is non-viable. A foetus is said to be viable after 28 weeks or 7 months of conception. Abortion could be spontaneous when it is called *miscarriage*, or induced when the cause is some deliberate outside intervention.

abridged life table: A type of life table in which the values of the life table functions are presented for certain age groups rather than for single years of age. An *abridged life table* is the most commonly used life table for the analysis of mortality conditions in a population.

abstinence: The avoidance of sexual intercourse. A prolonged abstinence is an effective method of contraception, while *periodic abstinence* is somewhat less effective.

age: Age of an individual is defined as 'the estimated or calculated interval of time between the date of birth and the time point in question expressed in completed solar years' (Bhende and Kanitkar, 2011:154). A distinction is, thus, made between exact age and age in completed years.

age composition: The proportion of population in each age category. The age structure of a population is the cumulative result of the past trends in mortality, fertility and migration. Graphically represented by a *Population Pyramid*, age structure reveals the entire demographic history of a population. Populations growing rapidly due to high birth rates are marked with a greater proportion of children, while populations growing slowly, or stationary populations, are marked with a greater proportion of adult and aged persons.

age heaping: A false concentration of persons at certain ages in single-year age returns of the census counts. This occurs due to misreporting of age in the wake of preference to ages ending with certain digits.

age pyramid: A special type of graph showing the age structure of a population.

***age transition*:** Change in age structure brought about by mortality and fertility transition.

***ageing of population*:** A process whereby the relative strength of aged persons over 65 years in the population increases over time. This is also manifest in an increase in the average or median age of population.

***age-specific birth or fertility rate (ASFR)*:** The number of live births occurring to women of a particular age or age group usually expressed per 1,000 women (or sometimes per woman). Since ASFR is worked out only for females, the measure is used without any reference to sex. ASFR is worked out for five-year age groups in the reproductive age span.

***age-specific marital fertility rate*:** The number of live births occurring to married women of a particular age or age groups expressed per 1,000 women (or sometimes per woman). Since childbearing in almost all the societies of the world is permitted only in a marital bond, the measure is sometimes preferred over ASFR while analysing change in fertility behaviour of a population.

***anti-natalism*:** A term used for policies or theories which contain an explicit element of birth control in order to limit births for restraining growth in population.

***baby boom*:** A significant increase in the number of births sustained for a reasonably long time. It is particularly used with reference to sudden increase in the number births in much of Europe, North America and Australia after the end of the Second World War.

***bilateral corridors*:** Migratory movements between pairs of countries are referred to as 'bilateral corridors'. The largest bilateral corridor in 2017 was that between Mexico and the United States of America. The latter hosted 98 per cent of all Mexican-born individuals (12.7 million) residing abroad.

***bills of mortality*:** Information collected about the incidence of mortality on a weekly basis within the jurisdiction of city authorities in Europe from the 16th century onwards.

***birth*:**

***birth cohort*:** A group of individuals born during a specified period of time. The birth cohort is the most commonly used form of cohort in population analysis, and, therefore, the term *cohort* is often used for birth cohort. Sometimes, the term *generation* is also used in place of birth cohort or cohort.

***birth control*:** The behaviour of couples with an aim of preventing the occurrence of births. The term is sometimes used as synonymous with *family planning* or *fertility regulation*, although birth control is the most general term referring to the behaviour of couples without any regard to specified methods.

***birth interval*:** The interval between any two successive births, or the interval between marriage and the first birth.

***birth order*:** The classification of births according to the number of previous births to the mother. Birth order is normally used with reference to live births, although stillbirths are also sometimes taken into account.

***birth rate*:** The number of live births per thousand persons in a population in a calendar year. *See also* crude birth rate.

***birth spacing*:** Deliberate action taken by couples to space births of children at particular intervals.

***brain drain*:** Emigration of highly skilled persons, often professionals, from the less developed parts of the world to the developed countries.

***carrying capacity*:** The maximum number of people that can be supported by an area under specific conditions. The term was first employed in ecological studies and is now frequently used by geographers.

***cause-specific death ratio*:** The percentage of all deaths due to a particular cause in a population during a calendar year. It is a very convenient and simple measure of the relative importance of different diseases in a population.

***celibacy*:** Staying away from having sex with anyone for a long time or over a particular period. It also refers to the state of remaining single or unmarried because of religious belief.

***census*:** The total process of collecting, compiling and publishing data on the demographic, social and economic characteristics of all persons in a particular territory at a particular time.

***childbearing age span or group*:** The age span in which a woman remains biologically capable to bearing a child. Age group 15–44 (or sometimes 15–49) is regarded as the childbearing age span, although some women are able to bear children even beyond this age group. *See also* reproductive age span.

***child-women ratio*:** The number of children age 0–4 years (or sometimes 0–9 years) per 1,000 (or per 100) women in the childbearing age span in a population at a particular time point.

***circular migration*:** A form of migration in which individuals or groups move out and then return to the place of origin over the course of a well-defined time.

***Civil Registration*:** The registration of vital events such as births, deaths and change in the civil status of an individual. *See also* Vital Registration.

***closed population*:** A population having no in-migration or out-migration. The rate of growth in such a population is the function of only births and deaths.

***cohort*:** A group of persons who experience the same significant events during a particular period of time. They are treated as one group in any analysis.

***complete life table*:** a life table based on single year age. It is also known as *unabridged life table*.

***components of population change*:** Births, deaths and migration, which bring about changes in the size of population in a territorial unit.

***contraception*:** Conscious efforts taken by couples to prevent conception.

***crude birth rate*:** The ratio of live births in a calendar year to average population (usually mid-year population) expressed per 1,000.

***crude death rate*:** The ratio of deaths in a year to average population (usually mid-year population) expressed per 1,000.

***de facto population*:** The population enumerated in a census count according to where people are found at the time of counting, and not on the basis of the usual place of residence. Population counted on the basis of the latter is known as *de jure population.*

***de jure population*:** Population counted on the basis of usual place of residence, and not according to where they are found at the time of actual counting. Also known as *resident population*, it includes temporary absentees but excludes visitors. *See also* de facto population.

***death*:** Permanent disappearance of all symptoms of life, at any time after the birth of an individual.

***death rate*:** *See* crude death rate.

***demographic ageing*:** *See* ageing of population.

***demographic dividend*:** An economic growth potential resulting from shifts in the age structure of population towards the adult working ages.

***demographic transition*:** The process of change in fertility and mortality levels from a stage when both fertility and mortality are high to a stage when they become low.

***demography*:** A branch of study that deals with human population in relation to the changes brought about by the interplay of births, deaths and migration – the three components of population change.

***density of population*:** Number of persons residing in one standard unit of area.

***dependency ratio*:** The ratio of economically dependent persons (i.e. children and elderly persons) to economically active persons in a population. Since it is based on age structure of a population, it is sometimes called as *age dependency ratio.*

***depopulation*:** A decline in the size of population in any area. This may result from loss of population through migration, or because of more deaths than births.

***de-urbanisation*:** A process of decline in the proportion of population residing in towns and cities over a period of time.

***differential fertility*:** *See* mortality differential.

***digit preference*:** A tendency among the respondents to misreport their ages showing preference to ages ending with certain digits.

***distribution of population*:** The way in which individuals in a population are physically dispersed over space.

***doubling time*:** The duration required for a population to double its size with the prevailing rate of growth. Since population grows at a compound rate, at 1 per cent annual rate of growth the population would double in about 70 years and not 100 years. The doubling time in a population, therefore, can be approximated by dividing 70 by the prevailing rate of growth. Thus, at a rate of 2 per cent per annum, the population would double its size in 35 years, and at 3 per cent in 23 years.

***dual report system*:** A system of collecting data on vital events in a geographic area or a sample population by two independent processes. Data collected by these two processes are then matched and corrections are made. Data thus obtained are more reliable and accurate. SRS in India is based on the *dual report system.*

***ecological footprint*:** Land and water area required to support indefinitely the material standard of living of a given human population.

***emigration*:** The process of out-migration from one country to another. Emigrants are persons leaving one country to seek residence in another country.

***emigration rate*:** The ratio between the number of emigrants during a specified period to the average population in the country.

***enumeration*:** The process of data collection at the time of census operation.

***epidemic*:** A mass outbreak of a particular disease in a locality or an area.

***epidemiological transition*:** A shift from the predominance of infectious and parasitic diseases to that of chronic and degenerative diseases of adulthood as the main cause of death.

***eugenics*:** The study of factors capable of improving the physiological and intellectual status of population by their effects on the conditions of human reproduction and on the physical environment. A prominent intellectual force in the late 19th and early 20th centuries in Europe and North America, eugenics later culminated in racism and sexism.

***expectation of life*:** *See* life expectancy.

***family planning*:** Conscious efforts of couples or individuals to control the number of births and regulate its spacing in a population.

***fecundity*:** The physiological capacity of a woman or couple to produce children. It is different from *fertility*, which refers to the actual reproductive performance.

***fertility*:** The childbearing performance of individuals, couples, groups or population. It is different from fecundity, which refers to the biological capacity to reproduce that may or may not lead to fertility. Sometimes, the term *natality* is used in the analysis of the childbearing process.

***general fertility rate*:** The ratio between the number of live births during a calendar year in a population to the mid-year population of women in the childbearing age groups (i.e. 15–44 or 15–49) expressed per 1,000.

***general marital fertility rate*:** The ratio between the number of live births during a calendar year in a population to the mid-year population of married women in the childbearing age groups (i.e. 15–44 or 15–49) expressed per 1,000.

***gravity model*:** A model used in migration analysis pertaining to the relationship between volume of migration, on the one hand, and population size of two interacting centres and the distance separating them, on the other. The model envisages that the volume of migration between any two centres is directly proportional to the product of their population size, and inversely proportional to the square of the distance separating them. The model has been widely used in geographical studies concerning a variety of flows and interaction between different centres.

***gross migration*:** The total migration into and out of a specified territorial unit during a certain period.

***gross reproduction rate*:** The average number of daughters that a woman is likely to bear during her lifetime if she is subjected to the given age-specific fertility rate in her childbearing age group.

***health*:** A state of complete physical, mental and social wellbeing and not merely the absence of disease or infirmity.

***health transition*:** *See* epidemiological transition.

***immigration*:** Movement into a territory from some other country. The equivalent term used for movement within a country is *in-migration*.

***indirect estimation techniques*:** Techniques employed to derive estimates on the levels and trends in fertility, mortality and migration using data on other related indictors. This is done when direct estimates are either not available or they are highly inaccurate.

***infant mortality*:** Death of a live born baby who has not yet completed his or her year of life. A distinction is generally made between exogenous and endogenous infant mortality. While the former is attributable to accidents and infections, the latter results from congenial malformation and birth trauma.

***infant mortality rate*:** The number of infant deaths per 1,000 live births in a population during a calendar year.

***infanticide*:** The practice of killing newly born babies at the time of birth or soon thereafter.

***in-migration*:** Movement into an area within the boundary of the same country.

***intercensal*:** A term used to denote the period between two consecutive censuses.

***internal migration*:** Migration within the boundary of the country.

***international migration*:** Migration across national boundaries.

***interpolation*:** The estimation of the values of a particular series of numbers at points intermediate between given values using either graphical or mathematical technique.

***intervening opportunities*:** The concept proposed by S. A. Stouffer, an American sociologist, in 1940 concerning migration. According to Stouffer, there is no necessary relationship between mobility and distance. Instead, the observed decline in the volume of migration with growing distance is due to an increase in the number of intervening opportunities.

***life expectancy*:** The average number of additional years a person is likely to survive if existing age-specific mortality conditions continue to prevail. Life expectancy of a newly born baby is known as *life expectancy at birth*.

***life table*:** A detailed description of mortality conditions in a population in the form of probability of dying and various other statistics at each age. The values of life expectancy at each age in a population are derived from the *life table*.

***literacy*:** The ability of a person to read and/or write.

***live birth*:** *See* birth.

***logistic population growth*:** Population growth which conforms to the mathematical form of a logistic curve. This makes the rate of growth a linearly decreasing function of population, producing an 'S' shaped curve with population size gradually approaching an asymptotic value.

***Malthusianinsm*:** Doctrines that derive inspiration from the writings of Malthus and that advocate a check on the rate of population growth.

marital status: The status of an individual in a population with regard to whether he or she is single (i.e. never married), currently married, divorced and separated or widowed. An important aspect on the composition of population, data on marital status are generally derived from census or surveys.

marriage: The legal union of persons of opposite sex, the legality of which is established by civil, religious or other means according to the prevailing customs and laws.

marriage cohort: Individuals who marry during the same time period.

marriage rate: Rates calculated to describe the occurrence of marriage in a population. The simplest form is the crude marriage rate, which is derived by dividing the number of marriages occurring in a calendar year by the mid-year population.

maternal mortality: Death of females related to the childbearing process. Maternal mortality rate is calculated by dividing the number of such deaths by the total live births recorded in a population during a specified period and is expressed per 100,000.

mean age at marriage: The average age at which individuals in a population marry.

menarche: The onset of menstruation among females, which usually occurs in early teens.

menopause: The permanent cessation of menstruation at the end of the reproductive span.

mid-year population: The size of population at the mid-point of a year, often derived as the arithmetic mean of the population size at the beginning of the year and at the end of the year.

migration: Movement of an individual or individuals from one place to another with either a permanent or semi-permanent change in the place of usual residence.

mobility: All forms of movement of individuals or a group of individuals from one place to another with or without any change in the place of residence.

morbidity: The state of illness and disability in a population. The term has its origin in the Latin word *morbus* meaning disease.

mortality: The process whereby deaths occur in a population.

mortality differential: Differences in mortality rates found in different sub-groups in a population at a particular point of time.

natality: A word used as an approximate synonym to fertility.

natural increase in population: Change in population size brought about by fertility and mortality alone.

natural fertility: Fertility that prevails in a population without any deliberate measure of birth control.

natural increase: The gap between the number of births and deaths in a population during a given period.

neo-Malthusianism: A doctrine which derives inspiration from the writings of Malthus. However, unlike Malthus, neo-Malthusians advocate contraception and induced abortion as means of birth control.

***neonatal mortality*:** Death of a newly born baby within the first month i.e. within 28 days. Sometimes, death occurring within the first week of birth is called *early neonatal mortality*.

***net migration*:** The difference between the number of persons moving into and moving out of a specified territorial unit during a particular time.

***net reproduction rate*:** The average number of daughters a woman is likely to bear during her lifetime if she is subjected to a given level of age-specific fertility and mortality rates.

***nuptiality*:** the frequency, characteristics and dissolution of marriage in a population.

***optimum population*:** A population size that gives the highest per capita income (if economic considerations are of paramount importance) or the highest possible level of overall wellbeing of the people.

***out-migration*:** Migration out of an area within the boundary of the same country.

***overpopulation*:** An excess of population in an area in relation to the resources available or to broader economic and social goals.

***parity*:** A term used for a category of women on the basis of number of children born alive to them. For instance, the first parity women are those who have given birth to one child; the second parity are those who have given birth to two children, and so on.

***peri-natal mortality*:** A term used for death of infants in the first week and stillbirths occurring after 20 or 28 weeks of gestation taken together.

***period life table*:** Also known as *current life table*, it is a type of life table that is based on a hypothetical cohort subjected to the prevailing age-specific mortality rates.

***population pyramid*:** *See* age pyramid.

***population registers*:** A system of data collection wherein information related to demographic, social and economic characteristics of the individuals in a population are continuously recorded in a register.

***post-neonatal mortality*:** Death of an infant occurring after 28 days but before one year of life.

***probability of dying*:** The probability that a person age exactly x years will die before reaching the age $x + n$.

***probability of survival*:** Opposite to *probability of dying* and can be expressed as the difference between unity and probability of dying.

***projection*:** The computation of future population size and other characteristics based on assumptions about future trends in components of population change viz. fertility, mortality and migration.

***pro-natalism*:** Opposite to *anti-natalism*, it refers to policies aiming at increasing the growth rate in the population by raising birth rates. A synonymous term to pro-natalism is populationism.

***proximate determinants of fertility*:** Biological and behavioural factors that directly influence fertility levels, and through which social, economic and other factors come to influence the childbearing process.

***replacement-level fertility*:** A fertility level, which in combination with mortality, leads to a net reproduction rate of one. The fertility needed to ensure this varies from country to country depending upon mortality conditions, but a TFR of 2.1 is generally taken as replacement-level fertility.

***reproductive ages*:** The age groups in which individuals remain capable of begetting children. Mainly used with reference to women, the term is sometimes used synonymously with childbearing ages.

***return migration*:** Migration in which individuals return to the previous area of residence.

***Sample Registration*:** Registration of vital events occurring in a representative sample of households or area.

***sex differential mortality*:** Differences of the mortality rates experienced by males and females in a population.

***sex ratio*:** The number of males per 100 females in a population at a given time point. In some cases it is expressed as the number of females per 100, or per 1,000 males. Sex ratio can be worked out for the total population as a whole (where it is called *overall sex ratio*) as well as for different age groups. The ratio pertaining to male and female babies at birth is called *sex ratio at birth* and is always expressed as the number of male babies per 100 female babies.

***singulate mean age at marriage (SMAM)*:** An estimate of mean age at first marriage derived from the proportion of single individuals in each age group of census data.

***stable population*:** A population which is closed to migration and which has unchanging age-sex structure, although population size may vary over time.

***stationary population*:** A stable population having a zero growth rate.

***sterilisation*:** An operation carried out on either males or females with the aim of ensuring sterility.

***stillbirth*:** The expulsion or extraction from the mother of a dead foetus after 28 weeks of gestation when the foetus is supposed to be capable of an independent extra-uterine existence.

***total fertility rate (TFR)*:** The number of children a woman would bear if she were to experience the fertility schedule as prescribed by age-specific fertility rates during the childbearing ages.

***undercount*:** Failure to cover all the persons or events in a census or survey. Also known as *under-enumeration*.

***under-enumeration*:** *See* undercount.

***vasectomy*:** An operation carried out on a man which entails tying or cutting the sperm duct. It is a very effective method of contraception.

***vital events*:** Births (both live births and stillbirths), deaths and such events pertaining to a change in the status of an individual as marriage, adoption, annulment, legitimisation, separation, divorce and migration. Vital events bring about changes in the composition of a population.

***Vital Registration*:** The registration of vital events occurring in a population.

REFERENCES

Adlakha, A. and Kirk, D. (1974) "Vital Rates in India 1961–71", *Population Studies*, Vol. 28, No. 3, pp. 381–400.

Agarwala, S. N. (1962) *Age at Marriage in India*, Kitab Mahal, Allahabad.

Agnihotri, S. B. (1995) "Missing Females: A Disaggregated Analysis", *Economic and Political Weekly*, (August 19), pp. 2074–84.

———. (2000) *Sex Ratio Patterns in the Indian Population: A Fresh Explanation*, Sage Publications, New Delhi.

Ahmad, A. (2002) *Social Geography*, Rawat Publications, Jaipur.

Alkema, L., Jones, G. W. and Lai, Cynthia U. R. (2013) "Levels of Urbanization in the World's Countries: Testing Consistency of Estimates Based on National Definitions", *Journal of Population Research*, Vol. 30, No. 4, pp. 291–304.

Amonker, R. G. (1974) "Demography: A Case Study of India", *International Review of Modern Sociology*, Vol. 4, No. 2, Autumn, pp. 194–214.

Ashford, L. S. (1995) "New Perspectives on Population: Lessons from Cairo", *Population Bulletin*, Vol. 50, No. 1.

Bailey, A. (2005) *Making Population Geography*, Hodder Arnold, London.

Bandarage, A. (1997) *Women, Population and Global Crises: A Political-Economic Analysis*, Zed Books, London.

Barclay, G. W. (1958) *Techniques of Population Analysis*, John Wiley and Sons, New York.

Barcus, H. R. and Halfacree, K. (2018) *An Introduction to Population Geographies*, Routledge, London and New York.

Barrat-Brown, M. (1976) "The Crisis of Capitalism and Commodity Production", in M. Barrat-Brown, T. Emersion and C. Stoneman (eds.) *Resources and the Environment: A Socialist Perspective*, Spokesman, Nottingham, pp. 5–9.

Bataille, L. (ed.) (1976) *A Turning Point for Literacy: Adult Education for Development. The Spirit and Declaration of Persepolis*, Pergamon, Oxford.

Beaujeu-Garnier, J. (1966) *Geography of Population*, Longman, London.

———. (1978) *Geography of Population*, Second Edition, Longman, New York.

Bhagat, R. B. (1998) "Recent Trends on Population Growth and Fertility Levels Among Muslims in Major States of India – 1981–91", in M. H. Qureshi (ed.) *Muslims in India Since Independence: A Regional Perspective*, Institute of Objective Studies, New Delhi.

———. (2002) *Early Marriages in India: A Socio-Geographical Study*, Rajat Publications, New Delhi.

———. (2005) "Rural-Urban Classification and Municipal Governance in India", *Singapore Journal of Tropical Geography*, Vol. 26, No. 1, pp. 61–73.

———. (2008) *Levels, Trends and Structure of Workforce in India: Census Based Study 1981–2001*, International Institute for Population Sciences, Mumbai.

Bhat, P. N. Mari (2002a) "On the Trail of 'Missing Indian Females': Search for Clues", *Economic and Political Weekly*, (December 21), pp. 5105–18.

———. (2002b) "On the Trail of 'Missing Indian Females': Illusion and Reality", *Economic and Political Weekly*, (December 28), pp. 5244–63.

Bhende, Asha A. and Kanitkar, T. (2011) *Principles of Population Studies*, 21st Edition, Himalaya Publishing House, Mumbai.

Blij, Harm J. de and Muller, Peter O. (1986) *Human Geography: Culture, Society and Space*, John Wiley and Sons, New York.

Bongaarts, J. (1978) "A Framework for Analyzing the Proximate Determinants of Fertility", *Population and Development Review*, Vol. 4, pp. 105–32.

Bose, A. (2001) "Census of India 2001 and After", *Economic and Political Weekly*, Vol. 36, No. 20, pp. 1685–7.

Boserup, E. (1965) *The Conditions of Agricultural Growth*, Aldine Publishing Company, Chicago.

Brock, Jan O. M. and Webb, John W. (1978) *A Geography of Mankind*, Third Edition, McGraw Hill Book Company, New York.

Case, R. A. M. et al. (1962) *Chester Beatty Research Institute Serial Abridged Life Tables, England and Wales, 1841–1960* (Supplement in 1970), London.

Chamie, J. (2016) "International Migration", in *Great Decisions 2016*, Foreign Policy Association, pp. 35–50 (URL: www.jstor.org/stable/44214820. Accessed: 12–09–2019 05:28 UTC)

Champion, T. (2003) "Demographic Transformations", in Peter Daniels et al. (eds.) *Human Geography – Issues for the 21st Century*, First Indian Edition, Indian Branch of Pearson Education (Singapore) Pvt. Ltd., New Delhi.

Chandna, R. C. (1986) *A Geography of Population: Concepts, Determinants & Patterns*, Kalyani Publishers, New Delhi.

———. (1987) *Jansankhya Bhoogol* (in Hindi), Kalyani Publishers, New Delhi.

———. (2002) *Geography of Population: Concept, Determinants and Patterns*, Fifth Edition, Kalyani Publishers, New Delhi.

———. (2009) "Population Geography", in L. S. Bhat (ed.) *Geography in India: ICSSR Survey of Advanced Research*, Pearson, New Delhi.

Chaubey, P. K. (2001) *Population Policy for India: Perspective Issues and Challenges*, Kanishka Publishers-Distributors, New Delhi.

Chung, R. (1970) "Space-Time Diffusion of the Demographic Transition Model: The Twentieth Century Pattern", in G. J. Demko, H. M. Rose and G. A. Schnell (eds.) *Population Geography: A Reader*, McGraw Hill Book Company, New York.

Clark, C. (1951) *The Conditions of Economic Progress*, Macmillan and Co. Ltd., London.

Clarke, J. I. (1972) *Population Geography*, Second Edition, Pergamon, New York.

———. (1977) "Population Geography, Progress Reports", *Progress in Human Geography*, Vol. 1, pp. 136–41.

———. (1979) "Population Geography, Progress Reports", *Progress in Human Geography*, Vol. 3, pp. 261–6.

———. (1984) "Geography, Demography and Population", in J. I. Clarke (ed.) *Geography and Population*, Pergamon, Oxford, pp. 1–10.

Coale, A. J. (1973) "The Demographic Transition Reconsidered", Paper Presented in International Conference, Liege.
Coale, A. J. and Hoover, E. M. (1958) *Population Growth and Economic Development in Low-Income Countries: A Case Study of India's Prospects*, Princeton University Press, Princeton, NJ.
Cohen, B. (2004) "Urban Growth in Developing Countries: A Review of Current Trends and a Caution Regarding Existing Forecasts", *World Development*, Vol. 32, No. 1, pp. 23–51.
Coontz, S. H. (1979) *Population Theories and Economic Interpretations*, Routledge and Kegan Paul, London.
Cortright, R. W. (1982) "Literacy", in *Encyclopedia International*, Vol. 11, Lexicon Publication Inc., Philippines and Republic of China, pp. 17–18.
Cox, P. R. (1975) *Demography*, Fifth Edition, Cambridge University Press, Cambridge.
———. (1976) *Demography*, Cambridge University Press, Cambridge.
Crane, R. I. (1955) "Urbanism in India", *American Journal of Sociology*, Vol. 60, No. 5, pp. 463–70.
Das, N. P. and Bhavsar, S. (1991) "Population Growth Rate in India: Emerging Trend in the Light of 1991 Census Result", *Demography India*, Vol. 20, No. 2, pp. 227–41.
Datt, G. and Mahajan, A. (2016) *Indian Economy*, S. Chand and Company Ltd., New Delhi.
Davis, K. (1968) *The Population of India and Pakistan*, Russell and Russell, New York.
Dereze, J. and Sen, A. K. (1989) *Hunger and Public Action*, Clarendon Press, Oxford.
Dikshit, R. D. (1997) *Geographical Thought – A Contextual History of Ideas*, Prentice-Hall of India Pvt. Ltd., New Delhi.
Dyson, T. and Moore, M. (1983) "On Kinship Structure, Female Autonomy and Demographic Behavior in India", *Population and Development Review*, Vol. 9, No. 1, pp. 35–60.
Easterlin, R. A. (1983) "Modernization and Fertility: A Critical Essay", in R. A. Bulatao and R. D. Lee (eds.) *Determinants of Fertility in Developing Countries*, Vol. 2, Academic Press, New York, pp. 562–86.
Ebdon, D. (1985) *Statistics in Geography*, Second Revised Edition, Basil Blackwell, New York.
Ehrlich, P. (1968) *The Population Bomb*, Ballantine Books, New York.
Ehrlich, P. and Ehrlich, A. (1990) *The Population Explosion*, Simon and Schuster, New York.
Encyclopaedia Britannica (1993) *Population*, Vol. 25, 15th Edition, Encyclopaedia Britannica Inc., Chicago.
Findlay, A. M. (1991) "Population Geography", *Progress in Human Geography*, Vol. 15, No. 1, pp. 64–72.
Findlay, A. M. (1995) "Population Crises: The Malthusian Spectre?" in R. J. Johnston et al. (eds.) *Geographies of Global Change: Re-Mapping the World in the Late 20th Century*, Blackwell, London.
Findlay, A. M. and Graham, E. (1991) "The Challenges Facing Population Geography", *Progress in Human Geography*, Vol. 15, pp. 149–62.
Fisher, B. and Ifeka, C. (1984) "The Indian Census Dilemma: Investigating Explanations for the Sex Ratio Between 1881 and 1931", *Demography India*, Vol. 13, No. 1–2.
Foster, J. B. (1999) "Malthus' Essay on Population at Age 200: A Marxian View", *Monthly Review*, Vol. 50, No. 7, pp. 1–18.
Galle, O. R. and Taeuber, K. E. (1966) "Metropolitan Migration and Intervening Opportunities", *American Sociological Review*, Vol. 31, No. 1, pp. 5–13.
George, P. (1951) *Introduction a l'etude geographique de la population du monde*, INED, Paris.
George, S. M. and Dahiya, R. S. (1998) "Female Foeticide in Rural Haryana", *Economic and Political Weekly*, Vol. 33, No. 32, pp. 2191–8.
Gosal, G. S. (1984) "Population Geography in India", in J. I. Clarke (ed.) *Geography and Population*, Pergamon, Oxford, pp. 203–14.

Government of India (2000) *National Population Policy 2000,* Ministry of Health and Family Welfare, New Delhi.

———. (2013) *A Strategic Approach to Reproductive, Maternal, Newborn, Child and Adolescent Health in India,* Ministry of Health and Family Welfare, New Delhi.

Goyal, R. P. (1982) "Nuptiality Trends and Differentials, Population of India", in *Country Monograph Series No. 10,* ESCAP, United Nations, pp. 109–33.

———. (1991) "First Results of 1991 Census – A Small Decline in Growth Rate", Paper Presented in the Symposium on the 1991 Census of India: Methodology and Implications of the First Results, Institute of Economic Growth, New Delhi, April 16.

Graham, E. and Boyle, P. (2001) "Editorial Introduction: (Re)-Theorising Population Geography: Mapping the Unfamiliar", *International Journal of Population Geography,* Vol. 7, pp. 389–94.

Grigg, D. B. (1976) "Population Pressure and Agricultural Change", *Progress in Geography,* Vol. 8, pp. 134–76.

———. (1977) "E G Ravenstein on the Laws of Migration", *Journal of Historical Geography,* Vol. 3, pp. 41–54.

Guilmoto, C. Z. (2009) "The Sex Ratio Transition in Asia", *Population and Development Review,* Vol. 35, No. 3, pp. 519–49.

Guilmoto, C. Z. and Rajan, S. I. (2001) "Spatial Patterns of Fertility Transition in Indian Districts", *Population and Development Review,* Vol. 27, No. 4, pp. 713–38.

———. (2002) "District Level Estimates of Fertility from India's 2001 Census", *Economic and Political Weekly,* Vol. 37, No. 7, pp. 665–72.

Hajnal, J. (1965) "European Marriage Patterns in Historical Perspective", *Population and Development Review,* Vol. 8, pp. 449–94.

Hartmann, B. (1995) *Reproductive Rights and Wrongs: The Global Politics of Population Growth,* South End Press, Boston, MA.

Hartshorn, T. A. and Alexander, J. W. (1988) *Economic Geography,* Third Edition, Prentice Hall of India, New Delhi.

Hartshorne, R. (1961) *The Nature of Geography: A Critical Survey of Current Thought in the Light of the Past,* Fourth Printing After Correction, The Association of American Geographers, Lancaster, PA.

Hassan, M. I. (1997) "Population Growth and Environmental Degradation: Malthusian Vision?" *Annals of the National Association Geographers, India,* Vol. XVII, No. 1–2, pp. 53–64.

———. (1998) "Population Pressure and Intensity of Landuse: A Study of Uttar Pradesh", *Asian Profile,* Vol. 26, No. 4, pp. 293–9.

———. (2000) "Sex Composition of Haryana's Population: Some Evidence of Persisting Gender Inequality", *Man & Development,* Vol. XXII, No. 1, pp. 61–8.

———. (2005) *Population Geography,* Rawat Publications, Jaipur.

Hassan, M. I. and Daspattanayak, P. (2007) "Internal Migration in India: Some Emerging Patterns in the Post-Reform Period", *Geographical Review of India,* Vol. 69, No. 1, pp. 69–76.

Hauser, P. M. (1975) "Demography in Relation to Sociology", in Kenneth C. W. Kammeyer (ed.) *Population Studies,* Rand McNally College Publishing Company, Chicago, pp. 6–9.

Heckscher, E. F. (1935) *Mercantilism,* Vol. 2, Allen and Unwin, London.

Heenan, Brian (1988) "Population Studies, Progress Reports", *Progress in Human Geography,* Vol. 12, No. 2, pp. 282–92.

Heer, D. M. and Grigsby, J. S. (1994) *Society and Population,* Third Edition, Prentice-Hall of India Pvt. Ltd., New Delhi.

Hornby, W. F. and Jones, M. (1980) *An Introduction to Population Geography,* Cambridge University Press, Cambridge.

IIPS (1993) *National Family Health Survey*, International Institute of Population Sciences, Mumbai.

———. (2000) *National Family Health Survey*, Second Round (1998–99), International Institute of Population Sciences, Mumbai.

———. (2017) *National Family Health Survey (NFHS-4), 2015–16*, International Institute for Population Sciences, Deonar, Mumbai.

Jain, N., Singh, A. and Pathak, P. (2013) "Infant and Child Mortality in India: Trends in Inequalities Across Economic Groups", *Journal of Population Research*, Vol. 30, No. 4, pp. 347–65.

James, K. S. (2008) "Glorifying Malthus: Current Debate on Demographic Dividend in India", *Economic and Political Weekly*, Vol. 43, No. 25, pp. 63–9.

James, P. E. and Martin, G. J. (1981) *All Possible Worlds – A History of Geographical Ideas*, Second Edition, John Wiley and Sons, New York.

Johnston, R. J. (1983) *Philosophy and Human Geography – An Introduction to Contemporary Approaches*, Edward Arnold Publishers Ltd., London.

Johnston, R. J., Gregory, D., Hagget, P., Smith, D. and Stoddart, D. R. (1981) *The Dictionary of Human Geography*, Basil Blackwell Publisher Ltd., Great Britain.

Jones, H. R. (1981) *A Population Geography*, Harper & Row, London.

Kapadia, K. M. (1966) *Marriage and Family in India*, Third Edition, Oxford University Press, Calcutta.

Knowles, R. and Wareing, J. (1976) *Economic and Social Geography*, W.H. Allen, A Howard & Wyndham Company, London.

Knox, P. L. and Marston, Sallie A. (1998) *Places and Regions in Global Context: Human Geography*, Prentice Hall, Upper Saddle River, NJ.

Kosinski, L. A. (1984) "The Roots of Population Geography", in J. I. Clarke (ed.) *Geography and Population – Approaches and Applications*, Pergamon, Oxford, pp. 11–24.

Krishan, G. (1997) "Population Geography in India", *Transactions Institute of Indian Geographers*, Vol. 19, No. 1, pp. 71–82.

Krishnaji, N. (2000) "Trends in Sex Ratio: A Review in Tribute to Asok Mitra", *Economic and Political Weekly*, Vol. 35, No. 14, pp. 1161–3.

Krishnan, S. Rajoo (2002) "Literacy in India: Current Scenario and Change During the Last Decade", *Demography India*, Vol. 31, No. 1, pp. 51–64.

Kumar, S. and Sathyanarayana, K. M. (2012) "District-Level Estimates of Fertility and Implied Sex Ratio at Birth in India", *Economic and Political Weekly*, Vol. XLVII, No. 33, pp. 66–72.

Kundu, A. (2011) *Trends and Processes of Urbanisation in India*, Urbanisation and Emerging Population Issues-6, Human Settlement Group, IIED, Population and Development Branch, UNFPA, London.

Kundu, A. and Gupta, S. (2002) "Declining Population Mobility, Liberalisation and Growing Regional Imbalances: The Indian Case", in A. Kundu (ed.) *Inequality, Mobility and Urbanisation*, Manak Publishers, New Delhi, pp. 257–74.

Kundu, A. and Sahu, M. K. (1991) "Variations in Sex Ratio: Development Implication", *Economic and Political Weekly*, (October 12), pp. 2341–2.

Lal, H. (1988) *Jansankhya Bhoogol* (in Hindi), Vasundhara Prakashan, Gorakhpur.

Lee, E. S. (1975) "A Theory of Migration", in Kenneth C. W. Kammeyer (ed.) *Population Studies*, Rand McNally College Publishing Company, Chicago, pp. 188–202.

Lowry, I. S. (1990) "World Urbanization in Perspective", *Population and Development Review*, Vol. 16, pp. 148–76.

Maharatna, A. (2002) "India's Family Planning Programmes: An Unpleasant Essay", *Economic and Political Weekly*, (March 9), pp. 971–81.

Mahmood, A. (1998) *Statistical Methods in Geographical Studies*, Fourth Revised Edition, Rajesh Publications, New Delhi.

Malaker, C. R. (1978) *Study of Indian Nuptiality*, Unpublished Ph.D. Thesis Submitted to the Indian Statistical Institute, Calcutta.

Malhotra, A., Vanneman, R. and Kishor, R. (1995) "Fertility Dimensions of Patriarchy, and Development in India", *Population and Development Review*, Vol. 21, No. 2, pp. 281–305.

Meacher, M. (1976) "Global Resources, Growth and Political Agency", in M. Barrat-Brown, T. Emersion and C. Stoneman (eds.) *Resources and the Environment: A Socialist Perspective*, Spokesman, Nottingham, pp. 42–7.

Meadows, D. H., Meadows, D. L., Randers, J. and Behrens III, W.W. (1972) *The Limits to Growth*, Universe Books, New York.

Meadows, D., Meadows, D., and Randers, J. (1992) *Beyond the Limits*, Chelsea Green Publishing, White River Junction, VT.

Miller, M. A. L. (1995) *Third World in Global Environmental Politics*, Open University Press, Buckingham.

Misra, B. D. (1982) *An Introduction to the Study of Population*, South Asian Publishers Pvt. Ltd., New Delhi.

Mitra, A. (1979) *Implications of Declining Sex Ratio of India's Population*, ICSSR Programme of Women Studies, Allied Publishers, Bombay.

Mohanty, B. B. (2003) "Educational Progress of Scheduled Tribes: A Discursive Study", *Man & Development*, Vol. XXV, No. 2, pp. 91–106.

Monkhouse, F. J. and Wilkinson, H. R. (1980) *Maps and Diagrams*, Indian Edition, B.I. Publications, New Delhi.

Murphy, J. C. (1970) "Literacy", in *Encyclopedia Americana*, Vol. 14, Americana Corporation, New York, pp. 775–7.

Naagarajan, R. (2010) "Demographic Dividend in India: A Challenge or Opportunity", in T. Lakshmanasamy (ed.) *Population Dynamics and Human Development: Opportunities and Challenges*, Vol. 1, Book Well, New Delhi, pp. 81–93.

Nagle, G. (2000) *Advanced Geography*, Oxford University Press, Oxford.

Navaneetham, K. (2010) "Demographic Dividend in India", in T. Lakshmanasamy (ed.) *Population Dynamics and Human Development: Opportunities and Challenges*, Vol. 1, Book Well, New Delhi, pp. 71–80.

Navaneetham, K. and Dharmalingam, A. (2011) "Demography and Development: Preliminary Interpretations of the 2011 Census", *Economic and Political Weekly*, Vol. 46, No. 16, pp. 13–17.

Newbold, K. Bruce (2012) *Population Geography: Tools and Issues*, First Indian Reprint, Rawat Publications, Jaipur.

Newman, J. L. and Matzke, G. E. (1984) *Population: Patterns, Dynamics and Prospects*, Prentice Hall, Englewood Cliffs, NJ.

NFHS (2000) *National Family Health Survey – Second Round (1998–99)*, International Institute of Population Sciences, Mumbai.

Norton, W. and Mercier, M. (2016) *Human Geography*, Ninth Edition, Oxford University Press, Ontario.

Ojha, R. P. (1989) *Jansankhya Bhoogol* (in Hindi), Pratibha Prakashan, Kanpur.

Overbeek, J. (1974) *History of Population Theories*, Rotterdam University Press, Rotterdam, Netherlands.

Pakulski, J. (2016) "Facing the Challenges of an Ageing Society", in H. Kendig, P. McDonald and J. Piggott (eds.) *Population Ageing and Australia's Future*, ANU Press Stable (URL: www.jstor.org/stable/j.ctt1rqc955.11. Accessed: Tue, 03–07–2018 09:10:59 UTC)

Pandey, A. (1984) *Determinants of Age at Marriage for Females in India* (Typed), International Institute of Population Sciences, Mumbai.

Pathak, K. B. (1980) "Law and Age at Marriage for Females in India", *The Journal of Social Work*, Vol. 40, No. 4, pp. 407–15.

Pathak, K. B. and Ram, F. (1998) *Techniques of Demographic Analysis*, Himalaya Publishing House, Mumbai.

Petersen, W. (1975) *Population*, Third Edition, Macmillan and Co. Ltd., New York.

Petrov, A. N. (2007) "Revising the Harris-Todaro Framework to Model Labour Migration the Canadian Northern Frontier", *Journal of Population Research*, Vol. 24, No. 2, pp. 185–206 (URL: www.jstor.org/stable/41110888. Accessed: 11–01–2019 08:49 UTC)

Phillips, D. R. (1994) "Epidemiological Transition: Implications for Health and Health Care Provision", *Geografiska Annaler.*, Series B, Human Geography, Changing Geography of Disease Distributions, pp. 71–89 (URL: www.jstor.org/stable/490591. Accessed: 18–07–2019 10:05 UTC)

Population Reference Bureau (2003) *World Population Data Sheet Highlights, Washington D.C., USA.*

Population Reference Bureau (2017) *World Population Data Sheet, Washington D.C., USA.*

Prasad, S. (2011) "The Numbers Game: Revisiting the 'Malthusian' Legacy" (A Review of Oxford Handbook of Population and Development by A K Shiva Kumar, Pradeep Panda and Rajani R Ved), *Economic and Political Weekly*, Vol. 46, No. 20, pp. 29–31.

Premi, M. K. (1991) *India's Population Heading Towards a Billion: An Analysis of 1991 Census Provisional Results*, B R Publishing Corporation, New Delhi.

———. (2001) "The Missing Girl Child", *Economic and Political Weekly*, Vol. 36, No. 21 (May 26–June 1), pp. 1875–80.

———. (2003) *Social Demography: A Systematic Exposition*, Jawahar Publishers and Distributors, New Delhi.

Premi, M. K. and Tyagi, R. P. (1985) "Distribution and Growth of Population in India", in K. V. Sundram and Sudesh Nangia (eds.) *Population Geography: Contributions to Indian Geography*, Vol. 6, Heritage Publishers, New Delhi, pp. 7–39.

Proyer, R. J. (1984) "Methodological Problems in Population Geography", in J. I. Clarke (ed.) *Geography and Population – Approaches and Applications*, Pergamon, Oxford, pp. 25–34.

Radkar, A., Kanitkar, T. and Talwalkar, M. (2010) "Epidemiological Transition in Urban Maharashtra", *Economic and Political Weekly*, Vol. 45, No. 39, pp. 23–27. Published by: Economic and Political Weekly (URL: www.jstor.org/stable/25742115. Accessed: 18–07–2019 10:28 UTC)

Raj, K. N. (1959) "Employment and Unemployment in the Indian Economy: Problems of Classification, Measurement, and Policy", *Economic Development and Cultural Change*, Vol. 7, No. 3, Part 1, pp. 258–78 (URL: www.jstor.org/stable/1151636. Accessed: 19–01–2019)

Rajan, I. and James, K. S. (2008) "Third National Family Health Survey in India: Issues, Problems and Prospects", *Economic and Political Weekly*, Vol. 43, No. 48, pp. 33–8.

Rajan, I., Mishra, U. S. and Navaneetham, K. (1991) "Decline in Sex Ratio: Alternative Explanation", *Economic and Political Weekly*, (December 21), pp. 2963–4.

———. (1992) "Decline in Sex Ratio: Alternative Explanation Revisited", *Economic and Political Weekly*, (November 14), pp. 2505–8.

Rajan, S. I. and Mohanachandran Nair, P. (1998) "Infant and Child Mortality Estimates for States and Districts", *Economic and Political Weekly*, (May 9), pp. 1120–40.

Rajan, S. I., Mohanachandran Nair, P., Sheela, K. L., Jagatdeb, Lalitendu and Mishra, Nihar Ranjan (2008) *Infant and Child Mortality in India: District Level Estimates*, Population Foundation of India, New Delhi.

Raju, S. and Premi, M. K. (1992) "Decline in Sex Ratio: Alternative Explanation Re-Examined", *Economic and Political Weekly*, Vol. 27, pp. 911–12.

Ramakumar, R. (1986) *Technical Demography*, Wiley Eastern Ltd., New Delhi.

Ranis, G. and Fei, J. C. H. (1961) "A Theory of Economic Development", *The American Economic Review*, Vol. 51, No. 4, pp. 533–65 (URL: www.jstor.org/stable/1812785. Accessed: 11–01–2019 10:12 UTC)

Rao, M. (1994) "An Imagined Reality: Malthusianism, Neo-Malthusianism and Population Myth", *Economic and Political Weekly*, (January 29), pp. PE40–PE52.

———. (2000) "Family Planning Programme: Paradigm Shift in Strategy", *Economic Political Weekly*, (December 2), pp. 4317–22.

Rees, J. (1985) *Natural Resources: Allocation, Economics and Policy*, Methuen, London and New York.

Rele, J. R. and Sinha, U. P. (1970) "Fertility and Mortality in India, 1951–60", in Ashish Bose et al. (eds.) *Studies in Demography*, George Allen and Unwin Ltd., London.

———. (1973) "Birth and Death Rates in India During 1961–70: A Census Analysis", *Demography India*, Vol. II, No. 2.

RGI (1988) *Child Mortality Estimates of India: Occasional Paper 5 of 1988*, Office of Registrar General, New Delhi, India.

———. (2001) *Indirect Estimates of District Level Child Mortality in India Based on Census 2001*, Office of Registrar General, New Delhi, India.

———. (2011) *Provisional Population Totals*, Census of India, Paper 1 of 2011, India Series 1, Office of Registrar General, India, New Delhi.

———. (2016) *Sample Registration System Statistical Report*, Office of Registrar General, New Delhi, India.

Riley, N. E. (1997) "Gender, Power and Population Change", *Population Bulletin*, Vol. 52, No. 1, pp. 1–48.

Robey, B., Rustein, S. O. and Morris, I. (1993) "The Fertility Decline in Developing Countries", *Scientific American*, Vol. 269, No. 6, pp. 60–7.

Rubenstein, James A. and Bacon, Robert S. (1990) *The Cultural Landscape: An Introduction to Human Geography*, Prentice Hall of India Pvt. Ltd., New Delhi.

Sacher, R. (2000) "Environment and the Poor", *Mainstream*, December 23, pp. 29–80.

Samers, M. and Collyer, Michael (2017) *Migration*, Routledge, London.

Saravanan, S. (2002) "Female Infanticide in India: A Review of Literature", *Social Change*, Vol. 32, No. 1–2, pp. 58–66.

Saxena, G. B. (1965) "Estimates of Fertility and Mortality in India from 1901 to 1961", Paper Contributed at the World Population Conference, Belgrade, 1965, Office of the Registrar General, New Delhi.

Sekhar, S. C. and Padmaja, R. (2013) "Rural Demographics of India", *Indian Journal of Industrial Relations*, Vol. 49, No. 1, pp. 157–65.

Sen, A. (1999) *Development as Freedom*, Oxford University Press, New Delhi.

Sharma, A. K. (2014) "The National Rural Health Mission: A Critique", *Sociological Bulletin*, Vol. 63, No. 2, pp. 287–301.

Shrivastava, A. (1992) "Overpopulation: The Great Red Herring?" *Economic and Political Weekly*, (September 19), pp. 2032–8.

Shryock, H. S. and Siegel, J. S. (1976) *The Methods and Materials of Demography*, Academic Press, New York.

Singh, I. J. (2004) "Improving Birth Registrations: Role of National Campaigns", *Economic and Political Weekly*, Vol. 39, No. 24, pp. 2435–6.

Sklar, D. S. (1974) "The Role of Marriage Behaviour in the Demographic Transition: The Case Study of Eastern Europe Around 1900", *Population Studies*, Vol. 28, No. 2, pp. 231–47.

Smil, V. (2000) *Feeding the World: A Challenge for the Twenty-First Century*, Cambridge, MA: The MIT Press.

Srinivasan, K. (1994) "Sex Ratio: What They Hide and What They Reveal", *Economic and Political Weekly*, Vol. 29, pp. 3233–4.

———. (1998a) "Population Policies and Programmes since Independence", *Demography India*, Vol. 27, No. 1.

———. (1998b) *Basic Demographic Techniques and Applications*, Sage Publications, New Delhi.

———. (2017) *Population Concerns in India: Shifting Trends, Policies and Programs*, Sage Publications, New Delhi.

Srivastava, O. S. (1994) *Demography and Population Studies*, Second Revised Edition, Vikas Publishing House, Pvt Ltd., New Delhi.

Stangeland, C. E. (1904) *Pre-Malthusian Doctrines of Population: A Study in the History of Economic Theory*, Columbia University Press, New York.

Staszewski, J. (1957) "Vertical Distribution of World Population", *Polish Academy of Sciences, Geography Studies*, Vol. 14.

Stouffer, S. A. (1940) "Intervening Opportunities; A Theory Relating Mobility and Distance", *American Journal of Sociological Review*, Vol. 5, pp. 845–67.

———. (1960) "Intervening Opportunities and Compelling Migrants", *Journal of Regional Science*, Vol. 2, pp. 1–26.

Tanzer, M. (1980) *The Race for Resources: Continuing Struggle on Minerals and Fuels*, Monthly Review Press, New York and London.

Tirtha, R. (1996) *Geography of India*, Rawat Publications, Jaipur.

Trewartha, G. T. (1953) "A Case for Population Geography", *Annals of the Association of American Geographers*, Vol. 43, pp. 71–97.

Tyagi, R. P. (1991) "Pattern of Population Change in India (1981–91)", Paper presented in the symposium on The 1991 Census of India: Methodology and Implications of the First Results, Institute of Economic Growth, Delhi, April 16.

UN (1956) "Methods of Population Projection by Sex and Age", *Population Studies*, No. 25, New York.

———. (1973) *The Determinants and Consequences of Population Trends*, Vol. 1, United Nations, New York.

———. (1976) "Fertility and Family Planning in Europe Around 1970: A Comparative Study of Twelve National Surveys", ST/ESA/SER, A/58, *Population Studies*, No. 58, New York.

———. (1995) "Population and Development: Program of Action Adopted at the International Conference on Population and Development", Cairo, September 5–13, 1994, New York, Vol. 1.

———. (2015) *World Population Prospects: The 2015 Revision*, Department of Economic and Social Affairs, Population Division, New York.

———. (2017) *International Migration Report*, Department of Economic and Social Affairs, New York.

_______ (2018) *World Urbanisation Prospects: The 2018 Revision*, Department of Economic and Social Affairs, New York.

_______ (2019) *World Population Prospects 2019: Highlights*, Department of Economic and Social Affairs, Population Division, New York.

UNAIDS (2019) "UNAIDS Data" (URL: www.unaids.org/en/topic/data. Accessed: 31–07–2019)

UNDP (2003) *Human Development Report*, UNDP, New York.

———. (2016) *Human Development Report*, UNDP, New York.

UNESCO (2006) *Education For all Global Monitoring Report*, UNESCO, Paris.

Visaria, P. M. (1968) *The Sex Ratio of Population of India 1961*, Monograph No. 10, Vol. 1, Office of the Registrar General of India, New Delhi.

———. (1969) "Mortality and Fertility in India, 1951–61", *Milbank Memorial Fund Quarterly*, Vol. 47, No. 1.

———. (1995) "Demographic Transition and Policy Responses in India", *Demography India*, Vol. 24, No. 1, pp. 1–12.

Wattal, P. K. (1916) *The Population Problem in India*, Bennett Coleman Company Limited, Bombay.

Weeks, J. R. (2018) *Population: An Introduction to Concepts and Issues*, Indian Reprint, Rawat Publications, Jaipur.

White, P. and Jackson, P. (1995) "(Re)-Theorising Population Geography", *International Journal of Population Geography*, Vol. 1, pp. 11–123.

WHO (2018) "Global Health Estimates 2016: Estimated Deaths by Causes and Region", Geneva, Switzerland (URL: www.who.int/healthinfo/global . . . disease/GHE2016_Deaths_WBInc_2000_2016.x. Accessed: 31–07–2019)

WHO (2020) "Health Statistics and Information System", Geneva, Switzerland (URL: https://www.who.int/healthinfo/statistics/indmaternalmortality/en/#. Accessed: 9–02–2020)

Wilson, C. (1985) *The Dictionary of Demography*, Basil Blackwell Ltd., London.

Woods, R. (1979) *Population Analysis in Geography*, Longman, London and New York.

———. (1982) "Population Studies, Progress Reports", *Progress in Human Geography*, Vol. 6, pp. 247–53.

———. (1984) "Population Studies, Progress Reports", *Progress in Human Geography*, Vol. 8, No. 2, pp. 247–54.

———. (1986a) "Population Studies, Progress Reports", *Progress in Human Geography*, Vol. 10, No. 2, pp. 258–66.

———. (1986b) "Theory and Methodology in Population Geography", in Michael Pacione (ed.) *Population Geography: Progress & Prospect*, Routledge, London.

Woods, R. I. and Rees, P. H. (1986) *Population Structures and Models*, Allen and Unwin, London.

Zelinsky, W. (1966) *A Prologue to Population Geography*, Prentice-Hall, Englewood Cliffs.

———. (1971) "The Hypothesis of the Mobility Transition", *Geographical Review*, Vol. 61, No. 2, pp. 219–49 (URL: www.jstor.org/stable/213996. Accessed: 09–01–2019 05:10 UTC

INDEX

abridged life table 214
adult literacy rate 123, **124**, 125, 126, 127, **131**, **135**, 137
Agarwala, S. N. 143, 149
age and sex specific death rate (ASSDR) 212
age at marriage *see* singulate mean age at marriage (SMAM)
ageing 97, 98
age pyramid 92
age-specific death rate 211
age-specific fertility rate (ASFR) 178
age-specific marital fertility rate (ASMFR) 178
age transition 97
agricultural density 29
agricultural revolution 70, 219, 221
annual compound rate, of growth 69
ante-natal care (ANC) 27
Anthropogeographie 1, 2
anti-natalist 310, 311, 312
arithmetic density *see* crude density
arithmetic progression 280
arithmetic rate of growth 68
Association of American Geographers 3, 4

baby boom 72, 185, 203
Barcus, H. R. and Halfacree, K. 7
Beaujeu-Garnier, J. 9
Becker, G. S. 206
behaviouralism 10
Beyond the Limit 300
Bhagat, R. B. 149, 152
BIMARU states 85, 90, 191, 193
biological theories 201–3
bird flu 232
Birth Control League 312
Blache, Paul Vidal de la 2, 3
Blacker, C. P. 289, 290
Boserup, E. 296
Botero, G. 278, 281
Brentano, L. 204
Brunhes, Jean 2

Caldwell, J. C. 205
camp approach of family planning 315
Cannan, Edwin 284, 285
carrying capacity 303, 306
Castro, Jo Sue de 203
census moment 16
Census of India 13, 20, 22, 60, 62, 128, 132, 133, 167, 168, 244, 268
census time *see* census moment
census towns 58
centre of minimum travel 31
Champion, T. 80
child marriage 150, 151, 152, 153, 159
Child Marriage Restraint Act 151
child sex ratio (CSR) 110, 112; in India 115–19
Child Women Index (CWI) 192
Child Women Ratio (CWR) 180
Chung, R. 79
civil registration system 13, 17, 23, 24, 187, 195, 210, 233
Clark, Colin 162, 296
Clarke, J. I. 4, 6, 8, 9

clinic approach of family planning 314
Coale, A. J. 146
Coale, A. J. and Hoover, E.M. 290
cohort life table 214
communicable diseases 220, 226
comparative density 29
Compendium of India's Fertility and Mortality Indicators 189
complete life table 214
Condorcet, M. 279
consumerism 305
Corn Law 283, 284
Cox, Peter R. 141
crude birth rate 177
crude death rate 211
crude density 28
crude literacy 129
cultural environment 6
cultural landscape 3
cultural theories 203–5
culture 2
current life table 214
currently married 142, 150, 156

Darwinian Tradition 288
Davis, K. 83, 92, 188, 267
de facto approach of enumeration 16
de jure approach of enumeration 16
demographic dividend 97, 98; in India 105–6
demographic sample surveys 17, 24, 149, 176
demographic transition 72, 77, 78, 79, 81, 82, 86, 87, 88, 96, 97, 102, 105, 111
demographic transition theory 288, 289, 292
Demographic Year Book 18
demography 5, 11, 12, 77, 98
dependency ratio 94, **95, 103**
Dereze, J. and Sen, A. 297
determinism 2
distribution and density: mapping of 33–4
District Level Household Survey (DLHS) 24
Doubleday, Thomas A. 202
doubling time 69
dowry system 145
Dumont, A. 204
Dyson, Tim 296

early expanding stage 88, 253, 290
Easterlin, R. A. 205
Ebola 231, 232
ecological deficit 303
ecological footprint 302, **304**
economic diversification 162
economic theories 205–9
ecumene 36, 37
Education Index 125
effective literacy 130
Ehrlich, P. 296, 300
emigration 243
Empowered Action Group (EAG) of states 85, 90
environmental degradation 300, 301, 303, 304, 306
epidemics 22, 70, 84, 232, 233, 234
epidemiological transition *see* health transition
eugenic movement 288, 312
ever-married women 21, 27, 176
exponential rate 69
extension approach of family planning 314

famines 70, 77, 84, 219, 221, 233, 280, 290, 298
fecundity 141, 176, 178
female mean age at marriage 180
fertility 176
fertility analysis, measures of 177–81
fertility differentials 197
fertility transition: in India 189–93; less developed parts of the world 187
flow data 15
foeticide 112, 118, 119
Food Planning for Four Hundred Million 313
forced migration 244
formal demography 11
functional literacy 120, 121, 123

general fertility rate (GFR) 177
general marital fertility rate 178
generation life table *see* cohort life table
Geographical Analysis of India's Population 12
Geography of Hunger 203
geometric law 69
geometric progression 280
George, P. 3, 9
Gini's coefficient 32
globalization 298, 305, 306
Godwin, W. 279
Gosal, G. S. 12, 13, 14
gravity model 247
Great Divide, year of 83
gross migration 244

gross reproduction rate 179
Guilmoto, C. Z. 108
Guilmoto, C. Z. and Rajan, S. I. 191, 192, 193, 194, 195

H1N1 231, 232
Hajnal, J. 143, 145, 146
Harris, J. and Todaro, M. P. 254, 255
Hassan, M. I. 13, 80, 88
Hauser, P. M. 11
health transition 229
Heenan, B. 8
Hettner, Alfred 2
HIV/AIDS 27, 231, 232, 322
Human Development Report 19, 122, 125, 305
humanism 10, 11

ICPD 318, 319
illiterate 120
immigration 243
index of concentration 32
industrial revolution 70
infant mortality rate 212
infectious and parasitic diseases 229, 231, 234
integrated approach of family planning 315
internal migration 243; in India 266–73
International Labour Organisation (ILO) 163
international migration 243
intervening opportunity model 249

Jones, H. R. 10

Kabo, K. M. 3
Kapadia, K. M. 144, 151
Karve, R. D. 312
Kirchoff, A. 2
Kosinski, L. A. 4
Kosinski, L. A. and Prothero, R. M. 9
Kulkarni, G. D. 312
Kumar, S. and Sathyanarayana, K. M. 195

labour force participation rate *see* work participation rate
late expanding stage 88, 254, 290
Law of Retail Gravitation 248
Lee, Everett 250
levels of urbanization 50
Lewis, Arthur 254
Liebenstein, H. 205, 206
life expectancy at birth 213
life table 213–18
Limits to Growth 300
literacy differentials 131
literacy transition 122, 123, 127, 128, 130, 131, 134, 138
logistic law of population growth 286, 288
Lorenz, M. O. 32
Lorenz curve 32

Macchiavelli, N. 278, 281
Malthus, Robert Thomas 279, 280, 281, 282, 283, 284, 285, 288
Malthusianism 294, 303, 306
Malthusian Population 69
marriage boom 146
marriage patterns 145, 149, 156
Marx, Karl Heinrich 285, 286, 308
maternal and child health 26, 27, 314, 323, 325
maternal mortality rate 212
mean age at marriage *see* singulate mean age at marriage (SMAM)
mean centre 30
mean point 30
median centre 30
mercantilism 274, 277, 278, 279, 308
migration 242; indices 244–6
migration effectiveness 245
migration streams 243, 251
Mill, J. S. 283, 284
Millennium Development Goals (MDGs) 123
mobility 243
modal centre 31
Monkhouse, F. J. and Wilkinson, H. R. 33
morbidity 25, **26**, **141**, 229, 310
Mukherjee, R. 312, 313

National Family Health Survey (NFHS) 25, 142, 149, 159, 197
National Health Mission (NHM) 323, 325
National Health Policy (NHP) 322, 323
National Health Resource Centre (NHSRC) 241
National Population Policy 316, 317, 320
National Rural Health Mission (NRHM) 323
National Sample Survey (NSS) 25, 149
National Urban Health Mission (NUHM) 323
natural increase 76, 78, 80, 87, 88, **89**
natural selection 288
Neolithic Revolution 70, 295
Neo-Malthusianism 303
neonatal mortality 142, 226, **235**, **236**

net migration 243, 244
never married 142
Nipah 231, 232
NITI Aayog 313
Noin, Daniel 7
non-communicable diseases 27, 229, 231
non-ecumene 36, 37
non-literate 120
north-south divide 85, 112, 116, 117, 193
Notestein, F.W. 289, 290
nutritional density *see* physiological density

occupational structure *see* workforce structure
optimum population 284

period life table *see* current life table
Phadke, N. S. 312
physiocrats 274, 278, 279
physiological density 29
Planning Commission 313, 320
Poor Law 281
Population and Vital Statistics Report 19
population bomb 79
Population Bomb, The 296
Population Division, UN (UNDP) 49, 122
population dynamics 6, 7, 8, 10, 16, 17, 102, 176, 304
population explosion 79
Population Explosion, The 296
population geographies 11
Population of India and Pakistan 83
population policy 307; in India 312–25
population potential 31, 248
Population Reference Bureau 19, 42, 122, 182
population registers 18
population studies 5, 7, 8, 11, 12, 13, 15, 19, 242
positive checks 280, 284
possibilism 2
Post Enumeration Check (PEC) 18, 111
post-modernism 11
post-natal elimination 112
post-neo-natal mortality 213
preliterate 120
prenatal elimination 110, 112
preventive checks 280, 282
primogeniture, institution of 144
Production Year Book, FAO 19
pro-natalist policy 310, 311
Proyer, R. J. 7
pull factors 244
push factors 244

quantitative revolution 9
quaternary 160, 162
quinary 162

radix of life table 214
Ranis, G. and Fei, John, C. H.
Ratzel, Friedrich 1, 2
Ravenstein, E. G. 246
reasons of migration 268
reference date *see* census moment
refugees 258, 262, 309
Registrar General and Census Commissioner 20, 21
replacement index 179
replacement level fertility 86, 90, 183, 184, 191, 194
Reproductive, Maternal, New-born, and Adolescent Health (RMNCH+A) 323
Reproductive and Child Health (RCH): approach 319, 324; programme 27, 319, 320, 321, 322, 324
reproductive span 177
Ricardo, David 274, 283, 284
room density 29
RTI/ STI 27

Sadler, Michael Thomas 201
Sample Registration System (SRS) 14, 23, 24, 187, 188, 195, 233
Saravanan, S. 119
sex age adjusted birth rate (SAABR) 179
sex ratio at birth (SRB) 106, 107, 108, 111, 115
Singh, Karan 316
singulate mean age at marriage (SMAM) 143
Sklar, D. S. 146
slave trade 256, 257
Slonaker, R. J. 203
Smil, V. 299
Social Darwinism 288
social physics 10
son-preference 108, 110, 112
spatial demography 7, 11
Special Economic Zone (SEZs) 56
Spencer, Herbert 203
standard distance deviation 31
State of the World Children, The, UNICEF 301
Statistical Year Book, UNESCO 19
statutory towns 58
Steuart, J. 281
stock data 15
Stouffer, S. A. 249

structuralism 10, 11
Sustainable Development Goals (SDGs) 123
Swaminathan, M. S. 318, 320
swine flu 232

Thompson, W. 289
Todaro, M. P. 254, 255
total fertility rate (TFR) 178
transhumance 243
Transnational Corporation (TNC) 305
Trewartha, G.T. 2, 3, 4, 5, 6, 7, 9, 12
triangular slave trade *see* slave trade

underemployment 168
undernourishment 299
unemployment 168, 173, 246, 255, 285, 295
United Nations Educational, Scientific and Cultural Organisation (UNESCO) 121
United States Agency for International Development (USAID) 25
universal literacy 123, 124, 125, 126, 127, 130, 134
unliterate 120
urban-rural distribution: India 57–67; world 50–7
Urban-Rural Growth Differentials (URGD) **58**, 59
urban-rural mix 63
urban-rural ratio 50, 53, 55, 66
urban transition 51, 53, 55, 56
utopian 274, 279, 286

vital statistics 16
voluntary migration 244

Wallace, Robert 279
Wattal, P. K. 312
welfare approach of family planning 318
William S. Gary 121
Winkelblech, Karl 284, 285
Woods, R. 8, 10
Woods, R. and Rees, P. H. 7
workforce: feminization of 170
workforce structure 160
work participation rate 160
World Development Report, World Bank 19
World Health Statistics Annual, WHO 19
World Marriage Data, UN 148
World Urbanization Prospects, UN 49

Year Book of Labour Statistics, ILO 19
youth bulge *see* demographic dividend

Zelinsky, W. 6, 8, 9, 252, 253, 254

www.ingramcontent.com/pod-product-compliance
Lightning Source LLC
LaVergne TN
LVHW021247011026
849160LV00010BA/761
9780367441548